LAKE ERIE'S LONG POINT

and the Company That Saved It

Stephen Selk

2nd Edition

Copyright © 2025 by Stephen Selk

All rights reserved.

Dedication

To conservation officers and prosecutors worldwide

who enforce their nation's wildlife regulations.

Selk

FORWARD TO THE SECOND EDITION

Almost half a century ago, Harry Barrett wrote a book titled *Lore & Legends of Long Point*. Although he had been a teacher, after retiring from that occupation, he worked briefly for the Long Point Company, the entity that owned most of the island of Long Point. His role was to protect his assigned area of the island from intrusion.

Barrett was an excellent writer who did an admirable job on a book that has since entertained and satisfied the curiosity of many readers. However, having been an employee of the Long Point Company, he was limited in what he could write about. At the time, the shareholders of the Long Point Company had decided to donate part of the island, and they were engaged in sensitive discussions with government officials. Because of that, and for other reasons, they were averse to publicity.

This book supplements Barrett's fine effort by covering matters he was unable to address. It can also serve as a standalone history of Long Point. I used a biographical approach when research made it possible. My reasoning was that the approach would facilitate further research by individuals who share an inclination for such exploration.

The decision to write this book followed one of my frequent visits to the Library of Congress in Washington, DC. Among the library's collection of tens of millions of books, there is a 1932 volume titled, *The Long Point Company*. It was compiled and printed after the Company's directors concluded that the members of the Company knew little about its history.

Staff at the Library of Congress categorized the Company's book as socially significant when it was cataloged in 1932, almost a hundred years ago. I expect readers of this book will recognize the significant sociological underpinnings that have remarkably preserved most of Long Point as a near-pristine wilderness and ecological wonder for the last 150 years.

This book is extensive, containing a great deal of information and nearly 500 references to source material. Instead of reading it sequentially chapter to chapter, you may prefer to begin with the chapters or appendices with titles that capture your interest.

SJS
Vienna, VA
May 2025

Contents

Selk

Introduction

This book recounts the history of Long Point, a 32-kilometre-long sand spit that reaches far into Lake Erie. Although it remains mostly a wilderness, a small portion of the spit has become a destination for summer beachgoers, vacationing cottagers, campers, fishermen, recreational boaters, kiteboarders, and bird watchers. Why the rest of the island has remained tranquil for more than 150 years, with minimal human intrusion except for logging —much of which was done long ago —is a consequence of a fascinating yet little-known history. This history is directly related to the leisure interests of elite British military officers during the early colonial period, class conflicts in pre- and post-Confederation Canada, and ultimately to the influence of Gilded Age wealth.

A biographical approach is frequently used herein to chronicle Long Point's history. Individuals who featured prominently in life on the island, which was public Crown Land until it was sold in parcels at auction by government authorities in 1866, are identified.[1] The motivations of a small group of wealthy Canadian businesspeople who bought almost the entirety of the island at the auction are discussed, together with why they promptly formed a corporation which they named the Long Point Company. Over 156 years, the corporation had just 140 shareholders, and never more than 20 at any given time. As a historical treatment, the book respects the privacy of current shareholders while identifying those who came before them and are since deceased. Their backgrounds are revealed, and where information has been located, so are their influences on the Company's development and policies.

Long Point is one of Canada's most southerly locales.[2] Extending from just south of the village of Port Rowan, in Ontario's Norfolk County, it stretches far into Lake Erie's deepest waters. The eastern terminus, or tip of the island, stands just 45 kilometers north of Erie, Pennsylvania and 27 kilometers south of the town of Nanticoke on the lake's north shore. Readers unfamiliar with the area can refer to the Canada Wildlife Service map on Page 9. (Figure 1)

While I refer to Long Point as an island, it is currently a peninsula. As a land mass comprised of sand with minimal relief, it is inherently unstable. Over the last few hundred years, Long Point has alternated from peninsular form to island. The primary factors influencing this infrequent transformation are fluctuations of the water level in Lake Erie, and storm impact. Very severe windstorms (such as those that might occur twice in a century) can cause Lake Erie to wash over Long Point at one location or another. Water currents during these events can scour away a great deal of sand, creating discontinuities. This phenomenon has occurred at various places from one end of Long Point to the other.[3]

---

[1] Note that historical treatises often refer to the entire region including the mainland as Long Point or the Long Point Settlement. In this text, Long Point refers to the island that reaches far out into the middle of Lake Erie.

[2] Lake Erie's Middle Island, located three miles south of Pelee Island, is the furthest place south in Canada. Pelee Island has the same latitude as Crescent City, California.

[3] Over the last 157 years breakwaters have occasionally been built to prevent Lake Erie from washing over into the island's marshes. The most recent is a sand berm about three miles in length that the Long Point Company created. Additionally, many property owners in the subdivided part of the island have installed shoreline protection.

Topographically, the island is reminiscent of the sandbar-built Atlantic barrier islands found off the coasts of Virginia, the Carolinas, and Georgia. Specifically, it has a quiescent marsh on one side, and a wave-battered beach on the other. However, unlike the flat barrier islands off the Atlantic coast, Long Point has a series of ridges, generally aligned from southwest to northeast. The ridges, which have elevations roughly 10 meters above lake level, may be thousands of years old, and are wooded. Between them are savannah, swales, or a combination of both. The swales sometimes take the form of wetlands or thicket-swamps. Like the coastal Atlantic barrier islands, Long Point is subject to erosion by high water, waves and wind. However, erosive forces have not flattened the ridges, at least not those on the eastern two-thirds of the island. One former western ridge, called the Oak Ridges, no longer has any noticeable elevation, but its path through a vast marsh remains perceptible.[4] It is possible that logging occurred along the ridge during the first half of the 19th century, making the ridge more susceptible to erosion.

The island shelters the waters of Long Point Bay, which is divided by a sand reef into two zones, the very shallow Inner Bay, and the deeper and larger Outer Bay. The climate-tempering impact of the bays, and the open water of Lake Erie to the south, contributes to the presence of flora atypical in Canada. Biologists who surveyed the island and nearby mainland almost 100 years ago noted the presence of trees, shrubs, and aquatic plants not generally found so far north. [1] Among them were sassafras, tulip, swamp oak, black oak, sycamore, buttonbush, and the American lotus —species more common to the Alleghenies and Carolinas. Since the 1931 survey was published, the region has often been described as Carolinian Canada.

Although it is an oversimplification, it is convenient to describe Long Point as having three zones. Most of the eastern 17-kilometers are designated and protected as a National Wildlife Area. There are two exceptions. One is a small plot at the island's tip that has been reserved for a lighthouse for almost 200 years.[5] The public is permitted to land and stroll in that immediate area. The other exception is a privately owned strip roughly one kilometer wide (known as the Anderson Property.) The plot runs south from the island's north shore, but doesn't quite reach the south beach. More than a dozen cabins are present on the plot. Shares in the property change hands infrequently and have done so since the late 19th century. Shareholders are tenants-in-common, who have access and crossing privileges for the entire plot. They reach the property by boat. While there are no utilities or roads, a couple of narrow sand paths, created long ago for logging, can be negotiated by all-terrain vehicles.

The central part of the island, which is largely marsh, is the private duck hunting preserve of the Long Point Company. A small tract that extends west from Company's boundary to Long Point Provincial Park (the "new" park) separates the third zone of Long Point —the public part — from the rest. The tract is also designated as a National Wildlife Area.

---

[4] Today, the Oak Ridges are also known as Wood Duck Alley. Although the former ridge has been flattened, a few trees still survive on the remaining land. Wood Ducks occasionally nest in these trees, hence the name.

[5] The first lighthouse at the tip of Long Point was lit in 1830 but was soon undermined by water. [465] The second lighthouse was lit in 1843 and suffered the same fate 73 years later. The current lighthouse was lit in 1916. The area around the base of the structure has been since been fortified to protect against water encroachment.

The far western part of the island is public. A park was first established there in 1921. The Long Point Park Commission (a governing body discussed further in the chapter titled The First Long Point Park.) sought to subdivide the park into building lots for lease. The subdivision plan was approved in 1923. Because Long Point could only be reached by boat at the time, and because the park was undeveloped, little activity beyond hunting occurred for almost a decade.

Immediately west of Long Point lies a marshy river delta. For eons reptiles and amphibians such as frogs, toads, and turtles, including jumbo-sized snappers traveled unimpeded back and forth between the delta and the open water of Long Point's Inner Bay.[6] Following the advent of automobiles and the establishment of the park, the Ontario government was persuaded by local politicians to fund the building of a causeway across the delta. Construction began in 1927, and the road was completed two years later, thus connecting the park to the nearby mainland. Wildlife continued their instinctive journeys by crossing the road. Over decades, as vehicle traffic increased, the Long Point causeway unfortunately became notorious for having one of the highest incidences of roadkill in North America. Even airborne Monarch butterflies meet their demise, by being struck. Recently, tunnels have been built under the road so amphibians can reach the marsh without traveling on the road. Authorities are currently installing exclusionary fencing just beyond the road's shoulders. The fencing is intended to further motivate wildlife to pass through the tunnels.[7] There are some private residences that have driveways on the east side of the causeway. Consequently, there are interruptions in the exclusionary fencing. Users of the road should be attentive to and give way to snakes, turtles, toads, and other wildlife.

Completion of the causeway in 1929 facilitated rapid development at the western part of Long Point. The Park Commission built roads of sand and gravel and marked out lots for lease.[8] By the early 1930s, about three dozen seasonal residences, generally humble fishing and hunting cabins, had been established. Later in the decade, the Commission widened a creek to create a canal and harbor that has since been called the Old Cut. Sand from the digging and dredging was spread to fortify lots in the marsh, allowing more cottages to be built. Thus, many of the lots present in the marshy area today should not be deemed natural. To a considerable degree they were man-made. All this early development activity unsettled groundcover, so the Commission widely planted pine seedlings to help stabilize the sandy park from wind erosion.[9] Many of those pines, all of which were non-native species, still stand throughout the Long Point community today.

In the late 1950s, a private enterprise named SpencTedKen (whose founders were Spencer Smith, Ted Whitworth, and Ken McCall) dug additional canals, creating more building lots. Since then, many of the original hunting and fishing cabins have been torn down, their lots raised further with additional fill, and more substantial residences constructed. Today, the built-up community

---

[6] During the late 19th and early 20th Centuries, turtles were commercially harvested at Long Point by American net trappers and exported by schooner to the United States.

[7] Some have suggested the exclusionary fencing might facilitate amphibian predation by coyotes, foxes and other relatively intelligent species. This hypothesis could be a worthy candidate for research.

[8] The roads have since been surfaced with asphalt.

[9] The pine species the Commission planted at Long Point were Scotch and Red Pine.

has about 900 dwellings. The majority, but by no means all, are occupied only during the warmer months of the year.

There are two provincially owned and administered public parks. The older of the two is laid out exactly as called for in the 1923 subdivision plan. The other, which is much larger, wasn't established until 1960. Both flank the south beach, operate during the warmer months, and offer overnight camping. Combined, the built-up residential and Provincial Park areas of Long Point extend for about five kilometers, just 15% of the length of the island.

The Mississippi and Atlantic flyways, two of the continent's four avian migration corridors intersect over Lake Erie. Long Point, centrally located in the lake, is consequently one of North America's most vital bird concentration areas. Indeed, the island has been designated a Ramsar site, a wetland of international importance.[10] Almost 400 species of birds stop to rest and nourish themselves by feeding on the dense population of insects, flora, and aquatic life that thrive in the island's marshes, sloughs, and ponds. About 175 species nest for the season. [2] During Fall migration, as many as 100,000 waterfowl may be present on a given day. This avian richness has resulted in Long Point being a place for ornithological research for well over a hundred years. Amateurs found rare species on the island no later than the 1890s. [3] The first professional ornithologist to do research at Long Point was W. E. Clyde Todd of the Carnegie Museum in Pittsburgh , who visited in 1907.

Systemized ornithological research commenced in 1960 when a group of individuals who had emigrated from the United Kingdom to Canada established a banding station. They called their new organization the Long Point Bird Observatory (LPBO). [4] Modeled after similar institutions in the United Kingdom that operated regularly and followed a scientifically rigorous protocol, LPBO has the distinction of being the first bird observatory in the Western Hemisphere. Previous undertakings had been unstructured and episodic. Since its founding, LPBO has banded more than a million birds.

As a largely uninhabited wilderness located along a migratory corridor, Long Point also serves as a staging place for Monarch butterflies. When I was a child, we would see them in the trees by the hundreds. Over the course of many weeks last summer, I saw just three. I expect the reasons for their diminishing numbers are many. Whatever the circumstances, via an agreement with Mexico, Long Point has been designated an International Monarch Butterfly Reserve. The species is officially listed as endangered in Canada, so everyone should avoid disturbing the few that still visit the island during their long journeys.[11]

The Seneca tribe referred to Long Point as Ganohogeh, meaning "the place filled up." The name was associated with the mythology that a Great Beaver had built a dam across Lake Erie. [5] [12] Current geological science indicates that the north and south shores of Lake Erie in the vicinity of Port Rowan and Erie, Pennsylvania, were indeed bridged to each other about 12,000 years ago.

---

[10] Ramsar is the organization that coordinates the implementation of the Convention on Wetlands of International Importance. More than 90% of United Nations states have entered into agreements with Ramsar.
[11] Monarch butterflies are proposed to be listed as endangered in the United States.
[12] Orsamus H Marshall began working as a lawyer in Buffalo in the 1830's. He died in 1884.

It follows that the name the Seneca tribe used for Long Point may have been based on factual geographic awareness orally passed down over thousands of years.

As for how long the island has been known as Long Point, in 1670 French explorer René Bréhant de Galinee, labeled the spit a peninsula, Presqu Isle du lac D'Erie. Writing in his journal, he characterized it as a *long point*. [6] When René-Robert LaSalle sailed by a few years later, he named the eastern tip of the island Cape St. Francis. [5] Louis Hennepin referred to it the same way, a few years later. [7] Writings by the Jesuit explorer Pierre Francois Xavier de Charlevoix suggest that the name Long Point had come into common use no later than 1721. That year he wrote:

> The 1st. of June being the day of Pentecost, after having sailed up a beautiful river for the space of an hour, which has its rise as they say at a great distance, and runs betwixt two fine meadows; we passed over a carrying place of about sixty paces in breadth, in order to avoid turning round a point which is called *the long point*; it is a very sandy spot of ground, and naturally bears a great quantity of vines. The following days I saw nothing remarkable, but coasted along a charming country, hid at times by very disagreeable prospects, which however are of no great extent. Wherever I went ashore I was quite enchanted by the beauty and variety of a landscape, which was terminated by the noblest forests in the whole world. Add to this, that every part of it swarms with waterfowl. [8]

Late in the 18th century, the British gave the island the official name North Foreland, probably because the colonial Governor John Graves Simcoe liked to adopt names of places in Britain that he was familiar with. [13] [9] [10] The name Graves chose never found much favor among the local populace, or any others for that matter, even though the government used it for official publications. The name North Foreland still appeared on early 20th century nautical charts, although together with the name Long Point.

While the island's beaches are beautiful and the surrounding water most pleasant during the warmer months, Long Point isn't a Shangri La. It is variably and seasonally infested with midges, stable flies, deer flies, mosquitoes and ticks. The stable flies, a species that came with livestock accompanying early European settlers on Atlantic crossings, can be particularly bothersome, especially to beachgoers. They first appear in late July and sporadically thereafter until frost. Although they present like a regular housefly, they target and stealthily alight on people who are stationary. Then, they inflict a sharp bite. Receiving too many bites can result in an allergic response. Some of the ticks can transmit Lyme's Disease, while others may transmit different afflictions. On one occasion, following a mere two-minute walk through an ill-chosen grassy shore dune, I found more than a dozen ticks affixed to my pant legs.

Spiders are ubiquitous. As is the case with snakes, some individuals have an instinctive fear of these arachnids. Most Long Point property owners' contract with pesticide applicators who spray entire cottage exteriors to eliminate the spiders. Fewer try to deal with the spiders by using

---

[13] Simcoe named Point Pelee the South Foreland.

a leaf blower or broom. Phobia typically isn't their motivation. Rather, if nothing is done, one's cottage might well appear haunted. At a minimum, it will be draped in spider webs and copiously splattered with black droppings that are persistent and very difficult to remove. While the pesticides have been approved by government authorities, and their use is entirely practical, I have begun to wonder whether widespread and long-term application to entire cottages might eventually have a detrimental impact on the local ecosystem. Instead of relying on a commercial pesticide applicator, I've begun to sparingly apply spot treatments myself.

Snakes (and far more frequently their squashed remains —a consequence of roadkill) are a common sight, although their numbers seem to be diminishing. Gordon Sinclair, a well-known Canadian journalist since deceased, overnighted on Long Point early in his career to report on the abundant serpent population. [14] His account of the adventure was published by *Maclean's* magazine and may be accessed online free of charge. [11] Nine species are present. None are venomous to humans, but they can be intimidating to individuals who have a naturally instinctive fear of snakes. The Eastern Fox Snake, an endangered species, is a tree climber that can easily grow to a metre in length.[15] Another, the Eastern Hognose Snake might rise when disturbed and threaten to strike. Uncharacteristically wide behind its head, it can appear slightly reminiscent of a cobra. While it might strike (rarely inflicting a bite,) it almost always ceases its bluster and plays dead if continually provoked.

John Spain, who built and operated a hotel on Long Point beginning in the 1850s, reminisced about the island's serpents:

> I have seen them in the trees, on my docks, in my boats, in my house, and in my beds. I have [sic] never killed a snake during my fifteen years residence there. I am a greater friend to snakes than mosquitos [sic] and believe the latter to be the greater pest to residents. There is an old saying that there is [sic] enough snakes on the Point to fence it all around. [12]

Norfolk County, the political entity having local governing authority for regions that include Long Point, asserts that the island and its marshes have a degree of ecological diversity second only to the Amazon. Whatever the validity of that claim may be, Long Point's fragile and relatively undisturbed ecosystem, along with its importance sustaining avian migration, was instrumental to its designation as a UNESCO World Biosphere in 1986.[16]

The County promotes the island as a tourist designation. However, as will be explained in the next chapter, very little of Long Point, including its most beautiful and interesting areas, is accessible to the visiting public.

---

[14] Sinclair developed a fascination for snakes —particularly venomous species —while working as a young journalist in southeast Asia.

[15] The Eastern Fox Snake is listed as endangered under Canada's Species at Risk Act.

[16] https://longpointbiosphere.com accessed January 2, 2025.

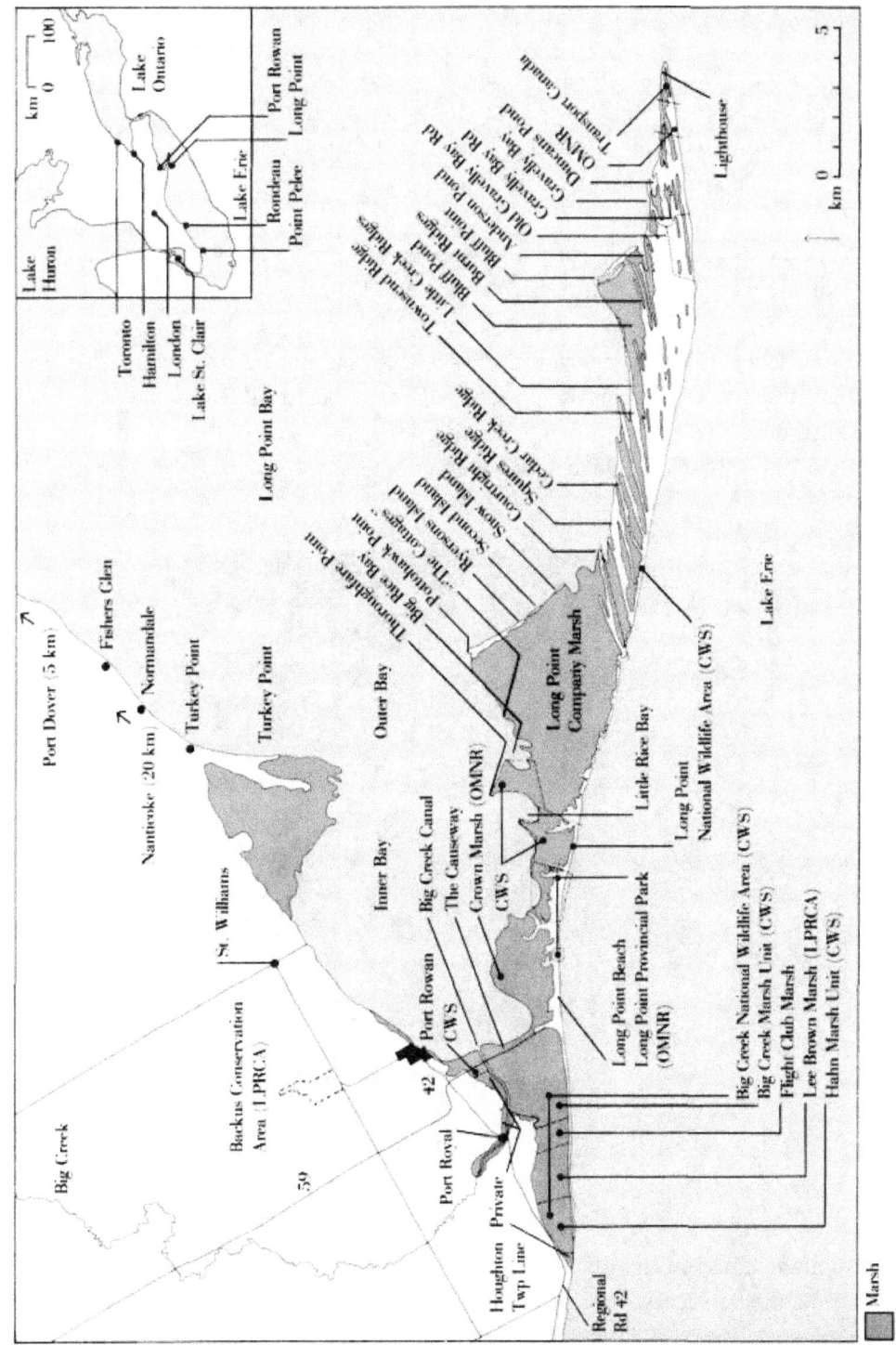

Figure 1. Long Point Area Map. [13]

Access Restrictions

Before the 1980s, if someone had a boat and was willing to risk unsheltered and unfrequented waters, they could go ashore along Long Point's 32-kilometer mile south beach. They would be trespassing on private property, but if they were not repeat offenders or had not ventured too far inland from the shore, the Long Point Company offered a gentle hand and would just ask the transgressors to leave.

While strolling the beach, particularly on the western part of the island, the visitors would have intermittently encountered thick beds of gravel. These are a testament to an end moraine left behind by a glacier that retreated 12,500 years ago. The gravel is replete with fossils, worn smooth by the erosive action of sand and water that has taken place since deglaciation. They are remnants from an ancient salt-water sea that was present in the area roughly 400 million years ago.[17] Wading ankle or knee deep in clear water while looking for fossils among the kaleidoscope of colorful gravel was an enjoyable interlude to a long boat voyage.

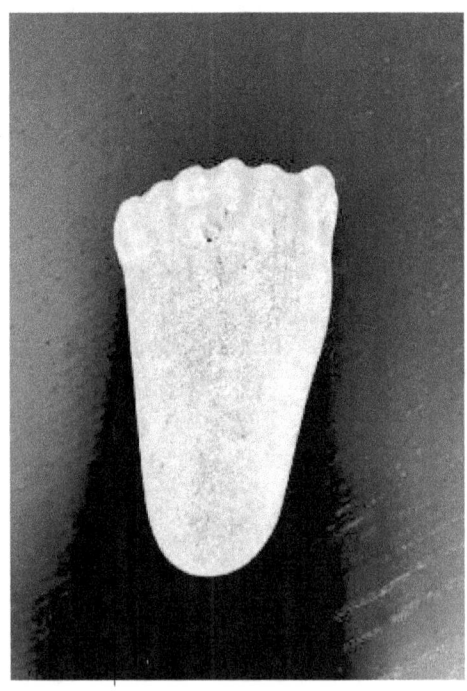

Photo 1 Long Point beach fossil. (Author's collection)

No more. Since much of the island was designated as a National Wildlife Area, the public has not been permitted access, except on two short lengths of beach, and only during the summer.

---

[17] Thick salt layers are present under the lakebed. The Cargill corporation operates a 42-square kilometer mine 450-meters beneath the lake off Cleveland.

One of these areas begins at the east end of the Provincial Park and ends at the Long Point Company's west boundary line. The other is a very short and rather unwelcoming stretch of beach on the north shore near Squire's Ridge. The Canada Wildlife Service even claims authority over swimming along certain parts of the island. [2] It might seem surprising that the government asserts such jurisdiction over one of the Great Lakes. The justification seems to be that the boundary of Long Point is referenced to a survey conducted in the 1850s.[18] Since then, the lake has flooded some areas that were solid ground when the survey was done.

Regulations under the Canada Wildlife Act expressly prohibit swimming in a wildlife area. They also prohibit the removal of any object, be it a fossil or driftwood. [14] Armed federal officers are sometimes present on the island. Because they are responsible for keeping the wildlife area free from human intrusion, do not expect them to respond favorably to an attempt at humor or profession of ignorance, even if you encounter them a few metres beyond the shoreline. Note also that the Canada Wildlife Act includes a false statements clause. The minimum penalties for encroachment in a National Wildlife Area are quite severe compared to a provincial trespassing offense.

The Long Point Company does not permit access to its property either. While the Company tends to be more lenient than its federal counterpart, it may gather evidence sufficient for prosecution and act on it. With respect to poaching, the Company has no tolerance whatsoever and many offenders have been convicted. Repeat trespassers can expect the same repercussion. During the mid-20th century, a certain Mr. Halcovich, a prosperous building contractor from Hamilton, moored his yacht offshore then entered the Company's marsh in a small dinghy to poach. He argued that he had the right to do so because the water in the marsh was navigable. While Halcovich's defense was plausible and it greatly worried the Company's members, it failed at trial, and he was convicted. The court held that the Company's marsh did not qualify as navigable water. [15]

Despite entry restrictions, boating along Long Point's distant shores is still a delightful experience on a warm summer day. There are many opportunities for swimming along offshore sandbars that flank both sides of the island. The water is much clearer and cleaner than at the public beaches of the provincial park and residential areas.[19] Afternoon onshore sea breezes are the norm on sunny summer days.[20] Consequently, the lake might be calm in the morning, but waves will form before noon and increase in height during the afternoon. A safe and easy morning voyage to the island's eastern tip or its south beaches can be followed by a downright uncomfortable and challenging return trip. When I was younger, I could tolerate the pounding from the waves. I can

---

[18] The survey was later used to delineate the land parcels that were auctioned by the government. Disputes subsequently arose about potential errors for the boundaries around Big Rice and Little Rice Bays. Additional surveying done during the late 19th century clarified the boundaries.

[19] The water along Long Point's public beaches sometimes contain a plentiful amount of algae, particularly during July and August. Occasionally, fecal coliform is present, a consequence of older, substandard septic systems in the built-up part of the island. Algae and fecal coliform are far less likely to be found in the waters surrounding the distant reaches of the island.

[20] Sea breezes are a type of shoreline effect. As the sun heats the ground on or inland from the shore, the air above it rises and is replaced by air from over the water.

no longer do so.[21] Before setting out on a voyage to Long Point's far reaches, it is advisable to obtain the official Environment Canada marine forecast as it usually includes whether waves are likely to develop in the afternoon and what their height will be.

---

[21] As we age our brain shrinks substantially, causing the space between the skull and brain to increase. A consequence is that the cerebrospinal fluid within the space becomes far less effective at cushioning the brain from sudden acceleration. Everyone develops this condition, making them susceptibility to injury from events which have little to no impact on younger people.

How Long Point Formed and Continues to Evolve

How Long Point formed over thousands of years is more complex than commonly believed. Lake Erie is a recent geological formation that developed roughly 12,500 years ago during deglaciation. [16] Its modern form, however, is only 4,000 years old, and it was during that later stage of development that conventional sand spit-forming processes impacted Long Point's development. An attestation is a delta at the western root of the island through which runs Big Creek. It is a small stream today, but it was formerly a more substantial river fed by melting glacial ice. Eluviation in the river deposited sand and silt throughout and beyond the delta.[22] This activity gave Long Point some estuarial characteristics.

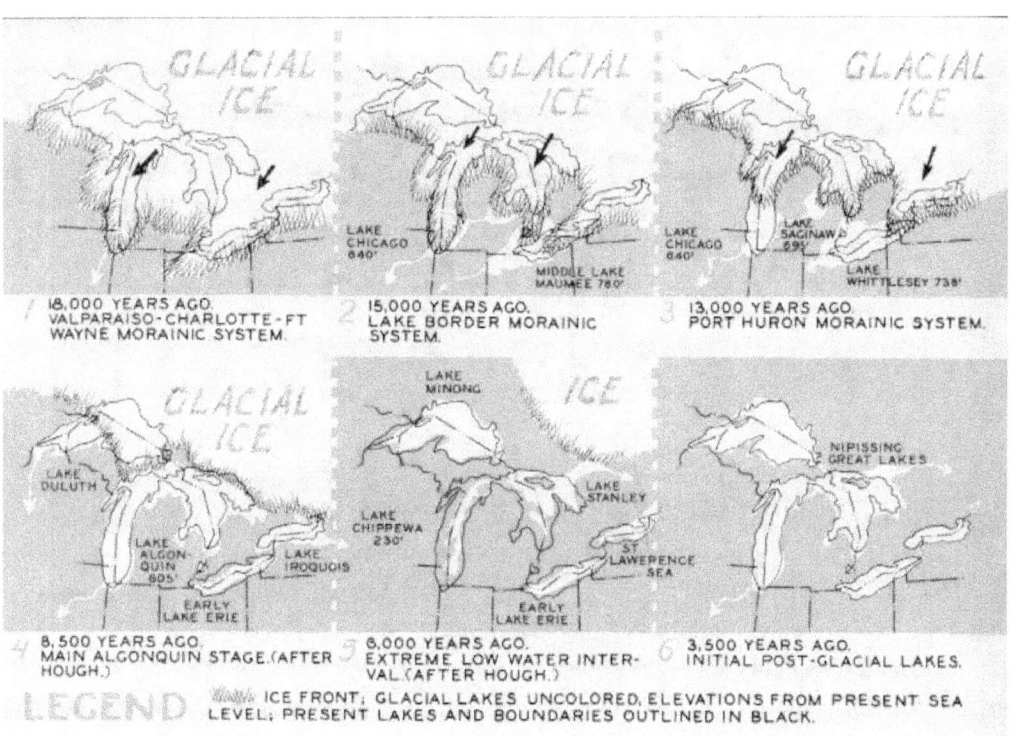

Figure 2. Glaciation history of the Great Lakes Basin. [17]

The other conventional process that played a role in Long Point's development over the last 4,000 years was the erosion of shoreline clifftop dunes located west of the island. Much of this occurred when the lake level was much higher than it is now. Sand from the collapsed dunes drifted eastward. One nearby dune (known as Sand Hills Park) remains to this day. (Photo 2) Others are long gone because erosion of the lake's shores is an ongoing process. Scientists estimate that over

---

[22] Eluviation is the transport of dispersed solids in a river current.

the last 2,000 years erosion has caused the surface area of Lake Erie to increase 15 to 20 percent. Over the same period, the lake has become 30 to 35% shallower. [18]

The source of the sand for the clifftop dunes was a formation known as the Norfolk Sand Plain. It extends over 1,200 square miles north and generally west of Long Point and was deposited when glacial Lake Whittlesey drained through the area at least 13,000 years ago, creating a delta. [19] The sand plain, which reaches the Lake Erie shore in some places, has an average depth of about nine metres, although, in some areas it is as deep as 25 metres. [20]

Photo 2, Sand Hills Park. (Author's photo)

Although these two conventional spit formation processes (river alluviation and the collapse of sandy shorelines) occurred, they are not sufficient to explain Long Point's formation. In a formidable 384-page analysis, earth scientist Dr. John Coakley concluded that Long Point "did not result from conventional sand spit formation".

Coakley explains that 12,500 years ago, a land mass (composed of gravel, sand, and silt) bridged the north shore of Lake Erie from present-day Port Rowan to the south shore near Erie, Pennsylvania. The bridge was an end moraine, the elevated line of debris left behind where a glacier had reached its maximum extension.

Around 10,000 years ago, as glaciers to the north continued to melt, the rising lake level disconnected the land bridge from the south shore, leaving a long peninsula extending from the north shore. Carbon dating of organic content from core samples taken during lakebed drilling demonstrates that the peninsula had become at least partially wooded 7,000 to 8,500 years ago. (Figure 4, Panel A) [21]

As the lake level continued to rise, the peninsula became more and more submerged, and lake currents carried sand and silt from the peninsula northeastward. It was that activity that laid the foundation for Long Point, Ryerson's Island, and Bluff Bar. Today, the former peninsula survives as an underwater ridge, known as the Long Point – Erie Ridge. (Figure 3)

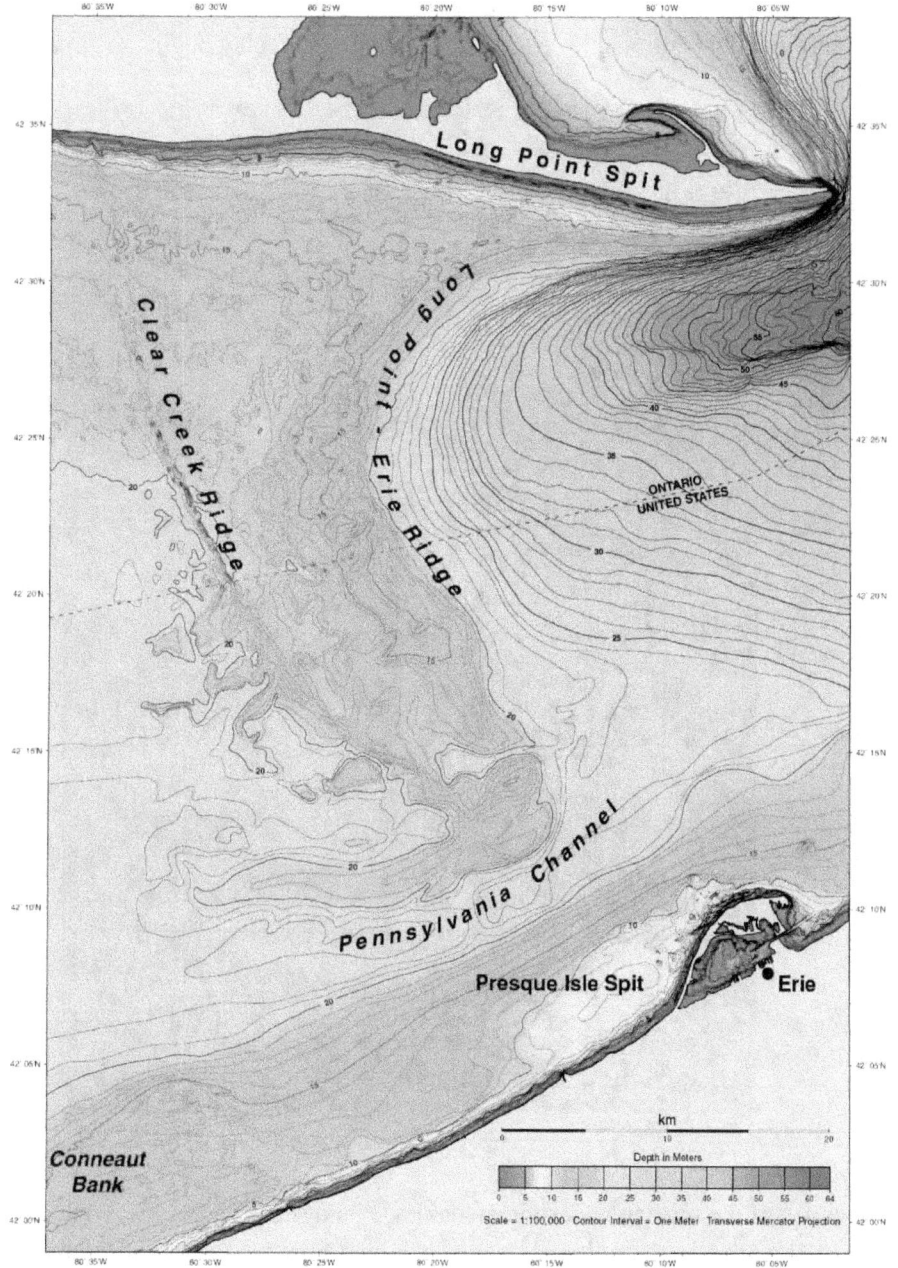

Figure 3. Lake Erie bathymetry.
(National Oceanic & Atmospheric Administration, U.S. Dept. of Commerce)

Coakley drilled boreholes on Long Point during the summers of 1980 and 1981, sampling every metre or so.[23] (Photo 3) Among his findings was that the sand layer on the western part of Long Point is relatively thin, about three meters in depth. It is underlaid by clay. [22] Eastward, the sand layer gets progressively deeper. At the tip of the island it is about 18 meters deep. Below that, there is a 40-metre-thick transitional layer of silt and sand before clay begins to appear.

Photo 3, John Coakley drilling on Long Point. [22]

While much of the science underlying Coakley's analysis is arcane, his conclusions can be readily presented. Figure 4 on the following page, extracted from his PhD thesis, depicts how Long Point evolved. In the figure, panel D illustrates Long Point's current configuration and the

---

[23] Coakley drilled near the south beach east of the Provincial Park, near the north shore of Cedar Creek Ridge, and near the shore of Gravelly Bay close to Anderson Pond. He also had access to data from Lewis who had drilled at the tip in 1966. The four boreholes ranged in depth from 40 to 122 metres.

underwater ridge. The other three panels temporally depict three evolutionary phases. Each phase is superimposed over the island's current configuration. Noteworthy are the diminutive peninsulas that extend northeast. These were precursors to the ridges which exist on Long Point today.

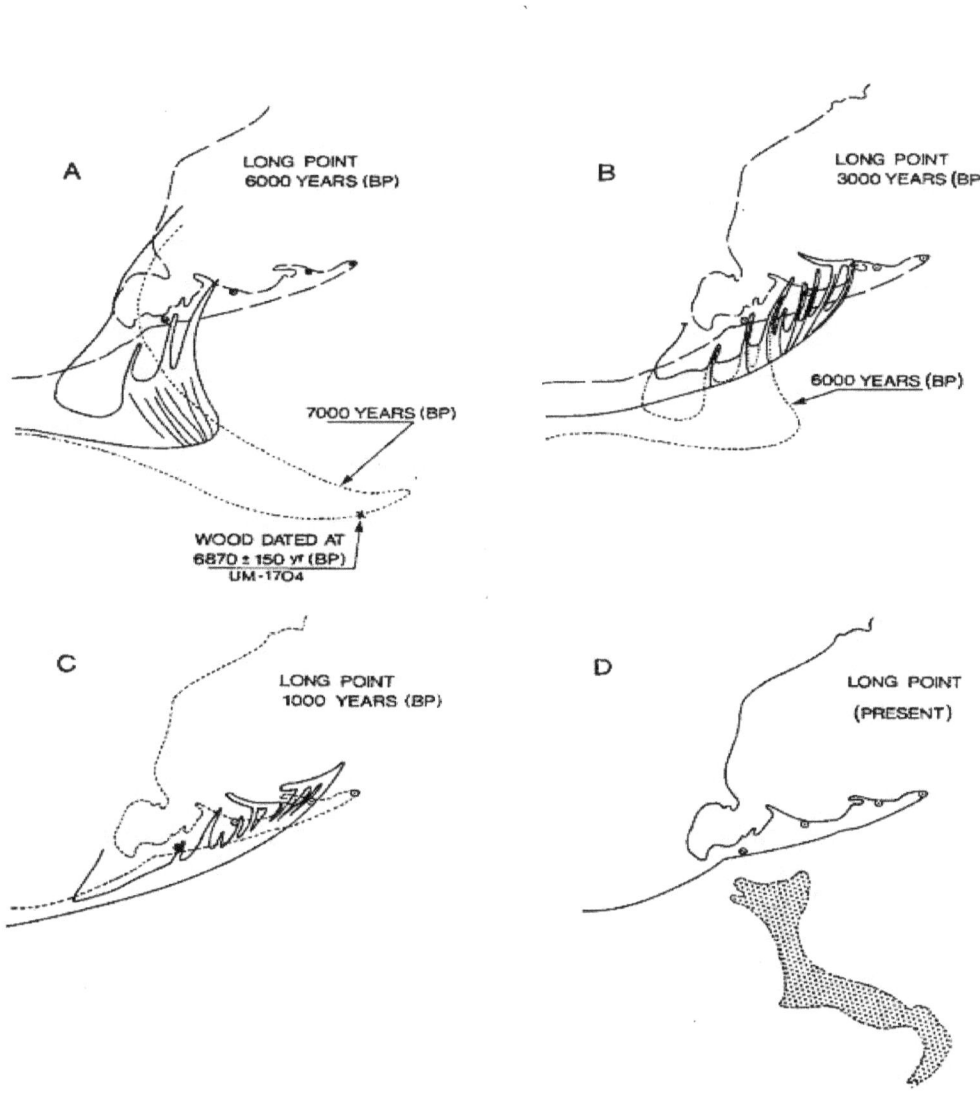

Figure 4. Coakley's pictorial evolution of Long Point. [22]

Today, small secondary islands extend northwestward from Long Point. (Figure 5) Three of them form a chain that terminates with Ryerson's Island, the end of which is known as Pottahawk Point. The chain may be a peninsular remnant, that later became a single island that subsequently eroded after timber was harvested during the 19th century. Long ago, the island extended further northward. That extension manifests today as a reef of sand. (i.e. a submerged sandbar.)

The other northwestward facing island is closer to the eastern end of Long Point. Although this island is unnamed, its northwestern tip is called Bluff Point.[24] This island too, once extended farther. What remains is an arcuate five-kilometer-long sandbar known locally as Bluff Bar. The bar has been submerged for much of the last 50 years, but it can be waded upon over its entire length. During the 1930s and the mid-20th century, when the level of Lake Erie was lower, the bar emerged above the water's surface.

The existence of all these secondary islands is consistent with Coakley's analyses of how Long Point was formed.

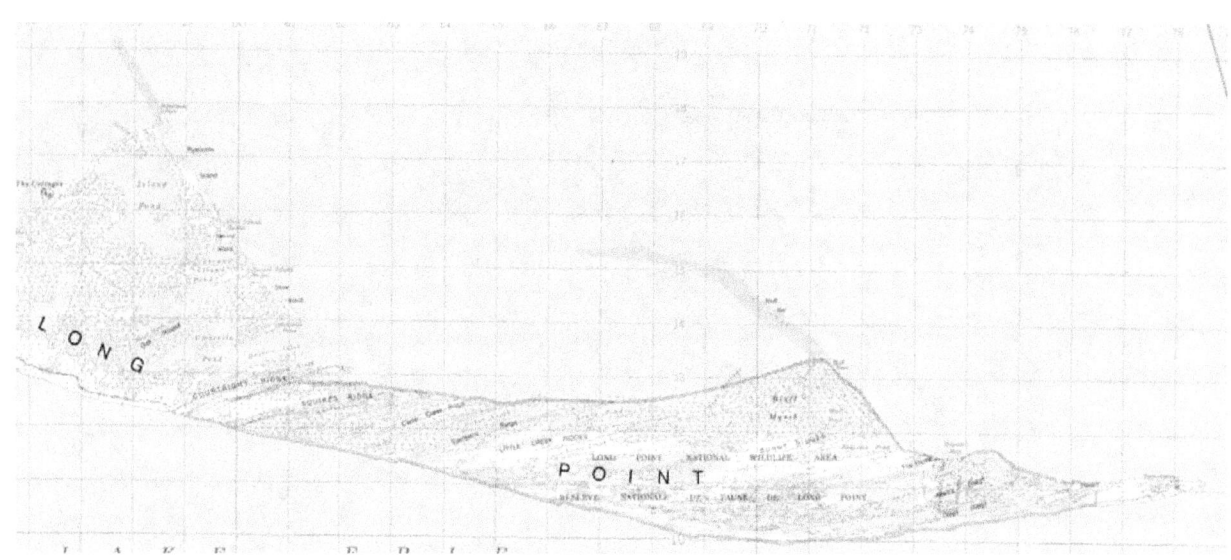

Figure 5. Topographical map of the eastern portion of Long Point.
The northwestward facing secondary islands and their extended sandbars are plainly apparent.
(Government of Canada, 1994)

---

[24] This island was known as The Bluffs during the 19th century.

While Coakley's work provides a data-driven, theoretical impression of how Long Point evolved over thousands of years, the directly observed historical record of the last 200 years demonstrates ongoing change. The most notable of these changes has occurred at each end of the island, not just because these have been continuously inhabited areas —where the changes were more likely to be observed —but also because, in general, these areas have minimal relief above the lake.

Except for some scattered gravel, Long Point is comprised of sand. Wind, waves, and currents of sufficient strength will fluidize the sand and move it around, causing land to be lost in one place and gained in another. Land will also be lost due to encroachment during long-duration periods of high water, only to be recovered years or decades later as the lake level recedes. The following charts show how Lake Erie's level has fluctuated over 164 years. The regular, sawtooth pattern in the data reflects seasonal variation: the lake level decreases in the Fall when evaporation is at its peak, then rises due to runoff from melting snow and rain during the Spring season.

However, it is the long-term variation that is most significant. Note that the range from the lowest water level to the highest is 2.1 metres (seven feet). This is an enormous variation, and one that has been impactful. The lowest level occurred in the 1930s —the Dust Bowl years —when construction commenced at Long Point to implement the subdivision plan that had been drafted in the early 1920s. The highest recorded level occurred in 2019. A near-high occurred during the mid-1980s, a time when many beachfront cottages were overtaken and carried away by a storm.

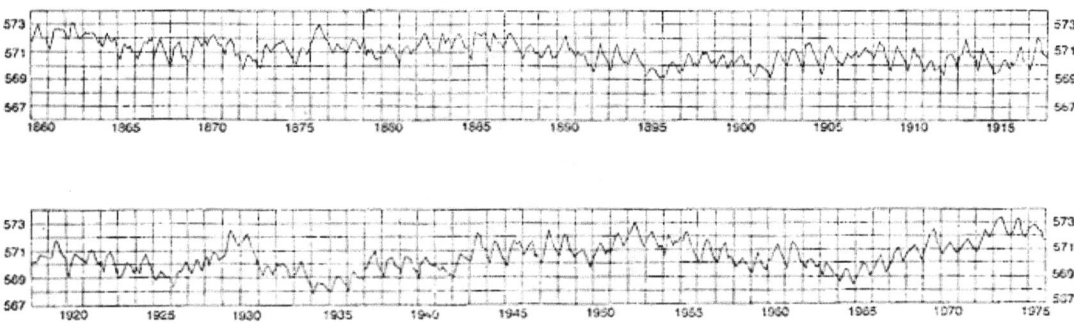

Figure 6. Variation in Lake Erie Water Level, (feet). 1860-1975. Annual peaks and troughs reflect seasonal variation. (Great Lakes Levels Board)

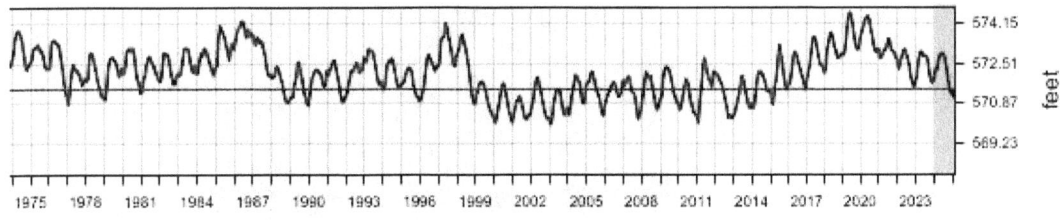

Figure 7. Recent variation in Lake Erie Water Level, (feet) 1974-2024. (U.S. Army Corps of Engineers)

Photo 4 The eastern tip of Long Point during 1935. Note the location of the lighthouse. (Wilton Lloyd-Smith) (Public domain)

Photo 5 The eastern tip of Long Point in 2016. (Author's photo)

Changes at Long Point can be rapid. Very severe storms, (for the sake of argument those that might occur every fifty years or so) can cause flooding, especially when a storm happens during a year when the lake level is higher than it typically is. That was the circumstance when Jeremiah (Johnny) Becker, husband of Abigail Becker, (the well-known Heroine of Long Point[25]) met his fate at Long Point. On New Years Day, 1864, as the lake raged toward his cabin, which was in the vicinity of the present-day new Provincial Park, Becker evacuated eastward. Tragically, he either drowned or succumbed to the cold while on his way. [23] The following Spring, his body and that of his dog were found five kilometers down the island. [24] In 1975, Long Point Company keeper John Dixon met a similar fate in the same area. [15]

An insidious event that can strike Long Point occurs after intense winds are sustained. Such winds cause water to pile up at the leeward (downwind) end of the lake. For example, an intense, enduring westerly blow causes the lake to rise at Buffalo, New York. Simultaneously, the level falls in the western basin near Toledo, Ohio. The technical term for this phenomenon is *wind set-up*. The surface of the lake becomes tilted.[26] If the wind suddenly changes direction or subsides abruptly (as may happen once a weather front passes by) the piled-up water will seek flatness. This manifests itself as a wave, and the occurrence known as a seiche.[27] In the common vernacular, seiches are sometimes referred to as the bathtub effect. That is a handy notion because it is reminiscent of water splashing back and forth in a tub, and all seiches do in fact oscillate while fading away.

Imagine yourself wading knee-deep on a sandbar in Long Point Bay. If a seiche were to occur, you would not see an approaching wave. Rather, if you could be sufficiently perceptive, what you would observe is the depth of the water around you slowly rising. What people can and do observe at Long Point is the water rising in their boathouses or along seawalls. Even then, they would probably have to look periodically, say every half hour or so, to recognize that the water has risen.

It isn't uncommon for a seiche to wash across the causeway that leads to Long Point. Such events might occur roughly every five years. Security cameras have recorded the phenomena. Water is seen to be rushing across the road from east to west. The flow is not periodic or wave-like; it is continuous and enduring.

In the most extreme instances, a seiche can wash across Long Point itself. The most severe occurrence in recorded history happened in late October or early November 1833. Richard Johnson, born in 1813, related that he had gone to Long Point to fish and camp. [25] The following day, the wind started to blow in the evening, first from the south-southeast before shifting from the southwest. Finally, it blew directly from the west. The lake broke across the Long Point isthmus

---

[25] In 1854, Abigail Becker assisted the crew of the schooner Conductor after it grounded on a sandbar during a late November storm. For her fortitude, she was widely recognized as a heroine. The recipient of two honorariums and a gold medal, she was able to leave the hardscrabble life she had endured on Long Point for a farm on the mainland.

[26] The cause of the tilt is friction at the air/water interface. Friction creates drag which forces water near the lake's surface downwind. Although the tilt may become steady, wind set-up is not a static condition because deep below the lake's surface return currents will be moving water in the opposite direction to the wind.

[27] While we can readily perceive wind-born surface waves such as those arriving at a shoreline, the wave that occurs during a seiche is a *standing wave* that we cannot be perceived in a similar fashion.

and began flowing into the bay. Sometime afterwards, Jackson observed the flow reverse. A seiche had arrived. The rushing water flowing from the bay to the lake carved a deep channel which would become known as The Cut, because it severed what had been a peninsula transforming it to an island. At the time, the occurrence was considered remarkable. Accordingly, it gave rise to press coverage in Canada, Britain, and the United States. [26] The *Advocate of Science*, a scientific journal published in Baltimore, reported that the cut was 900 feet wide (274 metres) and 10 to 12 feet deep (3 to 3.7 metres).

Severe seiches, while rare, can be life-threatening. In 1844, a sustained storm with winds from the northeast, perhaps a consequence of an Atlantic hurricane, piled up water at the west end of Lake Erie. On October 18th, the wind shifted, and water sloshed back eastward. The consequences at Buffalo were devastating. Dozens of people drowned when a flood overran the city. Estimates of the actual number of deaths vary. However, an article on the United States National Oceanic and Atmospheric Administration website states the death toll was 78. [27] The names of many of the dead were published in the local newspapers.

The crew of the steamer *Kent* reported that the seiche damaged the piers at Port Dover and Port Ryerse. The lighthouse at the tip of Long Point also incurred damage. [28] In a presentation to a historical society in 1906, local schoolteacher Edmund Pugsley, stated the seiche killed hundreds of cattle. [29]

Lake breakthroughs and seiches have severed Long Point at various locations over the length of Long Point. In his book *Lore and Legends of Long Point,* Barrett wrote that before the 1833 storm, Long Point had long been an actual peninsula. Geographer Jedidiah Morse (born in 1761) would have disagreed. He wrote that it wasn't unusual for Long Point (which he referred to as the North Foreland and also as Abineau) to be "overflown" from time to time, such that portage was unnecessary.[28] [30] The same perspective also appears in a gazetteer published in 1813.

> From the head of the bay there is a carrying place across, over a flat
> sand, about eight chains distance, into Lake Erie, which sometimes
> is sufficiently overflown to be used as a passage for small boats. [31]

Morse's view that Long Point was occasionally an island is also consistent with a British naval chart carrying a date of 1815. The chart shows a creek running through the Long Point isthmus. It also shows Big Creek entering Long Point Bay —not directly into Lake Erie.

A subsequent chart carrying an 1818 date depicts Long Point as a peninsula. (Figure 68) On that chart, the lake has washed over into the Big Creek marsh, thereby redirecting the creek outlet directly into Lake Erie. Both charts would have been accurate at one time or another. Charts were occasionally re-released. The date at the top of the chart would remain the same and the revision could appear elsewhere.

Today, near the entrance to the provincial park near the Old Cut stands a historical plaque. It states this was the location of a "carrying place" where early explorers would portage across the

---

[28] Jedidah Morse' use of the name Abineau for Long Point likely reflected his familiarity with the writings of the 17th-century Jesuit explorer Claude Aveneau. Point Abino, a small peninsula that juts out from the Lake Erie's north shore west of Crystal Beach, was named after Aveneau.

Long Point isthmus. The site of the plaque should not be deemed to mark a specific place of portage precisely. Over centuries various locations on the western part of Long Point would have offered opportunities to cross the isthmus. The journals of early French explorers strongly suggest that they passed from the Inner Bay into Big Creek before portaging to Lake Erie. Using that route, they would have traversed over a short section of beach to the lake in the area through which Hastings Drive now passes.

Cottage Creek, which flows southeast from the Long Point Company's headquarters, was known as Carrying Place Creek in the late 19th century. Yet, the creek is seven miles east of the causeway. Although most of the early travelers would have preferred to remain in the confines of the Inner Bay as much as possible before crossing into the main body of Lake Erie, a few may have paddled along Carrying Place Creek through what is today the Long Point Company's marsh to reach the southern beach and cross there.

In conclusion, future breakthroughs across Long Point at one location or another should be anticipated.

Early Habitation & Development

Seven hundred years ago there was an Indigenous People's settlement at Port Rowan. In 1976, excavation of the site revealed the remains of six long houses, a burial ground and a protective double palisade. The location, which is on private property, has since been designated the *Reid* site. [32]

In 1981, a burial ground was discovered on Long Point. This site, which is located far out on the island south of Bluff Point on a sandy hill overlooking Anderson Pond, has been designated *Varden*. Anthropologists hypothesize the burial ground was associated with a seasonal fishing camp used by Indigenous People for decades, if not centuries. Occasionally, someone died at the camp and was buried at the site. In 2010, anthropologists reported the *Varden* site to be "the largest Transitional Woodland human skeletal sample excavated in southern Ontario to date." [29]

In 1985, an excavation at a different location exposed the remains (and what were apparently many personal items) of an Indigenous man believed to have passed away about a thousand years ago. [33] Of course, Indigenous Peoples' use of Long Point would have reached much further back in time. However, the three instances mentioned are the ones for which archeological information is publicly available.

After the Treaty of Paris ended the eight-year long American War of Independence (1775 to 1783), many British loyalists and soldiers sought to avoid discrimination and retribution by relocating north to British-held lands. Among the first to leave were those whose businesses, land, and homes had been confiscated because they believed in the British king and the parliamentary system of government, not the new republic. [30, 31] Because New York City was a British stronghold, most of the loyalists gravitated there, and the British supplied ships to evacuate them to New Brunswick, Nova Scotia, or Quebec. There were also a few British ship departures from Charleston, South Carolina, and St. Augustine, Florida.

Smaller numbers traveled inland following routes such as the Hudson River to Albany, then the Mohawk River to Rome, and eventually following the Oswego River to Lake Ontario. [34] Another route from Rome went to Sacket's Harbor. A few emigres from the Washington area traced the path of the Potomac River and likely reached Lake Erie via French Creek. Some, on reaching Upper Canada, then headed west along Lake Erie's northern shore.

Two early parties were John Troyer's and his family, who came from Pennsylvania, and Lucas Dedrick's party. Troyer (who was a pacifist as opposed to a loyalist) settled at a creek outlet just east of Port Rowan on land that later became known as Troyer's Flats. [35] Dedrick settled near the mouth of a different creek and flat, further west. It is known that Dedrick's party arrived in the

---

[29] ibid

[30] There was also migration southward. Some individuals who were sympathetic to the Rebel cause, left Quebec and the Maritime provinces for the United States. [449]

[31] Others fled north because speculative articles in newspapers warned that in spite of the peace Britain would soon attack and further violence could be expected. [449]

area in 1793 because British surveyor James Chewett met them when they were passing the Grand River and entered this fact in his notes.[32]

The Secord, Mabee, McMichael, Ryerson, and Smith families were other early newcomers. Some of these families had previously relocated to the Maritimes. However, after they found the climate harsh there and the soil poor, they decided to leave for Upper Canada. Typically, multiple families set out together on an arduous journey, which could take more than a year to complete. They followed shorelines; some in the group walked on foot while others traveled in bateaux loaded with household items and supplies. Staples such as cornmeal sustained them on the journey. They also hunted and gathered what they could. Some may have consumed milk from a cow they drove along with them. [36]

Clearing, building shelter and establishing crops were the settler's urgent priorities. Because there was not yet any system for land grants which, the early arrivals were technically squatters. In time, they gained titles for the farms they had established. School was first taught in 1789, apparently by Troyer's son, Deacon Michael Troyer. [37] [38] [39] He later became a blacksmith. [35] The arrival of the Backhouse family, probably around 1797, is noteworthy because of the fine grist mill they built, which still stands just north of Port Rowan on the banks of Venison Creek. They were not technically loyalists because they had only arrived in the American colonies as the War of Independence broke out.

The settlement soon took on the name Long Point and over time that name was applied to a wide regional area with no official borders that roughly comprised today's North and South Walsingham townships and Charlotteville township.[33]

The virgin forests of the settlement were rich with hardwood and white pine, a species highly valued for its workability and for making ship masts and booms. Many pine specimens were hundreds of years old. The largest was reported to be more than seven feet in diameter (2.1 metres). [40] The claim is not unreasonable. An official government report on Upper Canada's natural resources prepared in 1862 stated that the average diameter of the white pine was greater than three to four feet and the height 140 to 160 feet (43 to 49 meters). [41] The report also stated that the largest specimens were found near the shoreline of Lake Erie where diameters of five to six feet and heights of 200 feet (61 metres) were not uncommon. The military utility of these trees for making ship masts did not go unnoticed. Upon surveying the area, British surveyors designated the finest specimens as the exclusive property of the Admiralty.[34] Contractors were issued no-fee licenses to cut the large pine for the navy's use.By 1827 a dues-based system applicable to general timbering on Crown Land had been established.

---

[32] Chewett was mapping the north shore of Lake Erie from June 9 to August 12, 1793. [444]

[33] The influx of settlers increased following Governor Simcoe's 1795 visit to the region, and after a survey was done a year later by Daniel Hazen.

[34] In 1711, British lawmakers, in the interest of national security, passed legislation decreeing that all white pine trees greater than 24 inches in diameter in the colonies were thenceforth the protected property of the Crown. This led to the large pines becoming known as *Queen Anne's*.

Photo 6 How the Long Point region's tall pine would have appeared. (Unknown date)
(Ontario Ministry of Natural Resources and Fisheries, Dr. Edmund Zavitz collection)

Although shipbuilding would have commenced first in regions to the east, such as Kingston and Niagara, it was underway in the Long Point settlement by the 1790s. John Troyer seems to have been the first individual to build a sailboat in the settlement. In 1797, he filed a petition requesting grant of the water's edge in front of his farm so he could build a dock there from which to launch the boat. A year later, he advertised it for sale in the *Gazette*.[35]

TO BE SOLD

On the stocks at the Bay of Long Point at any time before the 28th of June next, a GOOD SLOOP, ready for launching, in good order and warranted sound and masterly built. She is framed of the best black walnut timber, 38 tuns [sic] burthen, and calculated for carrying timber. With her will be sold her rigging and tackle compleat. [sic] She will be sold by consent of Mr. Troyer, and a good title with warranty given on the sale. The conditions are for cash only, one half down and the other in three months, with approved security of payment. "Wm. Dealy."

"I approve of the above J. Troyer." [42]

---

[35] The Gazette was Upper Canada's first newspaper. Printed at Newark (now Niagara-on-the-Lake,) content was restricted to government announcements, notices, documents, and propaganda, although an occasional commercial notice appeared. Social information such as births or deaths, editorials, stories, and political discourse were not published. The limitations were imposed by the Governor John Graves Simcoe

In a book he published in 1898, E. A. Owen portrayed (perhaps dubiously) Troyer to be a madman obsessed with a fear of witches. [43] Regardless of whether that is true or not, it is clearly evident that Troyer was a capable and extremely hardworking individual. He established a farm, constructed and ran a grist mill, and built a boat —all in rapid succession. [35]

Settlers who came north and could demonstrate they had been loyal to Britain during the American Revolution became the beneficiaries of land grants. Those who had served in the military received the largest parcels. A soldier was typically granted 200 acres. Officers received more. A captain might be granted as much as 2,000 acres and senior officers more. Joseph Ryerson (who would become the Long Point settlement's first Sheriff,) initially received 400 acres after being evacuated to the Maritimes at the rank of lieutenant. He continued his association with the military and his rank eventually advanced to Colonel. Ultimately, he accrued at least 2,000 acres.

Lesser numbers arrived directly from Great Britain. A British officer who had done duty afar some place in the world would be put on inactive duty at reduced pay (typically half-pay) after returning home. If he was adventuresome, he could retire and accept a land grant in Canada.

British policy had long held that the North American colonies be cleared of timber to make way for agricultural development. To retain their land grant, settlers were required to clear a portion of their land each year. Clearing in the Long Point settlement was widespread. It continued northward for almost a century, even though British geographers became aware in the 1840s that land in Norfolk County was highly susceptible to erosion after being cleared, potentially rendering it blow sand.

On the island of Long Point itself, a small number of Indigenous People took refuge. They were joined by a few settlers who did not qualify for or had not yet received a land grant. Intermarriage was common.[36] (Rare obituaries mention individuals born on the island at the beginning of the 19th century.) Those living on the island would have sustained themselves and their families through hunting, fishing, and maintaining vegetable gardens, as unlike today, there was thin soil at some locations. It is likely that some settlers also grazed a cow or other livestock.[37,38]

There were no land grants on Long Point. The reason was an elite group of British miliary officers who enjoyed waterfowling (and had the muskets, leisure time, and access to horses for travel) wanted the island to remain Crown Land. Late in the 18th century, they arranged for John McFarland, who held the lofty status of *Her Majesty's Builder of Ships,* to lobby the colonial Governor John Graves Simcoe. McFarland convinced Simcoe to exclude Long Point and the spit on Burlington Bay from grants. [44] [45] There would be just one exception. In 1808, Col. Joseph Ryerson, the Long Point settlement's first sheriff, submitted a petition for compensation, asserting a survey error had deprived him the proper amount of land on his farm on the 2nd Concession of Charlotteville Township. [46] [47] [48] Subsequently, Ryerson was granted 191 acres of the island that

---

[36] Specific references pertaining to Native People who resided on Long Point during the 19th century have been omitted from this book due to content that may be deemed offensive.
[37] Alexander Somerville, a well-traveled journalist, reported that by mid-century the number of settler units on the island might have numbered about 20. [128]
[38] After the formation of the Long Point Company, head keeper William Leary kept cattle on Ryerson's Island

includes Pottahawk Point. Although Ryerson never owned the entirety of the island, it came to be known as Ryerson's Island. For many years he and his family used the place for hunting and as a summer getaway. They also cleared and cultivated some of the lands.

Development of the entire Long Point region suffered a significant setback during the War of 1812. The British had both captured Buffalo and attacked the American fleet at Erie, Pennsylvania. In response, early in 1814, American infantry camped in defensive posture at Erie. On May 15th, a contingent of 500 troops sailed from Erie to the Canadian shore. The expedition, an initiative of a certain Colonel Campbell, was unauthorized. The American troops marched into Port Dover where they burned the grist mills, sawmills, tanneries and distilleries. They also torched homes. As they withdrew, the forces burned other villages along the shore. Although the rampage lasted just five days, it was devastating. The American troops were accused of war crimes, and even in the United States their actions drew condemnation:

Disgraceful Termination of the expedition to Long Point

> In our last we mentioned that an attack on Long Point, or Dover, was in contemplation, by the American forces stationed at Erie. We now publish the disgraceful and unmanly termination of that expedition. This paper has uniformly been the advocate of a fair, open, and honerable [sic] war; believing that the causes are abundantly sufficient to justify the American government in appealing to the last resort of nations —disgust and indignation from a scene in which the American character is disgraced by a wanton attack on defenseless women and children; where the military are suffered to become, not the honorable and proud defenders of their country's rights, but miserable incendiaries for the burning and destruction of private property! The demerit of such actions ought to rest only with our enemies; and if the American troops, have in the present instance, been guilty of such lawless conduct, let the public indignation fall on the heads of those who had the management of the expedition. [49]

U.S. General Jacob Brown ordered the arrest and court martial of Colonel Campbell. During the subsequent proceedings, Campbell was criticized for initiating the expedition in the first place, and for attacking homes and particular businesses. However, he escaped responsibility for the torching of the area's grist mills when the court deemed that action a strategic act of war. The British probably considered the court martial of Campbell to be a hollow act of placation. His brutal tactics, and an unrelated action against York (Toronto) are believed to have been significant factors in the British decision to attack and set fires in Washington, D.C., including to the Capitol building and White House.

Anti-American sentiment was acute in Canada following the war. British officials actively discouraged immigration from the United States, while not suspending it completely. [50] The local economy of the Long Point region had been weakened, but it received a boost after Englishman John Mason constructed a blast furnace adjacent to Potter's Creek near today's village of

Normandale. The furnace commenced operation in 1817 but ran just sporadically for a few months until Mason suffered an untimely death. His widow sold the furnace in 1820 to a group of six Americans that included Hiram Capron. Operating as Capron and Company, the new enterprise ran the furnace and cast some of the iron, albeit with quality issues. [51] After a fire in 1830 destroyed the furnace, the site was acquired by local contractors, the VanNorman brothers. They built a new unit using improved technology, that not only doubled capacity but resolved the quality issues with the metal.[39] The Normandale furnace was Upper Canada's first successful iron production facility, and it gave rise to three forges and multiple foundries that cast the iron into stoves, tools, pots, pans, kettles, and hardware. Blacksmiths took up shop to work the iron into more elaborate items such as agricultural implements. [52] At least one such facility was located in Port Rowan.[40] [53]

Between 1815 and 1850 roughly a million people emigrated from Britian to Canada. [50] A private initiative that promoted emigration, not only from Britain but other countries in Europe, was the formation of The Canada Company in 1825. The brainchild of a group of English merchants and capitalists, this company's business plan proposed buying then reselling to the public the land in Upper Canada that Britain had set aside as Crown Reserves, plus one-half of the land reserved for the Clergy. The group backed their application for a corporate charter with a capital sum of one million pounds. To further sway the British government and to preempt resentment from existing settlers, the group offered to ignore any land that had been occupied by squatters for ten or more years:

> Finally, there are within the Clergy and Crown Reserves, various parcels of land which have been occupied for ten years and upwards, by persons who have resided upon them, not only without any grant, but without any pretense of legal title, and who, in America, are usually designated by the appellation of "Squatters," but who, notwithstanding, have not been disturbed in that occupation.....it being understood that the several portions of the Crown and Clergy Reserves which, as above mentioned, have been granted or demised on lease, or occupied on the license or promise of the Government, or appropriated to public or clerical purposes or occupied without disturbance for ten years, or which may be peculiarly convenient or necessary either for the public service or the ecclesiastical objects already mentioned, are to be wholly exempted. [54]

The British government approved The Canada Company's request for a corporate charter, and the company proceeded to purchase almost two million acres of Crown Land to resell.[41] To entice Europeans to move overseas, the company offered them inexpensive crossing on good ocean

---

[39] ibid

[40] A previous attempt to manufacture iron had been made at Lyndhurst, Ontario. A blast furnace was erected there around 1800. However, the venture is considered to have been unsuccessful. [53]

[41] Most, but not all the land the Canada Company acquired was closer to Lake Huron than to Lake Erie.

ships. After the settlers landed, it sold them the tools and implements they would need to establish their farms.

The Canada Company became aware of the potential for Big Creek to serve as an artery for moving inland timber to Lake Erie. No later than 1841, it was advertising the sale pine forest near the creek. The advertisements specifically called out the opportunity the creek presented for getting timber to American markets. (Figure 8)

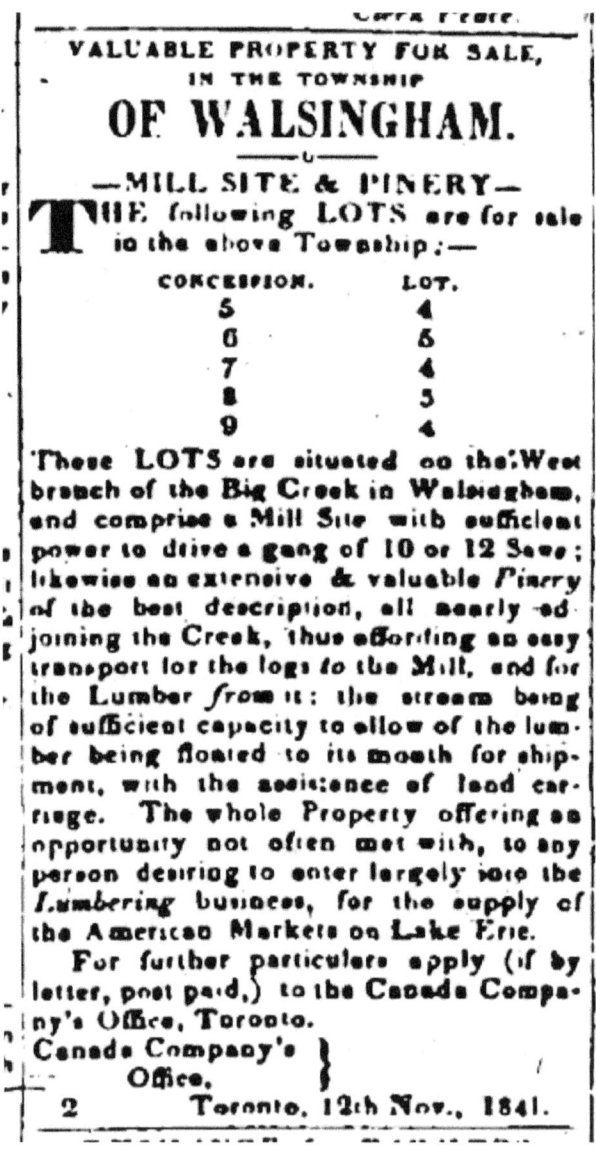

Figure 8. Canada Company advertisement offering timberland along Big Creek for sale. 1841.

Once the Erie Canal connected the Hudson River to Lake Erie in 1825, Buffalo became a gateway to Canada and the midwestern United States. Immigrants and freight arriving at New York City —the continent's busiest seaport —could transfer to steam-powered packet boats that plied the Hudson River to Albany.[42] There, most passengers and goods transferred to slow canal boats destined for Buffalo. Lesser volumes transferred to the Oswego Canal and onto southeastern ports on Lake Ontario. By 1833, passenger and freight vessels could pass between Lake Ontario and Lake Erie through the Welland Canal.

Steamboats running on a schedule began making calls to Port Rowan no later than 1836.[43] The *Thames* ran that year between Buffalo and Port Stanley with calls at Ryerse's Creek, Port Rowan, and Port Burwell. The total one-way trip took about two days, with departures dependent on the weather. [55] These early steamers rarely carried more than 24 hours of firewood for heating the boiler, making port calls a necessity. The captain would make on-the-spot purchases, preferably the best hardwood, either through barter or with cash.[44] [56] Making stops at multiple ports allowed the captain to bargain with vendors, some of whom were farmers seeking to supplement their income. Throughout the Great Lakes region, such vendors became colloquially known as woodhawks.

It was on the steamer *Thames* in 1836 that naturalist and ornithological illustrator William Pope completed his voyage from England to Canada. He sailed from London on March 28 and arrived in New York on May 7th. After an 11-hour 160-mile trip up the Hudson River to Albany on the steamboat *Erie*, traveling became slow and challenging for the genteel Pope. In his journal, he describes travel on the Erie Canal as miserable. Rather than ride on the crowded, stinking boat that carried his trunk, he often chose to walk with the horses on the towpath beside the canal — even at night. Where stages were available, he transferred to them. But he found the coaches so firm and the roads so rough that overland travel left him bruised, exhausted, and aching. Pope reached Port Stanley from Buffalo on the *Thames* on May 18th, having steamed through the cut that had formed across Long Point just a few years earlier. [57]

By 1843, the steamboats servicing Lake Erie ports were becoming larger and faster. The sidewheeler *Kent* could make the trip from Buffalo to Detroit in just two days with stops at Port Colborne, Port Dover, Port Ryerse, Port Rowan, and Port Stanley. Five dollars secured a passenger a place below deck shielded from the elements. For two dollars, one could make the trip on deck. [58] By 1850, the *Wave* was running twice weekly from Buffalo to Port Stanley, calling at Port Dover, Port Rowan, and Port Burwell. [59]

Reginald Fowler, a well-traveled English barrister, wrote this about his voyage:

---

[42] Packet boats were built to carry small freight and had no passenger cabins. However, paying passengers were often onboard the deck and in the hold.
[43] Prior to this time Port Rowan had been variably known as Cartwright's Landing, Dutcher's Corners, Wolven's Landing, and Wolvine.
[44] By the late 1840s, a canal was completed that connected Erie, Pennsylvania with the town of Beaver more than 125 miles south. The canal opened Pennsylvania's coal fields to Lake Erie. [372] Construction of the canal

> A steamboat took me to Port Rowan, where I intended to remain a few days. This boat being high pressure, panted and puffed through the water, making sufficient noise to prevent all sleep. One peculiarity of these boats, where the fuel for the fire is wood, is the great quantity of sparks and flakes of fire constantly thrown over the boat in all directions. The fiery shower gleaming in the air at night, and reflected by the water, is a pretty sight, but destructive to one's clothes, unless care be taken to knock off the sparks as they fall. [60]

For all its bustling trade and growth to a population of about 500 by mid-century, the village was still a recent frontier settlement. Fowler reviewed it unfavorably adding:

> Port Rowan is a wretched little collection of half ruinous log houses, woe-begone to a degree.... From Port Rowan a wagon conveyed me to Simcoe. The dust was horrible, the sun scorching; and the vehicle had no springs, either iron, or wood. Fortunately, the road traversed fine oak plains, and was, therefore, good. The light, sandy soil of these plains, produces good crops; and the woods were full of wildflowers —many very beautiful.

Timber and lumber accounted for a large portion of the local economy. The challenge was getting these commodities to market. Consequently, the forests near the shoreline were the first cut. In the 1840s, three men from well-to-do English families who had settled near Beachville, Ontario began buying land along Big Creek. They were Arthur Farmer, Capt. Henry DeBlaquiere, and Lt. Colonel Edmund Deedes.[45] [61]. They bought land east and west of the creek, eventually accumulating thousands of acres. In 1848, they mortgaged some parcels through an American bank to obtain capital to build steam-powered sawmills. They located one at the place now known as Rowan Mills and equipped it with a five-gang saw. They established another mill at Port Royal.[46]

DeBlaquiere personally managed the Rowan Mills facility. The village that rose there became known as DeBlaquiere's Hollow.[47] By 1847, the village had about 130 residents and DeBlaquiere was postmaster. A fascinating infrastructure related to the mill was the Laycock Line, a private railroad built to carry timber.[48] It had eastern and western sections. The western portion ran from the border of Houghton township near the village of Cultus, to the mill; the eastern section ran to the mill from the village of Walsingham. [62] The rails were not made from steel; they were hewed from ash, the hardest wood available. Nor was power brought to bear on the line. Teams of

---

commenced the transition to coal for vessel boilers. The development of railroads during the following decade furthered the transition. Railroads also made many canals obsolete.

[45] Henry DeBlaquiere was the son of the Honorable Peter Boyle DeBlaquiere, who became the first chancellor of the University of Toronto. Edmund Deedes was a veteran British military officer, who on his return England, had been placed on half-pay.

[46] Messrs. Jarom and Baker built a steam powered sawmill at or near Port Rowan about the same time.

[47] Rowan Mills was renamed Stisted during the late 1860s. No obvious signs exist today that there was ever a village there. The name of the locale on current maps is Rowan Mills.

[48] Originally from Buffalo, the Laycock family settled about four miles west of Rowan Mills near the present-day village of Cultus.

horses or oxen pulled the flat cars. Sawn lumber from the mill at Rowan Mills was forwarded down Big Creek to Port Royal, where it was staged for shipping.

DeBlaquiere and Farmer also had operations farther west in Houghton Township. They cut timber on the lands along Clear Creek and floated it to a shipping wharf they built at the mouth of the creek. During the winter months, their overall enterprise employed hundreds of tree cutters across the county. One of them, Colon LaFortune, claimed to have personally felled 400 four-foot diameter pines one winter.[49] During the warmer months, he worked as a river driver on Big Creek and as a ship crew member transporting lumber from Norfolk County to the St. Lawrence River and Lower Canada. No later than 1861, he was operating a business known as LaFortune & LaFayette that had a facility in Tonawanda. Vigorous labor did not prevent him from living a long life. He died at Port Dover in 1919 after suffering a fall. He was 102 years old. [63]

Oxen or horses pulled the sawn logs onto sleighs. A rope, chain, or cable was affixed to both ends of a log lying on the ground on one side of the sleigh. A horse or ox on the other side pulled the chain so that the log climbed a ramp and onto the sleigh. Two men, known as bull-ropers, would guide the log into position. (Photo 7) Once the sleigh was loaded, teams pulled it to the banks of Big Creek. Loading and unloading sleighs was hazardous work. Injuries and fatalities were not uncommon.

In the spring, most of the workforce returned to their farms and remained there for the planting, growing, and harvesting seasons. This arrangement was practical, and also beneficial for health. The dense canopy of the virgin forests inhibited sunlight from reaching the ground causing many areas to be damp, boggy, and pestilent. During the warmer months, a much smaller workforce of river drivers tumbled the logs into Big Creek. Wearing spiked boots (called caulks), they shepherded the logs, each stamped on the end with the owner's mark, to the mills or Port Royal. This too was hazardous work, and numerous newspaper reports tell of men injured or killed along or on Big Creek. In Port Rowan, on holidays such as the Queen's birthday, river drivers demonstrated their skill by engaging in log rolling competitions. [64] The workforce was likely paid in company scrip to spend in three retail stores that DeBlaquiere and Farmer operated, including one in Port Rowan.

From Port Royal, the lumber was shipped on barques and schooners. The logs were bundled into rafts and towed by steam tugs. Buffalo or Tonawanda were the most common destinations for logs. Some were milled there, and others forwarded by rail, or by boat along the Erie Canal. Shipments destined for Hamilton, York, or Lower Canada, went to Port Maitland, where the timber and lumber were transferred to canal boats that were towed along the feeder canal that linked to the Welland Canal.

Port Royal and Port Rowan were locations where considerable shipbuilding occurred. One database identifies at least 30 schooners constructed at the two ports during the years from 1848 to 1870. [65] Inspection of a private publication produced by the Association of Canadian Lake Underwriters identifies additional vessels. One, the *Margaret*, had Big Creek listed as its home port. [66] A few tugs and steamers were also built along the creek's banks. Port Ryerse had a sawmill

---

[49] At birth in 1818, Colon LaFortune was given the name Calixte Tellier dit LaFortune.

as well. Several schooners and one barque, the three-masted, 136-foot *Joseph S. Austin,* were built there.[50] Limited shipbuilding occurred at the port of Normandale.

The Exposition Universelle commenced in Paris in 1855. The Hudson Bay Company exhibited a collection of Canadian furs. DeBlaquiere, Farmer & Deedes exhibited planks and cross sections of oak, ash, maple, birch, cherry, ironwood, walnut, chestnut, beech, poplar, and cedar. More than five million people attended the exposition, and the DeBlaquiere firm's wares won a second-class medal for Canada. [67]

By the latter part of the decade, the enterprise's land had rendered all its profitable timber. Their Oxford County neighbor, Arnold Burrowes Jr. bought the Rowan Mills and Port Royal sawmills.[51] DeBlaquiere, Farmer & Deedes turned their attention to the development of the Woodstock and Lake Erie Railway and Harbor Co.[52] Arthur Farmer served as the president of the new company while the line was under development. The venture didn't go smoothly. DeBlaquiere and Farmer were accused in a contractor kickback scandal and brought before a criminal inquiry.

A heavy spring rainfall and flood in 1867 created an interesting incident on Big Creek. Delhi merchant James Whiteside had been retaining hundreds of logs in a pond. Flooding allowed the logs to get around his retaining boom and escape into the creek. Although all Whiteside's logs were branded with his JW mark, they intermixed with those of another party, which river driver David Jackson and his crew were shepherding along the creek to Port Royal. Faced with a dilemma, Whiteside retained Jackson on an emergency basis to drive the escaped logs as well.[53] The two men agreed to an unusual arrangement. Whiteside stated that if he himself shipped the logs from Port Royal down the lake to market, he would pay Jackson's fee upon receiving the proceeds from the sale. In the event the logs were sold to a party at Port Royal, Whiteside was to advise the buyer that Jackson had a lien on the logs, which the buyer would need to discharge.

The following year, Whiteside sold the logs to Port Rowan's Killmaster, Evans & Co. After Jackson was unsuccessful at collecting his fee, he sued for payment, asserting he had a lien on the logs. At trial, Henry Killmaster testified he was never informed of the lien. Whiteside and Jackson testified otherwise. After all the evidence had been heard, and the jury instructed, they found for Jackson. The decision didn't sit well with Killmaster, who happened to be a Justice of the Peace and the Reeve of the township. He appealed to a higher court in Vittoria, but a three-judge panel ruled against him, affirming the lower court's decision. [68] Killmaster found himself a defendant in another local matter. He owned a dock in Port Rowan and a fellow by the name of Taylor won a judgement against him after the shingles he had stored there went missing.

---

[50] ibid

[51] Burrowes operated a lumber business in Tonawanda under the name Burrowes and Lane. He later retired to England where he had been born.

[52] Although he was successful businessman by this time Edmund Deedes was also the sheriff of Norfolk County. Class distinction in colonial North America was not as unequivocal as in Europe. Consequently, holding public was one way that individuals in the colonies expressed their self-image of being upper class. Deedes also served as the president of the Mechanic's Institute in Simcoe.

[53] Driving hundreds of logs from the Lyndoch area to Port Royal was not a task that took mere days. Weeks of effort were required.

By the 1860s, Port Rowan was a notably vibrant community. The Port Rowan & Middleton Road Co., a private stock company, built a toll road to connect the town with points north. [69] One source states the road was surfaced with timbers of ash and pine. [70] [71]

Wood shingles, staves, barrels, and iron farm implements made in town were shipped from the port along with agricultural commodities such as barley, wheat, and apples. Records attest to the large scale of operations at the private wharves of the harbor and along the banks of the Port Royal Ship Canal. For example, the schooner *Belle* was reported to have arrived one day in Buffalo from Port Rowan with 248,000 shingles onboard. The tug *Jesse* arrived towing a log raft equivalent to 355,000 board feet of lumber. [72]

Figure 9. The DeBlaquiere & Farmer sawmill at Rowan Mills. [73]

Photo 7. Work crew loading a sleigh. (Library and Archives Canada)

FARMER, De BLAQUIERE & DEEDES.

WHEELER HOTCHKISS, Agent.

OFFICE--Cor. Niagara & Pearl Streets.
RECEIVING YARD--Ohio Basin & Elk St.

EDMUND DEEDES,
FIRM OF FARMER, De BLAQUIERE & DEEDES; RESIDENCE AMERICAN HOTEL.

The undersigned having a resident partner, Edmund Deedes, in this city, and having also entered into an engagement with Mr. Wheeler Hotchkiss, whose Lumber business they have recently purchased, as Agent for carrying on the said business, are now prepared to receive consignments of all kinds of Lumber, on which liberal advances will be made.

In addition to the large and well-selected stock constantly on hand at the old yard, at the corner of Niagara and Pearl streets, they have on the Ohio Basin and Elk street, adjacent to the Railroad freight depot, a large and commodious yard, flanked by 1200 feet of dockage, and 500 of sheds, where they land their own lumber, and buy and sell at wholesale or retail, all kinds of Lumber, Timber, Shingles, Lath, &c.

They will also receive and forward Lumber to the Eastern markets at the lowest rates.

N. B.—The highest market prices paid for all descriptions of Hemlock and other Lumber, Lath, &c., brought in by land or water.

To Rail Road Contractors and Ship-Builders.

The subscribers expect to receive immediately on the opening of navigation, a large and very superior lot of square Pine and Oak Timber, from 25 to 90 feet long, and from 12 to 24 inches square, which they will offer for sale in lots to suit purchasers.

FARMER, De BLAQUIERE & DEEDES.
WHEELER HOTCHKISS, Agent.

Figure 10. Advertisement, Buffalo City Directory. 1853.

Mid-century infrastructure Norfolk County infrastructure [54] [74]

Water-driven sawmills	72
Steam-driven sawmills	32
Shingle mills	1
Grist mills	21
Tanneries	6
Woolen factories	3
Distilleries	4
Breweries	2
Foundries	3
Villages	22
Post Offices	26
Plank or gravel roads	5
Railroads	1

[54] A later enumeration (1871) of Norfolk County businesses presents considerable detail, including ownership, employment figures for each business, and locations. [442].

Photo 8, An intentionally staged photo purporting to depict teaming. No team could ever pull such a large load. The sleigh was loaded and the photograph was composed for bragging rights. However, one fact the photo realistically depicts is the girth of Ontario's white pine. Location and date unknown. [75]

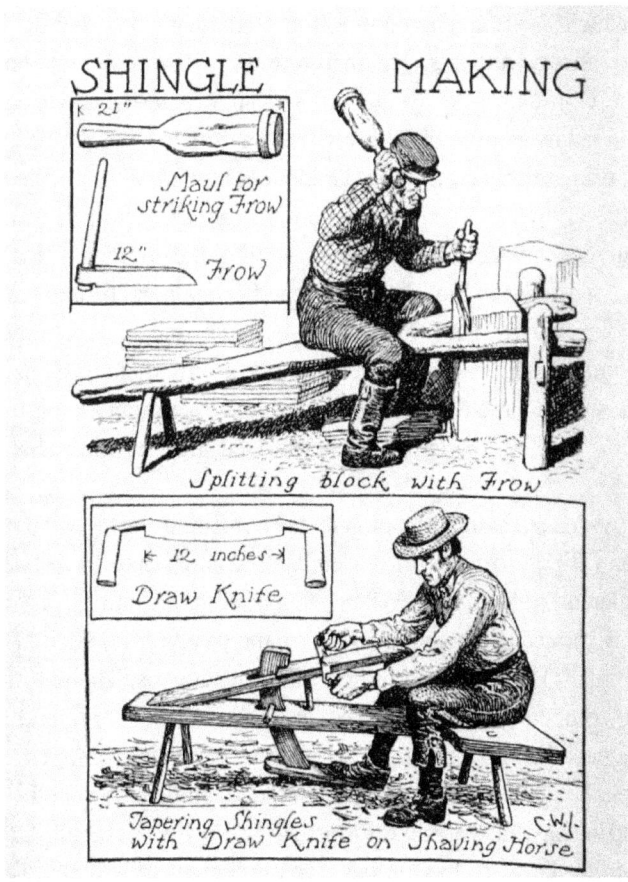

Figure 11. Making a tapered wood shingle. [76]

The village had also bloomed to become a merchandising center because returning vessels brought incoming freight. The local newspaper correspondent sometimes poked fun at the town's relatively prosperous merchant class. Although there was not yet a railroad right of way, a telegraph line was put through from the village to Simcoe in 1867. The poles for the line were not sourced locally. They were cut from the area around Georgian Bay, then forwarded by rail to Toronto and transferred to Port Rowan on the barque *Marsh*.[55] The intent had been the ship would deliver most of the poles to Normandale and the remainder to Port Rowan. However, the barque skipped the port stop at Normandale. The captain refused to stop there before sailing on to Cleveland. Consequently, the poles for the entire route to Simcoe had to be moved from Port Rowan by teams.

In the first edition of this book, I wrote that the United States opened a Consular Agency in Port Rowan in 1866. Further research has revealed that it was much earlier. William Stevenson, an American attorney, had been in place at Port Rowan as U.S. consul no later than 1861. His daughter Maria, married Dr. Joseph Tweedale in the Anglican church in town that year. [77] [78]

---

[55] A barque has three or more masts.

Consular offices, which were not uncommon at Canadian ports, handled notarial matters such as validating trade and other documents. The facility in Port Rowan operated out of a hotel room.

In 1882, the Consular Agency at Port Rowan was re-designated a Commercial Agency. It would soon be managed by George B. Killmaster, a naturalized U.S. citizen who had been born in Port Rowan. Killmaster was assisted by a Canadian deputy named William Meek, who was also the town pharmacist.[56] A little-known fact is the Commercial Agency in Port Rowan matured to become a full United States Consulate in 1906. A speculative theory for the upgrade is that some residents of Norfolk County had begun emigrating to the United States after the local timber had been depleted and much of the land reduced to barren sand. Northern Michigan, where the timber had not yet been fully harvested, was a popular destination. The creation of the United States Consulate in Port Rowan turned out to be a poor decision. By the time it was staffed and operational, emigration and trade had abated. Just two years after it opened, the United States closed the Consulate. Salaries were eight times the revenue collected.

Various activities attest to the sophistication of life in Port Rowan during the 1860s. A public stock company was formed to raise a town hall. [79] Shares may have been well subscribed, as the building was completed late that year. When winter set in, a skating rink was prepared. There was a trotting track. Racing moved to a course laid out on the bay after ice set in. During the summer, cricket was immensely popular. The town had junior and senior teams. The seniors, under the leadership of Col. Simon Mabee, competed against clubs as far away as Tillsonburg and Buffalo. [80]

In 1864, the deck hands of the tugboats *William Peck* and *N.P Sprague* (who, in all probability, were Americans,) challenged the senior cricket team to a game of baseball.[57] The tug hands carried the day by a wide margin, in what very likely Port Rowan's first baseball game. (Accounts suggest the cricket team was unfamiliar with baseball and an agreement was made to replay the game.) [81] Four years later, the town established its first baseball club. [82]

On Sundays, the militia conducted their regular target practice using an allotment of Crown ammunition. Donated funds enabled construction of a drill shed for their use. Traveling theatrical troupes entertained the townsfolk in tents, or in Killmaster's Hall. [58] Clubs and community organizations held meetings there or in one of the town's hotels. Robinson's circus attracted hundreds of attendees when it passed through town. [83] Well-planned festivals (organized by committees that included the town's merchants, tavern owners, and hoteliers) were held on holidays such as the Queen's Birthday. These too, attracted hundreds of attendees from the surrounding area who participated in or observed events such as field sports and sailboat races. River drivers competed at log rolling in the harbor. An ignominious entertainment was cockfighting. [84]

---

[56] George B. Killmaster was educated at Dufferin College in London, Ontario and at the Michigan Military Academy.

[57] Baseball started to become popular in the United States during the 1830s and 1840s.

[58] Lapham's traveling troupe were occasional visitors to town. The ensemble sang, played music, and performed clog dancing. Comic skits, ventriloquism, sleight of hand, and balancing acts were also on the bill. S. D. Brown, who had lived in Walsingham Centre, was the troupe's business manager.

Long Point's Ship Canals

In a previous chapter I described how in 1833 a storm and associated seiche severed the Long Point peninsula creating what the local community called The Cut, a navigable passage that vessels could use to access Long Point Bay without rounding the eastern tip of the island. It is not commonly known, but The Cut was not the only breakthrough across Long Point that became navigable. Before providing the historical details, it will be helpful, even if initially confusing, to address how the various canals were named.

> In either 1859 or 1860, the lake broke across Long Point about one and a half kilometres west of The Cut. By this time, The Cut had become too shallow to be navigable. The local community logically named the second breakthrough The New Cut and adopted the name The Old Cut for the earlier canal.

> There is another channel at Long Point today that carries the name The Old Cut. However, this channel was never part of the 19th century Old Cut canal. Rather, it was a minor creek that the Long Point Park Commission dredged and widened in 1937 to create a harbor for pleasure craft, and to collect sand to build up lots. On official community plans the channel is named Lighthouse Creek or Dickinson's Creek.

> The Port Royal Ship Canal, (alternately known as the Port Rowan Ship Canal,) was dug in 1860. Today, the remnant of the canal is the outlet of Big Creek, and it flows beneath the bridge on the causeway and into Long Point Bay.

> The Sturgeon Bay channel formed around the same time as The New Cut. It crossed Long Point where the new Provincial Park stands today. Although the channel was very wide, it was too shallow for use by lake vessels.

With hope that I have acceptably explained the nomenclature for these waterways, I shall now detail their history.

A petition requesting the construction of an artificial canal across Long Point reached the House of Assembly of Upper Canada in the late 1820s. By 1833, the government had allocated funds for a canal and in August of that year British civil engineer Nicol Baird and Royal Navy Captain John Harris conducted a survey to identify a suitable location. Baird recommended a channel 380 feet (116 metres) in length be dug west of the present-day causeway. His intent was for the canal to link the open waters of Lake Erie with Big Creek, which in the day meandered east before discharging into Long Point Bay near where the Sandboy Marina is today.[59] [10]

---

[59] The Sandboy Marina is situated east of the causeway, one-third of a mile north of Long Point's south beach.

Later the same year, a fierce storm and seiche formed the natural canal three kilometres east of Baird's proposed location known as the Cut. This made the construction of an artificial canal unnecessary. George C. Salmon and 70 others from Norfolk County promptly submitted a petition to the House of Assembly asking that piers be installed to protect the natural canal. Their request was received favorably and the *Act for the Construction of Piers at the Isthmus of Long Point, Lake Erie* passed the House in mid-January.[60] [85]

The VanNorman brothers received the contract to install the piers which one source states extended 600-feet (183 metres) into the lake. [29] A gale on November 11th the following year carried many of the piers away, but the canal remained navigable for almost two decades and found much use by schooners and steam powered vessels. In 1844, the government moored a lightship in the Inner Bay to mark the canal.[61] [86]

By the middle of the 1850s, erosion of the canal's banks had caused the Cut to become too shallow for large vessels. An 1854 newspaper article stated that L.S. Leslie, Esq, superintendent of the Welland Canal Office, ordered an evaluation of the circumstances:

> The object is, we are informed, to ascertain the practicability of effectually securing the Cut, and keeping the inner channel always in a perfect state for navigable purposes, so as to render the Bay, and its several fine anchorages, at all times accessible; and make it available as a secure and perfect harbor of refuge. [87]

The outcome of Leslie's inquiry is uncertain. What is known is that in 1857 the government, aware the canal had become unnavigable, relocated the Long Point lightship to Lake St. Francis in Quebec. [88]

Although it was no longer deep, the Cut had become much broader than its initial width of 900 feet (275 metres). James Black, a licensed professional surveyor under contract to the government conducted a comprehensive survey of Long Point in 1853. His map and the markers he put down reveal that the Cut was by this time about 1,200 metres wide. It crossed Long Point in the area that has since been built up with cottages. The east bank was just west of present-day Old Cut Blvd. Beyond the west bank, (where the western half of the present-day Long Point community stands today) there was little more than a narrow sandbar. (Figure 12)

Years of high water in Lake Erie during the 1850s weakened the western part of Long Point. [89] During the Fall or early Winter of 1859-1860, a storm severed the isthmus just east of the present-day causeway.[62] This breakthrough became the New Cut. (Figure 13)

---

[60] £3,000 was reallocated to procure and install the piers. That is the equivalent of about $500,000 dollars today.
[61] The lightship had three lanterns, the highest of which was 6 metres above water level. The British Office of Marine Affairs reported in its guide to mariners that light could be expected to be seen from 15 kilometres away in clear weather. Peter Blaikie was appointed keeper of the lightship.
[62] ibid

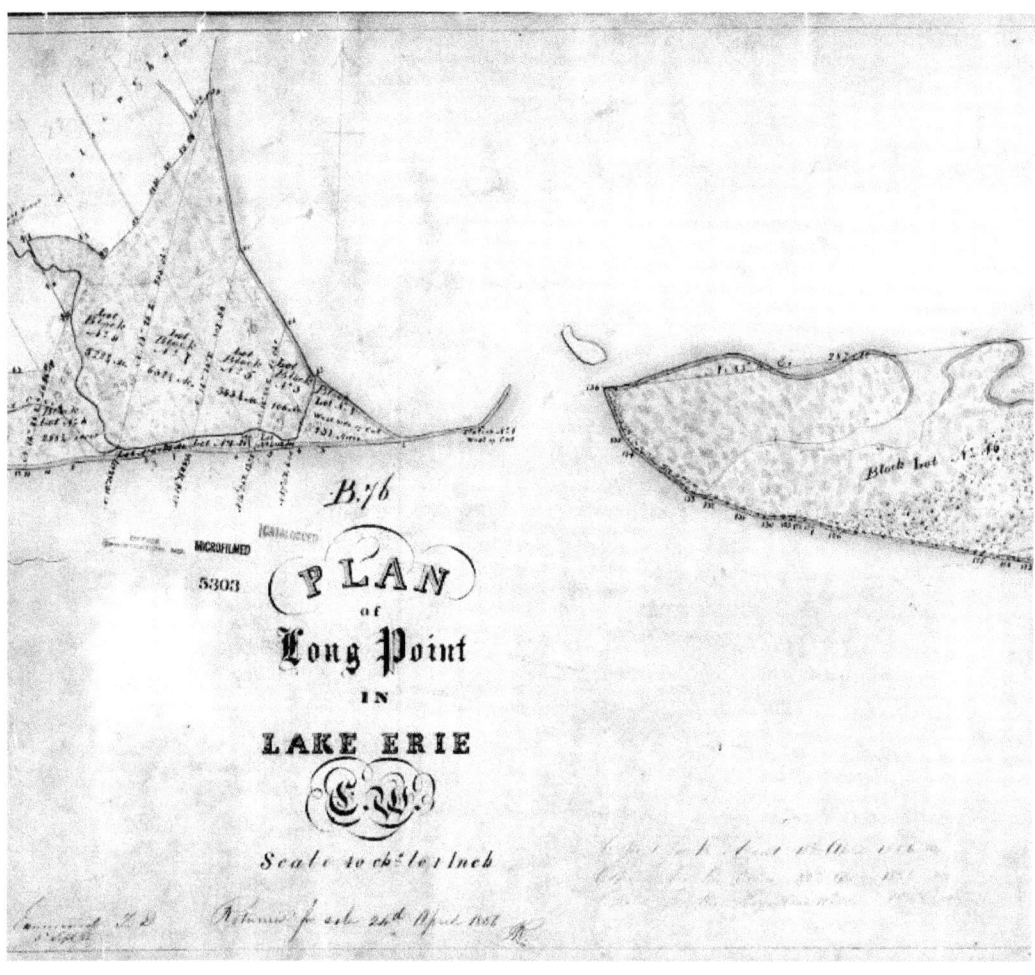

Figure 12. Excerpt from Black's 1853 survey of Long Point showing the Cut.
West of the Cut there is a lengthy sandbar (Ontario Ministry of Natural Resources)

At first, the New Cut wasn't navigable because the storm of 1859-1860 carried a great deal of sand into the southwest corner of the Inner Bay creating a horseshoe shaped sandbar and forever shallowing the area. However, after a few years, the breakthrough widened eastward into the area around present-day Poplar Road. An article published in the Norfolk Reformer attests that shallow draft schooners were passing through The New Cut by 1964.

> The scows *John A. MacDonald* and *Henry Jac*k arrived at Port Rowan on Thursday. They returned through the new cut. Their cargoes were Long Island watermelons, which are selling rapidly at double what they cost in Cleveland. [63] [64] [90]

---

[63] Scow schooners did not have a deep keel, allowing them to pass through water too shallow for other vessels.

[64] The John A. MacDonald was built at Port Rowan (likely on the Port Royal Ship Canal) by messieurs Glover and McLennan. She had a 98 by 23-foot deck (30-metres) and a 7.5-foot (2.3 metre) hold. A year or so later a similar vessel, the John S. MacDonald, owned by Messieurs Mabee and Newkirk was launched from the port.

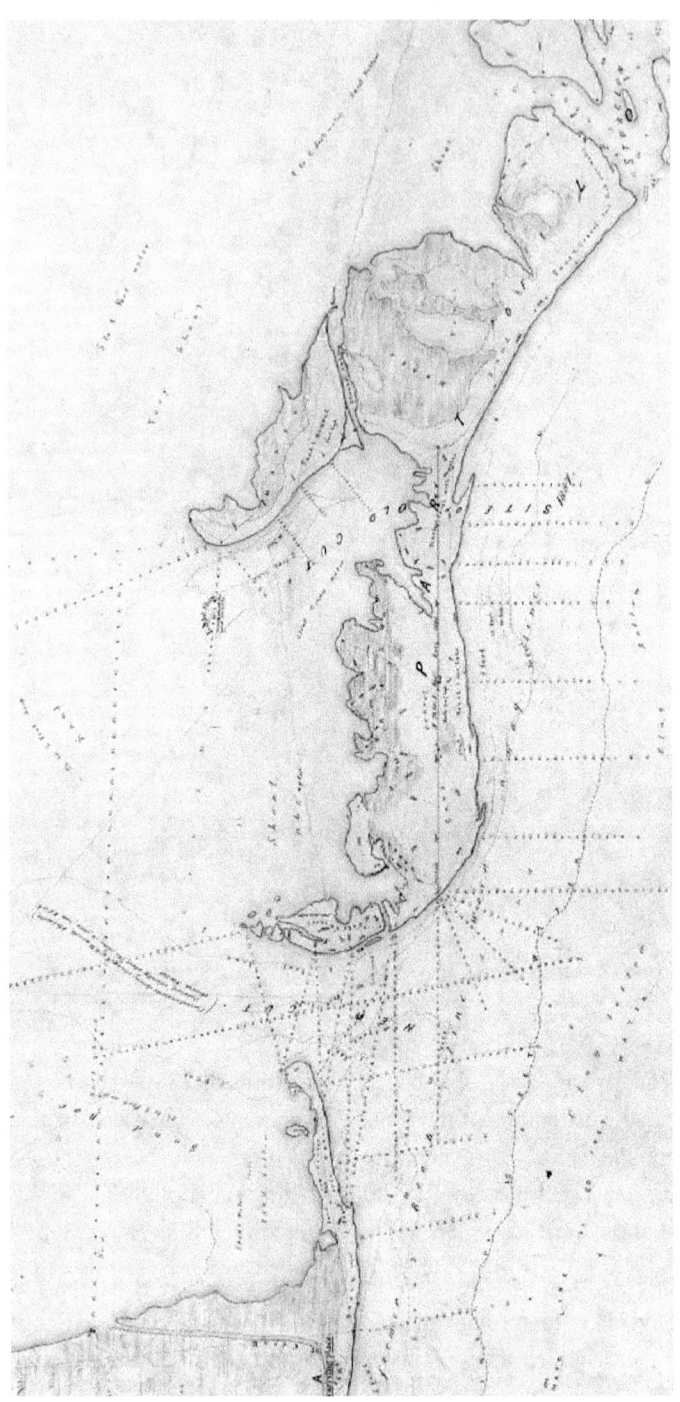

Figure 13. Sounding survey, Head of Inner Bay, 1869, (Archives Canada.)
Note the location of the New Cut, The Old Cut, the Sturgeon Bay Channel, and the future Lighthouse Creek.
Although the lightship was no longer present, its former location is included on the map.

Prior to 1860, the timber and lumber that came down Big Creek for local shipbuilding and for shipment to distant markets entered the southwest corner of Long Point Bay near where the Sandboy Marina is today.[65] The storm that created the New Cut pushed a great deal of sand into that part of the bay and it would have interfered with shipping. After the storm, local lumber barons formed the Port Royal Ship Canal Co. to address the circumstances. The company's business plan called for excavating a canal roughly one mile in length that would connect to Big Creek just south-east of Port Royal. The Big Creek Sault, which at the time ran southward approximately two kilometres west of the present-day causeway would be blocked off. (A lengthy remnant of the Sault is apparent in current-day satellite photographs.) In addition to the canal, a short channel would be dredged in the Inner Bay to allow vessels to approach the canal. Presumably, the lumber barons put up some of the capital necessary for the venture, but the enterprise was still set up as a public stock company.

John A. MacDonald, in his capacity as head of government for Canada West, swiftly authorized the canal company. Following the Spring thaw, the tugboat *Jennie Bell* towed a dredging machine from Buffalo to Port Rowan and digging commenced. [91] Big Creek was thus diverted. (Figure 14) Thereafter, various activities took place along the built-up canal banks including the staging of logs, the preparation of rafts for towing, sawmilling, and shipbuilding.

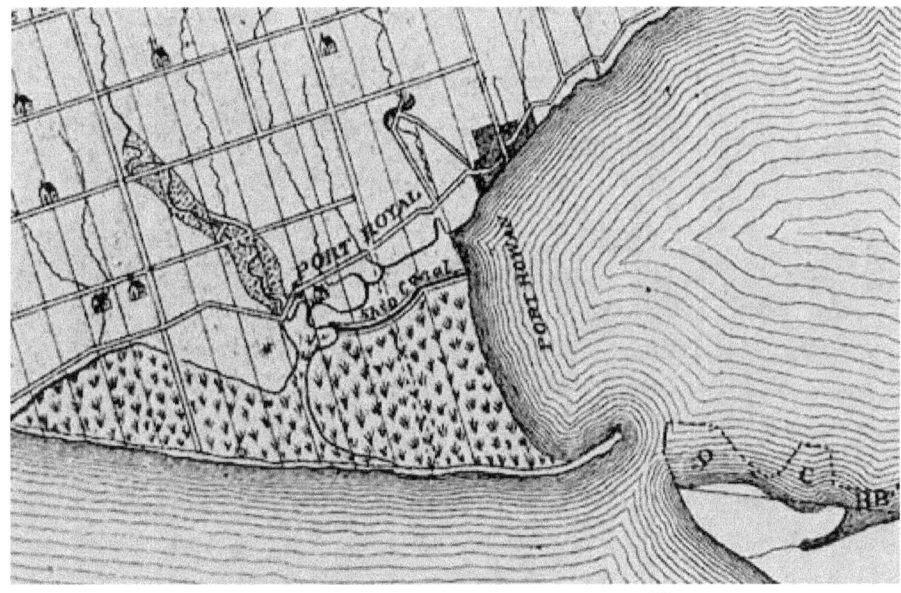

Figure 14. Route of the Port Royal Ship Canal [92]

---

[65] Logs and lumber were inventoried in marsh ponds west of this location. By 1849, Farmer and DeBlaquiere had built a wharf for loading lumber onto vessels just offshore in the Inner Bay.

Most of the vessels constructed on the canal's bank were schooners, but at least one tugboat was built.[66] The schooner *New Dominion* launched into the canal in 1867. At thirty-five metres of keel and three metres in hold, her owners Messrs. Woodward and Collett of Port Rowan and Monsieur McBurney of St. Williams expected the 164-ton vessel would carry 14,000 bushels of wheat. The main mast was reported to be 22-inches (one-half metre) in diameter and 83 feet (25-metres) in length. [93] Although the *New Dominion* had launched to great fanfare, during her first season she ran aground near The Old Cut during on a gale on November 29th while loaded with 20,000 bushels of corn. [94] The Phoenix Insurance Co. of Toronto retained salvagers who made use of the Buffalo-based tug *Frank Perew* to free the schooner in early May and tow it to St. Catherines for repair.[67] [95] [96].

Figure 15. The Schooner New Dominion was built on the banks of the Port Royal Ship Canal.
(Alpena George N. Fletcher Public Library)

Large sailing vessels such as *New Dominion* obviously couldn't enter or depart from the Port Royal Ship Canal unaided. While there may have been a towpath for teams of horses or oxen to pull vessels along the canal, harbor tugs (including the *New Era*, *Relief*, and the *Watchman*) would have towed and nudged them.

Occasional re-dredging maintained the canal's depth. [97] Toll collection and heavy volume made the venture a commercial success. Shareholders of the company were collecting dividends in 1861, just a year after the canal opened. That same year, the workforce cutting and sledding timber from the lands along Big Creek and driving logs numbered 900 men and 400 teams. The volume of timber exported was far higher than any previous year. [98] At the commencement of the shipping season in May of 1864, the canal company estimated there were 66,000 logs staged on

---

[66] The tug was the *New Era*. Some schooners recorded as built in Port Rowan that may have been built on the ship canal include the *Philo Bennett*, the *Rosa Stearns*, the *Bay Trader*, the *Erie Queen*, the *Northwest,* and the *Nettie Woodward*. The reason for uncertainty is that shipbuilding probably also occurred below the nearby Port Rowan bluffs.

[67] Following refurbishment, the *New Dominion* made Picton, on Lake Ontario her new home port.

Big Creek and the canal, in addition to 1,500 square lengths of oak, 3,700 square lengths of pine, 4,700 lengths of round timber, and 200 masts.[68] [99] The activity was sufficient to attract a group of investors to Port Rowan who were contemplating digging a parallel canal. [100]

The individuals who formed the Port Royal Ship Canal company were prominent businessmen. Edmund Deedes of Simcoe (who was also the Sheriff of Norfolk County) was the president and a director. The other directors were John Charlton, Arnold Burrowes, Henry Killmaster, and Buffalo shipyard owner Cornelius VanSlyke.

John Charlton resided in the village of Lyndoch at the north end of Big Creek. From there, he had managed the operations of Smith and Westover, a Tonawanda, New York lumber firm that was the other major timber operator along the creek.[69] [101] In 1861, with James Ramsdell of Buffalo, Charlton bought out Smith and Westover's Big Creek operation. They cut timber at their own sawmill in Tonawanda. Four years later, Charlton bought out Ramsdell's interest. [102] Although he had been born in New York State, he was elected a member of Parliament as a Liberal in 1872. Charlton used the profits from his local business to acquire timberland in Michigan. He relentlessly advocated for free trade and closer commercial ties with the United States. His more protectionist counterparts sometimes mocked him by referring to him as "the Honorable Member for Michigan." Charlton served in Parliament for decades.

Henry Killmaster was unquestionably Port Rowan's most prominent mid-century resident. He and his brother Benjamin were directors of the Port Rowan & Middleton Road Co.[70] Henry ran for election to Parliament in 1867 but lost by a slim margin.[71] While the two brothers operated a general store and a wharf, timber forwarding and milling, financing shipbuilding, railway development, and banking, eventually became their more significant interests.[72] The Killmaster's had a partner in the timber business named Edward Evans. Born in Haldimand County, Ontario in 1830, Evans became a Great Lakes sailor at the age of just sixteen.[73] The trio owned tugboats that made Port Rowan their home port. Two were the *N.P. Sprague* and the mighty 113-foot *General Grant*. A third was the smaller *William Peck*. All were built at Buffalo shipyards.[74] The principal

---

[68] The individual logs must have been very large. The canal company estimated the 66,000 logs were equivalent to 25-million board feet of lumber. An estimate for the yield from a log in board feet equivalent is: $BF = (d-4)^2 \cdot L/16$, where the unit d, (the log diameter) is measured in inches, and the length of the log, L is measured in feet.

[69] The principals of the Smith & Westover firm were Luther Westover and H.P. Smith.

[70] Other directors of the Port Rowan & Middleton Road Co. were at one time or another F. Bouck, M. Harris, and H. Holstead, T.R. DeWolfe, John H. Backhouse, and M. Holtby.

[71] Henry Killmaster was nominated to be the Liberal candidate for South Norfolk in 1872.

[72] Port Rowan's Captain Nathan Woodward managed the shipbuilding that was financed by the Killmaster's. One vessel they built at Port Rowan, the 124-foot, 260-ton schooner Garibaldi, launched on August 5, 1863. The vessel, which was designed by Oliver Wolven and intended for the Chicago to Buffalo grain route, fetched a sale price of $9,000 eight months later. [436] [451]

[73] Evans moved to Buffalo in the early 1860s where he took an active role in American politics. In 1872, he and Henry Killmaster established a bank in Tonawanda which they named the "Bank of Commerce." Following Killmaster's death in Port Rowan in 1876 at the age of 57, the bank was renamed Evans, Schwinger & Co. The bank became the largest depository of canal tolls in New York State. [466] Evans eventually became chairman of the National Reform Party in the United States.

[74] The *Willam Peck* was built in 1854. The *N.P. Sprague*, built in 1857, was named to honor Buffalo lawyer Noah P. Sprague, who was the Clerk of Erie County and a close associate of Millard Filmore.

engagement for these large tugs, which cost twice as much as similarly sized schooners, was towing log rafts to Tonawanda. The Killmaster brothers, Evans, and Cornelius VanSlyke operated a planning mill there. [103]

N.P. *Sprague* had a bad history. During her first year of service, she collided with another vessel on the Detroit River and her boiler exploded, leading to the death of ten people. Salvagers raised the tug from the river bottom and returned her to Buffalo for refurbishment. Killmaster and Evans then bought it.[75] Harvey Booth was Port Rowan's most esteemed tugboat captain, and he oversaw the voyages of all the Killmaster and Evans tugs at one time or another. During the shipping season of 1869, Booth reported that by mid-July he had already commanded *Sprague* on nine voyages from Port Rowan to Tonawanda. [104]

The *General Grant* entered service as a new vessel in 1864.[76] Killmaster and Evans proudly offered the townsfolk of Port Rowan the opportunity to take an excursion to Erie, Pennsylvania for Fourth of July celebrations. Southwesterly winds picked up in the afternoon causing many passengers to succumb to seasickness on the return trip. [105] (Alcohol use might have been a factor for some of the affected.) The following month there was an excursion to Buffalo. *General Grant*'s deck was covered with canvas, and chairs and tables from the town hall were brough on board. After departure from Port Rowan, additional passengers boarded at Port Dover. The fare was $2.00, and roughly 100 people made the trip spending two nights in Buffalo. Activities on board the tug included euchre, chess, and dancing. [106]

Lake Erie storms were not just a hazard to sailing ships. The *General Grant* encountered rough weather while towing a raft the next year and sunk near Point Abino. Salvagers recovered the vessel and removed it to Buffalo.

Vessels owned and harbored at Port Rowan were by no means the only craft that carried lumber or towed rafts of timber from the port. Brokers and agents arranged many third-party vessels. One massive tug that began towing from Port Rowan in the summer of 1862 was the *W.G. Fargo*, named for William Fargo, then mayor of Buffalo. [107] (Fargo and his business associate, Henry Wells, co-founded the American Express Co. at Buffalo in 1850 and later formed the Wells Fargo Company.) *W.G. Fargo* weighed 234-tons, was 37-metres long, and required 2.7 metres of water. At the time, there may have been a route with that depth from Turkey Point through the Inner Bay to the Port Royal Ship Canal that the tug could have traversed.[77] [108] Still, whether *W.G. Fargo* was actually able to reach the Port Royal Ship Canal is questionable. Smaller harbor tugs may have towed the timber rafts out to the *Fargo* while it waited in deeper water near Turkey Point. No information has been located to corroborate this speculative theory. As for the size of the rafts that left Port Rowan, Buffalo port arrival reports demonstrate that a single tow could amount to the equivalent of 350,000 board feet of lumber. [109]

---

[75] A few years after the Killmaster's and Evans bought the *Sprague*, the tug caught fire at Buffalo and again required repairs.

[76] The Civil War was ongoing in the United States. The tug was named to honor the American Union Army General Ulysses S. Grant.

[77] The Admiralty chart states that it includes amendments to 1861. However, it does not depict the Port Royal Ship Canal even though the canal existed by that year.

Just weeks after *W.G. Fargo* began towing rafts, it was involved in a collision while enroute to Port Rowan and had to be returned to Buffalo for repair. The following year, the Union Navy purchased the tug, refitted it, and then moved it to the Atlantic Ocean (presumably via the Erie Canal and Hudson River route.) Under a new name, *U.S.S. Honeysuckle*, the vessel remained in military service for the balance of the Civil War, plying waters as far south as the Gulf of Mexico. [110]

Figure 16. U.S.S. Honeysuckle, oil on canvas, Willliam G. Yorke. Unknown date. (Public Domain) [111]

The other founder of the Port Royal Ship Canal Co., Cornelius VanSlyke, co-owned the Van Slyke & Notter shipyard in Buffalo. Although he did not live in Port Rowan, he maintained some kind of premises there. Whether it was a second home, or solely a business premises is uncertain. Certainly, it reflected his interest in securing a continuous supply of hardwood for the Buffalo shipyard.

Day-to-day administration of the Port Royal Ship Canal was performed by Chauncey Bennett, the son of Philo Bennett, who was the collector of customs for Port Rowan. Although he had first worked as a broom maker, Chauncey was appointed the canal's secretary, treasurer, and toll collector. He held additional titles as a ship broker and raftsman.[78] To get to his post on the canal quickly, Chauncey acquired Port Rowan's first bicycle. It was a simple two-wheeled velocipede (or boneshaker as they became known.) The Port Rowan correspondent for the *Simcoe Reformer* referred to it as a velocipeddle. Chauncey predicted his bicycle would convey him to his work area on the ship canal in just five minutes. [112] His was likely an optimistic estimate.

---

[78] Raftsmen bundled and tied timber into rafts, presumably on the banks of the ship canal or at Port Rowan docks. One report mentions two tugboats working to "get a raft off."

The supply of timber from the lands along Big Creek had dwindled by the late 1870s, and the canal met its commercial demise. Chauncey Bennett found work in the American consular office in town.[79] Today, when automobiles travel over the bridge on the causeway leading to and from Long Point, they are crossing the former ship canal. We are left to wonder why the banks of the canal are no longer apparent. The reason may be as simple as continuous erosion. However, there is another possible explanation. The Toronto Big Creek Shooting Company was formed in 1889 with capital of $8,000 and 16 shareholders (most of them from Toronto and Niagara Falls.) The company soon built an 80-foot-long gated dam to choke the outlet of Big Creek thereby flooding the area west of the present-day causeway. They did this to make it more likely ducks would land in the area. The intentional flooding may have accelerated erosion of the canal's banks. What is known with certainty is the scheme went too far. Eventually, farmland located near the north boundary of the marsh became impacted. The farm's owners asserted the flooding was impairing their land, and during the summer of 1895 municipal authorities dismantled the dam. [114], [113]

---

[79] Chauncey Bennett remained prominent in Port Rowan for several years and served as Grand Superintendent of the town's Masonic Lodge. Late in the 1870s, he apparently suffered a middle-age health crisis, as he is listed as having become a resident of the psychiatric hospital in Hamilton at the age of 47. He died there in December 1881.

Long Point's Gardeners and Hotelkeepers

Early settlers who sought to hunt or fish would have accessed Long Point by bateaux or as soon as they could avail themselves of a canoe or skiff. By the late 18th century, the island's reputation as an exceptional location for shooting waterfowl was well-established. British officers from various garrisons in Upper Canada commonly traveled to Long Point to hunt. [115] No later than the 1840s, guides were offering services and renting shanties to visitors. That decade, a traveling Englishman wrote the following:

> But of all the places I know of in Canada, Long Point an Island, in Lake Erie, is the greatest rendezvous for ducks. There are quantities of wild rice swamps on the island which is about 9 miles in length; the neighboring settlements not being so thick as to be likely to cause very serious disturbance to the birds for many years. Here, they congregate in thousands, the supply being ample for the few parties that go up purposely in the course of the season. In fact, those that go are not sufficient to make any sensible diminution as to their numbers. You go thither about the month of November, and leaving your horses on the mainland, you engage a boatman, who takes you over to the island, where some log shooting boxes are erected for parties by persons who let them as may be agreed on. This, of course, you furnish with all necessary provisions and betting [sic], and then having established your party, the business of your man is to pull you in a canoe or punt, through the wild rice in a coaching [sic] position, when [sic] you shoot them in the little cagoons [sic] or toward night you post yourself in a convenient spot, amongst the rice, when they will often come in a cloud and settle quite close to you with a thundering splash, and you can then fire into them at your leisure.[80] Wild geese, also, frequent the place, and the ducks are some of the largest and finest I ever saw. I know of a party of gentlemen who went up from Toronto, and, in a very few days, got 500 ducks each to his share —the winter being so near, they were first well peppered and salted, and afterwards frozen, and this without any trouble. They had an ample supply of these delicious birds for themselves and their friends during the whole winter. [116]

Further development of transportation infrastructure brought hunters from afar. Americans from afar could reach Port Rowan quickly and comfortably once railroad service linked New York City with Buffalo in 1852. There, they could connect to the newly launched 450-ton sidewheel-steamer *Kaloolah*, which had upper-deck cabins that could accommodate 60 first-class passengers. (Figure 17) Hundreds more could occupy other cabins, the deck, and the hold. Despite its substantial tonnage, *Kaloolah* managed to navigate Long Point's shallow Inner Bay during her

---

[80] The presence of the words *betting, coaching, when, and cagoon,* in Christmas' passage are likely attributable to typographical error. The author probably wrote *bedding, crouching, where*, and *lagoon*.

maiden year.[81] The vessel departed Buffalo at 8 PM on Tuesdays and Fridays, making port calls at Dunkirk, NY, Port Dover, Port Rowan, and Port Burwell before terminating at Port Stanley. [117] At Port Rowan, arriving visitors could stay at one of the hotels or inns operated by Messieurs Bouck, Saxton, Stearns, or Turrill before crossing over to Long Point and roughing it in spartan shanties.

Figure 17. Advertisement for the Kaloolah. [118]

It was around this time, that Col. Samuel Ryerson sought an annuity to support himself in his old age. He sold his island to Richard Richardson in return for a mortgage. Richardson was a Port Rowan blacksmith who owned a foundry, a farm implement shop, a plaster mill, and a general store. His neighbors lightheartedly referred to him as Richie Riches. Richardson used the nickname himself.[82, 83]

As more and more American hunters visited Long Point, Richardson supposed he could profit from the circumstances. He decided to try and resell Ryerson's Island. In 1856, he targeted potential buyers by placing advertisements in various American publications. (Figure 18) His solicitation was unsuccessful. Several years later, he sold the island to Egerton Ryerson, one of Samuel's sons. Because Egerton lived and worked in Toronto, he could only visit the island occasionally. He arranged for William Bantam of Port Rowan to tend the island's gardens, vines, and peach trees and provided him with seeds.[84] (There were about 15 to 20 dry acres on the island, about 1 to 1.5 metres above lake level.) [119]. In 1865, fourteen thousand cabbage plants were raised on the island then shipped to the mainland for transplantation. Radishes, other vegetables, peaches, and plenty of grapes were also harvested.

---

[81] *Kaloolah* may have experienced challenges navigating Long Point's Inner Bay. The following year, 1853, the vessel did service on Lake Huron. The smaller *Mohawk* replaced it on the Buffalo to Port Stanley route. In 1855, the steamer *Ploughboy* was making the voyage.

[82] By the 1860s, Richardson was the township's Reeve. In 1875, he was elected to the Provincial Legislature as a Conservative, succeeding Simpson McCall.

[83] Farmers spread plaster sourced from gypsum mines along the Grand River, near Cayuga on their fields. Of itself, it provided no nutritional value. However, it made the soil more fertile by causing nutrients to be more readily absorbed by crops. Years of plaster application depleted the soil's nutrients.

[84] Bantam may have also cultivated the island for Richard Richardson. A multi-talented individual, he was a respected mariner, carpenter, and cobbler.

FOR SALE.
THE FINEST SPORTING PROPERTY IN CANADA.

THE place is known as "Ryerson's Island," and contains 191 acres per deed—is situated about one mile east of Long Point, in Lake Erie, and about eight or ten miles from Port Rowan and Normandale in Norfolk county.

The soil is very rich. Corn, cabbage, tomatoes, potatoes, and almost all vegetation is of the most luxuriant growth, and can be in market nearly three weeks before the same are produced on the main land. A small portion is under cultivation. It offers great advantages for raising Cows, Oxen, Sheep, and all kinds of Stock, as an extensive Grazing or Market Farm. Twenty to thirty or forty tons of excellent hay can be had just by cutting and curing Wild *Grapes* are very abundant and large. Every spring and fall it abounds with WILD FOWL—Wild Ducks innumerable, of almost every variety—(one gentleman shot and bagged 86 in part of one day last year)—Geese, some Swans, Plovers in flocks, Woodcocks, Pigeons, etc., all summer. Turtles of different kinds and size are very plentiful. Deer, Coons, Muskrats, etc., are in great numbers on Long Point. The FISHING ADVANTAGES ARE STILL GREATER, either with hook and line, nets, or otherwise. The fish are caught in *great quantities*, and are very large and fine. The delicious Muscalunge, weighing from 30 to 40 pounds; the Sturgeon, from 75 to 100 pounds; the Cat and White fish, and Herring are very plentiful. The PLEASURE BOAT is a great luxury here, being just far enough from the main shore not to be annoyed. It can be made a superior place of PUBLIC RESORT, being known to large numbers of sporting gents, all along from New Orleans, Canada, New York, etc. *It is very* HEALTHY, and can be reached from different points along the lake by Steamboat, which leaves Buffalo in the evening, and arrives early next morning; there are also Railroad advantages approaching. Terms very reasonable. Apply to

RICH. RICHES, Ryerson's Island,

Jan.—4t.   Normandale P. O., Canada West.

Figure 18. Newspaper Advertisement. 1856. [120]

Photo 9. Mrs. & Mr. William Bantam. (Unknown date, but c.1900.) (Bantam family collection)

American hunters sometimes brought enslaved black people with them to Long Point. [121] These servants handled baggage, provisions, and in some instances cooked in the shanties on the island.[85, 86] Barrett wrote that the body of a black man, whose throat had been slit, was found in Bouck's Pond, a lengthy, narrow inlet that flanks the Little Creek Ridges on the eastern half of the island. [122] Barrett provided no date or further details.

The number of fugitive blacks crossing into southern Ontario from the United States increased markedly in the 1850s. The reason was the passage of the Fugitive Slave Act. That federal legislation required all U.S. citizens to assist in capturing and returning formerly enslaved people to their supposed owners, regardless of whether the person had escaped to and was residing

---

[85] ibid

[86] Although the import of enslaved people became illegal in the United States in 1807 the practice continued for decades after that. The last ship to bring enslaved Africans to the United States is believed to have arrived in 1860.

in a northern "free state." The legislation made blacks in the northern states fear-stricken, and thousands fled to Canada. While they landed at many places, including the Niagara region, the Windsor area, and Lake Ontario ports, Yale University scholar Robin Winks concluded they also arrived at Point Pelee, Port Burwell, Port Stanley, Port Rowan, and Long Point. [123] In Canada, the blacks (on paper at least) had legal rights and protections. But, in many instances, they were unwelcome and met with discrimination. The murdered man's identity, and how he came to be at Long Point is lost to history. One speculative theory is that he was associated with an American hunting party and attempted to escape. Another is that he had rafted across the lake and landed at Long Point, where he found it necessary to steal to survive and his murder was a lynching.

In *Lore and Legends of Long Point,* Barrett also wrote that "so-called hotels" were present on the island. Again, he provided no other details except to briefly mention what he called "an encampment" located in an area known as the Little Sandhills. Barrett attributed the encampment's development to Harry Woodward, while suggesting that David Tisdale and a group of businessmen from St. Catharine's and Hamilton may have paid to have shanties built there.

Harry Woodward was a St. Williams brickmaker and carpenter. He was born in 1828 in County Wiltshire, England and he came to Canada with his parents and siblings in 1841.[87] The Port Rowan correspondent for the *Norfolk Reformer* characterized Woodward as enterprising and entrepreneurial. He referred to the encampment at Long Point as "Harry Woodward's sporting establishment," but the popular name was Harry's Place. [124] Woodward was referred to as the establishment's "proprietor."

The encampment was probably a collection of shanties, each with bunks and a fireplace, plus an additional structure that had a kitchen and eating area. At busy times, as many as 30 hunters and 30 punters might overnight there. [125] Woodward and his wife catered to them and supplied ammunition.

An 1880 map prepared by Edward Harris, who had become a member of the Long Point Company in 1877, and who was Egerton Ryerson's son-in-law, shows Harry's Place was located about seven kilometres east of the Old Cut lighthouse. Although Barrett wrote that the encampment was behind the foredune, Harris' map places it on the beach. An 1869 letter, written by W. Allan to George Gillespie, who was the Long Point Company's secretary and treasurer at the time, also states the shanties were located on the beach. I distinctly remember walking in that general area 60 years ago. About 30 metres out in the lake stood a brick chimney rising out of the water. What structure the chimney was a remnant from is for the time being a mystery. The south beach of Long Point is very changeable, and the general area where Harry's Place was located has been subject to heavy erosion. At least one of the original structures at Harry's Place was dragged across the ice-covered marsh around 1870 to where The Long Point Company cottages are today.

Besides Harry's Place, there were at least two accommodations on Long Point that claimed the title "hotel". One was a shanty owned by George Hutchison, a resident of the nearby mainland,

---

[87] Harry Woodward and Phineas Reeves were cousins. Information about Phineas Reeves is presented in the chapter titled Artists and Artisans.

and was well-reviewed by patrons. After Hutchison passed away in January 1864, Charles Brown leased and operated the premises:

> For a sportsman to attempt to pass the duck shooting season without visiting Long Point would be a hard task indeed. To pass the season at the Point without a good comfortable home to remain in when the inclination of the hunter led in that direction, would be an equally hard task. Sportsmen will therefore learn with pleasure that Charlie Brown has leased the hotel recently occupied by the late George Hutchison, at Carrying Place Creek, Long Point; and is prepared, with every comfort, for the reception of visitors. "Charlie" is well known throughout the Province as a caterer to the wants of the public, and knows "how to keep a hotel." In addition to this, experienced punters, as well as ammunition, etc., can always be had from him. [126]

Harry Woodward and Edwin Fenn eventually purchased Hutchison's hotel. As they had no title to the land beneath, when the Long Point Company acquired the island, it gave the duo a quitclaim settlement for the structure. The Company then selected Charles Brown to be the island's first steward. While that was the title used by members of the Company for decades, the vernacular name for the position became "head keeper".

Another establishment on Long Point, and one perhaps more worthy of the title hotel, was located at the northeast end of Courtright Ridge. (Figure 19) Available to visitors by 1861, and probably during the late 1850s, it was owned by a market gunner named John Spain, who claimed it was the largest accommodation on the island. [127] He probably meant the largest single structure. By 1866, a sizeable vineyard with 300 vines and an orchard with an unknown number of peach trees were associated with the premises. Presumably, there was a vegetable garden as well. After the Long Point Company acquired the island, Spain's wife advised Company representatives that she annually harvested peaches of excellent quality. [128] No records attesting to the hotel's size exist, although there is some evidence that it had a dining room.[88] Water might have overtaken the structure long ago.

John Spain was born of Irish descent in Middleton township, Norfolk County, in either 1832 or 1833. There does not seem to be any record of his family having received a land grant or that they owned a farm. Census data shows that Spain was working in Middleton as a cobbler at the age of 18. By the mid-1850s he had joined the market hunting rush at Long Point.

In 1863, Spain wrote a letter to the Hon. William McDougall, the government official who had authority for Crown Lands, pleading for a title to the land where his hotel, vineyard, and orchard were located:

---

[88] The evidence that suggests the hotel had a dining room has been omitted from this book. Also omitted is a reference to the published source material, which was controversial when it was published in the 1860s and would be deemed offensive today.

Dear Sir

I have just received a letter from Mr. Egerton Ryerson Chief Superintendent of Education Toronto in which he tells me he has been talking to you about the lot on which I have been making improvements.

He authorizes me to refer to him and his brother William Ryerson [illegible suffix] which [sic] gentlemen I am well acquainted with.

I use [sic] to come here to shoot ducks for my health as it was very poor and I found that I gained both health & strength but it still did not pay so I thought that I would build a sort of sporting establishment and try and get others to come for health and pleasure. But before I commenced to build I tried to buy the lot but it was not for sale so the Agent Mr. Duncan Campbell told me to come over hear [sic] and to forbid any persons from cutting timber and he gave me a written authority to seize all that was cut in the name of the Government. All of which I did and the government made about three hundred dollars out it … [129]

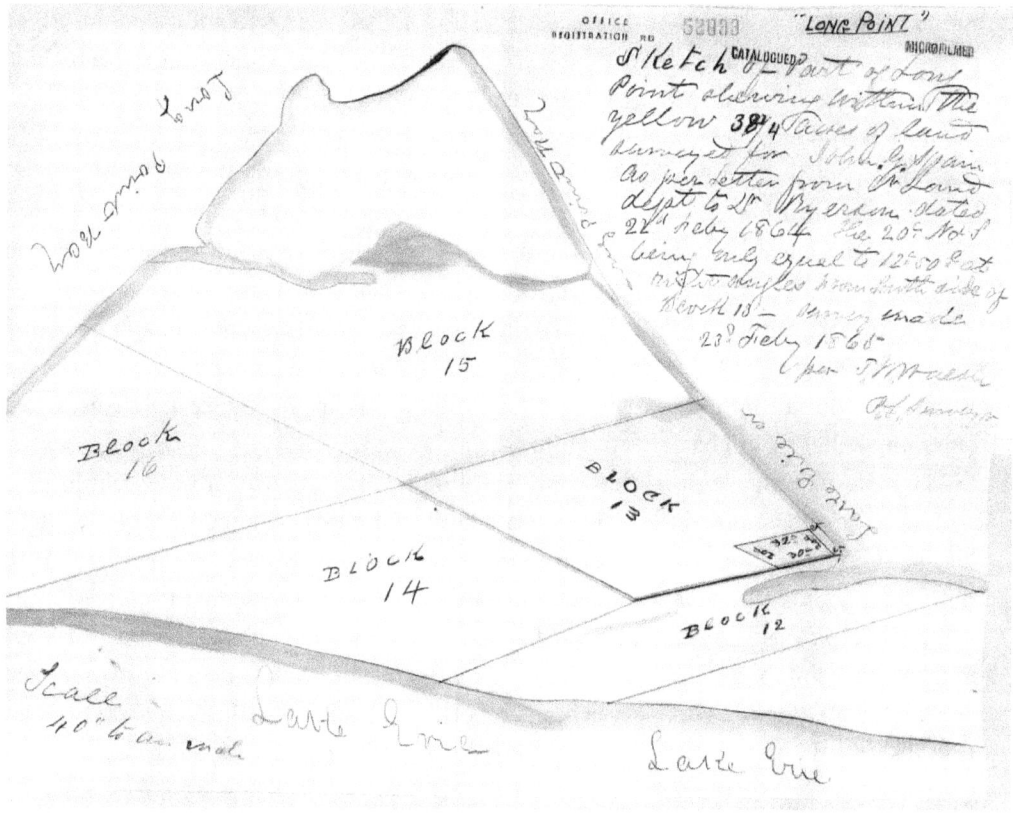

Figure 19. The location of John Spain's 39-acre plot on the northeast corner of Courtright Ridge.
The Long Point Company has long maintained a keeper's cabin on the plot.
Survey by J. Walsh. 1868.

Spain included a sketch of his lot and the surrounding area with his letter. He closed the note respectfully asking to be told what more he needed to do and signed as "Your Humble Obedient Servant." He added a postscript stating he had also submitted a petition to the legislature proposing new laws for better protection of game and had done so on behalf of "all the hunters and trappers." He stated, "I hope it will become law as the game will all be destroyed the way it is." Spain's entreaty was successful. The government granted him a land title in early 1866, just before it put Long Point up for auction.

There may have been something else at Spain's place on Long Point. In *Lore and Legends of Long Point*, Harry Barrett repeated the claim that there was a brothel on Long Point and he stated it was on Courtright Ridge. The Long Point Company's 100th anniversary yearbook also mentioned a brothel, saying the island "for a while supported a brothel, the inmates supplied from Buffalo." [130] The source for these assertions was Edward Harris, the Company's fifth president who served from 1886 to 1898. He wrote about the brothel using very similar words. [131] Harris ought to have known the facts; his father-in-law was Egerton Ryerson, someone with a long and deep knowledge of Long Point. But only Barrett, who had worked as a keeper for the Company, mentioned a location —Courtright Ridge, suggesting he had access to additional information.

As a matter of first impression, especially today, Courtright Ridge might not seem a plausible place for a brothel. More careful consideration suggests it was. Houses of ill-fame, as the press referred to them, were commonplace in Upper Canada. Every market gunner would have had cash in his pocket, as would all the visiting sportsmen. During the era, which was still the dawn of industrialization, most women, particularly younger women, had little or no money. For the vast majority engaged in prostitution, it was rarely a matter of lifestyle choice; it stemmed either from coercion or financial necessity. [132] As for the report that the inmates were supplied from Buffalo, it is entirely credible. Cross-border sex trafficking was prevalent.[89] A common ploy was to deceive women by telling them they were being taken to where there were factory jobs. For a woman from Buffalo, who was taken to Long Point's Courtright Ridge, the chances of escaping to something better would have been limited.

Hunters did engage prostitutes on Long Point. The violence inflicted could be extreme. One young woman engaged in prostitution on the island was murdered during the 1862 hunting season; her body was found in the marsh. [133] John Phelan, M.D., the coroner for Port Rowan at the time, went to Long Point and retrieved the body. He then convened a jury.

The victim was Elizabeth Berdan. Two years earlier, her father Jacob, had left the family's cabin on Long Point to get food for his hungry family. On his return trip, he froze to death while trying to cross the Bay. Newspaper accounts reported that after Ms. Berdan's father died, she had lived a "disgraceful life" —an encoded and untoward portraiture for prostitution.[90] [134] [135]

---

[89] One wire service article details a conspiracy under which young women were smuggled from upstate New York to Toronto under false pretenses, held there, and forced into prostitution. [403]

[90] Another newspaper account noted that Elizabeth Berdan moved from Long Point to Turkey Point after her father's death.

It was apparent to the jury that Phelan had convened that Berdan had been savagely beaten, and that they were therefore addressing a murder. Accordingly, they requested that a complete post-mortem examination be conducted. Phelan recessed them with the understanding that they would reconvene the following week. In the meantime, Phelan was to arrange for another Port Rowan physician, Byron Franklin M.D., to perform the post-mortem. Troublingly, research conducted during the preparation of this book turned up no further information to demonstrate that the investigation into Berdan's murder progressed, leaving a sinister impression.

All the facts considered, there isn't sufficient evidence to conclude that the brothel was associated with John Spain's hotel. If it was not, another possible location was a shanty located on Courtright Ridge closer to Harry's Place. After the Long Point Company took over the island, that shanty was improved, and an addition was built onto it. It served as the domicile for the Company's first two stewards, Charles Brown, and his successor, William Leary.

Descriptions of the general conditions on the island of Long Point during the mid-19th century are rare and narrow in scope. The account with perhaps the most breadth is found in a letter that government official W. Witcher wrote to the *Ottawa Citizen* in 1870. It is important to recognize the context of Witcher's letter; it was defensive rhetoric. Witcher was responding publicly to a group of sportsmen from Simcoe who had protested the privatization of Long Point. The following passage is taken from the letter but is abridged:

> During forty years it had been a fruitful source of trouble and expense to the Department. Barren of almost everything else profitable to the public, it produced an annual and abundant crop of annoyances. Americans and others pillaged the timber, destroyed the furs and fish and aquatic fowl, in season and out of season. Nobody seemed to care much about this havoc. The place was public, it belonged to the Crown, and was, therefore, thought fit for nothing else except to be plundered. Once-in-a-while some speculators from Buffalo or Cleveland would make a tempting offer in imaginary dollars of fabulous figures to buy it for cultivating grapes. Its apparent value would thus grow in the eyes of officials until they were afraid to do anything at all with it, either to sell it or to abandon it. Meanwhile the speculative strangers would run riot over the place--cull the remaining oaks, walnuts and cedars, harpoon and trap the half~ grown rats and minks, and burn down their habitations, shoot and hunt with dogs the half-fledged ducks, and net and spear the fish wholesale throughout the year. They had active allies from the mainland and among the squatters.
>
> Season after season things went on from bad to, worse, and the place was fast going to utter ruin. In 1857, I was instructed to inspect it. I did so. Afterwards I had it surveyed and subdivided into blocks.[91] The department then advertised it for sale. We paid $374 for publishing the auction to be held at Simcoe in May 1858. Sale day came round, and the local agent never got a bid for the valuable estate. [136]

---

[91] The survey was conducted in 1853 by James Black, P.L.S.

The Prize Fights

The isolation of Long Point and the maturation of American transportation infrastructure factored into how the island came to be the site of the October 20th, 1858, prize fight for the Championship of America. Prizefighting was illegal, and one of the fight's contestants, John Morrissey, had been in trouble with the law. He selected Long Point as the location for the fight because he wanted to avoid interaction with American law enforcement. The selection was unrelated to the island's reputation as a locale for unruly behavior.

John Heenan would be Morrissey's opponent. Both men were from New York City, where the fight was arranged. There were similarities in their backgrounds. They were Irish, and they both grew up in Troy, New York. Heenan was a first-generation American. Morrissey had immigrated to the U.S. from Templemore, County Tipperary, with his family while still a child. He received only a little formal schooling before being sent to work in a factory. A jury indicted him for attempted murder while he was still a youth, and it has been suggested that the Troy police eventually forced him out of town. By the time he was 17 years old, he was working as a deckhand on a Hudson River packet steamer running between Albany and New York City. He pilfered freight, selling it to supplement his wages.

During the gold rush era, Morrissey stowed away on a ship bound for San Francisco and found work there as a longshoreman. Away from work, he fought and gambled. In 1852, he won a match that yielded a substantial prize. Subsequently, he moved with his winnings to New York City. The following year, in a brutal fight that lasted 37 rounds, Morrissey claimed the title of Heavyweight Champion of America. He put his temperament and brawn to work by providing protection and intimidation for gambling houses and saloons, before opening his own establishment.

Morrisey was an exceedingly violent underworld character. He joined the Dead Rabbits, the notorious Irish street gang who often fought their nativist, anti-Catholic rivals, the Washington Street Gang. [92] His ability to intimidate others impressed the largely Catholic politicians of Tammany Hall, so they recruited him to work as an organizer for their corrupt political machine. In 1854, William (Bill the Butcher) Poole, the leader of the Washington Street Gang, savagely beat Morrissey in an arranged fight. A few months later, Morrissey's fellow gang members shot and killed Poole in retribution. Although Morrissey was indicted as a conspirator in the murder, he was never convicted because multiple juries could not reach a verdict about his precise role. [137]

Heenan also left Troy for California during the gold rush. Still a teenager, he did not strike it rich. Instead, he ended up swinging a sledgehammer for a living at the Pacific Mail Steamship Co., a Benecia shipyard. [138] A big and strong man, he earned a reputation as a dockyard enforcer. During off hours, he fought and gambled. Seeking to better profit from his fighting skill, Heenan moved with his trainer to New York City in 1856. By day, he worked as a blacksmith in Brooklyn. After work, his fighting skill gained him the sobriquet "Benicia Boy."

---

[92] The Washington Street Gang were later known as the Bowery Boys.

Political undercurrents greatly heightened public interest in the matchup between Morrisey and Heenan. Immigration to the United States had increased dramatically in the 1850s, particularly immigration from Ireland and Germany. Nativists assumed that the immigrants would upend societal norms. Accordingly, they aligned themselves with the anti-immigration Know Nothing political party. Because Heenan had been born in the United States, he was the nativist's favored contestant. Morrisey, on the other hand, was an immigrant Irishman aligned with Tammany Hall and the Democratic Party, which largely controlled the administration of the New York City. Another factor was religious strife. The nativists tended to be Protestants. Most of the recent immigrants who had arrived from Ireland and Germany were Catholics. Because the Tammany Hall organization was dominated by Catholics, the match echoed the hard-knuckled politics of New York City. After the fight, one reporter wrote of the latter group, "A worse set of scapegallowses' could scarcely be collected; low, filthy, brutal, bludgeon-bearing scoundrels — the very class of men who have built up the Tammany Hall party in New York and whose well-paid labors the party owes almost its existence." [139]

The contestants agreed to a purse of $5,000. Each man (supported by their associates) was required to pay $2,500 in installments. Morrissey was able to partly finance his portion of the purse himself. Because of his troubled history with U.S. law enforcement, he insisted the fight take place in Canada, and Heenan agreed. Those interested in attending the match were made aware they should plan to travel to Buffalo, although the selection of the site for the fight was shrewdly deferred until just before the event. In the months after the terms for the match were agreed to, Morrissey trained close to his former home near Albany while Heenan remained in New York City.

After Heenan displayed his prowess publicly in a sparring match on September 29th, chatter about the pending matchup picked up. The chatter tipped off the police, and they obtained arrest warrants for Heenan and Morrissey. Both men quickly went into hiding. They surfaced briefly to meet with each other and their associates at Buffalo on October 9th. There, Morrissey chose the final location, Long Point. The two men then went back into hiding, and their associates set about to make the necessary arrangements for the fight, such as chartering steamboats. A few days prior to the match, roughly 2,000 men, mostly New York City gang members, and gamblers, rode the rails to Buffalo.

On the evening of October 19th, with phony picnic excursion tickets in hand, the mob embarked for Long Point. Morrissey traveled on the screw-driven *Galena* and Heenan on the *Globe*. A third steamer, the paddle-wheeler *Kaloolah*, departed later that night. A *New York Tribune* reporter was onboard. Unimpressed by the *Kaloolah*, the Tribune reporter described the boat as a "floating coffin," and added that "every person who embarked on that illustrious craft, was swindled from the time he stepped on board till he left her deck." Of the disembarking mob, he wrote they were "the most vicious congregation of roughs that was ever witnessed in a Christian city." By early the following day all three steamers were moored on Long Point's Outer Bay, about two miles west of the tip. Because photography was still in its infancy, a newspaper illustrator was present.

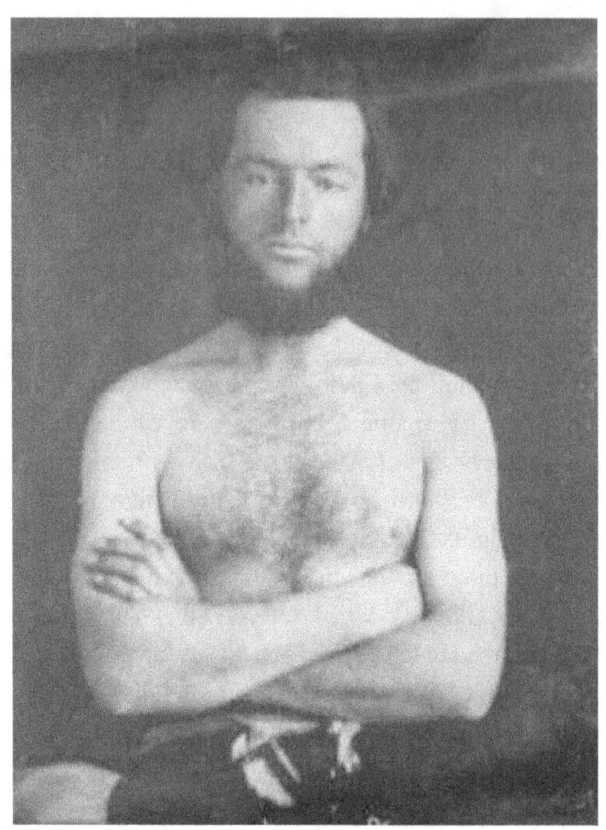

Photo 10 John Morissey. Unknown date. (Public Domian)

Photo 11 John Heenan. Unknown date. (Public Domain)

The passengers disembarked on yawls that carried them part way to shore until a sandbar impeded them. (Figure 20) Those who could afford a dollar paid a crew member to carry them on their shoulders from there to shore. Others, including the *Tribune's* reporter, waded through the chilly water from the sandbar to the beach and shivered for the rest of the day. The crowd was dismayed to discover the north shore of Long Point was largely marsh, beyond which were sandy knolls. The rules for the fight stipulated that the ring be set up on level turf, but there was none to be found. Seeking suitable ground, the crowd walked to the lighthouse plot at the tip of Long Point, where after some argument, it was agreed that the ring would have to be set up on sand.

Morrissey spent the next few hours waiting in the lighthouse keeper's cottage, likely in exchange for some money. A few others paid the keeper to let them observe the match from the top of the lighthouse. At about 3:30, the fighters and their crews gathered at the ring, betting activity frenzied, and the fight commenced.

After breaking a hand, Heenan was impeded for the rest of the fight. Twenty-one minutes later, in the eleventh bare-fisted round, he fell —and Morrissey carried the day. It had been a brutal spectacle. The *Tribune* reporter wrote, "Probably no human eye will look upon so much rowdyism, villainy, scoundrelism, and boiled-down viciousness …" He added that both men had to be carried away, side-by-side in a wagon, probably seized from the lighthouse keeper. A different report stated both men were "shockingly mangled and bruised" and each was carried away on a stretcher. [140] The steamers docked at Buffalo around 3 AM, and the results of the match were quickly sent to New York City by telegraph. [141] It was estimated that across the United States, the match drew $250,000 in wagers.[93]

ARRIVAL OF THE STEAMBOATS AT LONG POINT, CANADA WEST, THE PUGILISTS AND SPECTATORS LANDING.—FROM A SKETCH MADE ON THE SPOT BY OUR OWN ARTIST.

Figure 20. Going ashore from Gravelly Bay. (Public Domain) [142]

---

[93] ibid

Figure 21. Heenan vs. Morrissey, (Public Domain) [142]

GENERAL VIEW OF THE SCENE OF THE PRIZE FIGHT, AT LONG POINT, CANADA WEST.—FROM A SKETCH BY OUR OWN ARTIST.

Figure 22. The Setting. (Public Domain) [142]

THE LAST ROUND IN THE GREAT PRIZE FIGHT—THE BENICIA BOY FAILING TO COME TO TIME—FROM A SKETCH BY OUR OWN ARTIST.

Figure 23. The Last Round. (Public Domain) [142]

The contest prompted a great deal of controversy and heated discourse in the United States. [143] The *Tribune* published a scathing editorial two days after the fight condemning the violence. *The Clipper*, one of the other New York City newspapers that had sent a reporter to Long Point, responded by parodying the *Tribune* editorial on its front page. Academics have since suggested these differing editorial views reflected festering class distinction and struggle in New York City during the era. [144] Politicians took the Tribune's side and prepared a bill to revise the laws against prize fighting so that going forward not only could contestants be prosecuted, but spectators as well. It breezed through the New York State Assembly and passed the Senate without a dissenting vote. [145]

Morrissey retired from fighting. He leveraged his political connections and invested his winnings by setting up gambling establishments in upstate New York.[94] One of his early 1860s undertakings was the development of the racecourse and clubhouse at Saratoga Springs. He was elected to the U.S. House of Representatives as a Democrat in 1866, and to the Senate in 1875. [146] An affront to Canadian sovereignty, the 1858 fight at Long Point would have incensed British officials and subjects who held resentments related to the War of 1812.

The next fight in the Long Point region occurred between Port Dover and Port Ryerse on May 12, 1871. Two chartered steamboats, *Winona* and *New York*, departed Erie at two that morning. On board one was an ill-at-ease reporter from the *New York Herald* who wrote that the safest wager of the day would have been that nine out of ten attendees (whom he referred to them as roughs) were armed with either a pistol or a knife. [147] Accounts state the boats rendezvoused with others near the tip of Long Point. One source states the organizers intended to land at the tip but were dissuaded when they observed an armed group of men from the Long Point Company,

---

[94] Morrissey's extensive history of operating gambling establishments is discussed in the 1938 book *Sucker's Progress, an Informal History of Gambling in America from the Colonies to Canfield.*

led by head keeper William Leary. [148] By 7:AM, the boats were moored near Hay Creek, between Port Dover and Port Ryerse.

The yawls were lowered, and a crowd of 1,500 to 2,000 were rowed ashore. They climbed the creek ravine and followed it until arriving at Lot 5, the farm of a soon-to-be bewildered Daniel Woolley. (Figure 24) The ring was pitched on Woolley's field, kegs of beer were tapped, and Joe Coburn and Jem Mace from New York City set about to compete for another Championship of America. A source reported that men grabbed the few farm wagons and moved them near the ring, where they tipped them on their sides to afford makeshift seating. A few others mounted the Wooley's horses to get a better view. [149] It had been arranged that a certain Mr. McCallan, an Alderman from Philadelphia, would referee the match. At the last minute, he declined his duties (perhaps having been suspected of holding a wager,) and a fellow with a name that would today be considered quite fanciful was substituted. It was retired New York boxer Dick Hollywood. Dick was not from the West Coast; he had retired to Indianapolis. [150]

Canadian authorities probably received advance notice of the match from anticipatory articles published in U.S. newspapers. They were prepared to intervene. Not long after the fight commenced, Judge and Clerk of the Peace William Wilson arrived. He was accompanied by Colonel Edmund Deedes, the Norfolk County Sheriff.[95] To a chorus of boos and jeers, Deedes, sword-on-side, made his way through the crowd and climbed into the ring where in a jittery voice struggling to make himself heard he read a proclamation ordering the fight terminated in the name of Her Majesty the Queen. Deedes' fortitude earned him plenty of mockery. The crowd dispensed wisecracks about his official three-cornered hat. The *Norfolk Reformer* later reported that "two or three revolvers were leveled at the officers." As the insults kept coming, Deedes motioned to a woodlot about 100 yards distant. Thence, the 39th Regiment of Canadian Volunteers under the command of David Tisdale and numbering about 50, revealed themselves and began marching toward the mob, rifles raised. (The Regiment may have initially mustered at Port Dover, anticipating they would be intervening on Long Point.)

Dick Hollywood prorogued all wagers, and the spectators hurried back to the Hay Creek ravine and to the water's edge where they had landed. Judge Wilson, for his valor, was frustrated to learn he had been the victim of a pickpocket. In the days that followed, stories of the event appeared in newspapers across the continent. John Sandfield MacDonald, the Premier of Ontario, congratulated Sheriff Deedes, writing that it "required no small degree of courage to face such a set of miscreants…" The Mace-Coburn match resumed on November 30th at Bay St. Louis, Mississippi, near New Orleans. After 12 rounds, the referee stopped the fight, having determined that each man was too exhausted to continue.

---

[95] Deedes, a half-pay British officer, had emigrated from England to Beachville, Ontario. He was appointed Lt. Col. of the Oxford 2nd battalion by the Governor General in 1848. Deedes served as Sheriff of Norfolk County over three decades until his death in 1892. A successful lumberman, he was elected chairman of the Port Dover & Lake Huron Railway in 1873.

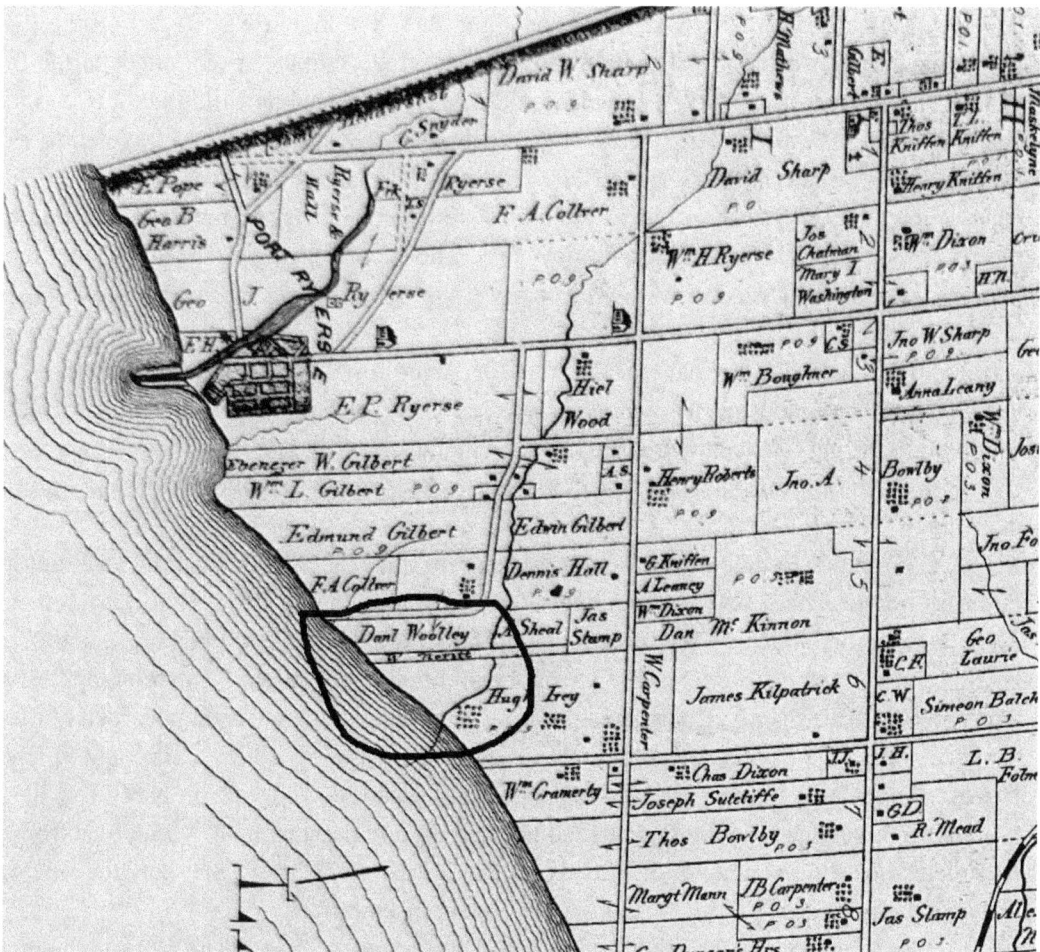

Figure 24. The location of Daniel Woolley's Farm. (Page's Illustrated Historical Atlas of Norfolk County, 1877)

In 1879, another crowd, mostly from New York City, embarked in the hundreds on a fleet of boats from Erie, Pennsylvania, to hold yet another prize fight. Officially, the match was slated to occur in Port Dover on May 8th. However, that planned location seems to have been a ruse because the night before the match, the two combatants signed papers switching the location to Long Point. [151] One of the combatants, John Dwyer, had been born in Saint John, New Brunswick. His family moved to New York when he was a child. When the fight was arranged, he was working on the printing press of the Brooklyn *Eagle*. The match at Long Point would be his first prize fight. His opponent was a homicidal criminal, James Elliott. He was a veteran of previous fights, including one that had been held on Pelee Island in 1867. That match, too, had brought a tough crowd to Canada. The *Chicago Tribune* reported an attendee had one ear and part of his nose bitten off while onboard a steamboat carrying attendees to the island. Before his Long Point fight, Elliott was well into a 16-year sentence in a Philadelphia prison, having been convicted of attempted murder for nearly beating to death Hughey Doberty, a well-liked black minstrel. He was granted early release, perhaps because the fight's promoters influenced politicians and officials.

Like the 1858 Morrissey vs. Heenan fight, the 1879 match was staged on the lighthouse plot at the island's eastern tip. The fighters, their entourage, and the spectators departed from Erie at 4:30 AM. Dwyer and his crew traveled on *George S. Frost* while Elliott and his party were on board *Thomas Thompson*. There were other steamboats, two of which had traveled to Erie from Canada to participate in the flotilla. The crowd was estimated to number about 400. The media tagged along to observe the spectacle. Both The New York Times and the Brooklyn Eagle printed the results of the fight later the same day. [152] The reporter, who referred to the attendees as "toughs," wrote that Long Point was "as dreary a spot as could well be selected" even though the weather was reportedly good that day.

Dwyer carried the day in the twelfth round by knock-out, securing the American heavyweight championship. He would be elected Clerk of Brooklyn's Third District Court the following year, but he died three years after the match at the age of 36, perhaps from alcoholism. [153] Things didn't go much better for Elliott; four years after his Long Point fight, he was murdered in Chicago's Tivoli Restaurant.

Boxing fans and gamblers were at it again on May 11th, 1880, when they set out for Long Point from Erie aboard several steamboats and a few small sailboats to stage yet another fight.[96] They were accompanied by reporters from Buffalo, New York City, Pittsburgh, and Cincinnati. By this era, newspapers were reaching distant communities by railroad, and telegraph service was widespread. Consequently, Canadian authorities were well prepared as they learned of the fight in advance. When the flotilla departed, the Erie police sent a telegraph to their counterparts in Port Dover. *Annie Craig* left the harbor carrying Sheriff Deedes (who was probably less nervous on this occasion,) Judge Huntington, a dozen constables, and a company of volunteers from the 39th Regiment under the command of Port Rowan's Col. Simon Mabee. She was the first vessel to arrive at the tip of Long Point, where the contingent disembarked.

The American vessels rounded the island and dropped anchor. The mobs on board became agitated when they realized they were about to be confronted. Sheriff Deedes yelled to them, that they would be fired upon, should they attempt to disembark. A negotiating party and a reporter did go ashore, where they were met by Deedes who made his formal proclamation that they could not land for the purpose of a fight. After a few more minutes of discussion, the landing party departed. When the crowd on board the vessels realized there wasn't going to be a match, they gestured and swore at the contingent ashore. The vessels pulled anchor, rounded the lighthouse, and made way westward along the island's southern shore, hoping to land elsewhere. However, Deedes and the contingent went back aboard *Annie Craig* and shadowed the flotilla along the length of Long Point until about 4:30 PM. At that time, the fight's organizers realizing they had no chance of going ashore, chose to return to Erie. [154] [155] [156]

The last attempt to stage a fight on Long Point occurred a year and a half later. This time the contestants were Frank White and George Holden. Together with their accompanying crowd,

---

[96] Vessels included the *Thompson, Dragon, Welsh, & Hunter* from Erie. The *Welsh* caught fire during the voyage, and the passengers on board were taken on by the *Annie P. Dorr*, a boat from Buffalo that rendezvoused with the flotilla.

they intended to depart from Erie for Long Point. Canadian authorities had expected them and prepared by chartering the *Annie Craig.* An article that appeared on the front page of the *New York Times* the day before the pending match stated that a militia and constables (who had with them 50 pairs of handcuffs), were planning to depart Port Dover at 3 AM the following morning. It wasn't just bluster. The *Annie Craig* steamed for Long Point with the No. 7 Company of the 39th Battalion on board, this time led by Capt. Biddle. [157]   As in the past, the contingent was accompanied by Sheriff Deedes and his constables. [158]

It turned out to be a rough day on the lake. The fight's organizers opted not to cross to Long Point. Authorities in Erie made it clear to them that they would not allow the contest to occur in Pennsylvania. The following day, the contestants and would-be spectators boarded a westbound train and got off just beyond the Ohio state line, east of Ashtabula. Outside town, a ring was pitched, and the match commenced. Shortly thereafter, a constable arrived and stopped the fight. Holden and White were arrested in Ashtabula later in the day. [159]

The Free for All

Perhaps nothing contributed more to the unrestrained slaughter of waterfowl than railroad development. Writing in 1848, Henry Herbert lamented the circumstances in the opening observations of his book titled, *Frank Forester's Field Sports of the United States, and British Provinces of North America.*[97]

All this has now changed —the railroads by which the country is everywhere intersected, enable the city pot-hunter to move about with his dogs, and to transmit the subject of his butchery to the market easily, cheaply, speedily. Nor is this all —the country now bids fair to monopolize the trade of pot-hunting. The young men and boys, nowadays all shoot on the wing; many of them shoot extremely well; and knowing the country, and being at it all the time, the devastation they make is enormous.

Their game is easily disposed of by the aid of the conductors, or other employees on the railroads, who share the spoils with the killers; and fathers, finding that the idle lad, who formerly did an hour or two of work, and bird nested or played truant quite unprofitably all the rest of the day, now readily earns his three or four shillings a day by loafing about in the woods with a gun in his hand and a cur at his heels, encourages him in this thoughtless course, and looks upon him as a source both of honor and profit to the family.

In the meantime, knowing nothing, and caring less than nothing, about the habits or seasons of the birds in question, he judges naturally enough that, whenever there is a demand for the birds or beasts in the New York markets, it is alright to kill and sell them.

And thanks to this selfish gormandizing of the wealthier classes of that city, there is a demand always; and the unhappy birds are hunted and destroyed, year in and year out, by the very persons whose interest it is to protect them, if it be only for the selfish object of making the most money of their killing. [160]

Long Point ducks, shot by market gunners, were reaching Hamilton on stagecoaches by the mid-1840s, after the Plank Road first connected the city to Port Dover.[98] However, by the late 1850s, road and railway infrastructure had developed sufficiently to allow waterfowl shipments from villages on Long Point Bay's shore to distant urban markets. Trade was bidirectional. Just as patrons of restaurants and hotels in mid-Atlantic cities such as New York, Philadelphia, &

---

[97] Henry William Herbert sometimes used the pseudonym, Frank Forester.

[98] The surface of the 47-mile Plank Road was constructed by nailing hardwood planks to logs set parallel to the roadway. At the village of Caledonia. a wooden swing bridge allowed users of the road to cross the Grand River. The route is presently Ontario Highway #6. The first plank roads in North America were built in Canada and were a curiosity to visiting Americans, who later adopted the technique.

Baltimore could dine on Canadian duck, residents of Simcoe indulged themselves with fresh Chesapeake Bay oysters. They were a delicacy well-advertised in the *Simcoe Reformer*.

Men descended on Long Point, seeking to earn extra cash by selling ducks. By 1860, the technological innovations of percussion-firing and breech-loading enabled the gunners to reload quickly and bring down more ducks.[99] The Port Rowan correspondent for the *Norfolk Reformer* reported as follows:

> A remarkably successful season for shooting is drawing nigh to a close. Harry Woodward came over from the Point on Monday with about 50 brace of large black and grey ducks, being about the last we may expect from that quarter for many a month.[100] A week ago, Harry shot 90 ducks in one day, and during the season Peter Price, who shanties by himself, succeeded in killing nearly 2,000. The probabilities are that there have been over 20,000 ducks taken from Long Point Marsh this fall! There will not be many more brought down this season, as since the appearance of snow the feathered tribe have been leaving in flocks for their summer land of Dixie. [161]

Photo 12 St. Williams resident Peter Price. Unknown date. [162]

---

[99] Earlier shotguns and fowling pieces had to be loaded through the muzzle with both the charge and shot. This was time-consuming. Percussion center-fired shotguns could be quickly reloaded with a cartridge.
[100] One brace is comprised of two ducks.

An outlandish occurrence was the arrival in Port Rowan in 1866 of an improvised gunboat, the 34-foot *Hattie Brown*. On board were seven men from Buffalo. Mounted on the deck was a gun weighing 36 kilograms that had a barrel two metres in length. The men claimed it was an early 18th century military weapon of English origin. [163] Similar guns were commercially built in England expressly for shooting waterfowl. The largest could weigh as much as 90 kilograms. They were typically fired from punts at night when ducks were resting on the water, killing dozens in a single blast. Legislation implementing the 1918 Convention Between the United States and Great Britain for the Protection of Migratory Birds made the use of such guns illegal, thankfully.

Hunting did not just occur during the fall season. Unscrupulous Long Point punters hosted shooters during the spring, even though concerned citizens had already succeeded in getting the legislature to ban spring duck hunting. (If birds are killed during the nesting season, whether male or female, progeny will decrease.) Enforcement of the regulations, however, was sparse. In April 1866, the Port Rowan correspondent for the *Norfolk Reformer* reported:

> We hear that some parties from Boston, Massachusetts, played sad havoc among the ducks in the marsh last week. It is a shame that while those living in the neighborhood observe the game laws, parties from a distance violate them with impunity. They should be attended to. [164]

Eventually, a small group of well-heeled sport hunters became concerned about the ongoing slaughter. They were particularly unhappy with how Harry Woodward was operating his establishment. The group recognized there were simply too many hunters on the island, shooting too many ducks. If the extent of hunting were to be left unchecked, the number of ducks would diminish, potentially rendering the island barren to sport shooters such as themselves. It wasn't an unfounded supposition. Their motivation was to secure for themselves the continued opportunity to engage in a sport laden with class distinction, in which privileged participants competed and demonstrated mastery by shooting as many ducks as possible.

Aware that the British government had tried once to privatize the island by putting it up for auction, they arranged for solicitor David Tisdale, an occasional Long Point hunter, to lobby the government to attempt a second auction. They planned to be well-prepared to acquire Long Point for themselves should the auction occur. In the Old World, hunting was the domain of the uppermost class for the simple reason that they owned the lands. The New World wasn't like that, at least initially. The founders of the Long Point company sought to impose an Old World style reordering on an exceptionally bountiful hunting ground.

The Auction and Aftermath

Eight years after the previous auction attempt at Simcoe failed to attract bidders, the Government made a second attempt, this time at Toronto.[101] The well-advertised sale took place at noon on May 4th, 1866. The land, all of which was encumbered by an existing timber license, was auctioned in parcels referred to as blocks.

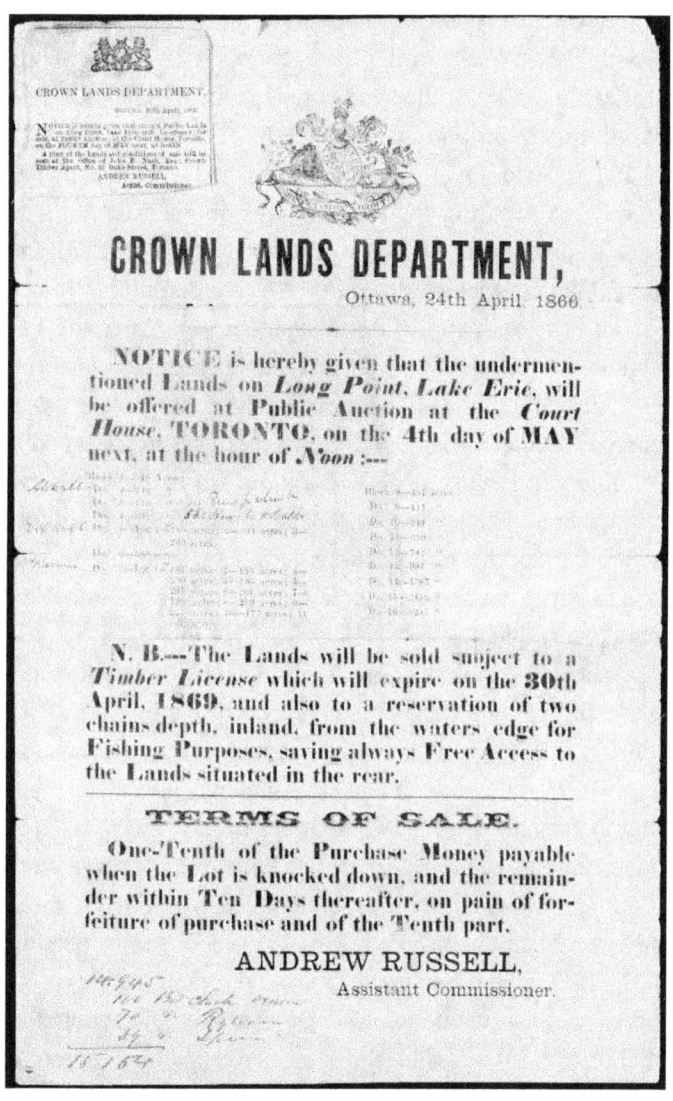

Figure 25. Crown Lands Department auction poster. 1866.

---

[101] Edward Harris, in his memoir *Recollections of Long Point,* stated the government made three attempts to auction the property. Long Point Company records and W. Witcher's retrospection state there were only two.

Henry Clark, the keeper of the lighthouse at the tip of Long Point, successfully bid for a 100-acre parcel on Bluff Point for 50 cents an acre. He did so because he had already established a vineyard on the fertile plot and wanted to protect the investment in labor he had made in previous years. John Aldwell of Toronto won 243 acres fronting Gravelly Bay, some for 51 cents an acre and the rest for 67 cents. A 196-acre block east of that parcel went to Bernard Saunders, also of Toronto, for 52 cents per acre.

The remaining parcels, comprising 14,324 acres, were successfully bid on by seven other individuals at prices ranging from 50 to 70 cents per acre. Although each of them made their bids separately, they were members of a syndicate. They were the individuals who, earlier in the decade, became disenchanted with Harry Woodward, plus a few others who later signed on to the scheme to acquire Long Point. Each member of the syndicate is identified below:

Lauchlin McCallum was born in Scotland in 1823. He owned a lumber and boat-building business at Port Maitland, Ontario. Over time, he established a fleet of canal boats and tugboats. One of them, the 128-foot, 180-ton tug *W. T. Robb,* was an occasional visitor to the Port Royal Ship Canal, from where it towed rafts of logs to Buffalo.[102] [165] McCallum formed and led his local militia. When the Fenian conflict occurred in 1866, he put the *W. T. Robb* to military service carrying his brigade from Port Maitland to the Niagara River. After the Fenians retreated west from the Battle of Ridgeway, McCallum and his forces engaged them in combat near Fort Erie.[103] [166] McCallum was elected a Member of Parliament in 1874 as a Conservative.

Samuel Deveaux Woodruff was born at St. Catherine's in 1819 and schooled there. After training to be a civil engineer in Lewiston, New York, he worked for the Erie Canal at Lockport. Woodruff returned to Canada to take a position for the Welland Canal and was later appointed its superintendent, a position he held for almost three decades. Concurrently, he invested in timber, railroad development, and paper manufacturing. When Woodruff died in 1904, he was reputed to be St. Catharine's wealthiest resident.

David Tisdale was born in Norfolk County in 1835. Called to the bar in 1858, he set about practicing law in Simcoe. In 1861, he was named Captain of the Fenwick Rifle Co. He saw action during the Fenian conflict in 1866 and later that year became Lieutenant-Colonel of the 39th Norfolk Rifles Battalion. Tisdale was adept at financial law. He ran regular newspaper advertisements offering to arrange large loans. It wouldn't have been his money; he was offering to structure financial agreements among parties. As his career progressed, Tisdale cut back on general law to focus more on business development. He was one of the founders of and the president of the Port Dover & Lake Huron Railway. That led to him becoming a shareholder of substance in the Grand Trunk when the two railways were amalgamated. Tisdale was elected a Member of Parliament as a Conservative in 1887. By that time, he also had extensive timber and sawmill interests in Michigan and Wisconsin, and some cattle ranching investments in Montana. [167]

---

[102] Port arrival records for Buffalo show the *W. T. Robb* could arrive towing the equivalent of 220,000 board feet of timber.

[103] Lt. James Robb, the tug's master, stood guard over 60 prisoners in the tug's hold. Robb and his brother Walter Robb, drowned in Long Point Bay two years later. The yawl they were fishing from capsized during a squall. [427]

Thomas C. Kerr of Hamilton was a principal of the firm Kerr, Brown & MacKenzie, wholesale importers of dry goods, groceries, wine, and liquor. He was also a director of the Canada Life Assurance Co., Canada's first life insurer. Upon incorporation of the Long Point Company, Kerr served as its first president.

John Brown of Hamilton was associated with Kerr, Brown & MacKenzie. He was also engaged in railway development.

George H. Gillespie of Hamilton, a principal of Brown, Gillespie & Co., wholesale importers of groceries, tea, wine, and general merchandise. He was a member of the Hamilton Board of Trade and its Board of Arbitration. Although he bid at the auction himself, an interest in his purchases accrued to a relative, John Gillespie, thereby effectively creating an eighth member of the syndicate.

William Little of London, Ontario, was a lumberman. His father, James Little, of Caledonia, timbered the near shore of Lake Erie from the Grand River westward, including lands flanking Big Creek.[104] Little was instrumental in expanding the private dock at Port Rowan and was among the earliest sawmill operators to export lumber to the United States.[105] His son, William, had a close business association with New York lumberman Col. Eli Clark. Jointly, they were the first to organize and conduct government licensed timbering on Long Point. They began cutting in the general area of Second Island and Snow Island, in the 1850s.[168] On the day the government auctioned Long Point at Toronto, **William Little** bid on and won various land parcels. However, a few months later he revealed to the others in the bidder's syndicate that **Eli Clark** held a position in the parcels he had won. The obvious hypothesis is Little's bidding at the auction in Toronto was done at the behest of Clark. As a matter of fact, it was Clark who was the lessee who held the timber license from the Government —for the entirety of Long Point.

Without delay, the syndicate applied to the Legislative Assembly to incorporate an entity they named the Long Point Company. Years later, in a letter to the Federal Government, **John MacKenzie**, the Company's secretary/treasurer, asserted the men had not coordinated with each other when they bid at the auction. He wrote:

> In May 1866, this property was advertised for sale at the City of Toronto. Seven gentlemen without any understanding or concert were present at that sale and they bid for the various blocks, being largely the main purchasers, thus finding themselves the owners of a white elephant. Eventually they held a conference and decided to buy out the few others to whom lots were knocked down, and to form a Joint Stock Corporation for sporting purposes.

---

[104] The Grand River was a toll route at the time, and James Little was the secretary of the Grand River Navigation Co.

[105] James Little and his son participated in and observed the denudation of Ontario's timber. However, by the 1860s Little realized America's demand for Canadian timber was destructive and unsustainable. Consequently, he lobbied for the imposition of a timber export duty, an initiative that earned him widespread ridicule. After the timber in southern Ontario was harvested, James and William relocated to Quebec. Both James and his son William eventually became advocates for more sustainable forestry practices.[469]

Photo 13. George Gillespie & Samuel Woodruff. [162] *(Public Domain)*

MacKenzie's assertion that the founder's bids were uncoordinated was disingenuous, as was his rhetoric characterizing the founder's purchases as a white elephant. He was a serial fibber, who in the early years of the Company, claimed that it didn't sell game, even though it did.

The syndicate applied to the Legislative Assembly in Ottawa to create a corporation less than three weeks after the auction. An item published in the *Norfolk Reformer* that month stated:

> We observe that notice has been given of an application to Parliament to incorporate the Long Point Company, for the purpose of pursuing, protecting and granting license to take game and fish upon lands and property owned by such company on Long Point, and Lake Erie; for the purpose of mining, boring for or manufacturing oil, salt and other mineral and vegetable substances, upon or under such land; For the purpose of cutting and manufacturing trees, timber and wood upon such land, for the purpose of planting and growing grapes and other vineyards upon the said land, and manufacturing the products thereof, and of selling, leasing, and making contracts concerning said lands. [169]

During the era when the auction was held, communication was significantly slower than it is today. It would have been impractical for the members of the syndicate to formalize an agreement to incorporate within such a short timeframe. It is highly likely the decision to incorporate was premeditated, with the necessary application papers prepared in advance of the auction.

By summer, the legislature had granted a corporate charter. The articles of incorporation created one hundred shares, each assigned a notional value of $500, thereby setting the total stated capitalization at $50,000. The capital valuation was an arbitrary declaration. The syndicate's members, and no one else, injected any funds whatsoever into the corporation. The first meeting of the Company occurred on August 16, 1866. A solicitor was tasked with preparing a set of bylaws.

The next meeting occurred on January 29, 1867, at the Royal Hotel in Hamilton. Directors and officers were elected. On the motion of Samuel Woodruff and David Tisdale the directors authorized the new corporation to acquire each of the land parcels individually held by the proprietors of the syndicate. In return for their land, each syndicate member would receive 12 shares of stock in the newly created corporation. A residual of four shares remained in the Company's account.[106] Paper share certificates were ordered from the British American Bank Note Company and distributed to the members on June 27th.

A couple weeks later, February 12th, 1867, the Company held another business meeting. At that time, William Little revealed to the other founders that his Long Point interest was obligated to his business associate, Eli Clark, and he wished to transfer the interest to him. Payment for Little's twelve shares was made by cheque in the amount of $1,040 drawn on the account of Clark's Albany lumber firm, Clark, Sumner & Co. That amount was essentially what Little had paid at the auction.

---

[106] The Company soon sold the residual four shares.

Figure 26. Share certificate, assigned in 1891. (Private collection)

One of the Company's earliest actions was to force Harry Woodward to relinquish his sporting establishment. He had no title to the land it occupied. The Company gave Woodward no compensation for the shanties at Harry's Place. However, by this time, Woodward also owned a partial interest in Hutchison's shanty on Carrying Place Creek together with Edwin Fenn.[107] The Company did agree to a quitclaim settlement for that structure.

Woodward spent the fall of 1867 in St. Williams, hosting visitors at his father-in-law's inn. He likely guided them to hunt in the marshes of Turkey Point. The correspondent for the *Norfolk Reformer* hinted jokingly that Woodward's wife might not have been unhappy to return to the more gentrified mainland:

> Harry Woodward has moved over from the Point and taken Dease's old stand at St. Williams, where he no doubt will do well as he is a "jolly good fellow" and his long experience as a caterer for the public on the Point, will ensure him a good share of public patronage. Mrs. Woodward is the right woman in the right place.[108] [170]

---

[107] Carrying Place Creek became known as Cottage Creek. The cottages of the Long Point Company are located at the north terminus of the creek.

[108] "Dease's stand" was likely a tavern or inn operated by the father of Woodward's second spouse, Jane Dease.

Mrs. Woodward was perhaps twice unlucky. Harry was hired the next year to replace Henry Clark as the lighthouse keeper at the isolated tip of Long Point. She and her children would need to join him at that lonely place. Mrs. Woodward is reputed to have become highly skilled at taxidermy during her years there. The family tended the light until 1893.

After Harry was established as the lighthouse keeper for a few years, the Long Point Company, knowing full well its relationship with him was strained, made the pragmatic decision to pay him an annual stipend over and above his government salary. Woodward's assignment was to keep poachers and others from trespassing on the far reaches of the island. Samuel Woodruff, the Company's second president, supported Woodward's employment but expressed concern that his earlier troubled relationship with the founders might hinder his earnest pursuit of assigned duties. [171]

The Company hired Charles Brown, the former host at Hutchison's hotel, to be its first steward. Brown promptly arranged for Port Rowan's Mitchell Proux to cater to sportsmen at Harry's Place. Proux filled the role for two years. [109] [172] During the 1869 season, he temporarily fell ill, and the position seems to have been assigned to Harry Woodward's brother, William.

On the mainland, the public who were unhappy that Long Point had become private property, began to sarcastically refer to Charles Brown as the "Governor of Long Point." Nonetheless, he seems to have been well-respected. The Norfolk Reformer had the following to say about him:

> Governor Brown still remains in charge of the premises.

> > He is monarch of all the surveys;
> > His rights there are none to dispute;
> > From the marsh round to the cut,
> > He is lord of the rat and the duck.

> > The governor is a jolly goodfellow, and although he has a difficult post to fill he does it very satisfactorily; It would be hard to fill his place. He has issued nearly 100 licenses this year and a greater number of ducks have been killed this season than in any previous year. [172]

By this time it was becoming difficult for John Spain to attract hunters to his hotel because of the Long Point Company's ownership of the surrounding hunting marshes. Recognizing his life was about to change, Spain commissioned the construction of an 80-foot, 40-ton sidewheel steamer, which he named *Norfolk*. [110] [173] The vessel launched in 1868, and Spain initially moored it near his hotel on Courtwright Ridge. [174] The Board of Trade in Erie, Pennsylvania offered him $2,000 to put the vessel on a fixed route serving Port Rowan, Port Ryerse, Port Dover, and Erie, but the proposed arrangement was never implemented. [175]

---

[109] On the county voter's list, Proux was identified as an oarsman, suggesting he was a punter. Company records show him as having punted in 1869.

[110] Commissioning the construction of the *Norfolk* would have required significant capital. A speculative theory is that one or more of the Long Point Company's founders had benevolent feelings toward Spain and may have assisted him with financing. They may have occasioned his hotel during the years prior to the auction.

Consistent with the Company's long-term plan to acquire the entirety of Long Point, the following year Company secretary-treasurer George Gillespie convinced Spain to sell his plot and hotel. Gillespie placed the property in trust. The Company's financial records show it acquired the plot and booked a charge of $1,100 for the transaction. That equates to about $28 per acre. Considering the Company's founders had purchased almost 15,000 acres at auction for about 50 cents per acre, the premium Spain received demonstrates how determined the Company's members were to exclude other hunters from Long Point.

Spain relocated his household and the *Norfolk* to Port Rowan, from where he captained the vessel to distant ports including Buffalo and Hamilton. Locally, he transported passengers, oxen, hay, or provisions to Long Point. On festive occasions, such as the Queen's birthday, the townsfolk delighted in pleasure excursions aboard the steamer.

Spain soon became well-respected for his expertise at navigating around Long Point Bay's sandbars and shallows. The Long Point Company asked him to ensure the safe passage of Prince Arthur, a son of Queen Victoria, and His Excellency the Governor General, from Port Dover to Long Point. Spain was to captain the *Norfolk* as a pilot boat. The Prince and his entourage were to reach Port Dover by land, where they would board another steamer, the *Ivanhoe*. That vessel was to follow the *Norfolk* to Long Point. [176] Never one to forego a business opportunity, Spain sold excursion tickets to the residents of Port Rowan for his trip on the *Norfolk* from Port Rowan to Port Dover so they might get a glimpse of royalty. When the planned day came in late September, Spain set out from Port Rowan with a complement of paying passengers.

Upon reaching Port Dover, Spain was informed that the *Ivanhoe* had yet to arrive because of strong opposing winds. Officials demanded that Spain make the *Norfolk* available solely for the Prince, the Governor General, and their entourage. He refused on the basis that his vessel was in charter, and he did not want to abandon his passengers, who would have to spend the night in Port Dover. The outcome was that the Prince, Governor General, and their entourage joined Spain's passengers on the *Norfolk*. The understanding was that the Prince and Governor General would have the cabin to themselves. Others were to remain on or below deck. After the vessel got underway, Prince Arthur exited the cabin and took to the deck, where much to their delight, he mingled with the Port Rowan townsfolk for the remainder of the three-hour voyage. [177] At Long Point, Prince Arthur was guided by Company keeper William Leary. Company records state the Prince downed 18 ducks one day and 11 the next.

Spain went on to acquire a second vessel, the 13-ton screw-driven harbor tug named *Watchman*. However, in 1872 he set about planning another career change and decided to sell it and the *Norfolk*. He advertised that the *Watchman* had a boiler that was rated at 24 horsepower, and he convinced a certain Captain Davis of Collingwood to purchase the tug for the next season. An American sailor, who happened to be waiting out the winter in one of the hotels at Port Rowan that year, challenged Spain regarding the concept of horsepower. He argued that the *Watchman* could not overcome ten men, let alone 24 horses, and he was willing to support his contention with a wager. The following contest was scheduled to occur following the spring thaw:

That 20 men on a rope could hold the tug from getting underway,

That ten men could do the same, and

That 25 men could bring the vessel to a stop after getting underway.

Many spectators and a few reporters were present at Port Rowan when the contests took place on April 10, 1872. Thirty metres of rope was uncoiled; two minutes were allotted for each event. The *Watchman* succumbed to human strength in all three contests, leading plenty of money to change hands. A good deal of press coverage resulted, including a few lines in the *Chicago Tribune*, New Zealand's *The Cromwell Argus*, and *The Engineer,* a highly sophisticated technical journal published in Britain, that regularly included pages of mind-numbing calculus and vector algebra. Port Rowan was by no means a dull place 150 years ago.

After selling his vessels, Spain returned to the hospitality business by buying the Stearns Hotel in Port Rowan. Another notable fact about him is that he was a collector of antiques and artifacts. He particularly favored items that had been created by Indigenous People such as arrowheads, axes, and pipes. Over his lifetime, he accumulated hundreds of these. A partial inventory of his collection mentions 175 stone axe heads, 30 pipes, and hundreds of flints. [178] Late in life, he donated a copper axe to the Royal Ontario Museum that is cataloged as originating in Ontario sometime between 3,500 and 2,500 BCE. It is uncertain when Spain first developed his interest in such artifacts, but during his early days on Long Point in the mid-19th century, he would have encountered Native People.

Spain later moved to Simcoe where he operated a printing business. Among the materials he produced were postcards, and he registered copyright for at least one.[111] Under the pseudonym *Rambler*, he wrote an occasional column for the *British Canadian* newspaper. He traveled the county seeking artifacts for his collection. Spain would offer residents a free subscription to the newspaper in exchange for an artifact. To display and profit from his collection, he established Simcoe's first museum. Patrons paid an admission fee to see what he called "curiosity rooms."

By the dawn of the 20th century, Port Dover was attracting tourists and Spain moved his museum there. His interest and knowledge of the hospitality business led him to buy the Commercial Hotel and to create Orchard Beach Park, a place for tourists. Late in life, he was unsuccessful in convincing the government to buy his museum collection and was forced to liquidate most of it piecemeal. The Ontario Agricultural College did purchase a few of his artifacts. [179] Some others, Spain donated to the Royal Ontario Museum, including his native copper axe. [180] [181] He died at Port Dover in 1914.

Freewheeling, unrestrained market hunting on Long Point had finally come to an end. A few former guides who had assisted patrons at Harry's Place and at Spain's accepted employment with the Long Point Company. They were not only permitted, but encouraged to continue hunting, although they would do so via a revenue sharing program under the auspices of the corporation.

---

[111] The postcard is titled, *Adrift on Lake Erie.*

Photo 14 Captain John Spain and his second wife Emily, whom he married in Buffalo. (Date unknown). [182]

Share Sales, Timber Extraction, and Further Land Acquisition

At the Company's next annual meeting in 1868 the directors established an extraordinary benefit for the founders. On the motion of Samuel Woodruff, seconded by Lachlan McCallum, they agreed to create a corporate bylaw granting lifetime hunting and fishing rights to the original syndicate members, regardless of whether they sold all their shares in the Company. Consequently, the only incentives a founder had to hold his shares was an expectation they would increase in value or a personal desire to maintain voting rights.

Sell, they did. Lauchlin McCallum disposed of all his shares in less than two years. The other founders sold portions of their stock. It is a certainty that all of them, except for William Little, banked handsome profits. Their initial investment had amounted to less than $90 per share. Thomas Kerr, the Company's founding president, asked $250 for each share he sold.

Five of the individuals who purchased shares from the founders were well-established wholesale grocery importers from Hamilton, which at the time was second only to Montreal as a location in Canada for wholesale commerce. They were George Forster, Henry Routh, John MacKenzie, James Turner, and Adam Brown.[112] Brown was a principal of Brown, Gillespie, & Co., and Routh was a salesman for the firm. The number of grocery wholesalers from Hamilton who were members of the Company had risen to nine.

Except for John MacKenzie, none of the Hamiltonians would hold their shares for long. It is possible a few had contemplated the commercial opportunity of selling ducks. That wouldn't have been an unreasonable aspiration. In time, the Company would become Upper Canada's prevailing supplier. Other purchasers may have been speculating that they could flip shares and make a profit.

There is evidence some of the founders were aggressive in promoting the sale of their shares. Edward Harris, a lawyer who became president of the Company two decades later, was critical of the founders. In an 1879 letter to shareholders, he wrote that the founders had been "promoters" and stated, "The company was in fact formed with a view to realize an immense and immediate profit ..." While Harris' assertion should not be assigned total credibility, it wasn't unfounded. The very act of creating a corporation facilitates the transfer of interests. The issuance of assignable paper share certificates (which are essentially a form of currency) made it easy for the founders to sell either their entire or partial interests in the Company. As soon as they had their stock certificates in hand, that's what they did. Moreover, they had reserved for themselves the right to hunt at Long Point, even if they sold all their shares —an arrangement that particularly irritated Harris. He wanted the bylaw that gave the founders lifetime rights struck down, and he seems to have been taking aim at John Brown, George Gillespie, John MacKenzie, and David Tisdale.

Although some of the founders may have promoted the sale of their shares aggressively, there is little doubt that several buyers were fully content with their purchases. One of them was

---

[112] Turner was the president of the Hamilton Board of Trade. Adam Brown was the business partner of George Gillespie. He would later be elected a Member of Parliament as a Conservative in 1887.

William Hunter of New York, who acquired half of David Tisdale's shares immediately after the Company's formation. He would have a powerful impact that could be felt for two decades. Hunter learned the wholesale grocery business in Hamilton. No later than 1852, he was residing and doing business in New York City. [183] Within a decade, he had established himself as one of the continent's leading importers of English tea and was a member of the New York City Chamber of Commerce and the Grocer's Exchange. [184] [185]

Hunter had a clear vision for the Long Point Company, one that his business relationships with prominent people in New York would help him realize. He wanted the Company to be a stable, exclusive, and enduring club for elite sportsmen. His first recruit was James Hewlett, whose business premises were located at 69 Wall Street, just two blocks from Hunter's. Together with his partner, Montreal-born Henry Torrance, Hewlett imported tea, coffee, tobacco, spices, fruit, sugar, and other commodities.[113] [186] [187] Hewlett bought his shares in 1868, and his tenure with the Long Point Company would last 23 years.

Hunter also recruited sportsman John T. Lord, a British subject who was living in the United States and overseeing the merchant firm Lord & Taylor, which his father, Samuel had co-founded. [114] Lord was onboard by 1869. While Company records state he was from New Brunswick, the reference does not refer to the Canadian province. Rather, Lord had homes in New Brunswick, New Jersey, as well as New York City and at 38 Park Lane in London.[115] Lord moored a private steam launch at Port Rowan for his personal use. He was relatively young when he became a shareholder, and his membership endured for 31 years.

Photo 15 Steam launch owned by John T. Lord. The crew onboard were Lafayette Gifford at the tiller and

---

[113] Torrance's father was the first merchant to import tea from India and China to Canada directly. The younger Torrance was adventuresome. He traveled abroad, handling the procurement side of the business. In 1870, he scaled Europe's Mont Blanc. [375]

[114] The Lord and Taylor company wasn't only a retail merchant. The firm also sold wholesale and occasionally acted as an intermediary in the sale of Long Point Company ducks.

[115] New Brunswick, New Jersey, then and now, is the site of Rutgers University.

Alvin Becker is operating the boiler. (Public Domain) [188]

Eli Clark was a member who had no interest in hunting ducks whatsoever. His father owned a sawmill in Albany. He left it to Eli after heading west to participate in the Pennsylvania oil boom. Because the availability of white pine to feed the Albany mill had become very scarce in New York State, Eli Clark began buying Crown timber rights in Ontario in the 1850s. That was also the decade when Canada and the United States agreed to abolish tariffs on timber and lumber. Typically, a license was sold for an annual payment of 50 cents per square mile plus dues on the amount of timber cut. Clark acquired the license for the entirety of Long Point. When the island was auctioned in 1866, his Crown license was valid up to April 1869. After that date, any remaining timber on Long Point would become the property of the Long Point Company. Consequently, during the Company's first years of existence, Clark and William Little raced to cut as much timber as they could. They employed contractors, such as Rial Canfield of Jarvis, to perform the logging. Long Point's tall white pine was relatively easy to harvest. Unlike timber inland, there was no need to hire drivers to convey the logs miles downriver to the private facilities at Port Royal. During the winter months on Long Point, teams of oxen, nourished with hay shipped to the island the previous fall on John Spain's steamer, dragged the logs the short distance from the ridges and savannah to inlets and shorelines. [189] After being staged, the logs were tied into rafts for towing during the warmer months to Tonawanda, New York, or Buffalo. From there, they were either forwarded by rail to Albany or on boats plying the Erie Canal. At Albany, the logs were sawn at Clark's mill. The finished lumber was then shipped down the Hudson River to New York City to meet America's rapacious demand. An article in the *New Dominion* newspaper provided a measure of the extent of cutting on Long Point. It reported in the spring of 1869 that contract crews had staged 5,000 logs, the equivalent of two million board feet, on Long Point ready for shipment.[116]

Facing the upcoming expiration of his Crown timber license, Clark proposed compensating the Company double the fee he was paying the government, plus one dollar per thousand board feet harvested. His proposal was not well received. A letter from the Company's secretary/treasurer to Samuel Woodruff indicates the Company sought better terms. [190] Eventually, Clark acceded to the same revenue arrangement the Company used for ducks and furs. Revenue would be split evenly. In 1869, the first year of the agreement, the Company booked annual revenue of $4,999 from timber. That sum was triple the revenue it gained from selling about 10,000 fur pelts that year. Considering the syndicate had only paid about $8,000 for Long Point at auction, the income generated in 1869 was considerable. The cash flow from timber would not continue, however. Clark had already stripped much of the island's tall white pine. In future years, the Company's timber revenue fell to approximately $500 annually. In 1874, cutting ceased. Colonel Clark, who had no interest in Long Point beyond its timber, liquidated his shares to David Tisdale, Samuel Woodruff, and William Hunter. Some years later, he built a grand stone mansion in Saratoga Springs. A high roller, Clark involved himself in speculative ventures such as silver mining. In 1908, he defaulted on the mortgage for the mansion, and it was ordered to be sold at auction. Clark died almost poor at his winter home in

---

[116] ibid

Galveston, Texas, five years later. [191] Today, we can only imagine what Long Point would have been like before its tall white pine trees were removed.

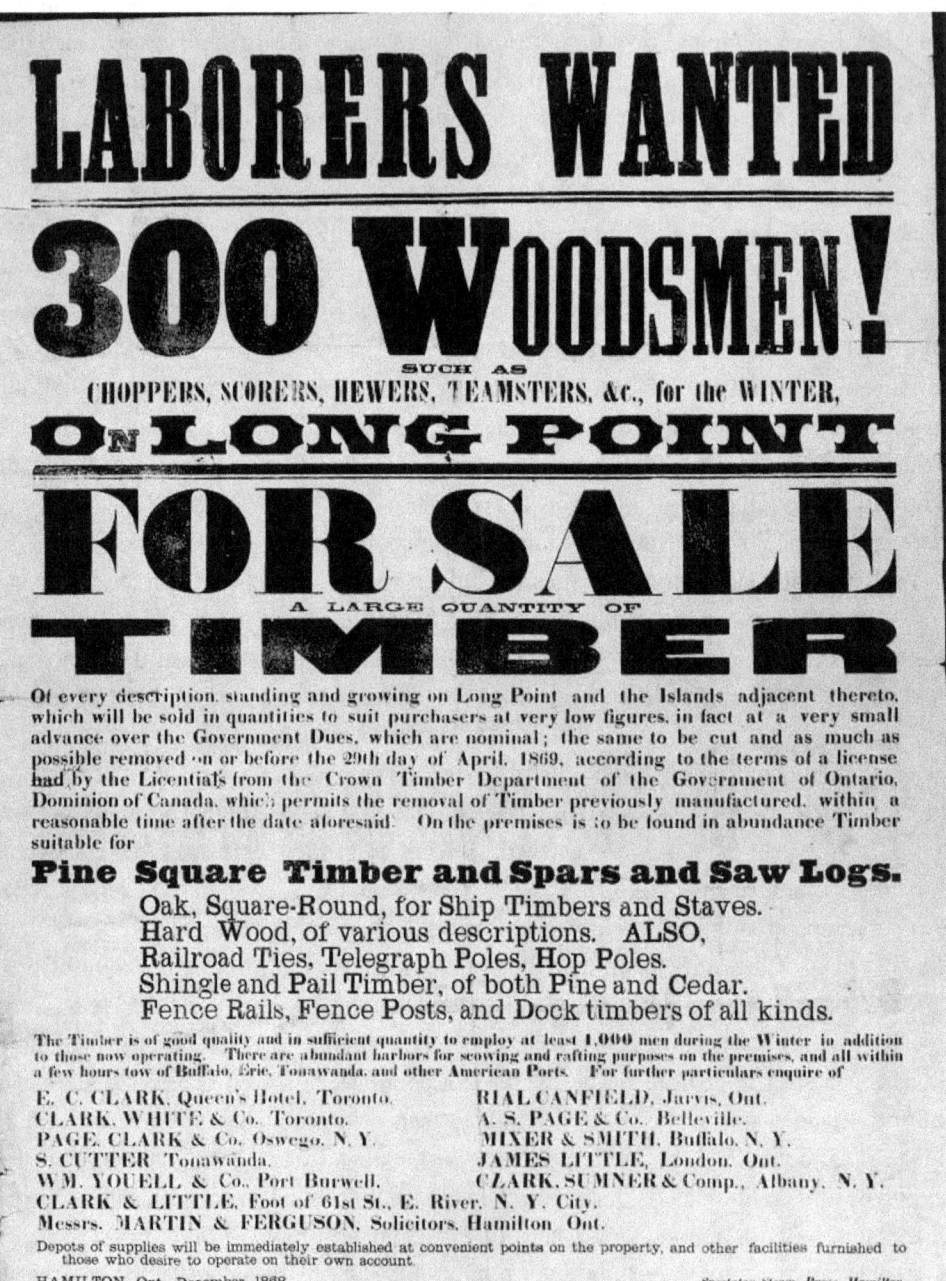

Figure 27. Poster soliciting labor and offering products for sale. 1868. (Public Domain)

In an operational sense, another early focus of the Company was security. It expelled or resettled most of the squatters. [192] A few were hired as trappers, and they were also assigned to guard the island from intrusion.[117] Prolific market gunner Peter Price of St. Williams claimed title to his shanty and a small plot in the marsh south of Rice Bay. He asserted there were defects in the survey the Government had earlier commissioned. The Company's negotiations with Price progressed expediently. A quitclaim settlement for his shanty and an employment offer, which he accepted, was the outcome. Price went on to shoot more ducks annually than most of the members, benefiting from a revenue sharing agreement with the Company. He was still shooting ducks in 1893, at the age of 87. [193] One reason Price fared so well in negotiations with the Company was he happened to be David Tisdale's uncle. During his lengthy employment, he not only provided security against poachers, but he also oversaw the leases the Company sold to fishermen. Price died in 1896.

In its effort to secure the island, the Company mounted an aggressive plan to acquire the few plots owned by others. The directors authorized certain members to negotiate directly with these parties, buy them out, and place the properties in trust for the Company. David Tisdale bought the 196 acres Bernard Saunders had purchased at auction. Henry Clark yielded his similarly acquired 100-acre Bluff Point plot.

Getting Egerton Ryerson to part with his island was more challenging. When he was approached by members of the Company who were seeking to buy the island, Ryerson contemplated a lease instead, stipulating the Company not remove the remaining timber. [194] He also expressed his view that the island would be the best place for the Company to locate its base of operation. It was not to be. By 1868, David Tisdale, George Gillespie, and Long Point Company president Thomas Kerr convinced Ryerson to sell. As part of his compensation, Ryerson received a commitment that he could establish a residence on Cottage Creek.[118] Both he and his son Charles also received lifetime hunting and fishing rights. (Figure 28) The exact sum Ryerson received for the island is uncertain, but the Company booked a $603.39 charge related to the transaction. Ryerson then proceeded to have a two-room, white cottage and an adjoining boathouse built. These were completed by 1870, and the cottage was equipped with two stoves, two washstands, kitchen facilities, walnut tables, and two beds. An icehouse for storing natural ice that was cut during the winter was added later. His cottage was where Ryerson did much of his writing during the latter years of his life. If members and their punters were present when he was staying there, he would read prayers to them on Sundays in the Company dining room. Ryerson's nephew, Major General George S. Ryerson, M.D., attributed his uncle's death to his zeal for hunting at Long Point. He wrote:

> In November, 1880, he sat out all night in his punt to shoot wild
> geese at dawn, being then seventy-eight years of age. He shot

---

[117] Early employees were Charles Brown, William Leary, Andrew Helmer, James Larose, William Woodward, Worthy Ayers, John Dennis, William Jackson, Bing Spencer, Morris Fitzmorris, and Phineas Reeves. [222]
[118] Cottage Creek is where the Company located its base of operation and cottages.

seven, but got a severe chill which resulted in pneumonia and his death. [195]

Photo 16 The Reverend Egerton Ryerson. Unknown Date. [195]

For the betterments he had made on Ryerson's Island, William Bantam received a modest $55 quitclaim settlement. However, the Company contracted with him to ferry people and supplies on his 40-foot yacht, *Adra,* which he had recently built. Bantam's relationship with the Company would sour many years later when he was accused of facilitating poaching. After the Company acquired Ryerson's Island, it gave Charles Brown, the Company's first head keeper the perquisite to graze cattle there. [196] His successor, William Leary, also grazed cattle on the island.

At the auction held in Toronto in 1866, John Aldwell had won 242 acres fronting Gravelly Bay that extended deeply but not fully across the island. He also won an additional 183-acre parcel. In 1870, Aldwell sold the 242-acre parcel to a partnership comprised of James Salmon, M.D. of Simcoe, Walter Anderson, a local lumberman, Simpson McCall, a member of the Legislative Assembly, from Vittoria, and David Duncombe. The other plot of 183 acres, he sold exclusively to Salmon. Soon after, Salmon bought out the interests of Duncombe and McCall. This left him owning three-quarters of the 242-acre parcel on Gravelly Bay and Anderson the other quarter. The acreage was undivided, making the two men tenants-in-common. In 1871, Salmon agreed to sell the 183-acre parcel, together with his three-quarter interest in the 242-acre plot, to Company members David Tisdale, John Mackenzie, and Thomas Kerr. They took these properties into trust for the Company. Records suggest Salmon received the generous sum of $1,750. Additionally, he entered into a contract with the Company that granted him non-transferable, lifetime hunting and fishing rights and the right to build and occupy a cottage either on Bluff Point or to the west on the

Little Creek ridges. The rights, given in exchange for a one-time fee of $200, restricted Salmon's activities to the area east of John Spain's hotel through to Bluff Point. It also stipulated that while Salmon hunted, he had to be accompanied by one of the Company's regular punters or by a punter vetted by David Tisdale. The punter was not permitted to shoot. Harry Barrett, in *Lore and Legends of Long Point*, wrote that the Company also agreed Salmon could harvest 4,500 cedar posts from his former parcel. Because Salmon's 242-acres was undivided, the overall transaction awkwardly left the Long Point Company as tenants-in-common with Walter Anderson. In time, the two parties would find themselves in a deeply strained relationship.

By 1871, the Company, through its member-agents, had captured all the property on the island of Long Point except for the common acreage it held as tenant-in-common with Anderson. It claimed to have spent more money buying out these small plots than the members of the original syndicate had paid at auction for 14,324 acres. The marshlands at the far west of the island (those that currently flank the west side of the present-day causeway) were owned by the Port Rowan Marsh Company, an entity formed in 1870 for the purpose of duck hunting and muskrat harvesting.[119]

Photo 17 James Salmon's cottage on Bluff Point. Unknown date, but likely early 20th Century [197]

---

[119] The first president of the Port Rowan Marsh Company was a Port Rowan resident who had the surname, Spencer. He was likely Lot Spencer. [423]

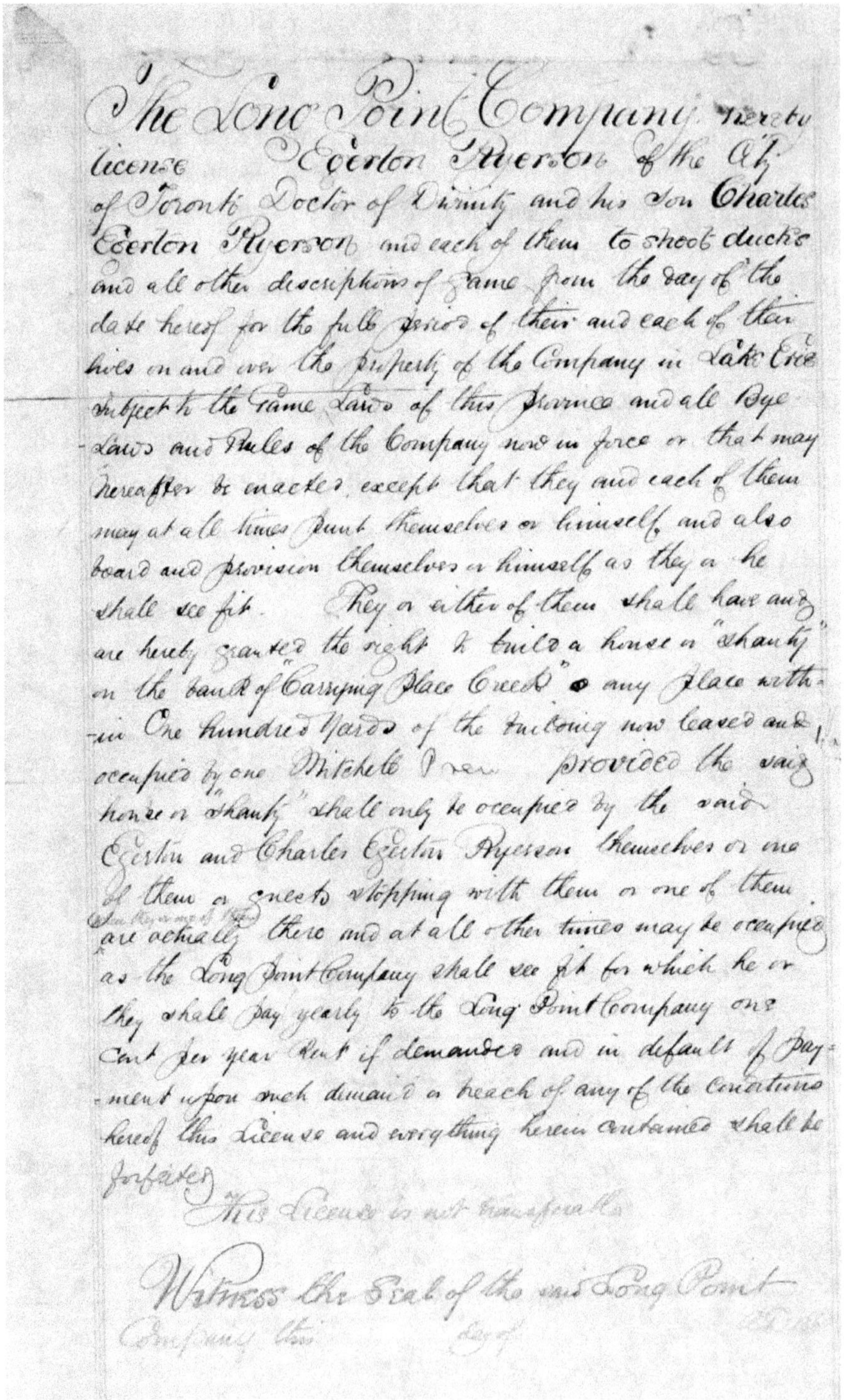

Figure 28. Agreement Between the Long Point Company and Reverend Egerton Ryerson.
(Private collection)

Scows and Poachers

After Long Point was privatized in 1866, individuals in Port Rowan devised a new way to host and cater to hunters —both local and from afar. They mounted shanties on scows and moored them in the water off Rice Bay. Assisted by local punters, hunters would disembark from the scows on skiffs and then encroach into the marsh to shoot. Hundreds of ducks were taken each day using this scheme. The owners of the scows received plenty of encouragement from the townsfolk.

Photo 18 A sailboat moored beside a scow, close to the Long Point Company marsh.
Because Long Point Company member John T. Lord had a steam-powered launch moored in Port Rowan for his personal use, the local community was aware of his identity. The lettering on the scow mocks him.
(Public Domain) [162]

In 1871, the Long Point Company launched a civil suit against five men involved in the operation of what may have been the first such scow. George Fick, his son George Fick the Younger, George Park, Blythe Woodruff, and John Payne were named as defendants. (Figure 29)

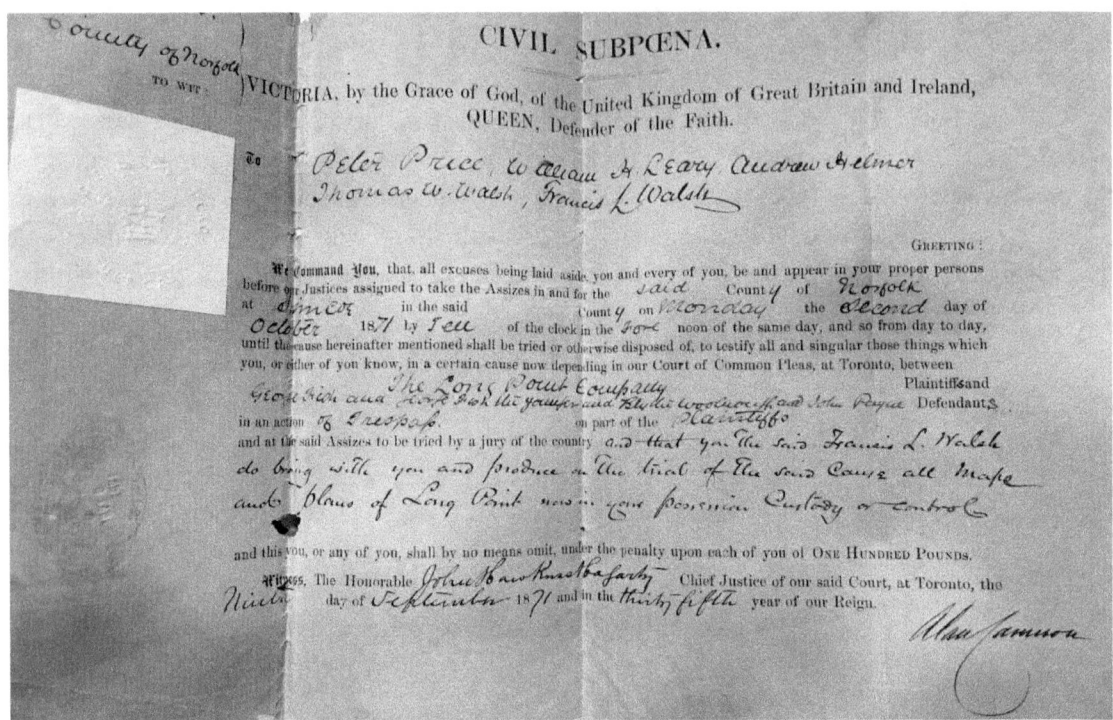

Figure 29. Subpoena commanding the attendance of land surveyors and Company employees. 1871.
Long Point Company vs. George Fick, George Fick the Younger, George Park, Blythe Woodrough, and John Payne.
(Norfolk County Archives)

The outcome of this early litigation is uncertain. The Company would not have been able to prevent the scows from mooring offshore, but it may have been successful in obtaining relief related to the skiffs. However, one thing is certain; nature occasionally worked in the Company's favor. Because the scows had living quarters, they presented a high profile to the wind. When a strong northwest wind blew, a scow might break its mooring. Over the years, several drifted into the marsh, where the Company impounded them.

In 1876, James Secord moored his scow too close to the marsh. One day, the Company removed it from its mooring and took it into possession. Secord responded by retaining barrister David Duncombe, who filed a lawsuit against the Company. While the outcome of this litigation also could not be located, evidence suggests the Company never did return Secord's scow, instead settling the suit by giving him monetary compensation. This was a strategic approach on the part of the Company. If the owner used his compensation to build a new scow, that effort would take considerable time. Meanwhile, the number of ducks poached temporarily decreased.

Poachers also crossed the Company's western boundary and then traveled farther east to reach favorable shooting areas. To make that approach less expedient, the Company attempted to acquire the one remaining parcel of land that was further west, but the effort was unsuccessful.

After the government completed construction of the Old Cut lighthouse in 1879, it appointed William Dickinson as the initial keeper. The Company approached Dickinson asking if he would guard the western boundary from intrusion. He accepted in return for an annual stipend of $25. His would not be an easy assignment. During his first year, poachers threatened to kill him. The Company responded by offering a $200 reward for information leading to the apprehension and conviction of the offenders. Although that was a handsome sum at the time, there is no indication the perpetrators were ever identified.

A decade later, Port Rowan resident Jerome Fick was testing the Company's resolve. He would row visiting hunters by yawl from Port Rowan to his sailboat and then ferry them to his scow. Onboard, he catered to his guests and served them alcoholic beverages. Fick permitted local punters to take his patrons from the scow on skiffs into the Company's marsh. The punters, who were local men, often wore hoods to conceal their identity. There were occasions when they exchanged gunfire with Company employees.

During the hunting season of 1888, a gale caused Fick's scow to drag anchor and it drifted into the marsh where the Company impounded it. [198] Although the loss of the scow temporarily put Fick out of business, he acquired a new hull and began building a shanty on it. Bragging publicly, he claimed to have made enough money that he could afford to cope with the challenges the Company presented. Noting it would cost him $400 to complete the new scow, he asserted it would net $14 dollars per day in income. [199] Over the duration of a hunting season, he would come out ahead with a profit. The townsfolk cheered him on.

The Company sued Fick, asserting he had abetted trespassing. David Tisdale's law firm represented the Company, and Port Rowan's C. E. Barber represented Fick. That Fick's scow had been moored in navigable water and not on the Long Point Company's property was not in dispute. Nor was the fact that the poachers, in aggregate, were shooting hundreds of ducks per day. Barber, in preparing his defense strategy, arranged for Port Rowan's most prominent and respected residents to submit affidavits stating they had shot ducks in the area in question for years. The case, in essence, became a boundary dispute. The court held for the Company and granted injunctive relief. Whatever the particular circumstances were, Fick remained defiant. The Company's next response was severe. Tisdale had a motion filed in Toronto to have Fick incarcerated for contempt of court. (Figure 30)

Whether Fick spent any time in jail is uncertain, but a later development suggests he probably did. The following Spring, Company president Edward Harris wrote a letter to David Tisdale relating that Fick had settled with the Company amicably in return for compensation of $350 and that it was expected he would no longer be an aggravation. Fick, for his part, remained in the hospitality business —on the mainland, not on the water.

Not long later the Company had further, but limited success, when constables arrested a group of trespassing punters and their clients. The punters were local men, but the clients were not. from the local community and were well-heeled. Displeased to have been arrested and detained, and anxious to return home, they pled guilty the next day and paid their fines. The punters, William Bantam, Charles Wood, Fred Spain, and James Spain pled not guilty. At trial, local Magistrate Mathew Brown convicted them.

IN THE HIGH COURT OF JUSTICE

Common Pleas Division

BETWEEN

The Long Point Company

-and- Plaintiffs

Jerome Fick

Defendant

TAKE NOTICE that a motion will be made on behalf of the above named Plaintiffs before the presiding Judge in Chambers at Osgoode Hall, Toronto, on Friday the 15th day of November 1889 at the hour of II o'clock in the forenoon or so soon thereafter as the motion can be heard, for an order that the defendant Jerome Fick be committed to the Common Gaol of the County of Norfolk for a term not exceeding twelve months for his contempt of Court in disobeying the Injunction Order made herein and dated the 30th day of September 1889 and the subsequent order made upon the Plaintiffs' motion to continue the said Injunction which last order is dated the 8th day of October 1889, in that the Defendant has since the making of the said Orders and contrary thereto entered upon and trespassed upon the land of the Plaintiffs at Long Point Island in the Township of Walsingham in the said County of Norfolk and the marsh lands and the lands covered with water of the Plainciff-company adjacent to the said Long Point Island within the staked boundaries thereof, such disobedience to the said Orders is shewn by the affidavits and material filed and for such further or other order as to the said Judge may seem meet-

AND TAKE NOTICE that on and in support of such application will be read the affidavit of W.P.Ferris, the said Orders dated the 30th day of September 1889 and the 8th day of October 1889 and the affidavits of Edward Harris, Frank Reeves, R.CLark, William Smith, W.P.Ferris (2) filed in support of the motion made herein on the 5th day of November instant and the affidavits and ex -

Figure 30. David Tisdale's motion to have Jerome Fick incarcerated. November, 1889 . (Norfolk County Archives)

The Spain brothers then retained Port Rowan attorney C. E. Barber, who succeeded in having their convictions overturned on appeal. [200] In a separate case, Magistrate Brown convicted Port Rowan's Alvin Becker for pointing a loaded shotgun at Company keeper James McLaughlin. The wily Barber appealed that conviction as well and successfully had it quashed on a technicality. [201]

Magistrate Brown's firm stance on convicting poachers didn't come without a personal cost. The poachers mounted a campaign to have him removed from the bench. Because of the Long Point Company's longstanding unpopularity, the movement gathered plenty of support among the local community. Brown did lose his position as Magistrate.

Poaching at Long Point didn't cease. It was a class struggle, and one that was about to become more violent. The following season masked punters had an altercation with head keeper Walker Ferris. They struck his head with an oar seriously injuring him. (Figure 31) The *Norfolk Reformer* reported Ferris had been left for dead in the marsh. A week or so later, the paper ran a second article stating that Long Point was such lawless place that it could be expected someone would soon be killed there. The newspaper then followed that piece with another that asserted that the Long Point Company did not own the whole bay, and was being too aggressive in enforcing its boundary.

THE ATTACK ON KEEPER FERRIS.

Figure 31. Newspaper sketch offering a depiction of the attack on head keeper Walker Ferris. [202]

The boundary dispute went unresolved. Finally, Norfolk M.P. John Charlton, a Reformer and a long-time political rival of the Conservative David Tisdale, demanded the government re-survey the Company's property around Rice Bay. [203] The boundary was clarified and by the turn of the 20th century facilitated poaching had diminished.

Photo. 19 Example of what may be a late evolution of a Long Point scow. Unknown date.
(Pratt and Rohrer family file, Port Rowan/South Walsingham Heritage Association Archives)

A Semi-Commercial Enterprise

One of the Company's first actions (although it was an initiative that would last only a few years) was to invite hunters to Long Point. The Company placed advertisements in newspapers offering access to the island for $5 per week. (Figure 32) That was hefty amount, given that the average daily wage at the time was about a dollar.[120] For a lesser occupation, such as a lighthouse keeper, it could be a mere 22 cents per day.[121]

The Company's high access fee annoyed the local populace. Additionally, they were finding it difficult to find a market gunner from whom they could buy a duck. They scorned the Company and began to refer to it as *the monopoly*. The press, politicians, and electoral candidates adopted the term as well. Some went so far as to make the dissolution of the Company part of their electoral platform. Simpson McCall was one of them. After he won the election to become the representative to the provincial legislature for Norfolk South in 1867, he introduced a bill that, had it passed, would have nullified the auction under which Long Point had been sold. [204]

During its first years, the Company sold about 100 hunting licenses annually. [205] While the revenue might have been welcome, the nuisances that the licensees caused were troublesome. In a letter to his daughter, Egerton Ryerson wrote that Company staff found many of the licensees to be uncontrollable "roughs" whose behavior was disorder, insulting, and abusive. Among them were British military officers from Toronto who significantly aggravated head keeper Charles Brown and Captain Spain, on whose steamer *Norfolk* they crossed to the island. [206] The Company's response to these behavioral issues was to cease selling licenses and to lock out members of the public permanently. This was a watershed event in the Company's evolution. It marked the transition of Long Point to a place where only members and their guests could hunt.

The Long Point Company was formed with sport in mind. Still, it operated as a semi-commercial enterprise, albeit one that never rewarded its shareholders with a dividend. To examine how income beyond the sale of game might be generated, the Company hired professionals to survey the island for its agricultural potential. [207] This led to further planting of peach trees on the island's orchards. The vineyards were tended and the grapes harvested. Various strategies were implemented to capitalize on the available opportunities. For the first three years, operations were financed by the sale of grapes, pelts, and ducks (even though the Company asserted in some quarters that it did not sell ducks.) Beginning in 1869, when Eli Clark's exclusive timber license expired and through to 1873, the Company booked $6,558 in timber proceeds under a revenue-sharing agreement with Clark. During the same period, revenue from pelt sales totaled $4,379.[122]

---

[120] The average wage figure was estimated using an American source. [416]

[121] A lighthouse keeper could also receive non-pecuniary compensation such as accommodation, pasture, and a garden plot.

[122] At the fur auction held annually at Port Rowan mid-decade, muskrat pelts sold for 29 cents, mink for one dollar, and racoon for 40 cents. [455]

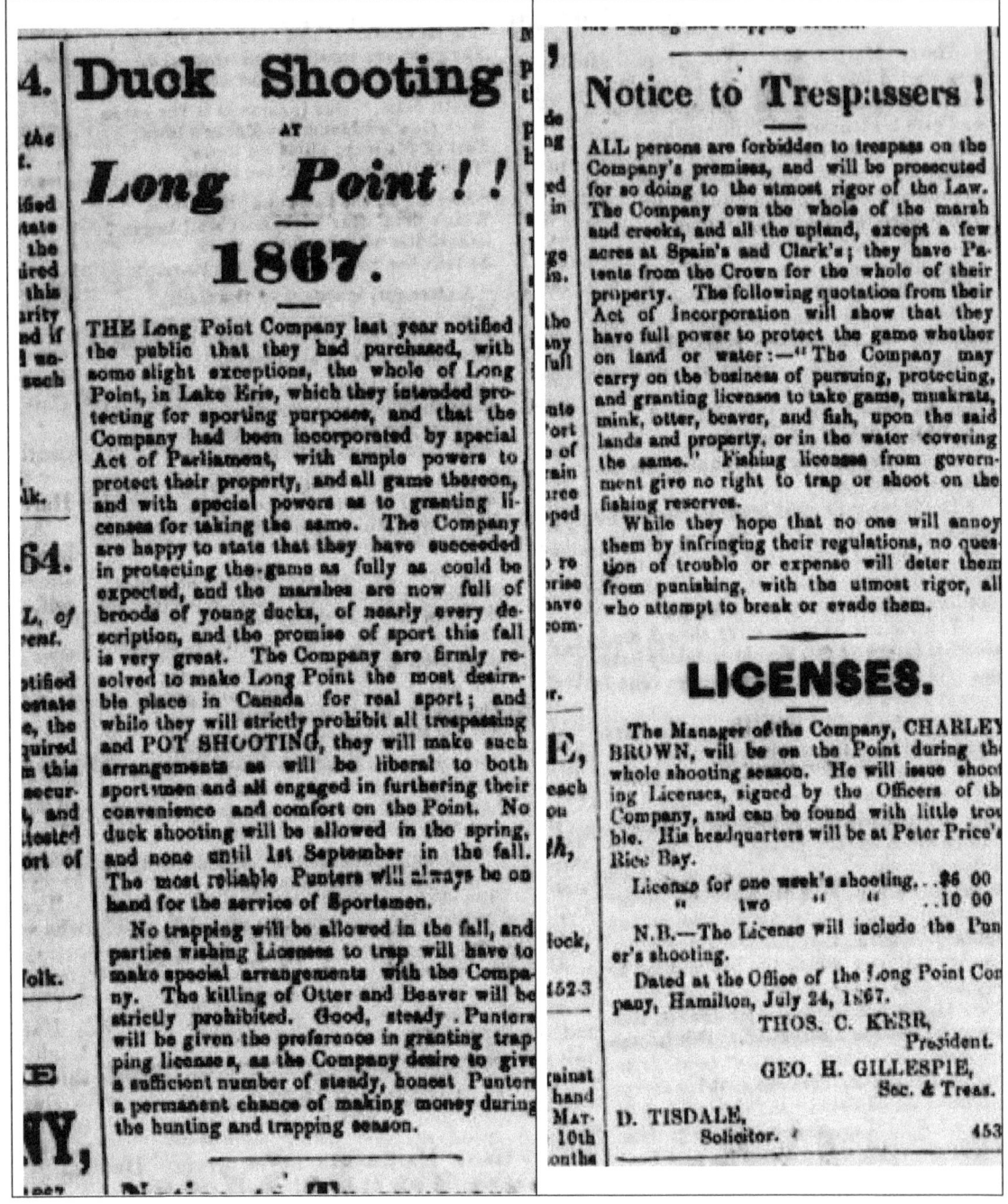

Figure 32. Long Point Company advertisements posted in the Norfolk Reformer Newspaper. July 25, 1867.

Staff were permitted to shoot after the members left at the end of the season, provided they turned the ducks over to the Company. They received compensation through revenue-sharing. Muskrat harvesting was handled under the same terms. In a year, staff could trap and skin as many as 11,800 muskrats. Fox and mink were trapped in lessor numbers. Because fox preyed on nesting ducks and ate their eggs, the Company occasionally held multi-day fox hunting events and local community members such as Col. Simon Mabee and John Backhouse would take their hounds to the island. [208]

Having established control of hunting, the Company's board of directors set their sights on fishing. In 1869, they assigned founding shareholder David Tisdale to negotiate with officials in Ottawa for fishing rights to the area around Long Point. Tisdale's effort was successful, yielding a wide-ranging nine-year lease that commenced in 1871. The covered area extended halfway across the Inner and Outer Bays, and all the water five miles out into the main body of Lake Erie along the entire length of Long Point's south beach. With control in hand, the Company then sublet zones to various commercial fishermen. W. Witcher was the government official who signed the lease. Not surprisingly, the Company granted him hunting privileges. The lease was renewed for a further nine-year period commencing in 1880. The annual fee was just $100. [209] Witcher was again the signatory for the Government. He traveled from Ottawa to hunt at Long Point regularly until he retired from government service.

The expenses of salaries, improvements, litigation, and the cost of acquiring the rest of the land on Long Point outran revenue. Beginning in 1870, the Company imposed annual dues. Initially, each member had to pay $70. That doesn't sound like much, but at the time that was about two months pay for a typical worker.

Township officials knew the Company was bringing in revenue and were well-aware the public resented the Company for locking them out of Long Point. William Anderson in his capacity as Deputy Reeve for the Township of Walsingham, moved in February 1870 to annex the island of Long Point into the township's #4 road division. [210] This redistricting made the island subject to "statute labor" taxes. During that era, property owners were required to contribute labor for the construction and maintenance of roads. If they could not provide labor directly, they had to remit funds in lieu of it. The township assessed the value of Long Point for tax purposes to be $8,500, essentially the amount the syndicate had paid at auction.[123]

David Tisdale subsequently appeared before the township council and tried to convince them not to levy the statute labor tax. The Company's unpopularity no doubt worked against him, and his entreaty was unsuccessful. The Company then commenced litigation against the county, arguing there were no roads on the island, nor was it likely that there would be any in the future. It also stated its costs to maintain Long Point exceeded revenue, and therefore taxation was inappropriate. The latter argument was somewhat disingenuous because a considerable portion of the Company's costs had been related to acquiring the few plots of land on Long Point that had been owned by others.

The Company prevailed at the county court level. However, the township appealed the judgement to a higher court where its authority to annex Long Point for tax purposes was affirmed. As for the assessed value, the higher court reduced it just slightly. [211].

_____

[123] For the 14,800 acres of Long Point, the tax levied by the County in 1870 amounted to about 80 days of labor.

Having had one success, the township then targeted Long Point for school taxes. The Company refused to pay. Again, the parties appeared before the county court. The Company presented the fact that while there was a school in Port Rowan, there wasn't one on the island. The court held that the county had no authority to annex for taxes a part of the township where there were no schools and awarded costs to the Company. [212] The judgment was a temporary reprieve. Records indicate the Company was paying a school levy to the township no later than 1890.[124] One might think that individuals who were members of the Company by that time were so wealthy that such taxes would have been immaterial to them. But that doesn't seem to have been the case, as the parties were before courts again in 1906. The township had assessed the value of the island at $100,000, on the basis that valuable timber was still present. The Company argued that an appropriate value was $25,000. The court set the value to $61,690. [213]

Ducks were a premium item on the menus of the best restaurants, hotels, and Atlantic-crossing steamships and the sale of ducks was a source of income for the Company from its inception. Employees of the Company shot on a revenue-sharing basis. Members and their guests were free to do whatever they pleased with their ducks until property taxes were levied on the island. After that occurred, the Company's board of directors decided to generate further revenue. In 1874, they put in place the following rule:

> One half of the ducks shot during the autumn season, by competent members, transient holders, and guests, shall be appropriated and sold for the use of the Company towards defraying expenses. The Board of Directors may, by resolution, exempt special cases from this rule.

The new policy necessitated the development of a marketing program suitable for selling more ducks. Consequently, the Company looked to the American market. It placed an advertisement in a business publication, *The Buffalo Commercial*, offering wholesale availability of 6,000 to 8,000 ducks. (Figure 33) There were icehouses at the Company's headquarters and fishermen holding licenses granted by the Company were required to supply natural ice cut on the Bay during winter. That would have kept the ducks from spoiling on site. How they first made it to distant markets without spoiling is uncertain. They may have been salted prior to shipment. By the end of the 1870s, the ducks were transferred to a freezing facility in Port Ryerse. Built to freeze fish by an American firm based in Conneaut, Ohio, the facility probably used a method S. H. Davis of Detroit had just patented. His approach involved placing the items to be frozen in seamless, waterproof rubber sacs. These were placed inside large but portable wheeled containers to which natural ice and salt had been added. [214] As anyone who has made ice cream the old-fashioned way knows, when ice and salt are combined, the result is an aqueous solution having a temperature well below the normal freezing temperature of water. The items inside the sacs would freeze.

---

[124] How it was ultimately resolved that the Company was required to pay school taxes could be an interesting topic for further research.

William Innes of Simcoe acquired a partial interest in the Port Ryerse freezing plant.[125] Late in the decade, he became its sole owner. Innes approached the Long Point Company in 1879, offering to freeze their ducks for nine cents each, and his offer was accepted.

A few years later, the Port Dover Freezing Co. captured the contract for the ducks and freight forwarding. Records indicate the Company sold ducks not only to distributors and retailers but directly to persnickety hotels and clubs that were willing to pay a premium. A few customers were the Walker House hotel in Toronto, the Tecumseh House hotel in London, the Toronto Club, and in New York, both the Merchants Central Club and the Union League Club (where more than a dozen U.S. Presidents have been members.) Duck sales continued into the 20th century until the passage of legislation that implemented the Convention Between the United States and Great Britain for the Protection of Migratory Birds. Because that agreement prohibited the sale of wild ducks, the Company donated the more than one thousand it had in freezer storage to the Canadian military for consumption by service members. Going forward, surplus ducks were distributed gratis in the community.

Figure 33. Three to four thousand brace offered for sale. One brace is comprised of two ducks.
(The Buffalo Commercial, 1874)

---

[125] William Innes was an early leader in the Canadian food preservation industry. His interests included freezing, dehydration, and canning. He was instrumental in the development of the apple evaporator that was built at Port Rowan.

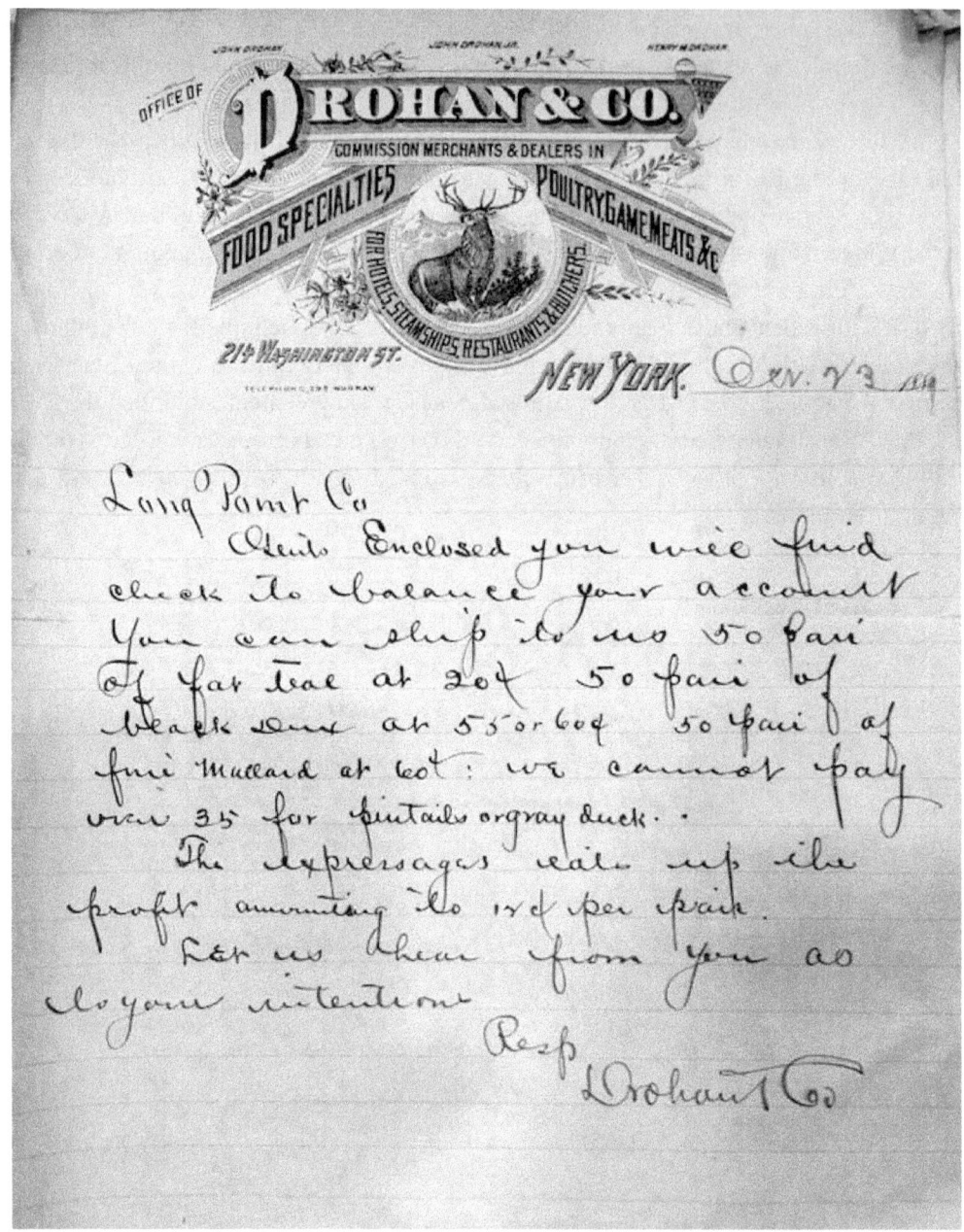

Figure 34. Letter from New York City wholesaler Drohan & Co., ordering 300 ducks. c. 1885.
(Norfolk County Archives)

In the interest of good public relations, the early Company was lenient by allowing the public shoreline access for summer picnics. Another accommodation it eventually made pertained to Sunday labor. Sunday happened to be the day of the week some members preferred to travel to or from Long Point. Typically, they crossed the bay on one of the Company's early yachts, *T. C.*

Kerr or *Dan*. This necessitated a crew member work on the Sabbath. Any sighting of a member crossing on Sunday, infuriated the Port Rowan clergy.

> Remember the Sabbath day, to keep it holy, is an injunction we all admit the correctness of; but few follow this commandment as correctly as they feel they should do, and there are many palpable violations of the sanctity of this holy day, indulged in by people who profess to be Christians. There is a good deal of murmuring about the members of the Long Point Company using Sunday for the purpose of going over to the Point and returning with their loads of ducks and luggage. The arrival of the *Dan* from the point every Sunday about church time gives the port quite a business day appearance, with young loading of luggage and bags and boxes of ducks, which are teamed up to the hotels and re-loaded and off for Ingersoll. The company have done much towards civilizing the Point; All Sunday shooting has been stopped, but the Sunday traveling is in full blast yet. We hope another year to see this also done away with. Governor Brown has inaugurated a good responsible government on the Point and we hope he will issue his edict and put an end to shipping ducks by wholesale on Sundays. If not, a missionary will have to be sent over to the Point to try to convert the "poor heathen." [215]

To appease the clergy and townsfolk, in 1870 the Company decided to forego Sunday water transfers. Notices were printed and posted stating that *Dan* was to be laid up on the Sabbath, and no unnecessary labor was to be performed for the Company that day. [216] (Figure 35) The policy was sustained for about 15 years.

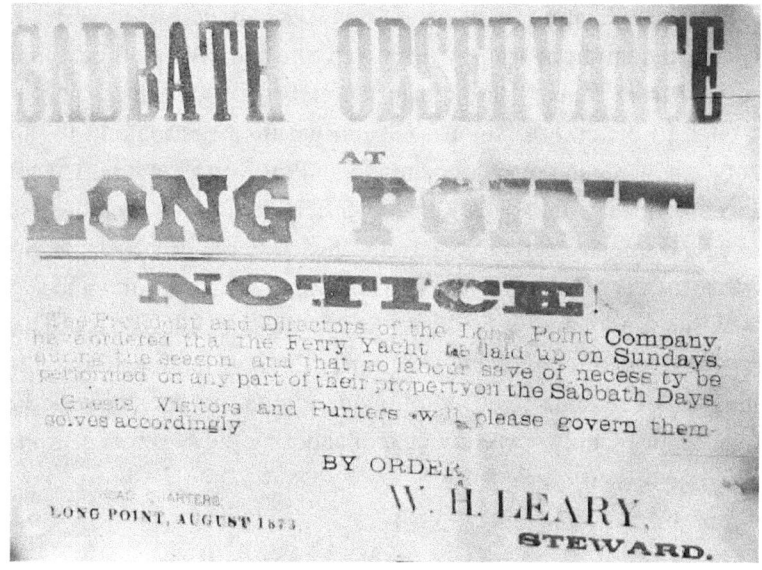

Figure 35. Poster stating the Company's yacht is not to be used on Sundays. 1873.

Early Members Were Not Conservationists

Some have suggested that the founders of the Long Point Company were conservation minded. There is little evidence to support that notion. Perhaps the sentiment arose because the Company ended the spring hunting that had plagued waterfowl at Long Point. Hunting licenses were only offered to the public for the fall season, and the Company touted that policy. The sporting press took note of it:

> It took years for the proprietors of the Long Point enterprise, on Lake Erie, to convert the prejudices of the native residents in the vicinity, but now they could desire no more earnest and efficient allies. Their profits in fur and feather have increased fourfold. Upon such rough woodsman, sturdy in their blows, but honest in their nature, a good word or a good example often has great influence, and we believe that an appeal to their sober judgment and the dissemination of proper information among them would work wonders toward reform; and we would therefore suggest that judiciously prepared circulars be printed and disseminated throughout the country by the agency of the numerous sportsmans' clubs and protective societies, appealing to the farmers, market hunters, and backwoodsman, to protect and spare the Game and Fish in designated closed seasons, setting forth in simple language the reasons therefor and beneficent advantages to accrue thereby. [217]

What *Forest and Stream* reported did not fairly represent what had occurred at Long Point. By the 1860s it was very well known that out-of-season hunting was destructive because it reduced progeny. While there had already been some restrictive game laws, following Confederation in 1867, Ontario prohibited hunting most species of ducks, woodcock, and snipe from March through to the end of August, quail from January through to the end of September, and turkeys, pheasants, partridge, and hare from January through to the end of August. Deer hunting was restricted to December through to the end of August. Citizen groups began taking the initiative to promote enforcement of the new regulations. For example, in Port Rowan, a group of concerned individuals convened a meeting at Johnson's Hotel on July 11, 1868, to address out-of-season hunting. That day, they formed a Game Protection Society for the township. Lot Spencer was elected president, and Simon Mabee the division court clerk in town was elected treasurer and secretary.[126] The other officers were William Woodward, William Anderson, and John Baker. They resolved that the society would fund and offer five-dollar rewards for information leading to the conviction of anyone shooting out of season. [218] The following month, the society issued its first reward after a member of the Secord family was convicted of shooting ducks out of season in the Turkey Point marsh.

---

[126] Colonel Simon Mabee was known to shoot as a guest of the Long Point Company. He was a staunch promoter of the hunting regulations that banned Spring shooting of waterfowl. [468]

While the Company prevented the public from shooting in the spring, the same policy was not enforced for members, and presumably not for their guests. Nor was it imposed on those the Company had granted lifetime hunting rights to, namely Dr. James Salmon and Egerton Ryerson. Company records show that during the spring of 1873, James Salmon shot 136 ducks. In a letter to his daughter written at Long Point in April 1869, Ryerson mentioned he had been out shooting ducks on several days. He added that Company members John MacKenzie, Alexander McInnes, and George Forster were also out shooting and laments he didn't bring down as many ducks as they did. [219] There is also evidence Company employee William Woodward, who would have been shooting on a revenue-sharing basis (or cheating the Company) engaged in the practice. [220]

Long Point Company co-founder Samuel Woodruff opposed conservation measures, such as limits on the number of ducks a person could shoot in a season, for his entire life. He wrote a letter to the Ontario Game and Fish Commission in 1893, in which he opposed limits on hunting ducks. Woodruff provided just one reason to support his opinion. He stated, "those not shot here go away and are liable to be shot elsewhere." One year, while he was serving as president of the Company, Woodruff was convicted of shooting snipe out of season. [221]

During the fall, the founders and members of the Company. and their guests shot enormous numbers of ducks. When considered today, the figures are disquieting. However, such slaughter was not uncommon during the 19th century. Whether duck, pigeon, crane, turkey, plover, snipe, swan, goose, bison, elk, or deer, people from all backgrounds and positions in society shot them in huge numbers. Waterfowl were slaughtered on the sounds of Long Island and Currituck; the Chesapeake and Delaware Bays; in Florida and California; and along the rivers of the Illinois prairie. Across Lake Erie on Ohio's Sandusky Bay, hunters might set 300 to 400 decoys in open water, then fire relentlessly from low-profile batteries —sometimes four at a time.

Long Point Company records reveal members and their guests brought down 8,739 ducks at Long Point in 1869. In each of the following two years, the number exceeded 11,000. John MacKenzie alone brought down 786 in 1870. Peter Price, the former market gunner the Company employed, took 978 in 1871. David Tisdale bagged 186 in a single day. William Hunter was credited with a total of 1,478 in 1874.

Photo 20. A boatload of Long Point ducks approaching the mainland. Unknown date. (Public Domain)
One of the individuals in the photograph is purported to be Dr. James Salmon. Note the denudation of the coast.

ANALYSIS OF SHOOTING FOR SEASON 1869

Total number of Ducks brought in from 20th September, to 30th November, 1869.   8,739.
",   "   at 3 lbs per Duck, equal to 26,217 lbs, or upwards of 11¾ tons.
Average number of Ducks to each Sportsman in September:—   24.
"   "   "   October:—   32.
"   "   "   November:—   21.
Highest number of Ducks brought in on any one day of season:—   491, on 25th October.
Average number to each Sportsman on this day :—   49, "   "   "
Highest number of Ducks brought in by a Sportsman in one day in Sept:— 80, Ducks, N. C. Ford.
"   "   "   "   Oct:— 92,   "   C. L. Andrews,
"   "   "   "   Nov:— 72,   "   C. C. Rapeljie.
Highest average in September:— 38 Ducks, A. McInnes.
"   "   October:—   46   "   G. J. Forster,
"   "   November:—   35   "   C. C. Rapeljie
Four highest numbers brought in, in one day—27 Oct. 92 ducks, C. L. Andrews.
            29   "   91   "   W. B. Hunter.
            18   "   88   "   Archd. Campbell.
            28   "   88   "   G. J. Foster.

Three largest bags of season.   {   W. B. Hunter,   571   "
                          Arch. Campbell,   513   "
                          Jno. Brown,   464   "

                                               GEO. H. GILLESPIE,
                                                 Sec'y Treas'r.

Figure 36. Shooting scores for 1869. [222]

ANALYSIS OF SHOOTING FOR SEASON 1870.

Total number of Ducks brought in from 1st of October to 23rd December, 1870.........................11,030
"   at 3 lbs per Duck, equal to 33,090 lbs or 14¾ tons.
Average number of Ducks to each sportsman in October..26
"   "   "   "   November...19
"   "   "   "   December 21
Highest number of Ducks brought in on any one day of Season, (on 1st Nov.)................................537
Average number to each sportsman on this day...48
Highest number of Ducks brought in by a sportsman on any one day in October......110,—J. I. MacKenzie
"   "   "   "   "   "   November.. 94,—J. Turner.
"   "   "   "   "   "   December... 26,—A. McInnes.
Highest average in October.. 49,—J. I. MacKenzie.
"   November .... 40,—S. P. Mabee.
"   December... 26,—A. McInnis·
Four highest numbers brought in on one day......110 ducks, 15th October, J. I. MacKenzie.
"   "   "   " 102   "   17th   "   "
"   "   "   "   94   "   1st November, J. Turner.
"   "   "   "   93   "   1st October, J. I. MacKenzie.

Three largest bags of Season.   {   J. I. MacKenzie..............786 ducks.
                                W. B. Hunter,........ 606   "
                                Peter Price,.................... 593   "

                                               J. I. MACKENZIE,
                                                 Sec'y Treas

Figure 37. Shooting scores for 1870 (ibid)

ANALYSIS OF SHOOTINGF OR SEASON 1871.

Total number of Ducks brought in from 15th September to 30th November...... 11,287
    "   at 3 lbs per Duck, equal to 33,861 lbs, or upwards of 15 and 1–10th tons.
Average number of Ducks to each sportsman in September...... 92
    "   "   "   "   October.... 172
    "   "   "   November......... 117
Highest number of ducks brought in on any one day of Season .....464, on 15th of September.
Average number to each sportsman on this day....................... 35
Highest number of ducks brought in by a sportsman on any one day in September, 138, W. B. Hunter.
    "   "   "   "   "   "   October, 116, Col. Tisdale.
    "   "   "   "   "   "   November, 90, Mr. Lord.

Highest average, per day, in September, 95, W. B. Hunter.
    "   "   October,   57, Col. Tisdale.
    "   "   November, 49, Mr. Lord.
Four highest numbers brought in on one day .....138 ducks, 15th September, W. B. Hunter.
    "   "   "   "   .....116 "   9th October,   Col. Tisdale.
    "   "   "   "   .....102 "   15th September, Mr. Mulkins.
    "   "   "   "   .....102 "   26th October,   G. A. Drummond.
Three largest bags of Season. { Peter Price ....978 "
                         { W. B. Hunter....519 "
                         { Col. Tisdale, ...442 "

J. I. MACKENZIE,
Sec'y Treas

Figure 38. Shooting scores for 1871 (ibid)

ANALYSIS OF SHOOTING FOR SEASON 1873.

Total number of Ducks brought in from 18th August to 13th November................. 11,063
    "   at 3 lbs. per Duck, equal to 33,189 lbs., or 16½ tons.
Dr. Salmon—Spring shooting, 28 Geese and 136 Ducks ; Autumn, 747 Ducks.................   911

                                                            11,974

Average number of Ducks to each Sportsman in August........................... 23
    "   "   "   October........................370
    "   "   "   November......................146
Highest number of Ducks brought in on any one day of season, (on 7th October)........660
Average number to each Sportsman on this day................................. 87
Highest number of Ducks brought in by a Sportsman in one day in August......... 38—A. Campbell.
    "   "   "   "   "   October ......173—W. B. Hunter.
    "   "   "   "   "   November.....105—S. D. Woodruff.
Highest average of Ducks in August .... 26—A. Campbell.
    "   "   October .... 92—Col. Tisdale.
    "   "   November .... 49—S. D. Woodruff.
Four highest numbers of Ducks brought in in one day, 18th October...............173—W. B. Hunter.
    "   "   "   "   8th   "   ....163—S. D. Woodruff.
    "   "   "   "   3rd   "   ....163—Col. Tisdale.
    "   "   "   "   17th   "   ....149—W. B. Hunter.
Three largest bags of Season, { W. B Hunter..............1,206 ducks.
                               { G. H. Gillespie............ 998 "
                               { J. I. Mackenzie............ 866 "

Figure 39. Shooting scores for 1873 ibid

ANALYSIS OF SHOOTING FOR SEASON 1874.

Total number of Ducks brought in from 1st October to 19th November...............................11,832
    "   at 3 lbs. per Duck, equal to 35,496 lbs., or 17¾ tons.
Average number of Ducks to each Sportsman in October.................................255
    "   "   "   November.....................184
Highest number of Ducks brought in on any one day of season, (on 2nd November).....566
Average number to each Sportsman on this day...63
Highest number of Ducks brought in by a Sportsman in one day in October.......163—W. B. Hunter.
    "   "   "   "   November..... 96—J. A. Hewlett.
Highest average of Ducks in October....................................... 54—D. Tisdale.
    "   "   November.................................* 84—Mr. Greene.
Four highest numbers of Ducks brought in in one day, 3rd October...........†163—W. B. Hunter.
    "   "   "   "   1st   "   114—D. Tisdale.
    "   "   "   "   12th   "   110—D. Tisdale.
    "   "   "   "   6th November.............. 96—J. A. Hewlett.

Three largest bags of Season, { W. B. Hunter.............1,478
    Col. Tisdale............... 805
    P. Price 695

* Only out one day.   † 12 picked up by Helmer next day (Sunday), and 9 by Mr. Hunter on Monday, 21; making a total of 184.

Figure 40. Shooting scores for 1874 (ibid)

ANALYSIS OF SHOOTING FOR SEASON 1876.

Total number of Ducks brought in from 1st October to 14th November...........................8,406
    "   at 3 lbs. per Duck, equal to 25,218 lbs., or 12½ tons
Average number of Ducks to each Sportsman in October.................................252
    "   "   "   November.....................138
Highest number of Ducks brought in on any one day of season, (on 2nd October).....761
Average number of Ducks to each Sportsman on this day................................95
Highest number of Ducks brought in by a Sportsman in one day in October....*182—D. Tisdale.
    "   "   "   "   November.. 41—G. H. Gillespie.
    "   "   "   "   41—R. Woodruff.
    "   "   "   "   †116—J. H. Backus.
Highest average in October..................................27—J. A. Hewlett.
    "   November..................................*182—D. Tisdale.
Four highest numbers brought in in one day, 9th October......................176—R. A. Lucas.
    "   "   "   2nd   "   138—S. D. Woodruff.
    "   "   "   2nd   "   135—J. H. Backus.
    "   "   "   10th   "

Three largest bags of Season, { Peter Price.............976 Ducks.
    D. Tisdale............·954 "
    R. A. Lucas............609 "

* 11 Ducks picked up next day not scored, making 193.   † Only shot two days.

Figure 41. Shooting scores for 1876 (ibid)

It wasn't uncommon for the Long Point Company to be in the news during 1870s. Shooting many ducks on a single day was considered an athletic achievement. Members were proud to report their scores publicly, and these were sometimes reported in publications such as *Forest & Stream*. One article mentions that an unnamed individual returned to Hamilton with 476 ducks. [223]

In 1880, the Company's board of directors took issue with such public releases and adopted a new policy that "on no account shall these scores be given to the public." This did not dissuade William Hunter. After he took claim to the all-time single-day record —243, he returned to New York City and bragged about his achievement. Several publications reported his score, noting he had set a record for shooting ducks in Canada. [224] (Figure 43)

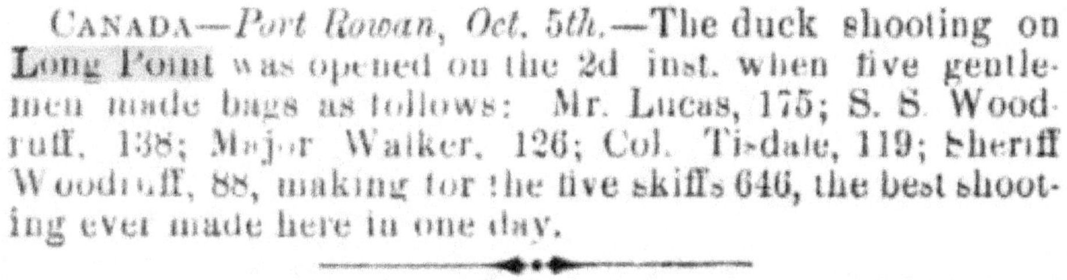

CANADA—*Port Rowan, Oct. 5th.*—The duck shooting on Long Point was opened on the 2d inst. when five gentlemen made bags as follows: Mr. Lucas, 175; S. S. Woodruff, 138; Major Walker, 126; Col. Tisdale, 119; Sheriff Woodruff, 88, making for the five skiffs 646, the best shooting ever made here in one day.

Figure 42. Individual daily shooting counts. [225]

As the decades progressed, the number of ducks visiting Long Point steadily declined, and so did the number that fell to the hunter's gun. Much of the decrease was a consequence of widespread drainage of wetlands across North America to create land suitable for agriculture.

SHOOTING.

NOTABLE PERFORMANCES.

TRIGGER.

100 single birds tame doves killed in succession in two hours. A H Bogardus, Chicago, July 21st, 1869. 99 birds out of 100 single, Bogardus, 30 yards rise, 80 yards fall, five ground traps, 1¼ oz shot, 10 bore, 10 lb 6 oz gun, English rules, Coney Island, July 2nd, 1880. 300 glass balls broken in succession, Bogardus, Lincoln, Ill., July 4th, 1877.

70 pigeons out of 100 by Charles Brown, a boy only 8 yrs old, 4ft high, 66 lb weight, at 18 yards rise, 80 yards fall, 3 traps, 5 yards apart, at fast blue rock pigeons, at Nottingham, England, Jan. 25, 1883.

500 glass balls broken in 24'min, 2 sec, out of 514 shot at. by J C Haskett match against time, 25 min 15 sec, two Bogardus traps, 12ft apart, 14 yards rise, at Lynn, Mass., May 30th, 1881.

501 clay pigeons broke in 34 min 7 sec, out of 543 shot at, by Bogardus, loading his own guns, one bird sprung at a time and thrown from three to ten feet above the ground, several traps ; 444 pigeons in 30 min, at Cincinnati, O, April 15th, 1882.

1000 glass balls broken in 1h 1 min 54 sec, by Bogardus, using two sets of barrels. 15 yards, two traps, twelve feet apart, at New York City, Dec. 20th, 1879.

5,500 glass balls broken in 7h 19 min 2 sec, out of 5,854 shot at, by Bogardus, at 15 yards, two traps, twelve feet apart, loading his own gun and changing barrels about 54 times, New York City, Dec 20th, 1879.

Mr. W B Hunter, of New York, killed 243 ducks in eight hours at Long Point, Ont., in October 1884—This is the largest bag ever made in Canada within the same number of hours and we believe it to be the best on record.

In 1878 Colonel Tisdale, of Simcoe, also shooting at Long Point killed 186 duck between 10 a.m. and 6p.m.

100 Clay Pigeons out of a possible 100 by W F Carver at Des Moines, Iowa.

Clay Pigeon shoot—100 each, 30 yards rise, Carver 94, Bogardus 94 at Dayton, O.

50 double birds (pigeons) 21 yards rise, Bogardus 81, Carver 79.

100 birds (pigeons) 30 yards rise, one barrel, F. Kimball 88. F. Keling 84.

100 birds (pigeons) 2 ground traps, 30 yards rise, 80 yards fall, Carver 83, Bogardus 82.

The purest "fiz" in the market is **Goulay**. It catches the judges' verdict ahead of all others.

Figure 43. Article calling out William Hunter's single-day record of 243 ducks. [224]

A Membership Shakeup

As soon as share certificates had been printed and distributed to the founders, sales began to occur by assignment. Evidence suggests that some close associates of the founders expected shares in the Company would be a worthwhile investment. Three were Adam Brown, Henry Routh and John MacKenzie. All acquired shares in 1867. Adam Brown wasn't just a brother of founder John Brown, he was a principal in Brown, Gillespie & Co., so he knew founder John Gillespie well. Henry Routh was a partner in the same firm. John MacKenzie was a partner in Kerr, Brown, Mackenzie & Co.

Although aforementioned wholesale firms were distinct entities, they cooperated with each other in business deals. In 1867, they entered a combined arrangement to procure a very large shipment of sugar from Halifax. They issued $30,000 (equivalent to more than $500,000 today) in commercial paper to pay for it. These notes had different maturity dates. Attesting to the high degree of cooperation between the two firms, after the sugar was delivered Brown, Gillespie & Co. discharged the first note by paying the entire balance to the Bank of Montreal, even though both firms were responsible. Soon thereafter, Kerr, Brown, Mackenzie & Co. reciprocated by paying the entire balance of the second note.

Later that year, things went awry. Brown Gillespie & Co. suffered serious financial difficulty. Messrs. Brown and Gillespie advised Kerr, Brown & MacKenzie that if they were to pay half their share of the pending third note, they would surely be bankrupted, and their families ruined. As all involved were on good terms, Kerr, Brown & MacKenzie agreed to provide relief for Brown, Gillespie & Co. and paid the full amount due on the third note.

Although it had received significant financial consideration, Brown, Gillespie & Co. tumbled into bankruptcy anyway. John Brown apparently avoided personal bankruptcy, but Gillespie was in trouble. His bankruptcy trustee, John Gillespie, himself a Long Point Company member (who may have resided in Edinburgh, Scotland) took control of his shares. Notwithstanding, George Gillespie remained secretary and treasurer of the Company for several years, an indication that despite his financial problems he still enjoyed considerable goodwill and confidence from the other founders. He hunted for many years using his lifetime rights.

The history of Gillespie's shares and those of his trustee, John Gillespie, are difficult to decipher, although some of them fell back in the hands of the Company for resale and ended up with Samuel Woodruff, Alexander McInnes, George Forster, and George Drummond.

Drummond was a Scottish-trained chemist who had married the daughter of the founder of Montreal's Redpath Sugar. He would eventually become the president of the Bank of Montreal. Alexander McInnes was the co-owner of a clothing factory in Hamilton.[127] Henry Routh was a partner in the Brown, Gillespie firm. He held his shares for just a year. George Forster was another wholesale grocer from Hamilton. His membership also didn't last long. In his only season with the

---

[127] The Sanford, McInnes Co. clothing factory in Hamilton employed more than 400 workers. [429] The associated shoe factory had about 130 employees. [360]

Company, he got into a dispute over who would be allowed to bring guests and when. [226] The result didn't sit well with him and he promptly sold his shares to David Tisdale.

John Brown sold some of his shares to John Rankin, a British shipowner and worldwide trader. He held on to them briefly before New York merchant John T. Lord bought them. Brown's other shares went to industrialist George Clark of New York City. Clark was a scion of a family in Paisley, Scotland that manufactured thread on a massive scale. While still a teenager in 1840, he was sent from Scotland to Hamilton, Ontario, to serve an apprenticeship with Thomas Kerr and his brother, which likely explains how he became interested in Long Point. Although Clark returned to Scotland after completing the apprenticeship he emigrated to the United States in 1856 with two of his brothers. They set about importing thread from the family business in Scotland. After the United States imposed import duties, Clark, his brothers, and Peter Kerr established a large thread factory in Newark, New Jersey. [227] Construction began in 1864 and was completed in 1866, with George overseeing the enterprise. Clark's membership in the Long Point Company was brief, as he died in 1873.

In 1870, Company president Thomas Kerr sold shares to William Tudor of Boston. Tudor's father, Frederic, had amassed a fortune by establishing the natural ice trade. The ice was cut from New England ponds then loaded onto outbound sailing vessels. Initial efforts to sell the ice in tropical and subtropical markets were unsuccessful. Tudor persisted and demand for eventually caught on. He built up his own fleet of sailing ships to carry ice to the far reaches of the globe, where it had never been seen before. The ships brought back return freight. One of Tudor's most profitable routes was to India, from where his ships returned with tea, spices, and perishables.[128] Import summaries and litigation documents demonstrate Tudor's firm was a major importer of tea to the United States. [228] [185] That may explain how Kerr and Tudor were acquainted. Kerr likely purchased goods Tudor's firm imported.

By 1873, an extraordinary shakeup had changed the character of the Long Point Company forever. All the members from Hamilton, except for John MacKenzie, had disposed of their shares. MacKenzie later revealed that some shareholders had never visited Long Point and others just once or twice. [229] The minutes from a Company meeting held in 1874 show that setting aside George Clark's five shares, which were tied up in his estate, just eight members remained. (Figure 44) William Hunter was holding 40% of the Company's stock — a near-controlling interest. His friend David Tisdale, and Samuel Woodruff, were the only remaining shareholders who had been founders. The Company commenced a recruitment effort for new members by placing an advertisement in the *Montreal Gazette*. (Figure 45)

---

[128] In addition to ice, Tudor shipped American commodities such as flour, tobacco, and perishables. Records demonstrate his ships sometimes arrived in India carrying American apples. [437, 438]

8 MINUTES OF THE LONG POINT COMPANY.

Hamilton, 18th June, 1874.

The special general meeting of the Shareholders of the Long Point Company was held at the Royal Hotel this day, at twelve o'clock. Present:

S. D. Woodruff, President,	owner of	10 Shares.
John I. MacKenzie, Sec'y-Treas.	"	5 "
W. B. Hunter,	"	40 "
David Tisdale,	"	15 "
Shareholders not present or represented.		
J. T. Lord,	"	10 "
J. A. Hewlett,	"	5 "
Geo. A. Drummond,	"	5 "
Wm. Tudor,	"	5 "
Heirs of Geo. A. Clark,	"	5 "
		100

Minutes of previous meetings were read and confirmed. The report of Special Committee being read,

It was moved by Mr. Hunter, seconded by Col. Tisdale, that the Report of Special Committee on Long Point, as now read, be received and adopted.—Carried.

Moved by Col. Tisdale, seconded by Mr. Hunter, that the Directors be authorized to carry out the recommendations made by the Special Committee, and to obtain the funds necessary for that purpose.—Carried.

It was moved by Col. Tisdale, seconded by John I. MacKenzie, and resolved, that the By-Laws heretofore in force shall be repealed, and that the following shall be adopted as the By-Laws of the Company.—Carried.

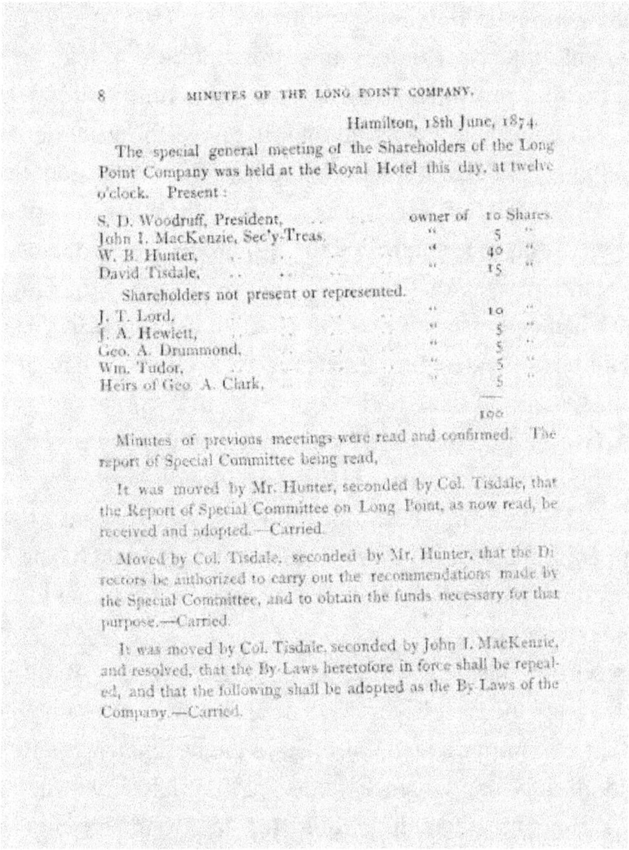

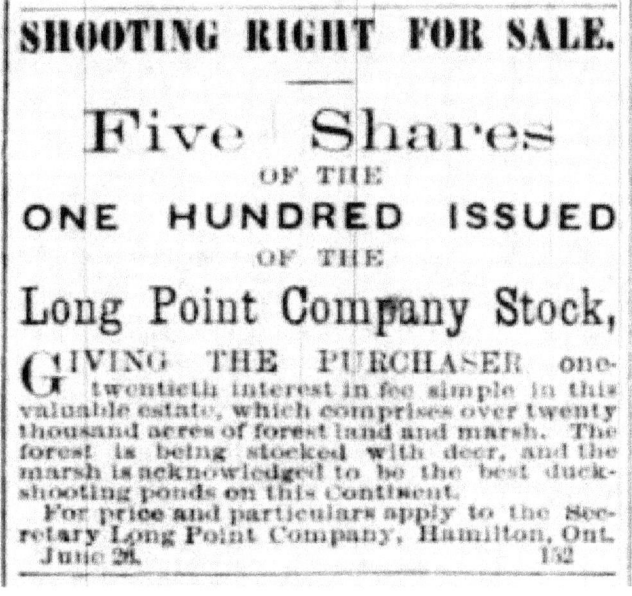

Figure 44. Share ownership in 1874. [230]

SHOOTING RIGHT FOR SALE.

Five Shares

OF THE

ONE HUNDRED ISSUED

OF THE

Long Point Company Stock,

GIVING THE PURCHASER one-twentieth interest in fee simple in this valuable estate, which comprises over twenty thousand acres of forest land and marsh. The forest is being stocked with deer, and the marsh is acknowledged to be the best duck-shooting ponds on this Continent.

For price and particulars apply to the Secretary Long Point Company, Hamilton, Ont.

June 26. 152

Figure 45. Company Advertisement. Montreal Gazette. 1874.

A severe recession followed the Panic of 1873. By 1875, it had caught up to William Hunter. His business went bankrupt. [231] Hunter had suffered losses on tea and admitted the value of his real estate and securities portfolios had shrunk. Apparently, he was successful in reaching agreements with his creditors but facing an ongoing need for cash, he started unloading shares in the Long Point Company. The first tranche went to Company president Samuel Woodruff. Another went to Montreal's Andrew Allan. His brother, Sir Hugh Allan, was perhaps the most aggressive capitalist in Canadian history. He controlled the Montreal Ocean Steamship Company, also known as the Allan Line, and was one of the world's wealthiest men. Hugh Allan bought into the Company in 1881. His membership was brief. He died the following year.

In 1876, Hunter unloaded further shares to Richard Lucas of Hamilton and Col. John Walker of London, Ontario. Lucas had taken over the wholesale grocery business of former Company member George Forster. Walker had been one of the earliest producers of oil, and he had established a refinery and sulfuric acid plant in London.[129] It was consolidated with two other London refineries in 1878 to form the Mutual Oil Refining Company. Two years later, Mutual was one of several companies that banded together to create Imperial Oil and Walker was on Imperial's initial board of directors.[130] [232] He was likely acquainted with David Tisdale, as both men were veterans of the Fenian conflict.

Hunter's importing business was located on the corner of Wall Street and Front, just steps from the wharves flanking the East River. Two doors away on the same block was the B. G. Arnold Company, a firm that also imported tea. Partners in the business were Benjamin Green Arnold, his son Francis Arnold, and Lyman Green. Hunter sold the latter two men shares in the Long Point Company in 1877. Their memberships would not last long. By the 1870s coffee had become increasingly popular in the United States, and the Arnold firm had diversified beyond tea, establishing itself as the country's largest coffee importer. For many years, the firm acquired green beans by bidding on shipments as they arrived in the port of New York. Aiming to further dominate the market, in the late 1870s the Arnold company adopted a revised strategy. Instead of bidding on beans when they arrived, the firm established an integrated supply chain based on fixed contracts with foreign growers. Having bet big, the partners in the B. G. Arnold Co. would soon lose just as heavily. The price of coffee collapsed in 1880. Stuck with too many beans, the Arnold firm suffered a spectacular bankruptcy. [184] [233] [234] [235] Lyman Green and Francis Arnold were financially ruined, causing their association with the Long Point Company to abruptly end. Green's shares remained tied up in legal proceedings for many years. Eventually, they passed from a trustee to Oliver Payne, a partner of John D. Rockefeller in the Standard Oil Co.

The following year, two brothers born in the Long Point region who were practicing law in London, Ontario acquired shares. They were George and Edward Harris. Edward was Egerton Ryerson's only son-in-law. He had long wanted to join the Long Point Company, but his efforts had previously been rebuffed.

---

[129] There were many small oil refineries in London at the time.
[130] Late in the 19th century, Rockefeller's Standard Oil Co. of New Jersey acquired a controlling interest in the Imperial Oil Co.

The corporate bylaw that imbued the Company's founders with lifetime shooting rights, regardless of whether they disposed of their shares didn't find favor with Edward Harris. Moreover, his relationship with the founders was somewhat strained because his earlier attempts to join the Company had been thwarted. When he did gain membership, he dealt the founders a hefty measure of criticism. In a letter he wrote to shareholders in 1879, he reminded them of what the founders had done:

> The Company consisting solely of the above seven persons, were authorized to purchase from themselves for the Company the said lands, for such price or sum of money, or for such a number of paid-up of the capital stock of the Company as they might agree upon. These persons at their first meeting (whether legally so or not is yet undecided) absorbed the entire capital of the Company by taking advantage of an apparently extensive power. They at their first meeting divided among themselves one hundred $500 shares as fully paid up —the actual expenditure being about $80 per share. For this $50,000 subsequently reduced to $48,000, they conveyed to the Company land which they had purchased a few months previously for $8,115. Courts of Law have recently judged transactions similar to the above with great severity, but it is not my intention at the present time to dwell upon the legal points. The Company was in fact formed with a view to realize an immense and immediate profit, and upon distribution of the shares to the promoters $250 per share was the price asked by the President. As no further expenditure had been made by the promoters beyond the $8,115 paid at the auction and expenses of charter, the cost of each share would have been under $85. The promoters having thus absorbed the entire capital of the Company, proceeded to a further act of spoliation, for which no possible justification can be found. Perpetual free licenses to shoot and fish on the Company property, without contributing to the support of the Company, were in some way claimed by the original proprietors, commonly called promoters.

A decade later, Harris would be elected president of the Company, a position he held for 12 years.

Influential Members from Boston and the Roots of Stability

While the early years of the Long Point Company were unsettled, its second decade was characterized by a reconstitution that led to stability. This was partly due to the 1877 purchase of founder Thomas Kerr's remaining shares by Major Louis Cabot of Brookline, Massachusetts. Cabot would have a long tenure and impact. The son of one of New England's wealthiest merchants, Cabot graduated from Harvard, where his studies included zoology and entomology. He then commenced a European sojourn, learning German and traveling around the continent. After Cabot had returned to the United States, the Civil War undid his privileged lifestyle, at least temporarily. He joined the Union Army, was commissioned as a lieutenant, and was soon injured in combat. Persuasive evidence suggests Cabot suffered severe post-traumatic stress disorder. Following a lengthy recovery, he returned to service, was elevated to commander of the third battalion of the 4th Massachusetts Cavalry, then saw further action. [236]

Following the war, Cabot married Amy Hemenway, the daughter of trader Edward Hemenway, who owned east coast timber and lumber operations, a Cuban sugar plantation worked by enslaved people, mines and warehouses in Chile, and a fleet of sailing vessels to service his enterprises.[131] Hemenway died in 1876, and his estate was determined to be the largest thus far appraised in Massachusetts history. Amy's inherited wealth, and that of Cabot's own family, allowed the couple to eschew all forms of hands-on business. Louis adopted an undemanding lifestyle of study and recreation that included natural history, botany, entomology, hunting, and salmon fishing. He purchased almost the entire lower portion of the Gaspé peninsula's Grand River and made it his private fishing reserve. [237] He joined the Pointe Mouillee Duck Club located at the western end of Lake Erie and afterward, the Long Point Company.

Cabot took an active interest in the management of the Company's affairs. Edward Harris, who became a member around the same time, reminisced that Cabot was cognizant waterfowl could be hunted to excess, having observed depletion of marshlands in New England. [131] It was only after Cabot and Harris joined the Company that the directors reduced the shooting limit for each member to 500 ducks per season. The previous Company limit had been 2,600. [238] They also ceased allowing punters to shoot with members and shortened the period the punters and employees were authorized to hunt at the end of the season after the members had left to just three days. While these were conservation measures, they were a means to an end. They were aimed at ensuring the contest that members of the Company longed for would endure, an outward competition against others to shoot the most ducks and an internal challenge to better one's previous score.

Louis Cabot acquired further blocks of shares from Samuel Woodruff (whose interest by this time had turned away from the Long Pont Company in favor of assembling land for a new venture, the Turkey Point Company), and other members. Telegrams exchanged between Cabot and Woodruff demonstrate Cabot was comfortable paying the face value of $500 per Company

---

[131] Hemenway's Chilean mining interests included silver, copper, and saltpeter.

share. (Figure 46) Over a period of years, he assigned them to his Boston contemporaries. All but one would retain their membership for decades, making the Company a very stable entity. The individuals Cabot recruited were:

> Horatio Hathaway
>
> Gen. Charles Paine
>
> George Richards
>
> Augustus Hemenway
>
> Col. Henry Higginson
>
> Dr. Arthur Cabot

Horatio Hathaway was New England's foremost textile industrialist.[132] His membership endured for 21 years, until just before he died. His son Thomas Hathaway followed him, and upon his death, Horatio Hathaway Jr. inherited the shares.

The next of his contemporaries Cabot recruited was sportsman General Charles Paine. A Harvard graduate and lawyer, Paine had commanded all-Black Union Army troops during the latter period of the Civil War. He married the wealthy Julia Bryant, granddaughter of far east trader John Bryant, and re-invested the family's wealth in copper mines and railroads —the growth sector of the age. Paine was an avid yachtsman who captained three America's Cup racers, the *Mayflower, Puritan* and *Jubilee*.

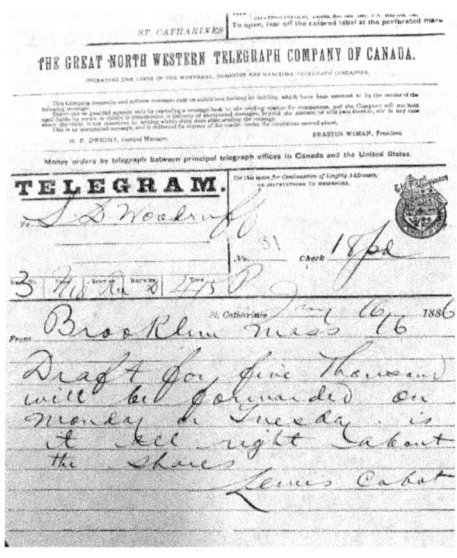

Figure 46. Telegram from Louis Cabot to Samuel Woodruff. (Brock University)

General Paine's most faithful crew member, attorney George Richards, was the next individual to join the Company. Richards and Cabot were also good friends. They sometimes traveled together to the Gaspé peninsula to fish for salmon on Cabot's private preserve. Richards

---

[132] The roots of Berkshire Hathaway corporation, led by Warren Buffett, can be traced back to Horatio Hathaway's initial enterprises.

was an amateur naturalist, while Cabot had formal training in biology. The two would return from Canada with flora samples and then submit them to colleges in Boston for examination. In another instance, Cabot took a Long Point duck which he thought might be a hybrid to Harvard for study.

Richards went on to be the managing director of the Long Point Company and was later elected president. He also served a term as president of the North American Fish and Game Protective Association. During his tenure, he advocated for a ban on hunting waterfowl at night. While the conservation principle behind his proposal was to give the birds an opportunity to rest and feed, the issue of class distinction surfaced. Working people argued that because they had to be at their jobs during the day, only the well-to-do would be able to hunt.

Correspondence exchanged between Richards and David Tisdale indicates Richards was sincerely concerned about conservation and that he fervently believed governments were not acting sufficiently to protect wildlife. He rationalized that private game preserves such as the Long Point Company were the only effective means of conservation at the time. While Richard's opinion had a some measure of validity, it was also hypocritical. Because there were no regulatory limits for the number of ducks an individual could shoot, Long Point Company members and their guests shot as many ducks as they were able, up to the Company's individual seasonal limit of five hundred. Richards remained a member of the Company for 39 years and served as president for eight.

Louis Cabot also recruited two relatives. One was a nephew, Dr. Arthur Cabot. After graduating from Harvard's medical school, Cabot went on to receive advanced training in London, Berlin, and Vienna. He then established himself as one of Boston's most innovative surgeons. Later in life, he dedicated the balance of his career to the prevention of tuberculosis. The bacterium that causes the disease survives well on surfaces. Cabot understood this and steadfastly advocated for better hygiene standards in schools. His membership in the Company lasted for 17 years.

The other relative Louis Cabot recruited was his brother-in-law, Harvard benefactor Augustus Hemenway. He would hold membership for almost half a century. Toward the end of his tenure, Hemenway ceased visiting Long Point every year, preferring instead to delegate his hunting and guest privileges to his friend, the artist Frank Weston Benson.

Records indicate Hemenway, like other members, would shoot as many ducks as he could when he was at Long Point. Such feats would not have impressed his wife, Harriet. She was a ground-breaking avian conservationist. [133] Wild bird feathers became popular for adorning women's hats during the 1880s. Harriet was deeply opposed to the use of feathers for millinery and the associated slaughter of birds for the commercial feather trade. She used her stature as a member of Boston's high society to bring pressure to bear against the slaughter. Together with her cousin, socialite Minna Hall, she held tea parties at which invitees were cajoled to cease wearing hats with feathers. Moreover, attendees were counseled to cast public shame on those who continued to do so. Both women were excellent organizers. They assembled more than 900 followers. By leveraging her husband Augustus' clout as a philanthropist, and former member

---

[133] Harriet Hemenway was also associated with suffrage, immigrant education, women's physical education, historic preservation, and Native American cultural preservation efforts.

of the Massachusetts legislature, Harriet and her group were successful in getting a bill before the legislature to ban the trade of wild bird feathers. It passed in 1887, the first such law in North America. This was achieved more than three decades before women were given the right to vote. Harriet and her cousin went on to form the Massachusetts Audubon Society. The first meeting of the organization was held in the Hemenway residence. A national movement followed. Within two years, similar organizations had been formed in 16 states.

The first federal action toward protecting birds came in 1900 when the U.S. Congress passed the *Lacey Act*. The Act prohibited poachers from transporting game across state lines. In 1913, the legislature went further by passing the Weeks-McLean Act.[134] While this Act prohibited the importation of wild bird feathers for use in millinery, and federally outlawed spring hunting, it met with opposition. Litigation ensued and the act was ruled unconstitutional.

Photo 21. Harriet Hemenway. Date unknown. (Public Domain) (Massachusetts Audubon Society)

Just a few years later, Canada and the United States entered negotiations aimed at creating a treaty to protect dwindling numbers of birds. That the negotiations underway included discussion about banning the sale of wild ducks caused considerable consternation among the residents of Port Rowan and other communities on the shore of Long Point Bay. [239] The act of selling a wild duck did become illegal within a few years. Regardless, Biddle's general store in Port Rowan was still selling ducks (with a wink and a nod) as late as the 1960s.

---

[134] John Weeks was a member of the House of Representatives from Massachusetts. The bill's co-sponsor, George McLean was a U.S. Senator from Connecticut.

In Washington, on September 16, 1916, the Convention Between the United States and Great Britain for the Protection of Migratory Birds was signed. The treaty's preamble reads as follows:

> WHEREAS, Many species of birds in the course of their annual migrations traverse certain parts of the United States and the Dominion of Canada; and
>
> Whereas, many of these species are of great value as a source of food or in destroying insects which are injurious to forests and forage plants on the public domain, as well as to agricultural crops, in both the United States and Canada, but are nevertheless in danger of extermination through lack of adequate protection during the nesting season or while on their way to and from their breeding grounds; The United States of America and His Majesty the King of the United Kingdom of Great Britain and Ireland and of the British Dominions beyond the Seas, Emperor of India, being desirous of saving from indiscriminate slaughter and of insuring the preservation of such migratory birds as are either useful to man or are harmless, have resolved to adopt some uniform system of protection which shall effectively accomplish such objects and to the end of concluding a convention for this purpose have appointed as their respective pleni-potentiaries:
>
> The President of the United States of America, Robert Lansing, Secretary of State of the United States;
>
> and
>
> His Britannic Majesty, the Right Honorable Sir Cecil Arthur Spring Rice, G. C. V. O., K. C. M. G., etc., His Majesty's Ambassador Extraordinary and Plenipotentiary at Washington;
>
> Who after having communicated to each other their respective full powers which were found to be in due and proper form, have agreed to and adopted the following articles:

The articles of the Convention defined seasons closed to hunting, imposed a ten-year moratorium on killing certain species at any time of the year, and banned the shipment of game across state, provincial, and international borders during closed seasons. The treaty was ratified within a few months. To put the principles of the agreement into force Canada's Parliament passed the Migratory Birds Convention Act in 1917. Similarly, the United States passed the Migratory Bird Treaty Act the following year. The American legislation was challenged as unconstitutional, but the Supreme Court upheld it.

The Duck Hunters—A day at Long Point, Canada.

Copyright 1890 by Geo. Barker.

Photo 22. Late 19th century stereophotograph showing Company punters with their kill of ducks and shorebirds.
George Barker. (Public Domain) (Library of Congress collection)

Col. Henry Higginson was also a recruit of Louis Cabot. (Figure 47) Higginson had studied music overseas in Vienna, before returning to the United States in 1855. Like Cabot, he entered the Union Army at the outset of the Civil War. On the battlefield at Aldie, Virginia, he was slashed and shot. Left for dead at first, he survived then suffered a difficult journey back to Boston, lying in a wagon, Higginson was attended to by Dr. Arthur Cabot's father Samuel, who was also a surgeon. Cabot removed a musket ball from near the base of Higginson's spine. After recovering from his injuries, Higginson went to work for his father's investment bank, Lee, Higginson & Co. His lasting passion for music led him to establish the Boston Symphony Orchestra.

The lengthy memberships of these men from Boston contributed to stability within the Long Point Company.[135] It also presaged the era of control by Americans. After the turn of the 20th century, annual meetings of the Company would no longer be held in Canada, but rather, in Boston's fashionable Sears building, where George Richards had his law office.

The early Company had taken measures to appease the local community. While it had no tolerance for poachers, it was lenient regarding occasional pleasure excursions that might land for a picnic. In 1881, after a severe forest fire occurred on Long Point, the Company became less tolerant. Captain Foster of Port Dover, who held the contract with the Company to furnish transportation and mail service, sought permission to build a dock on the shore of Gravelly Bay to aid public excursions in landing there. The Company denied his request. At the annual meeting that year, the following policy was laid down:

---

[135] The only member Cabot recruited whose tenure did not endure for a long period was General Charles Paine.

121

It is the aim of the members of the Company to make and maintain their property a private estate.

Company staff were then ordered to destroy all Long Point's vineyards, which from the 1860s had yielded annual harvests of several tons of grapes. The rationale was they attracted curiosity seekers who trespassed. The island's peach orchards fell to the same directive.

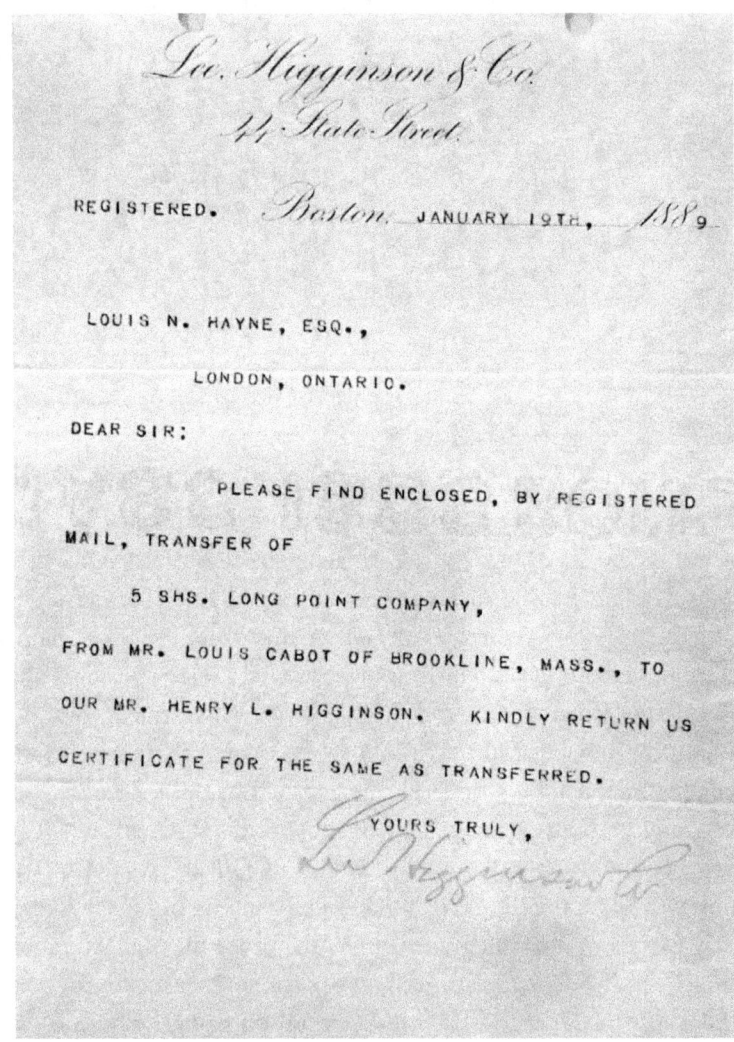

Figure 47. Memorandum related to the transfer of shares from Louis Cabot to Henry Higginson. 1889. (Norfolk County Archives)

Sunday arrivals and departures by members resumed, despite the clergy's furor. The *Norfolk Reformer* chastised the venerable David Tisdale for arriving at Port Rowan on the Sabbath and transferring to Long Point. Reporters fumed even if they did not know the identity of some of the offenders:

> On Sunday morning two sports from Boston arrived here with trunks and baggage on the Long Point Company's boat, *Hunter* [sic] landed their effects on the dock and sent them by team to Waterford, entirely regardless of the Sabbath day. [240]

Nor did the Company have any apprehension about challenging local authorities. Company agent James McLaughlin charged highly prominent Port Rowan resident and Magistrate Benjamin Killmaster with poaching. He was convicted and fined. Killmaster retaliated by having McLaughlin charged with assault for pulling off the full-face balaclava of Port Rowan poacher Alvin Becker. [241] Judge James Robb of Simcoe acquitted McLaughlin, who later gave evidence before the Royal Fish & Game Commission, publicly asserting Killmaster should be removed from the bench. [242]

During the 1870s and 1880s there were new Canadian members. One was Ottawa lumberman Allan Gilmour, whose steam-powered sawmill at Trenton, Ontario, was reputed to be the largest in Canada. Samuel Woodruff brought his brothers Richard and Joseph into the Company. Joseph, who held the position of sheriff for Lincoln County for many years, was reputed to have been popular among the members, regaling them in the dining room with his wisecracks and jokes. British military surgeon John MacKenzie, who had retired as a professor at the Grant Medical College in Bombay, bought John Walker's shares. MacKenzie had recently moved to Kingston, Ontario, where he may have been teaching at the newly formed Royal Military College. Reflecting his sense of class distinction and privilege, MacKenzie was extremely critical of pot shooters, those who hunt for food rather than sport. He held the view American pot shooters were depleting Canadian wildlife. At a game conference held in Ottawa in 1883, MacKenzie advocated that Canada should prohibit the export of game to the United States. [243] His recommendation would not have been a popular idea among the American members of the Long Point Company. Perhaps they were unaware of his viewpoint when they admitted him.

David Tisdale, who had turned his attention from general law to railway development — the ascendant businesses of the era, recruited Great Western railway manager Frederick Broughton. He had been sent to Canada in 1875 to turn around the British-owned railway after it had suffered financially during the severe recession that followed the Panic of 1873. A hard-nosed cost cutter, Broughton became deeply unpopular with Great Western's workforce. When he was called before a provincial inquiry that had been struck to examine the problem of worker fatalities on the railways, Broughton testified that a railway job was no more hazardous than any other occupation. He put forth that opinion even though the Great Western's workforce of about 800 typically suffered five fatalities and dozens of serious injuries each year. Broughton remained a member of the Long Point Company for just two years.

There were a few other notable occurrences during the 1880s. Prince George, who was accompanied by Sir Hugh Allan's son, hunted at Long Point in 1883. The Prince shot 82 ducks on his first day and 59 on his second. [244] He would later be crowned King. The Company implemented a program to poison foxes.[136] The lake broke across the south beach and into the

---

[136] Strychnine was the chemical the Company used to poison the island's foxes.

marsh, even though the Company had built at least one breakwater. The dining room was expanded to the form that still exists today. The Township of Walsingham reassessed the value of Long Point for tax purposes from $15,000 to $75,000, a fivefold increase. Steward William Leary and keeper Andrew Helmer retired, and David Tisdale helped resettle them in Manitoba by assisting in their procurement of land grants. Alfred March, a policeman from St. Catharines who earlier had been a game keeper in England, replaced Leary but he was dismissed a year later, purportedly because he had a female companion living with him at headquarters. James Pope was named the next steward.

Photo 23. (L. to R.) Louis Cabot, John Manuel, George Richards, Horatio Hathaway, James Hewlett, John MacKenzie, and John Lord. c. 1885. [162] *(Public Domain)*

The 1890s and the Commencement of the 20ᵗʰ Century

Walker Ferris replaced James Pope as chief steward in 1890. Ferris was a beekeeping enthusiast, and he introduced apiaries to the island while running a side business selling queen bees. Company president, Edward Harris enthusiastically supported Ferris and he contemplated the Company would eventually export honey to the United States. On one occasion, Harris escorted journalists to Long Point to show them the island's plentiful Basswood trees that were conducive to beekeeping and the apiaries the Company had established. [245] [246] Whether any honey was ever sold is uncertain. After Harris ceased being president in 1898, the Company disposed of the apiaries by sale. Interestingly, a Brantford beekeeper named R. F. Holterman temporarily relocated his apiaries to Long Point on several occasions in the ensuing years. The bees were transported from Brantford to Port Rowan by railcar, then taken to the island by boat. (Photos 24 & 25) [247]

Photo 24. Apiary enroute to Long Point in 1908. (Public Domain) [247]

Photo 25. Apiary on the marsh shore. 1908. (Public Domain) [247]

At the Company's annual meeting in 1906, the members were presented with a proposal to resume cutting and selling timber. Whoever first suggested the idea could not be ascertained, but John Manuel, the president of the Company at the time had spent his entire career in the lumber business. When the proposal was finally put to vote it was unanimously rejected. Two years later the directors authorized the removal of fallen timber from the ridges on the island that had been subject to forest fire.

During the period from 1890 to 1911, only one Canadian joined the Company. It was Sir William Mulock. Like others at the time, he paid $9,000 for five shares. Mulock is perhaps most remembered today for his donation of the Mulock Cup, reputed to be Canada's oldest sporting trophy. It was first awarded for rugby and later, football. Mulock's more important roles were Chief Justice of the Supreme Court of Ontario, Lieutenant Governor of Ontario, vice-chancellor of the University of Toronto, Member of Parliament, Postmaster General, and Minister of Labor. During the same 21-year period, as older members died or dropped out, 13 Americans joined. From the 20th century forward, Americans would comprise the majority of Company members.

In 1891, stockbroker and investment banker Watson Dickerman acquired the shares that were part of James Hewlett's estate. The previous year, he had been elected president of the New York Stock Exchange. Samuel Woodruff likely introduced Dickerman to Long Point, as both men were members of the Jekyll Island Club, which at the time was America's most exclusive resort. (Woodruff and his son Welland would be the only Canadians ever to be members there.)

Jekyll Island is an Atlantic barrier island located in the state of Georgia. Like Long Point, the inland-facing coast is largely marsh. The ocean side is beach. The club formed in 1886, and waterfowl hunting was a favored activity.[137] Over time, it evolved into a country club with member cottages, a golf course, and the first condominium in the United States. Members vacationed there accompanied by their families. Only a few Long Point Company members held memberships.

Like Long Point, Jekyll Island was connected to the mainland by a causeway during the 20th century. The experience driving these roads is notably similar. One reminds you of the other. The Jekyll Island club was closed for security reasons during World War II and never re-opened. Today the island is a state park. There is some residential development, particularly on the ocean-facing shore. The original clubhouse and dining room, a few member cottages, and the condominium survive. The clubhouse has been expanded, shaping what is today a rather magnificent hotel. (Photo 26)

Dickerman took an active interest in managing the affairs of the Long Point Company. When he was unavailable to attend an annual meeting, his business partner, William Dominick, acted as his proxy and made use of Company privileges. The firm the men founded, Dominick and Dickerman, still operates and is one of the oldest financial enterprises in the United States. Chances are high that Dickerman acquainted individuals with the Long Point Company who he wanted to maintain close business relationships with. One was likely Oliver Hazard Payne, who joined the same year as Dickerman.

---

[137] The Jekyll Island Club was the location where bankers such as J.P. Morgan managing director Henry Davison met secretly in 1910 to conceptualize what would be the Federal Reserve Bank. They traveled to the island under the guise of being duck hunters.

Photo 26. The Jekyll Island Club House and Hotel. 2019. (Author's photo)

Photo 27. Watson Dickerman at Long Point. Unknown date. [162] (Public Domaine)

Photo 28. William Dominick and Edward Harris. Unknown date. [188] *(Public Domain)*

Oliver Payne was the son of a Cleveland lawyer who became the president of the Cleveland and Columbus Railroad. He attended public school in Cleveland before his father sent him for further schooling at the Phillips Academy in Massachusetts. After graduating, Oliver enrolled at Yale. When the Civil War commenced, he left the university to join the Union Army and was commissioned as an officer. At Chickamauga, Georgia, where the Confederate Army had a significant victory, Payne was gravely injured. Following a lengthy recovery, he returned to duty. Payne retired with the rank of Colonel after three years of service and returned home to Cleveland.[138] Using a loan from his father, he entered the steel industry, and soon after, oil refining. It had been less than a decade since the first well had been drilled in the United States, making

---

[138] When the Civil War ended, Payne was honorarily brevetted to the rank General. However, he avoided use of the title, preferring Colonel instead.

Payne an early player in the oil business. By 1870, the Clark, Payne & Co. Star Works refinery in Cleveland was the largest in Ohio, and Payne was its principal shareholder. [248]

John D. Rockefeller had attended primary school with Payne in Cleveland. In 1871, he approached Payne and proposed a merger. Payne agreed, and he exchanged his stock in Clark, Payne & Co. for Standard Oil shares. The transaction made Payne the third largest shareholder in Rockefeller's fledgling company. The other major shareholder at the time was Henry Flagler. Over time, and with the addition of Charles Pratt's business, Standard came to control 90% of the refineries and pipelines in the United States. When the businesses were rolled up into the Standard Oil Trust in 1882, Payne was appointed the trust's treasurer.[139, 140]

Payne moved to New York City in 1884. He used the income from his ownership in the Standard Oil Trust to invest in other rising businesses of the day, including railroads, financial institutions, and the American Tobacco Company. [249] [250] He lived extravagantly, paying $700,000 for a home on New York's fashionable Fifth Avenue. He also purchased John Jacob Astor's 600-plus acre estate at Esopus on the Hudson River. Payne razed Astor's mansion and replaced it with a 42,000-square foot Mediterranean-style palazzo that overlooked the river where he would later moor his 300-ft (91-metre) steam yacht *Aphrodite*.[141] (Photo 31) The yacht carried him around the world once and to Europe each summer until World War I commenced. He also used it to reach New Brunswick, where he would fish for salmon. The yacht would moor on Chaleur Bay below the Gaspé Peninsula. As there were no roads in the area, Payne traveled from the bay up the Restigouche River to Camp Harmony on a houseboat specially designed for him by architect Stanford White. (Photos 29 & 30)

Photo 29. Long Point Company members Oliver Payne and Frank Ellis on the deck of Payne's houseboat. Restigouche River, New Brunswick. Unknown date. [251] *(Public Domain)*

---

[139] ibid
[140] Corporations are paper entities. The contrivance of bundling multiple companies into a trust is attributed to Standard Oil lawyer Sam Dodd. Shareholders surrendered their shares in the individual companies in return for certificates in the governing trust. The profits from all the individual companies flowed to a board of trustees who then distributed the money to the trust certificate holders. The trustees also selected the officers and directors of the various operating companies. The effect was to allow a very small number of individuals —the trustees —to exert control over multiple companies in different states in a monopolistic manner. The Sherman Act of 1890 spelled the end of anticompetitive trusts. However, a similar contrivance —holding companies —soon emerged.
[141] Payne named the palazzo Omega. The site is listed in the U.S. National Register of Historic Places.

Photo 30. Oliver Payne's houseboat moored at Camp Harmony on the Restigouche River. Unknown date. [251] (Public Domain)

Photo 31. Oliver H. Payne Estate, Esopus, NY. Payne's yacht Aphrodite is shown moored in the foreground. Unknown date. (Public Domain)

Oliver Payne never married. Karl Berntsen, a Cornell medical professor emeritus who had access to the Payne family papers, wrote that the reason for Oliver's bachelorhood was his Civil War injury had been to his genitalia. With no children of his own, Payne was generous to others and in his philanthropy. He eschewed publicity, was rarely photographed, and often kept his donations secret. He provided four million dollars for the construction of Cornell University Medical College, and later an additional 4-million dollars. Phillips Academy, Yale University, the New York Public Library, and Cleveland's Lakeside Hospital were also the recipients of seven-figure gifts.

Payne also doted on his sisters, including his favorite Flora, who married his former Yale roommate, the wealthy William Whitney. The couple had several children, two of whom were Payne Whitney and Harry Payne Whitney. Yet, for all his generosity, Oliver Payne could be vindictive. After Flora died, William Whitney made plans to remarry. Oliver's sentiment was the pending marriage was announced too soon after his sister's death, and he expected everyone to take his side in the matter. Payne Whitney, William's second son, cast his allegiance to his uncle Oliver, while Harry Payne Whitney sided with his father in the matter. The consequence was Payne Whitney became Oliver's most-favored nephew. When he married Helen Hay in 1902, Oliver bought the couple their own private railcar, a yacht, an Italian Renaissance townhome on New York's Fifth Avenue, and gave them a cash gift of $50,000. He also dazzled the bride with a diamond necklace worth $150,000 at the time. [252] Oliver Payne's shares in the Long Point Company passed to Payne Whitney in 1911.

Three years later, after Louis Cabot had died, Payne Whitney's brother, Harry Payne Whitney, quickly acquired the shares from Cabot's estate. Oliver Payne died in 1917. The portion of his estate that passed through probate amounted to 32 million dollars. Due to his lack of allegiance to his uncle, Harry Payne Whitney received just a single item from the estate, an oil painting. He did alright though; he married Gertrude Vanderbilt, daughter of railroad tycoon Cornelius Vanderbilt, and he inherited $24,000,000 dollars from his father, William Whitney. [253]

Oliver Payne's fortune was far greater than the 32-million dollars that was processed through probate. Evidence suggests the bulk of the fortune was conveyed confidentially through a trust to Payne Whitney.

Another individual who Watson Dickerman introduced to Long Point was Dean Sage. Sage had attended Albany Law School; whether he ultimately graduated is uncertain. A legal education would become a common attribute among Long Point Company members, not because they anticipated becoming practicing attorneys, but rather because a legal education was considered appropriate for young men whose parents were going to pass down a Gilded Age fortune.

Dean Sage's father, Henry W. Sage, was a well-established Ithica, New York lumberman. Aware that a railroad was about to be built to connect Toronto with Barrie, he began acquiring land around Lake Simcoe and added to his already large enterprise by having a steam-powered sawmill constructed at Bell Ewert, near the foot of the lake. Logs from the entire surrounding area could be floated to the mill. Sage encouraged farmers in the region to clear the rest of their land and he purchased their timber. Lumber production at the mill commenced in 1853. [254] After being forwarded to Toronto by rail, the sawn lumber was loaded onto lake vessels and exported to New York State.

Sage later provided loans to his sons, Dean and William, so each of them could acquire a ¼ share in his enterprises. Over a period of approximately 15 years, the Sage's stripped nearly all the viable timber from the area around Lake Simcoe. Then, they set their sights on Muskoka. Getting timber from there to the mill at Bell Ewart would require additional infrastructure. Consequently, it was Sage and his sons who led the consortium that built the canal and tramway that connects the Muskoka Lakes to Lake Simcoe via the Black River, Lake St. John, and Lake Couchiching.[142] The canal and tramway survive to this day, essentially for pleasure use.

Like other lumber barons, after logging one area the Sage's simply took their accumulated capital and moved on. Their next acquisitions were in lower Michigan, where with a partner, they built a world-scale mill at Bay City. It was another strategic location from which lumber could be readily shipped anywhere on the Great Lakes.

Sage and his son Dean eventually moved to New York City where they invested their fortune passively in railways and other rising enterprises of the era. Flush with investments, Dean indulged himself by engaging in leisurely activities such as hunting, breeding trotting horses, collecting rare books, and most notably, salmon fishing. He founded the Camp Harmony Angling Club, the famed fishing camp on New Brunswick's Restigouche River, and he commissioned New York architect Stanford White to design a lodge for the club. [251] Membership was restricted to seven individuals. Most of the initial members were also Long Point Company shareholders.

In 1887, Dean Sage completed writing a book titled *The Ristigouche and Its Salmon Fishing*. He had 105 copies of the book extravagantly assembled by a printer in Edinburgh. The book was and still is highly regarded.[143] Sage apportioned copies as follows:

Public libraries	5
Private presentation	50
Sale in the United States	25
Sale in the United Kingdom	25

Not all Dean Sage's avocations were as genteel as salmon fishing. He was a fan of brutal boxing matches, and he bred fighting cocks.[144] Rumored to be governed by a relentless temper, he could leavet a lasting impression on others, earning him the nickname Fierce Dean.

Sage's introduction to, and subsequent membership in the Long Point Company may well have been a strategic endeavor on the part of Watson Dickerman. Both men were directors of the Norfolk and Southern railroad. Dickerman had just been named President-as-Receiver of the railroad because it was struggling with financial challenges. He started bringing Sage to Long Point as his guest. In a letter to Company member George Richards, Dickerman tactfully alluded to Sage's temper. He wrote that Sage was "rather peculiar" and therefore an effort ought to be

---

[142] The entity that built the tramway and canal was the Rama Timber Transport Co. Henry Sage, Orillia's John Thomson, and Thompson Smith of Bradford, Ontario, were the company's initial shareholders.

[143] Original copies of *The Ristigouche and Its Salmon Fishing* sell for about US$ 27,000.

[144] Today, in both Canada and the United States, attendance at a cock fighting match is a criminal offense.

made not to further aggravate him by re-requesting advance payment of a government-required annual goose hunting license. (Dickerman, 1986) Given Sage's volatile nature, one might speculate that Dickerman, in his role as President of the Norfolk and Southern railroad, may have socially recruited Sage as part of an effort to keep him close and curry favor. After Sage joined the Company, the two men had a shared cottage built at the Company's premises on Rice Bay.

Ironically, the year Sage —who had made a fortune as a timber stripper —became a member of the Long Point Company, was the same year the Company began reforestation on Courtright Ridge by planting hickory and walnut seedlings.[145] [255] Sage died at Camp Harmony on the Restigouche in 1902. Present with him that day were Long Point Company members Watson Dickerman, Frank Ellis, and Oliver Payne. [256] Dean's son Henry M. Sage inherited his Long Point Company shares.

Philadelphia shipping magnate Clement A. Griscom became a member in 1900, also most likely at the invitation of Watson Dickerman. With assistance from J. P Morgan, Clement had monopolized the transatlantic shipping business by consolidating the Inman and Red Star Lines, the White Star Line, the American Line, the Leyland Line, the Atlantic Transport Line, and the Dominion Line, into a massive trust called the International Mercantile Marine Co. In addition to his marine interests, Clement had a close relationship with Standard Oil. He not only held certificates in the Standard Oil Trust, but he also served as president of the National Transit Co., Standard's pipeline business.

Also joining from Philadelphia was Frank Ellis, a year later. His lumberman father developed and owned Philadelphia's first streetcar system. The younger Ellis, to a degree, followed his father's lead by financing the development of other rail systems. He was a good friend of Oliver Payne and is known to have spent much of his life pursuing sports. He is particularly remembered for breeding harness racing horses.

Alexander Cochrane Jr., an heir to his father's major chemical enterprise at Billerica, Massachusetts, joined in 1902 [146] The younger Cochrane invested portions of his capital in several of the first telephone companies, becoming a director of many. In 1900, those investments led him to briefly serve as acting president of the American Telephone and Telegraph Company (AT&T). Cochrane was also a member of the Restigouche Salmon Club.

Investment banker Capt. Robert Dudley Winthrop acquired fellow banker Henry Higginson's shares in 1906. When he died six years later, the shares passed to his brother Frederic Winthrop, who wasn't particularly interested in Long Point. He soon sold the shares.

Company founder Samuel Woodruff died in 1904. The Province of Ontario asserted that some of his assets, particularly his holdings in the United States, were being concealed to avoid taxation. This delayed the settlement of Woodruff's estate. Consequently, the transfer of his Company shares to his son Welland didn't occur until 1912. Samuel's other son, Alfred, became a member in 1919 by acquiring shares that had flowed from John Manuel's estate to his

---

[145] In addition to the tree plantation at the north end of Courtright Ridge, there are plantations at the north end of Squire's Ridge and on Bluff Point.

[146] Cochrane's chemical business would eventually merge with another to form Allied Chemical Corporation. Today's Honeywell Corporation's roots can be traced back to Allied.

beneficiary.[147] Harry Johnson, the owner of a tannery in Toronto that was a significant supplier to the footwear industry during World War I, acquired shares that year from the same estate.

During the first two decades of the 20th century, some of the members from Boston reached old age and became ill or died. New Yorkers replaced them. Consequently, in 1922, the annual meeting of the Company was not held in Boston, but instead at New York City's University Club. A few of the New Yorkers were Harvard graduates or had connections to the institution, such as New York textile mogul Horace Stebbins.[148]

Reflecting the class differences of the era, all the new 20th century members were graduates of Ivy League universities. This was an era when fewer than 5% of Americans had the opportunity to receive any post-secondary education whatsoever, let alone an Ivy League schooling. While Harvard had been the alma mater of the Boston members, for the New Yorkers it was typically Yale. Otherwise, they were graduates of Colombia, Princeton, or Cornell.[149] Attesting to the fact that Company members competed against one another for shooting achievements, they often flew their school colors from their skiffs.

William Barnum was the first of the 20th century New Yorkers to join the Company. Inducted a Skull & Bones Society member in his final year at Yale, he went on to Columbia where he studied law.[150] After working as a lawyer on corporate matters for two decades, he became an investment banker with Harvey Fisk & Sons and assembled the financing for large New York City infrastructure projects such as the tunnels that pass below the Hudson River. Barnum would be the first member from New York City elected a president of the Long Point Company.

The brothers Payne Whitney and Harry Payne Whitney were Yale graduates. Payne had been captain of the crew team, which would have contributed to his being inducted into the Skull & Bones Society. He would see the fortune he inherited from his uncle Oliver grow. When Payne Whitney died in 1927, just a decade after his uncle had passed, his estate was appraised to be $191,000,000. Because John D. Rockefeller had not yet passed away, that made Whitney's estate the largest recorded in America history at the time. [257] [258] Payne Whitney's shares in the Long Point Company passed to his son, John Hay Whitney.

Harry Payne Whitney's great passion was breeding thoroughbred horses, but he was still very much a businessman. Around the time he became a member of the Long Point Company, he put some of his capital to bear on a risky venture that created a historically significant Canadian enterprise. The venture warrants a short digression from the topic of the Long Point Company.

---

[147] The beneficiary was James Manuel.

[148] Horace Stebbins was a highly successful and wealthy agent for New England's huge textile mills. He would have been acquainted with the Hathaway family.

[149] The other Ivy League universities are Dartmouth, Brown, and the University of Pennsylvania.

[150] The Skull and Bones Society is an exclusive and secretive fraternity. Members are drawn from the class of seniors at Yale. Those selected for admission have typically distinguished themselves through service to the university in one way or another.

Prospectors in Manitoba discovered a remote body of ore 450 miles north of Winnipeg. They named it Flin Flon, after the fictional character Josiah Flintabbatey Flonatin.[151] Because the ore quality was unusual, and because it was located far into the bush country, the deposit went undeveloped for several years. To shorten a lengthy and technically involved story, suffice it to say that Sir Henry Pellatt's Mining Corporation of Canada, the company that held the option on the Flin Flon deposit, was aware Harry Payne Whitney had other mining investments and approached him in 1924 to learn if he might be interested in developing a mine. In conducting his due diligence, Whitney dispatched his 24-year-old son, Cornelius Vanderbilt (Sonny) Whitney, to inspect the site of the deposit. Sonny paddled his way through Manitoba's lakes and rivers to reach the site. Meanwhile, the elder Whitney was careful to obtain reliable technical advice regarding the feasibility of processing the formation's unusual ore. [259] In 1927, Whitney applied for and received a corporate charter for the Hudson Bay Mining and Smelting Company. He furnished much of the capital for the enterprise himself, although there were minor partners. These were Col. William B. Thompson's Newmont Mining Corporation., and Sir Henry Pellatt's Mining Corporation of Canada. (Pellatt was the financier and electrical power developer who built the lavish home in Toronto that he named Casa Loma.)

Whitney's personal attorney served as the first president of Hudson Bay Mining and Smelting. However, it was Sonny Whitney who oversaw the development of the mine and its operation. Neither were minor undertakings. Development of the mine necessitated the construction of an electric plant on the Churchill River, building transmission lines to the mine site, a railway, and of course the smelter and recovery facilities. Until the railway was completed, teams of horses skidded the necessary materials and equipment to the site, a location that could be described as the middle of nowhere.

Open pit mining commenced in 1930, yielding gold, silver, copper, and zinc. The same year, the enterprise raised capital in public markets through the issuance of bonds underwritten by J. P. Morgan & Co. The capital infusion was used to develop an underground mine. (Time, 1935) The Whitney family retained control of Hudson Bay Mining and Smelting for decades and it was highly profitable. Sonny remained fully dedicated to the enterprise. After he and socialite Marie Schroeder were wed in Nevada on January 25, 1958, they attended their reception in Beverly Hills before immediately departing for bitter-cold Flin Flon, where they spent their honeymoon.

---

[151] One of the prospectors had read a 1905 book by author J. E. P. Muddock, titled, *The Sunless City: From the Papers and Diaries of the Late Josiah Flintabbatey Flonatin.*

The Introduction of Deer and the Conflict with Walter Anderson

Excessive hunting had extirpated deer from Long Point well before the founding of the Long Point Company. In 1874, the Company imported 15 deer from Clearwater, Minnesota and released them on the island.[152] The herd fared well, and seven years later Walter Anderson brought in an additional four. In 1885, the acreage he held as tenants-in-common with the Company's agents was finally partitioned. Anderson received about 90 acres as his exclusive property and the Company's agents the remainder. By this time, the deer had intermingled.

After Anderson shot a deer on his own land, the Company asserted the animal was its property and launched a lawsuit against him in county court. At trial, the fact that Anderson shot the deer on his land was not disputed. The judge ruled that one who creates confusion — being Anderson in this instance by introducing more deer —forfeits property rights willfully mixed with those of another. The judge concluded all persons were prohibited from shooting deer on Long Point unless they obtained permission to do so from the Company and ordered Anderson to pay $15 in damages. Anderson then appealed to the Divisional Court, where the judgment was overturned with costs awarded. The members of the Long Point Company were not pleased to lose their case.

Partly out of spite, Anderson then began syndicating the 90-acre parcel by selling shares in the property. Early purchasers were six young men from prosperous Woodstock families. They were Dan Kendall, J. Ralph (Rafe) Thompson, W.A. Karn, P. H. McLeod, Dan Miller, and Andrew Laidlaw. [260] Thompson, a Woodstock hotel proprietor, would later be prosecuted by the Long Point Company for poaching ducks near Sawlog Creek.

Suspecting that others who were using the Anderson property were also poaching, the Company sought out someone who could infiltrate them. The individual selected was Canadian-born Benedict Allen (a.k.a Allan) of London. Local lore is the Long Point Company retained him through the Pinkerton agency. While Allen may have been working under contract to Pinkerton, he was employed as a deputy game warden in Middlesex County. [261] Holding that official position would not necessarily have prohibited him from accepting a private assignment from Pinkerton.

In October 1893, Allen took on an assumed identity calling himself Mr. Graham of Goderich. He traveled to St. Williams around the middle of the month, where he claimed to be a new shareholder in the Anderson syndicate. He hired trapper William Helmer to take him to Long Point and serve as his guide for a fee of two dollars per day. On a Saturday, they traveled to a scow moored on Rice Bay and overnighted there. The next day they went on to their destination, a cabin on the shore of Gravelly Bay. They were reported to have toured the Anderson property on Monday and fished on Tuesday. On Wednesday, Allen shot a deer, and Helmer dressed it for him. The following day they met Stephen Price and Henry Bennett, (both of whom were from St. Williams,) and they agreed to hunt with them on Friday morning. [262] When morning came and Price and

---

[152] The Company booked charges totalling $479 for the deer.

Bennett had not yet arrived, Allen went out alone with his shotgun. Helmer heard a shot shortly thereafter.

Bennett and Price then arrived at the lodge seeking Allan to go out with them. Helmer told them Allan had already left on his own. They then left, taking the same path that Allan did. On walking a short distance, they came across Allan's lifeless body. A load of buckshot had entered his forehead a little over his right eye, plowing a hole and cutting a ridge from the top of his head. The shot came out at the base of the brain a little to the right. His eyebrows were apparently scorched by powder. Within a few yards lay his gun with one barrel discharged, a hunting knife, and the carcass of a huge buck, which had been shot and its throat cut, presumably by Allan. [263]

The Company retained attorney Britton Osler, the eminent criminal lawyer of his day, and one with a reputation for a high degree of competence for addressing medical evidence, to investigate Allen's death. Osler told reporters Allen wasn't the first detective to be murdered on Long Point. He said that two others had been killed twelve years earlier. [264]

An inquest into Allen's death presided over by Coroner James Hayes took place at Simcoe in early November.[153] The evidence describing the condition of Allen's injury was so graphic it unsettled the court stenographer, and the session had to be temporarily adjourned. [262] After all the testimony had been heard, the jury concluded that while Allen had died from a shotgun blast to his head, there was insufficient evidence to conclude how and by whose hand. [265]

Being a game warden by occupation, Allen would have been skilled in the use of firearms. A shotgun blast to the head is not an occurrence one would expect to be self-inflicted. The jury's verdict that they could not conclude Allan died at the hand of another was unreasonable. The verdict may have reflected the longstanding resentment the local public harbored toward the Long Point Company, which had locked them out of what had formerly been public land. Bad will between the members of the Anderson syndicate and the Company continued for decades. The Company posted notices that it intended to prosecute anyone who shot a deer anywhere on Long Point. (Figure 48)

Deer were not the only game the Long Point Company introduced to the island. In 1908, four elk were imported. [266] The effort failed, and it is believed the animals were killed by poachers. [267] Elk remains have since been found on the island. Although one specimen has been subjected to carbon dating, the method's resolution is only sufficient to conclude the animal lived sometime after the middle of the 17th century.

---

[153] The Crown attorney at the inquiry was J. H. Ansley. The Long Point Company was represented by David Tisdale, who also testified before the jury about the conflict between the Company and the Anderson property owners, who were represented by W. E. Kelley. London lawyer W. D. Edwards represented Allen's family.

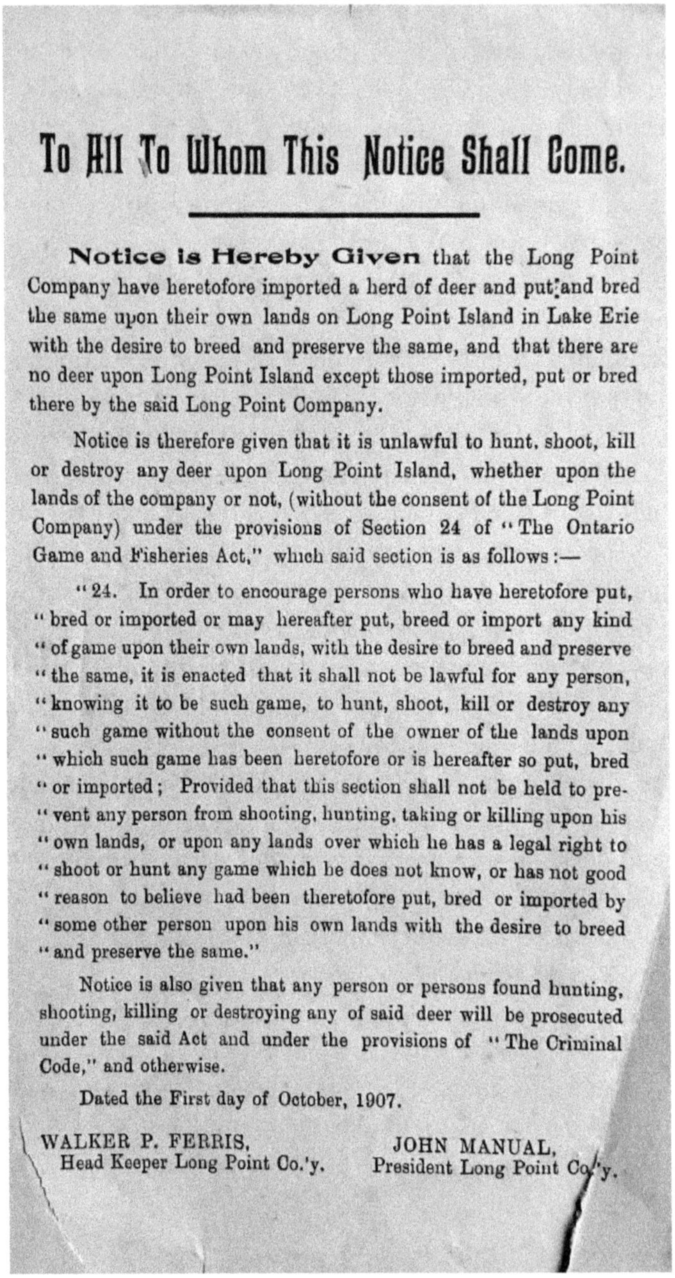

To All To Whom This Notice Shall Come.

Notice is Hereby Given that the Long Point Company have heretofore imported a herd of deer and put and bred the same upon their own lands on Long Point Island in Lake Erie with the desire to breed and preserve the same, and that there are no deer upon Long Point Island except those imported, put or bred there by the said Long Point Company.

Notice is therefore given that it is unlawful to hunt, shoot, kill or destroy any deer upon Long Point Island, whether upon the lands of the company or not, (without the consent of the Long Point Company) under the provisions of Section 24 of "The Ontario Game and Fisheries Act," which said section is as follows :—

"24. In order to encourage persons who have heretofore put, "bred or imported or may hereafter put, breed or import any kind "of game upon their own lands, with the desire to breed and preserve "the same, it is enacted that it shall not be lawful for any person, "knowing it to be such game, to hunt, shoot, kill or destroy any "such game without the consent of the owner of the lands upon "which such game has been heretofore or is hereafter so put, bred "or imported; Provided that this section shall not be held to pre- "vent any person from shooting, hunting, taking or killing upon his "own lands, or upon any lands over which he has a legal right to "shoot or hunt any game which he does not know, or has not good "reason to believe had been theretofore put, bred or imported by "some other person upon his own lands with the desire to breed "and preserve the same."

Notice is also given that any person or persons found hunting, shooting, killing or destroying any of said deer will be prosecuted under the said Act and under the provisions of "The Criminal Code," and otherwise.

Dated the First day of October, 1907.

WALKER P. FERRIS,
Head Keeper Long Point Co.'y.

JOHN MANUAL,
President Long Point Co.'y.

Figure 48. Notice pertaining to poaching deer. 1907.
(Norfolk County Archives)

The First Long Point Park

During 1919, the water level in Lake Erie fell abruptly. Additional dry land emerged at what is today the subdivided western part of Long Point. The happenstance contributed to the Department of Lands and Forests initiating a survey of the area the following year. The survey brought to light that while the Long Point Company held 141 acres west and north of the Old Cut Lighthouse, there was an adjacent parcel of about 420 acres to the west that was Crown Land.[154] Some people referred to the area as "the sandbar," and they were aware it would be a risky place to build.

Word that the 420 acres were Crown Land spread rapidly, resulting in hopeful anticipation among the local populace. Having been locked out of Long Point for decades, they longed for a modicum of access for fishing, hunting, and leisure. The Company's unpopularity was rekindled when many speculated it would acquire the parcel. The apprehension wasn't unfounded, and Joseph Cridland, the member of the legislative assembly for South Norfolk, fumed at the possibility, as did Port Rowan Reeve John Buck. [268] Buck asked to meet personally with Ontario's new Premier, Ernest Drury, to discuss the situation and Drury agreed to his request.

At their meeting, Buck showed Drury a map of Long Point and explained the island's ownership history. He convinced the Premier that the province should make the 420 acres a public park. Drury subsequently assigned a deputy minister to work with Buck to fulfill the vision. The possibility of a park on Long Point didn't impress Boston lawyer George Richards, who was the Long Point Company president at the time. The Company retained attorney Harry Collier to oppose Buck's plan. Collier argued that if the acreage was made a park, it would soon be populated by summer cottages. He stressed that any such development would be wholly discordant with the "wild nature" of Long Point, which the Company had preserved for decades. His entreaty was unsuccessful.

As a matter of ideology, Ontario governments during this era had little interest in creating or funding parks. There were just three Provincial Parks and two lesser ones. These were Rondeau, Algonquin, & Quetico Provincial Parks, and the locally administered parks at Niagara Falls and Burlington Beach. The history of these parks and how they were administered is interesting and worthy of a tangential digression from the topic of Long Point.

During the 19th century, Niagara Falls was one of the continent's most renowned natural wonders. Although it was a major tourist destination, it was controlled solely by commercial interests from as early as 1820. Places that offered views of the Falls were fenced off, forcing tourists to pay to access commercial viewing points. Visitors were preyed upon by unscrupulous individuals of all kinds, and criminal activity was prevalent. Eventually, the circumstances became an embarrassment to Canada, so in 1873 the federal government struck a Royal Commission to investigate the situation. The commission ultimately put forward numerous recommendations, including that a government-owned park be created. However, political bias against public parks

---

[154] On survey documents, the 141-acre plot west and north of the Old Cut lighthouse is designated Block "C."

remained strong, and Premier Oliver Mowat rejected the idea. Not much came from the Commission's recommendations beyond increased law enforcement resources.

A few years later, an American group of landscape architects that included Frederick Law Olmsted, together with some prominent New Yorkers, began lobbying governments to do something to preserve the natural beauty of the area. As part of their effort, they reached out to Lord Dufferin, the Canadian Governor General. Dufferin was supportive, and in 1878, he proposed the governments of Ontario and New York work together to develop an international park. By the following year, New York State Governor Lucius Robinson was supporting the plan. The group's influence led New York State to establish a public park on its side of the Niagara River. The American initiative stimulated Ontario to act as well. However, ruling politicians remained resistant to provincial administration of a park and opted in favor of a local governing structure by creating the Niagara Parks Commission. This body was given municipal powers, including the authority to issue bonds. In spite of the provincial government's lack of enthusiasm, a mechanism had finally been established to administer Ontario's first public park.

Awareness that Ontario's natural resources required management didn't surface until about 1860. One of the first to raise the issue was lumberman James Little, father of Long Point Company founding member William Little. He believed America's demand for lumber was insatiable and would result in the total destruction of Canada's forests. Although he had been among the first Canadian lumberman to export to the United States, Little began advocating for an export tariff. For this, his fellow lumberman widely ridiculed him, and his proposal found no traction. The notion that cutting was out of control finally took hold in the late 1870s through a conservation movement organized by the Fruit Growers' Association of Ontario, whose members were concerned about spreading areas of blow sand:

> The Fruit Growers' Association need to put forth their best efforts to husband our Dominion and Provincial resources in their timber limits —to carefully instruct the farming community how much depends on the judicious planting of forest trees, their presence producing abundant rainfall, preserving and distributing moisture and therefore forming a preventative against drought and devastating floods. [269]

The Growers Association's advocacy was instrumental in the province's decision to send a delegation to the founding meeting of the American Forestry Congress in Cincinnati in 1882. At the conference, at least ten presenters explained the consequences of uncontrolled cutting of timber. Subsequently, the province appointed Robert Phipps to an official position in the Department of Agriculture, and he set about developing an educational campaign to discourage farmers from clearing all the trees on their land.

The idea that forests and the wildlife they supported were a resource requiring conservation and scientific management was beginning to take hold. In 1883, New York State froze the sale of public lands around the headwaters of the Hudson River and began to move to create the

Adirondack Park. In Western Canada in 1885, the federal government, taking a cue from the formation of Yellowstone Park in the United States, created the Banff National Park.

Phipps recommended Ontario follow New York State's lead. He found support from the province's chief of public land sales, Alexander Kirkwood. In 1885, Kirkwood proposed the creation of Algonquin Park. Others who were interested in game protection, and understood how it was related to forest preservation got involved as well. However, ruling politicians resisted for several years.

Long Point Company president Edward Harris weighed in when he published a pamphlet titled, *Is Game of Any Value to the Farmer?* [270] Harris's principal motivation was to advocate for an end to the notion of game as common property. He appealed to farmers, expecting they would be supportive of regulatory reform because pot shooters regularly encroached on their land.

In his publication, Harris also promoted the concept of a national park, believing game would find refuge there and recover their depleted numbers. His appeal had some influence, but the final impetus for a park came from the report of the Royal Fish & Game Commission, a body on which Robert Phipps and Alexander Kirkwood served. In 1893, the Ontario legislature passed *An Act to Establish the Algonquin National Park of Ontario.* (The text of the authorizing legislation borrowed substantially from what the federal government had written for the creation of the park at Banff.) Although Algonquin Park was established at the provincial level, the intent was for it to have national stature. Despite the effort made to create the park, little to no consideration was given to the impact it would have on Native People.

Also during the 1890s, local officials in southwestern Ontario recognized ducks were being overharvested on the Pointe aux Pins peninsula. They encouraged the province's legislative assembly to address the situation. In 1894, a bill passed that created the Rondeau Provincial Park.

For the next 20 years, the administrators of the province resisted further creation of parks. The only exception was Burlington Beach, the sand spit which divides Lake Ontario from Burlington Bay. The City of Hamilton held a lease from the province for the spit. By the 1890s the property had been subdivided and developed. There were many substantial summer cottages, a yacht club, and at least ten hotels. The cottage owners, seeking better municipal services, petitioned the Ontario government to incorporate the spit as a village. The province didn't deem the request appropriate for a place that had become a mixed-use recreational area. The cottagers continued their plea for almost a decade. Finally, the province pulled the lease from the city, opting for a type of local self-determination in the form of an administrative commission, as had been put in effect earlier for Niagara Falls. It was all for naught. Air and water pollution soon made Burlington Beach a foul place. The cottagers departed, the hotels drew few visitors, and the spit deteriorated into a rundown area that was eventually encumbered by a freeway.

In the early 20th century, Minnesota Commissioner of Forests Christopher Andrews, who had canoed through the area known as the Boundary Waters, convinced his state legislature to set aside a tract of untouched wilderness amounting to about 140,000 acres. He advocated for Ontario to do the same for the abutting wilderness on its side of the border so that an international preserve could be created. Ontario shunned the idea. Some years later, the North American Fish and Game

Protective Association, which Boston native and Long Point Company president George Richards would soon head, began to lobby for Andrews' proposal. This initiative, too, was unpersuasive. Then, in 1909 President Theodore Roosevelt authorized the creation of the Superior National Forest, broadly extending the Minnesota park. Caught flatfooted, so to speak, Premier James Whitney and his cabinet relented and issued an order-in-council to create an abutting forest preserve. In 1913, by a further order-in-council, Quetico Provincial Park was fully created, fulfilling Andrews' vision. Long Point Company member Robert Laidlaw, through the Laidlaw Foundation, would become a significant contributor to Quetico Park.

Returning to the topic of the envisioned Long Point Park, the deputy minister who was assigned to work with Port Rowan's Reeve Buck suggested that if a park at Long Point was to be created, it would be best administered by the Port Rowan municipal council. For reasons unknown Buck was very resistant to the idea. He argued for a local governing commission, as had been implemented for Niagara Falls and Burlington Beach. In the end, Buck's recommendation was adopted. The legislature passed *The Long Point Park Act* which designated the entire 420 acres of public land at Long Point a "park, forest reservation, and health resort for the benefit, advantage, and enjoyment of the people of Ontario." [271] 155 The acreage was flanked by the Long Point Company to the east and the Toronto Big Creek Shooting Club Ltd. to the west. The authority to administer the park was entrusted to a three-person commission. Norfolk M.P.P. Joseph Cridland was given the pleasure of appointing whomever he wished to be the commissioners and he selected Dr. William Broddy, Jack Gleadall, and Thomas Pierce, all of Port Rowan. Thus, through a rapid sequence of events, Long Point Park was created —at least as a legal entity.

The enabling statute gave the Long Point Park Commission virtually all the powers of a municipality. These included creating by-laws, issuing debt, levying taxes, issuing leases, collecting rents, hiring police constables, etc. Authority was even granted to imprison individuals who violated bylaws the commission might establish. The legislation directed the commission to "layout, build, improve, develop, and enclose the park in such a manner as it thinks fit."[156] In short, it had free reign, although major initiatives required clearance through the office of the Lieut. Governor-in-Council. In a move that reflected the local community's hunting history, in its first year the commission sold duck hunting licenses. [272] The commission also had exploratory gas wells drilled. (Reeve Buck had been one of the founders of the Port Rowan Natural Gas Co.) It explained the drilling as a search for fuel for anticipated street lighting. At the time, the only way of reaching Long Point (where there were no roads) was by boat. The commission had probably embraced a vision whereby gas production royalties could have helped fund the park's development.[157] A search of a commercial database (WellDatabase) found no record of any extant wells in what is today Long Point's built-up community.

Just as the Long Point Company's outside counsel, Harry Collier, had predicted, the commission promptly set about planning to subdivide the park into lots. It retained the Toronto

---

[155] The Long Point Park Act was amended in 1927. See Ontario: Revised Statutes: Vol. 1927: Issue 1, Article 88.
[156] ibid
[157] Port Rowan Reeve J.L. Buck owned natural gas wells in the Township of South Walsingham.

firm, Speight and VanNostrand, to draw up a subdivision plan. Two years later, the commission submitted the plan to the office of the Lt. Governor-in-Council, which numbingly gave it rubber-stamp approval. (Figure 49) The plan provided for three areas of bona fide parkland. One was the plot that is today known as Cottonwood Park, or as it is sometimes called, the Old Provincial Park. A much larger plot was reserved for an amusement park. Today, it appears as a low marsh north of Erie Boulevard, between Howey Avenue and Austin Parkway. During the 19th century, that had been the area through which the Old Cut ship canal passed. The reason the vision for an amusement park was never fulfilled may have been that the undertaking would have required an impractical volume of fill. The third plot, originally designated as a park, ultimately served a different purpose. That land became the subdivided eastern parts of Erie Boulevard and Beach Avenue.

In 1926, Reeve Buck sought to have a road built to connect Long Point to the mainland. He was again successful in obtaining a face-to-face meeting with the Ontario Premier, who by this time was Howard Ferguson. Later that year, when announcing his approval of the project for a causeway, Ferguson declared it would open Long Point to the local community and thousands of tourists. Construction began in 1927. The original road had three bridges. One that crossed the Port Royal Ship Canal, and two further south, which crossed locations where Big Creek had formerly entered Long Point's Inner Bay.

Photo 32 The causeway bridge over Big Creek, circa 1929. (Port Rowan Women's Institute)

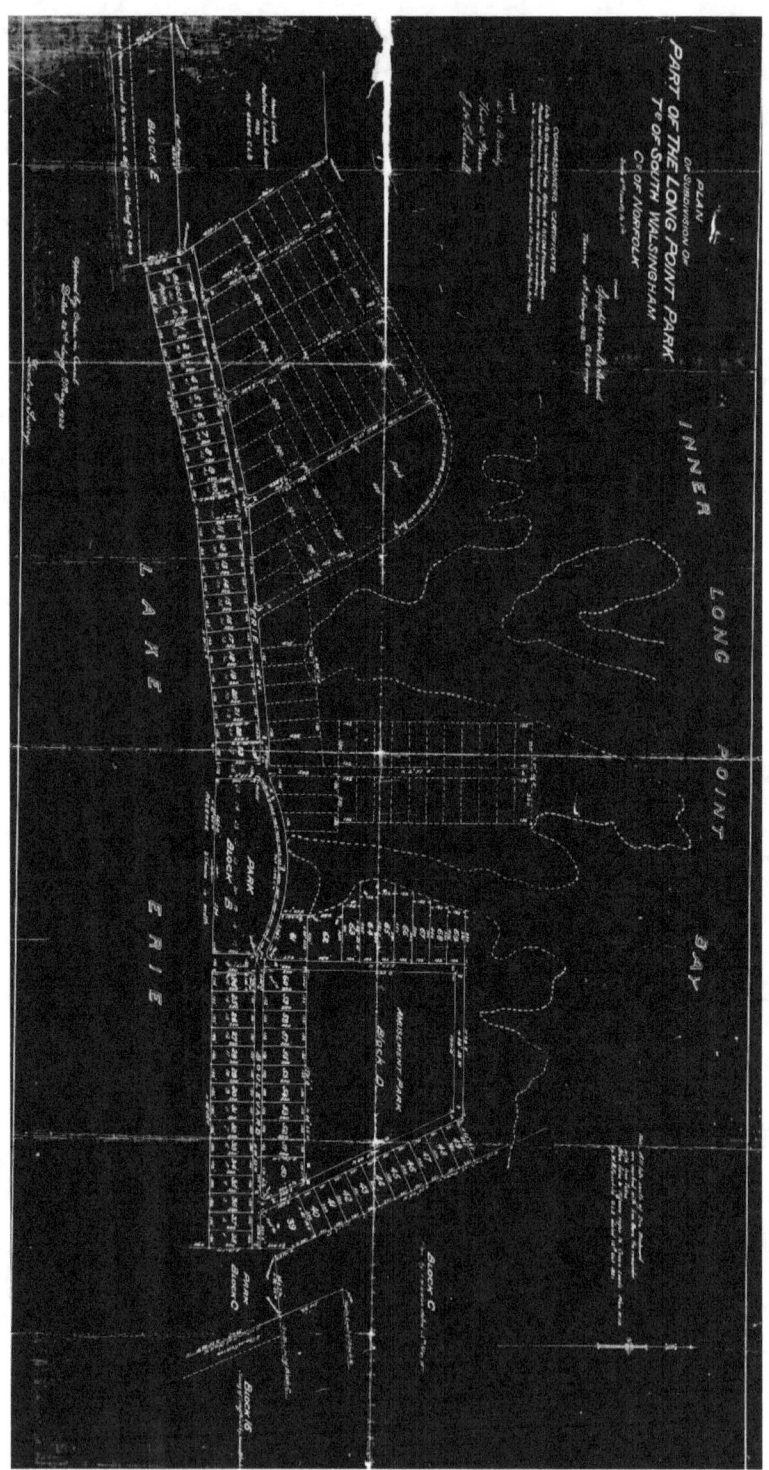

Figure 49. Original Long Point Park Commission subdivision plan.
Park Block B is the site of the Cottonwood campground.
Woodstock and Beach Avenue were not part of the original plan. (Speight & Van Nostrand, 1923)

For some reason, the three initial members of the Long Point Park Commission resigned in 1928. They were replaced by John Buck, Ken McCall, and Angus (Gus) Ferris. While the 1923 subdivision plan showed two natural inlets or ponds, it did not show or foresee any artificially built channels. In the 1930s, the new Commissioners oversaw the development of the first roads, lots, and channels. Excavated and dredged sand from the creation of the channels was used to build up the roads and lots. Dr. Edward Zavitz, who was by this time the Deputy Minister for Forestry, encouraged the Commissioners to have pine trees planted to reduce erosion and help stabilize the lots. Development was slow but steady. By 1933, about 30 premises had been built. In 1940, the number had increased to about 100. In 1956, one year after the Commission was disbanded, there were about 450. Over the last 50 years, the number has been steady at about 900.

Premiere Ferguson's prediction that the park would be a place for thousands of tourists to enjoy was never fully realized. By 1940, the Long Point Park Commission was administering a total of 561 acres, as the Long Point Company had yielded 141 acres west and north of the Old Cut Lighthouse. [158] Yet, just 15 acres were parkland. The Commission had fostered the development of a largely private community, not the forest preserve, and park envisioned in the provincial legislation of 1921. In a manner reflecting the private character of the place, in 1932 the Commission installed a stone-pillared gate on the mainland at the entrance to the causeway. I remember arriving there late on Friday nights in the family car with my parents and siblings. Pete Overbaugh, who was employed by the Commission, would come out dressed only partly in the uniform he had just pulled on. He would verify our identity, then allow us to pass through the gate to proceed down the causeway to the island.

Photo 33 Gated entrance to the Long Point Causeway, 1955. (Port Rowan Women's Institute)

---

[158] In 1940, there were two individuals on the Park Commission. One was Dr. D. A. Archibald of Port Rowan. The other was J.J. Miller of Simcoe. A third individual, D.C. Foster of Port Rowan, had resigned and was yet to be replaced.

Photo 34. Willow trees flanking the Long Point Causeway. J.E. Evans, 1959.
These non-native trees were planted by the Long Point Park Commission to increase the stability of the road shoulders.
(Courtesy, University of Western Ontario Archives)

Commissions are a highly concentrated form of governance because executive authority is combined with rulemaking authority. Moreover, the number of commissioners may be few, and their accountability limited because they are appointed as opposed to being elected. It is worth noting that the Long Point Park Commission not only fostered the development of a private community but restricted to whom leases would be given. Attesting to its constitution, and arbitrary exercise of jurisdiction, the Commission Secretary wrote a letter to leaseholders in 1941, reminding them of the following policy:

> "It has been the steady policy of the park Commission ever since its organization to prevent any infiltration by Jewish leaseholders, or for that matter any others, who for any reason, either political or religious, would be unable to unite in the general idea of a congenial gathering for the summer months." [268]

Antisemitism and xenophobia were pervasive in North America during the first half of the 20th century. It wasn't at all atypical for Jews to be excluded from Ontario resort communities. At Grand Bend on Lake Huron, the property covenants prevented both Jews and Blacks from acquiring property. Ontario courts upheld the covenants until 1950, when in a non-unanimous ruling, Canada's Supreme Court found the covenants unlawful. The Court's decision wasn't based on the discriminatory nature of the covenants, but rather a technicality.[273] The Long Point Park Commission's longstanding willingness to cast judgment "about any others, who for any reason, either political or religious, would be unable to unite in the general idea of a congenial gathering" leaves the question open whether individual leases were denied and if so to whom, or that the policy was pretentiousness.

Lifesaving Stations and the Old Cut Lighthouse

Shipwrecks were common on the sandbars off Long Point's south beach, particularly on high surf days during late autumn. Most of the wrecks occurred along the western part of the island. In many instances the consequences were tragic. People drowned when the yawls they tried to reach shore on capsized in the high surf. Occasionally, some would reach the largely uninhabited island, only to freeze to death. Long Point Company secretary/treasurer John I. MacKenzie found the frequent loss of life troubling.

The wrecks attracted cargo thieves, illegitimate wreckers, and curious trespassers. Eventually, legitimate insurance salvagers followed. All this activity was a nuisance and contrary to the island's status as a private game preserve. In 1877, the Directors of the Company petitioned the Canadian government asking that an additional lighthouse be built at the west end of Long Point. [229] They also asked that a lifesaving station be established. At the time, many of the members of the Company were influential Canadians, which likely contributed to the government's favorable response. The following year funds were allocated for the lighthouse. Construction was completed in August 1879 on land owned by the Company. The government appointed William Dickinson as keeper and allotted him five acres around the lighthouse for his livestock and a garden —land also owned by the Long Point Company. Although it was known simply as the West Lighthouse in its day, the structure later took on its current name as the Old Cut Lighthouse.

John MacKenzie took a special interest in promoting the creation of the lifesaving station. He not only advocated for the Long Point station but also for another at Port Colborne. He traveled to Buffalo where he personally examined the self-bailing, self-righting boats that were in use in the United States. The Canadian government subsequently chose Buffalo's Hingston Brothers to build the boats for Long Point and Port Colborne. Each was lapstraked cedar and weighed 1,100 pounds (500 kilograms). They measured 26 feet in length (7.9 meters) with a beam of six feet (1.8 meters) and were equipped with six oars. [274]

The Long Point boat was placed in a boathouse on the south beach just west of Courtright Ridge, making it the first lifesaving station on the Canadian side of the Great Lakes. MacKenzie encouraged the government to appoint William Leary, the head-keeper of the Long Point Company, as coxswain, and it complied.[159] He wouldn't serve long in the position. Three years later, Leary advised the Company that he wished to move to Manitoba. The federal government was granting farmland there and there were few restrictions on who could apply. Although the officers of the Company were disappointed to lose Leary, evidence indicates David Tisdale graciously assisted him in applying for a land grant.

Courtright Ridge was not a very practical location for a lifesaving boat because it was time consuming for some responders to get there. I wrote in the first edition of this book that after Leary relinquished his position, authorities relocated the lifeboat to a location west of Long Point and

---

[159] William Leary was likely recognized to be a competent mariner, as he owned the sloop, *Teal*.

appointed William Woodward of Port Rowan to be the new coxswain.[160] I also wrote that if a wreck occurred the keeper at the west lighthouse would summon the crew by shining a steady beam toward Port Rowan. [275] Recent research performed by a colleague demonstrates that the lifesaving boat was actually relocated to the village of Port Rowan. The relocation to the west of Long Point didn't occur until 1902.

Things didn't go smoothly for Woodward. During a gale the night of November 14th or 15th, the 300-ton barque *E. Fitzgerald*, carrying wheat, wrecked west of Long Point, leaving her crew in distress. After being notified of the wreck, Woodward set out on a 10-kilometre wagon journey westward from Port Rowan to evaluate the circumstances. He may have been informed that the ship's crew of seven had already perished after trying unsuccessfully to reach shore in a yawl. In any event, after observing the wreck offshore laden with ice, and the waves still high, Woodward decided there was no point taking any action. The lifeboat was far away, and the options were to deploy from Port Rowan and attempt a long journey through high seas or cart the 500-kilogram boat along the lakeshore road to a place from where it could be launched.

The *E. Fitzgerald* was an American vessel. During the days following the tragedy, newspapers in both Canada and the United States published dubious accounts of what had occurred. Woodward was disparaged. A frontpage article in the *New York Times* on November 27th reported that a government inquiry into the incident had commenced in Ottawa. The article closed with the sentence, "Woodward is reported as an incompetent man, whose first duty is to protect himself where danger presents itself."

Although the lifesaving boats were self-bailing and self-righting, courageously rowing a long distance through the waves off Long Point's south beach during a freezing gale would obviously have been a very hazardous proposition. Woodward vigorously defended himself, pointing out that the government had not yet appropriately outfitted his crew with life jackets, lifelines, or mortars.[161] Although he was eventually exonerated, Woodward was aggravated by the accusations against him, and he moved from Port Rowan to Vancouver where he manned the lighthouse near Stanley Park for many years. The government hired J. W. McCall to replace him as the coxswain of the Port Rowan crew.

Twenty years later, the government built a boathouse and living quarters on the beach just one kilometer west of Long Point. The location is known precisely because coordinates for the station were published in a 1902 Notice to Mariners. Interestingly, today that location is 150 metres offshore from Hastings Drive, a reminder of how far the lake has since encroached in the area. It is known that the crew were present full-time during the shipping season because the Notice to Mariners stated that it would no longer be necessary for the lighthouse keeper to shine his light toward Port Rowan when a wreck occurred.

In 1909, because the cut at the west end of Long Point was no longer navigable, authorities again relocated the lifesaving station. The new location was 32-kilometres to the

---

[160] William Woodward had been an early employee of the Long Point Company.
[161] Well-equipped mid-19th century lifesaving stations had mortars that could fire a rope from shore to the vessel. The rope could then be used to guide a lifeboat. Alternately, a sailor wearing a lifejacket or affixed to a buoy could hold on the rope and pull himself to shore.

east, on the south beach just 2-kilometres west of the island's tip. A full-time crew of eight men and a coxswain manned the facility during the shipping season. About two years later, the station was moved a short distance to its final location, which was on the north beach near the lighthouse that had been built in 1873.

Photo 35. The Lifesaving station at the east end of Long Point. Date Unknown. (Public Domain) [276]

By the turn of the century, the New Cut had shallowed and was no longer navigable. Sailing vessels were a rarity. Consequently, the government terminated the operation of the west lighthouse. Around 1917, it initiated activity aimed at disposing of the structure and its five associated acres by filing a plan for expropriation with the county land registry office.

Unbeknownst to the Long Point Company, the government put the property up for auction. Thomas Hancock, a Toronto lumber retailer, was the successful bidder.

Photo 36. The West Lighthouse (known today as the Old Cut lighthouse). Date unknown. (Public Domain)

When the Company became aware the property had been auctioned, it objected and requested the sale be nullified. The Minister for the Department of Marine and Fisheries was sympathetic to the Company's request. He agreed to cancel the expropriation plan and reverse the sale to Hancock, provided the Company put up a bond indemnifying the government from any action Hancock might bring. Hancock's deposit was refunded. However, the action to expropriate was never rescinded.

Almost five years later, in 1921, a subsequent government led by the United Farmers of Ontario party adopted a different posture. It expropriated the property and completed the sale to Hancock. The Company responded with a court filing that asserted expropriation might be appropriate if the property was going to be used for public purposes but was wholly inappropriate and illegal if the government was going to release the property to a private buyer, such as Hancock. The immediate result was a fiat against the government, awaiting relief. The Company then reached out to Hancock, suggesting it might be amenable to grant him a lease. Hancock rebuffed the initiative, retained legal counsel, and made it clear he would oppose the Company in any litigation. As time progressed, the Long Point Company's directors became increasingly wary of the potential for adverse publicity. Additionally, they were facing the possibility that their legal action might not be successful. Eventually, they accepted that they had a contest on their hands that might not be worth pursuing. It had taken years, but expropriation and closure of the sale of the five acres and the lighthouse were finally set to rest when title was transferred to Hancock in April of 1925. Soon after, the Ostrander family acquired the property from his estate. In 1998, the Westaway family purchased it and undertook a major renovation of the lighthouse.

Photo 37. Thomas Hancock. Unknown date. (Public Domain) [277]

Following the expropriation of the five acres, the Long Point Company still held a 141-acre tract west and north of the lighthouse. How that property, which flanks the Old Cut, came to be relinquished is a fascinating story related to the area's natural gas history and to the unrelenting ambition of an engineer from Niagara Falls named Harry Symmes.

Photo 38. The Old Cut lighthouse, c. 1925. (Public Domain)

Yielding of the Land Around the Old Cut Lighthouse

Before 1905, residences in Port Rowan were lit by oil lamps and candles. A few of the better buildings in town had acetylene lamps.[162] That year, Messrs. Killmaster, Buck, and Pearsall, formed The Port Rowan Natural Gas Company, Ltd., a stock company.[163,164] [278] [279] The company drilled gas wells and established the town's first distribution facility.[165]

At the same time, Harry Symmes, a graduate of the University of Toronto's School of Practical Science, who had first worked on the construction of hydroelectric power generation at Niagara Falls and on the electrification of Ontario's railways, was organizing the Volcanic Oil & Gas Company. He formed it to transport gas from the rich fields at Tilbury, Ontario, to the town of Chatham. The line Volcanic built was Canada's first cross-country gas pipeline. Symmes's vision went well beyond the use of natural gas for lighting and cooking. He wanted to see it used for electric power generation and for fueling industry. Accordingly, he aimed to expand the pipeline and sought additional capital. Long Point Company member Samuel Woodruff had died in 1904, and his son, Welland, was the recipient of a generous portion of his father's large estate. Symmes was married to Samuel Woodruff's daughter, Eloise. In his pursuit of capital, he reached out to his brother-in-law Welland Woodruff. Together with one other associate, they formed the Iroquois Pipeline Company with the objective of enlarging the pipeline from Tilbury to Chatham. [280] Symmes was on his way to becoming a major player in the oil and gas industry. For a short period, he claimed to be Canada's largest oil producer.

Seven years after the formation of the Port Rowan Natural Gas Company, it became understood that there was a sizeable reservoir of gas beneath the town and in the immediate vicinity. The consequence was a drilling frenzy. By 1912, the Oklahoma-based trade publication *Oil and Gas Journal* began reporting on the "Port Rowan Pool." Wildcatters started moving into the area, but most wells were sunk by the Dominion Natural Gas Co., a firm that dominated in Norfolk and Haldimand Counties.[166] While it had offices in Simcoe, and a name evoking Canadian ownership, Dominion was controlled by investors in Pittsburgh. Dominion didn't just drill that year. It took control of the Port Rowan Natural Gas Co. by purchasing two-thirds of its stock. It then upgraded the distribution plant in Port Rowan, turning it into a hub that serviced nearby Walsingham and St. Williams. [281] A year later, the Port Rowan Natural Gas Company and the Dominion Natural Gas Company offices were located in a Buffalo skyscraper, the Marine Bank Building.

---

[162] These included the Bay Cliff Hotel, the Bay View Club, the Baptist Church, & Pearsall House. [393] [394] [398] The acetylene was produced by onsite generators that reacted calcium carbide pellets with water.

[163] This was the same year drilling commenced at Selkirk, 37 miles east of Port Rowan. The Selkirk wells were so productive a pipeline was built to forward the gas to Brantford and Hamilton. Drilling was underway on the shore of Long Point Bay at St. Williams by 1908.

[164164] Other directors of the Port Rowan Natural Gas Co. were W.O. Franklin, J. Hanson, and E. Meek. The company was likely taken private in 1916.

[165] An earlier public stock company may have drilled for gas in Port Rowan as early as 1895. [453]

[166] The Dominion Natural Gas Co. hired contractors such as the Craise Bros. of Petrolia to conduct drilling in Port Rowan. Two individuals who labored on the wells were George Brown and Alex Holmes of Petrolia. Both had foreign drilling experience before working in Port Rowan. [470]

The Ontario government's GeoHub database identifies about 60 gas wells from Port Royal to St. Williams. There are many flanking Dedrick's Creek. A fee-based commercial database identifies additional wells beyond those in the government database, about 100.[167]. There may be others, because wells sunk by wildcatters that were not put into production may not be documented.

Photo 39. A drilling rig on the bank of Dedrick's Creek. (Public Domain) [282]

The extensive drilling activity and associated publicity attracted a shark from New York City named Henry Doherty. An oil and gas monopolist, Doherty acquired Dominion, its 786 Ontario wells, and every other natural gas distribution facility in Norfolk County. He then rolled the assets into an entity he named the Southern Ontario Gas Co. and made it a subsidiary of his giant continental holding entity, the Cities Service Co.[168] [283] [284]

Meanwhile, Harry Symmes's Volcanic Oil & Gas Co. merged with two other companies to form a new entity called Union Gas. The first headquarters was in Symmes's hometown of Niagara Falls. When he was not chosen for the new company's board, Symmes dropped his operational interest in Union Gas and formed his own firm, the Glenwood Oil and Gas Co.[169]

---

[167] The commercial database I used to ascertain the figure of 100 was WellDatabase®.
[168] Citgo is the descendent of Cities Service Company. Although recently owned by Venezuela, it has since been divested.
[169] Glenwood is a locale close to the shore of Lake Erie, near Port Alma.

Union Gas later relocated its offices to Chatham and dominated the industry in the southwest part of the province.

Symmes surmised the biggest pools of oil and gas were to be found beneath the waters of Lake Erie. He was the first to drill the lakebed, doing so by building caissons or cofferdams in the water offshore from Kingsville.[170] It was an innovative approach, but highly controversial. Two hundred fishermen and farmers petitioned the federal government to stop the drilling. [285] The fishermen asserted sulfur and salt from the gas wells would be detrimental to fish stocks, and they complained the caissons presented a navigation hazard. The farmers, for their part, were already collecting gas production royalties for wells on their land. Their concern was the entire industry might move offshore, causing them to lose revenue. The outcome was the government suspended the lease that permitted Symmes to drill offshore in the area. [286] He would need to test his theory elsewhere.

Aware of the ampleness of the "Port Rowan Pool," Symmes set his sights on Long Point. What better place for him to determine if bigger reservoirs of gas were to be found offshore? Instead of building caissons or cofferdams, as was necessary on the open lake near Kingsville, rigs could be towed across the winter ice on Long Point Bay, and wells could be easily drilled into the lakebed.

In 1913, through his solicitors, Symmes applied to the province for a lease to drill on the shore of Long Point and a short distance offshore. Interestingly, the application was submitted about one year after Symmes co-investor and brother-in-law, Welland Woodruff, became a member of the Long Point Company. Whether Woodruff had anything to do with Symmes's plan to drill on Long Point is uncertain, but chances are he did. Woodruff would likely have known that when the Long Point Company received title to its land in 1866, the government retained a shore reserve two chains in length around the outer perimeter of the island and it held the mineral rights to the reserve.[171]

> Reserving along the water's edge of Lake Erie a strip of land two chains in depth inland from the said water's edge for fishery purposes but granting always free access across the same to the lands in the rear thereof.

Symmes's lease application took the members of the Long Point Company by surprise. They retained solicitor W. W. Douglas to launch a protest with the Minister of Lands, Forests, & Mines. There was a sound basis for dispute. The Company pointed out that the language in its deed regarding the shore reserve mentioned just one activity —fishing. Additionally, the Company contended that oil and gas production would be wholly incompatible with the island's status as a game reserve.

Around the same time, the federal government envisioned that natural gas might be used to operate the lighthouse and heat the lifesaving station. It made plans to drill on or in the water

---

[170] A caisson is a dam, often circular. Once installed, it can be pumped free of water, thereby exposing dry ground.

[171] Two chain lengths is equivalent to 132 feet or 40.2 metres.

around the tip of Long Point. [287] An interesting question is whether Symmes had promoted this idea to the government.

What happened next is complicated, and all the details are not readily available. It is clear that the Company enjoyed early success when at first, the province denied Symmes's lease application. However, he was an affluent and relentlessly aggressive man, who had the backing of the huge Cities Service Co. Symmes continued to pursue a lease. The Long Point Company, even though comprised of wealthy and otherwise powerful men, had long been unpopular among the Ontario public. In 1916, the province, hell-bent on progress, reversed course and granted Symmes a lease to drill on the fishery reserve and out into the water for one quarter mile, the right to produce oil and gas, and permission —to lay whatever pipelines might be necessary.

Three months later, Symmes received approval from the government to assign his lease to Cities Service's subsidiary Dominion Natural Gas Company. Dominion then surprised the Long Point Company by informing it that it had secured the Symmes lease for the shore reserve. A bigger surprise was that Dominion was also seeking an additional lease from the Company that would allow it to drill on Long Point Company property beyond the shore reserve. - It is reasonable to assume the Long Point Company's members were displeased.

Both parties then entered joint negotiations with the government that went on for many months. The government, being highly interested in industrial development and having the upper hand, bullied the Company. Finally, in 1918 a compromise of sorts was reached. The Company agreed to lease the shore reserve from the government for an annual fee of $500. The government retained for itself the right to grant the Symmes lease —as assigned to Dominion Natural Gas Company, —to renew it, and to assign it to some other party should Dominion choose not to renew. A further term was more complicated, but it demonstrated how intent the government was to promote oil and gas production. The government agreed it would not issue additional leases for the shore reserve, provided the Long Point Company would agree to lease the reserve to further parties should they come forward. The Company was given the right to put provisions in any leases it granted that would make drilling and production less likely to interfere with the property being a game preserve.

Finding itself on the losing end of a lengthy dispute, in 1920 the Company gave a lease to Dominion Natural Gas Co. to drill on its land beyond the shore reserve. Dominion then spent about $100,000 drilling. All the wells that were sunk showed gas. Regardless of those somewhat positive results, Dominion ultimately decided producing gas on the island would not be as profitable as other opportunities it could apply its capital to. [288] It dropped the land lease the government had forced the Long Point Company to grant, and a few years later surrendered to the government the shore reserve lease as well.

So, what does the aforementioned drilling history have to do with the 141 acres of land west and north of the Old Cut lighthouse that the Company owned? Well, in 1929 the Long Point Park Commission, seeking to expand the park, sought to acquire further acreage. Recognizing once again that it was up against a powerful aspirant —a province armed with the power of eminent domain, the Company sought counsel. Harry Collier of St. Catharines, who had frequently served as Samuel Woodruff's personal lawyer and had handled his estate, agreed to take on the matter. After considering both the legal issues and the political environment, Collier advised the Company that it faced a formidable contest. Accepting its hand was weak, the Company asked Collier to negotiate what he could from the province.

Negotiations dragged on for three years. Finally, in 1932 an agreement was reached whereby the Company yielded its 141 acres to the province in return for revisions to its lease for the shoreline reserve around the perimeter of Long Point. The lease amendments gave the Company the sole right to restrict or grant oil and gas leases for the shoreline, while the Crown retained the right to issue commercial fishing leases thereon.

Following the settlement, the Long Point Park Commission set about in earnest developing the acreage around the lighthouse. It built roads, and in 1937 dredged the inlet that is today referred to as the Old Cut (but was officially named Lighthouse Creek.) The channel was widened by further dredging a few years later.

The 1920s

In the early 1920s the Long Point Company authorized logging of maple and cedar in the areas around Townsend and Cedar Creek Ridges. [168] What the impetus was is uncertain. There had been many forest fires on Long Point, and the logging was likely a thinning program designed to reduce spreading in the event of fire.

After head keeper Walker Ferris died in 1921, his son Hanson assumed the head keeper's position. The Company was never averse to employees having avocations to supplement their income. For Walker Ferris it was beekeeping, and for Hanson it was maple syrup. He established a collection, cooking, and filling station on Squires Ridge. The operation, which is reputed to have been conducted on a large scale, was overseen by William Wells. How many years it operated is uncertain. Damage from the forest fire of 1933 was likely the reason production ended.

Ducks were becoming scarcer by the 1920s and governments responded with conservation measures. Ontario imposed a daily limit of 25 ducks and a seasonal per-person maximum of 200. The Company protested the new limits but amended its field rules to comply. Restrictions imposed by migratory bird conservation laws had ended the sale of wild ducks. Those that members didn't ship home for their own consumption or for gifting to friends were distributed gratis among the local community. Anyone shipping a duck across the border had to fill out a customs declaration stating the duck had been defeathered.

As for new members, family linkages, inter-mutual business directorships, and other shared interests run deep in the Long Point Company. After Welland Woodruff died in 1920, his shares passed to Reuben Leonard. Leonard had founded and was president of the Coniagas Mines in Cobalt, Ontario, and the Coniagas Reduction Company in Thorold. Welland Woodruff was an investor in Leonard's ventures and a vice-president of the Thorold business. St. Catharines lawyer Harry Collier, a familiar face around the Long Point Company, served as the secretary for both Coniagas companies. Ore from the mine in Cobalt was shipped to Thorold because electricity from the stations at Niagara Falls was plentiful and inexpensive. There, valuable silver, nickel, & cobalt were rendered from the ore by electrolytic reduction.[172]

Company president George Richards died in 1922, leaving Thomas Hathaway and Augustus Hemenway the only remaining members from Boston. Consequently, the annual meetings of the Company shifted to New York City, and the first meeting held there took place at the University Club. Two years later, in 1924, three more New Yorkers became shareholders. Two were J.P Morgan & Co. partners Dwight Morrow and Thomas Cochran. J.P. Morgan & Co. had facilitated the creation of International Harvester, and the third new member was the former International Harvester treasurer Richard Howe, who had married the daughter of the conglomerate's co-founder, William Deering.

---

[172] The name Coniagas was derived from the symbols of four metals as they appear in the Periodic Table of Elements. Namely, Co (Cobalt), Ni (Nickel), Ag (Silver), and As (Arsenic). These elements were all components of the ore that was shipped from the mine to Thorold, Ontario for processing.

The business activities of J.P. Morgan & Company were contentious due to John Pierpont Morgan's efforts, starting in the 1880s, to consolidate competing companies in the same industry into single entities. Examples of sectors where Morgan facilitated consolidation are steel, railroads, and ocean shipping lines. He was highly instrumental in the creation of United States Steel. With the arrival of the Progressive Era, public concern about concentration in industrial ownership strengthened, and J.P. Morgan & Company was caught up in the controversy.[173] The bank attracted the attention of terrorists, or anarchists as they were known at the time. In 1920, a terrorist parked a horse-drawn wagon loaded with a large bomb in front of the bank's Wall Street headquarters. Detonation of the device killed more than 30 people, including two J. P. Morgan & Co. employees. Hundreds of others were injured. The crime was never solved. [289]

Thomas Cochran and Dwight Morrow were very influential politically. They were personally close to Calvin Coolidge. Cochran and Coolidge were classmates when they were teenagers attending Phillips Academy. Coolidge knew Morrow from their time at Amherst College. Both men played significant roles in promoting Coolidge to be the Republican vice-presidential candidate. More than school friendships were at play. Jack Morgan, the son of deceased John Pierpont Morgan and the new leader of the firm, also cozied up to Coolidge.[174] All the firm's partners expected that Coolidge's stridently pro-business, anti-regulatory, and laissez-faire politics would benefit them. The roaring twenties over which Coolidge ultimately presided when he assumed the Presidency would indeed be a sparingly regulated, unrestrained, and frothy era that presented the eleven partners of the J. P. Morgan firm an almost unrestricted opportunity to line their pockets. The Morgans themselves continued to enjoy financial success, and the other partners in the firm who had not initially had great wealth such as Cochran and Morrow, accumulated their own large fortunes. Late in his second term as President, Coolidge nominated Morrow to be his Ambassador to Mexico. [290]

Aviator Charles Lindbergh visited the Long Point area in July 1927, just two months after his celebrated trans-Atlantic crossing. He had taken a weekend break during a flight tour throughout the United States that was sponsored by the Daniel Guggenheim Fund for the Promotion of Aeronautics. After landing in Buffalo, Lindbergh traveled by car to Turkey Point where he spent several days relaxing. He swam, fished, and sailed on Long Point Bay, and tried his arm punting in the Turkey Point marsh.

Lindbergh would later marry Anne Morrow, the daughter of Long Point Company member Dwight Morrow. He met her after he flew non-stop from Washington, D.C. to Mexico City, where her father was serving as the U.S. ambassador. Although widely admired for his flying achievements, Lindbergh's opinions on some topics have made him a subject of controversy in modern times. Despite this, he also had a lesser-known side as a conservationist who cared about the environment and wildlife. He served on the advisory board of the Nature Conservancy and was a director of the International World Wildlife Fund. In 1964, Lindbergh wrote:

---

[173] The Progressive Era is generally considered to have run from 1896 to 1917.
[174] Jack Morgan held a 25% interest in J.P. Morgan & Co. His son Junius held 5%. Henry, his other son, presumably held 5% as well.

I realized more clearly facts that man should never overlook: that the construction of an airplane, for instance, is simple when compared to the evolutionary achievement of a bird; that airplanes depend upon an advanced civilization, and that where civilization is most advanced, few birds exist. I realized that if I had to choose, I would rather have birds than airplanes. [291]

Photo 40. Charles Lindbergh and Phillip Love punting in the Turkey Point Marsh, July 30 weekend, 1927. [292] (Public Domain)

Photo 41. Charles Lindbergh on board (stern-port side) the yacht Lightnin' on Long Point Bay, July 30 weekend, 1927. [292] (Public Domain)

Thomas Cochran had distinguished himself when he attended Yale by playing football and serving as editor of the *Yale Record*. These activities and his leadership ability led to him being "tapped" for Skull and Bones membership.[175] After graduating in 1894, he returned to his home state of Minnesota to take on the role of head coach of the Golden Gophers football team. Eight years later, he moved to New York City where he founded the Ardlsey Hall Co., a real estate investment firm. By 1910, he was a vice-president of the Astor Trust Company; by 1917 he was a senior partner in J. P. Morgan & Company, a position he retained until his death in 1936.[176]

Cochran happened upon good fortune and bad. His only child passed away on the day of her birth, and his wife died shortly afterwards. He was greatly impacted and never remarried. Nostalgic, he found comfort in philanthropy and took on a rather silent, but less than passive role in the further development of Phillips Academy, the preparatory school he had attended alongside Coolidge. He would shower virtually his entire fortune on the school. Most of his gifts funded new or improved infrastructure. Never a collector himself, Cochran anonymously arranged the purchase of many pieces of art. All were forwarded to the Addison Gallery of American Art, a facility on campus that Cochran had paid to construct.

It was Cochran who introduced Dr. Joseph Wheelwright, a surgeon who was one of the founders of Doctor's Hospital where Cochran was president, and Junius Morgan, grandson of John Pierpont Morgan to Long Point.[177] He invited them to be his guests in 1926. Company president William Barnum had just passed away, and Cochran was seeking a new member. Junius' Morgan's father, Jack, had hunted at Long Point, but this would be Junius' first attempt at duck hunting.[178] Cochran gave Morgan a list of gear to purchase, and they agreed to meet at Cochran's apartment that evening. When Morgan arrived, Cochran introduced him to Dr. Wheelwright. Notwithstanding their lack of duck hunting experience, Morgan and Wheelwright would soon become the next generation of Long Point Company leaders. [293]

The party boarded an overnight train in Manhattan and arrived in Waterford, Ontario, the next morning. From there, they traveled by car to Port Rowan. Because it was Sunday, there was no hunting. Curious to see more of Long Point, Morgan and Wheelwright pulled a punt from a boathouse and paddled deep into the marsh. They ventured too far, too late, and then struggled to find their way back, arriving at the cottages after dark. They were met by relieved, but annoyed members and staff who had been mustering a search party.[179]

The two guests arrived late to the dining room, where the members were already eating. In his memoir, Morgan recalled the mood being "grim." No one offered them a drink; they found themselves quite uncomfortable. Morgan's reaction to his experience in the dining room may not

---

[175] Inductees to the Skull and Bones Society learned they had been invited to join by being tapped on the shoulder from behind by a member.

[176] Cochran was also a partner in J. P. Morgan's associate firm, Drexel & Co., and London-based Morgan-Grenfell.

[177] The founding vision for Doctor's Hospital was it would offer premium care and accommodate patients in hotel-like comfort. As such, it was where wealthy New Yorkers sought care. Founded in 1929, it was folded into the Beth Israel Medical Center in 1987. The original building was torn down in 2005.

[178] J. P. Morgan Sr. never visited Long Point. However, his son, Jack, did. [293] On at least one occasion, J. P. Morgan's private railcar was seen at the Port Rowan train station. [390]

[179] ibid

have just been one of mere hurt self-pride. He concluded the ambiance was undignified, and he may well have felt insulted. In his Long Point memoir, he wrote:

> I well remember that when we were walking back from the dining room that night the Doctor and I agreed that if ever he and I had anything to do with the Company the atmosphere in the dining room was going to be a whole lot different from what it then was.[180]

Wheelwright and Morgan must have been quite taken by Long Point. Wheelwright acquired the shares from William Barnum's estate in time for the next hunting season. Junius would get his chance two years later. Barnum had been the president of the Company at the time of his death. The members elected Henry Sage to succeed him. Just two years into Sage's tenure, a dispute arose among the members and Sage resigned from the Company.[181] He sold his shares to J. P. (Jack) Morgan who assigned them to his son, Junius.

John Hay Whitney had just joined the Company a year earlier, following the death of his father Payne Whitney. He was only in his mid-twenties. In 1930, Whitney suggested surgeon Joseph Wheelwright should be the next president. He wrote:

> The Long Point Company is in great need of some directing at this time and it occurred to me that Doctor Joseph Wheelwright would be the man to take charge and I am writing to him by this mail asking if he will do so. [294]

Whitney would eventually have a great many business interests. He and his cousin Sonny Whitney invested in a young chemical engineer's innovative photographic technology called Technicolor. [182] Convinced the technology would be groundbreaking, Whitney financed Hollywood's first color movies. They were not blockbusters, but Whitney soon found success. As the financier behind Selznick International Pictures, and its chairman, he demanded a reluctant David Selznick produce the movie *Gone with the Wind*.

The members subsequently did elect Dr. Wheelwright president of the Company at the annual meeting that year. Effective leadership would be needed —the Company was heading into trying times.

---

[180] ibid
[181] ibid
[182] Technicolor was founded by MIT graduates Herbert Kalmus and Daniel Comstock. Kalmus obtained a Ph.D. in chemistry from the University of Zurich and taught at Queens University in Kingston, Ontario, prior to forming Technicolor.

Photo 42. Joseph Wheelwright. (Public Domain. [295]

The Parched 1930s

In 1932, there were just 15 active members in the Long Point Company. One new member was high-profile New York City realtor William Wheelock. He had assembled the property for Penn Station, Central Post Office, the second Waldorf Astoria Hotel, and several department stores such as Gimbel Brothers. Only two members were Canadians. They were Sam McLaughlin, the president of General Motors Canada, and William Woodruff of St. Catharines. Junius Morgan had likely recruited McLaughlin. They were acquainted, as both men served on the board of General Motors Corporation. Junius's brother, Henry Morgan, had also joined the Company. Among the Americans members, five were neighbors who had grand estates on Long Island's Gold Coast. The shares of Augustus Hemenway and Dwight Morrow were tied up by their estates.

The stock market crash of 1929 and the Great Depression that followed created concern that the underwriting activities of a few large institutions, and particularly J. P. Morgan & Company, were putting the bank deposits of the general public at undue risk.[183] The defeat of President Herbert Hoover and the election of Franklin Roosevelt facilitated the passage of the Banking Act of 1933, otherwise known as the Glass-Steagall Act. The legislation forced the separation of investment banking from commercial banking. Banks that accepted general deposits from the public could no longer engage in the business of underwriting equity offerings.[184] Harold Stanley had replaced Dwight Morrow as a partner in J. P. Morgan & Co. in 1927 when Morrow accepted the position of U.S. Ambassador to Mexico. After the passage of the Glass-Steagall Act, Stanley and Henry Morgan chose to separate from J. P. Morgan and Co. and pursue investment banking exclusively. They formed Morgan Stanley in 1935. Harold Stanley was admitted to the Long Point Company two years later.

Junius Morgan, who remained with J.P. Morgan and Co., recruited prominent Wall Street lawyer Wilton Lloyd-Smith to the Long Point Company. While many Company members had law degrees, Lloyd-Smith was the rare member who actually practiced as an attorney. In his memoir about Long Point, Morgan credited Lloyd-Smith for working with attorney Francis Reid of Simcoe to address issues with the Company's complex land titles and leases.[185]

Wilton Lloyd-Smith was himself well-to-do, but it was his wife Marjorie who possessed great wealth. She was the daughter of Canadian-born Arthur Fleming, who had amassed a fortune in the United States from timber and mining. Marjorie and her father's donations provided the land and money for the construction of the California Institute of Technology (Cal Tech) campus in

---

[183] When underwriting, J.P. Morgan & Co. would reduce its own risk through syndication with smaller banks. Sometimes directors of these banks were also directors of J.P. Morgan & Co.

[184] The separation restrictions imposed by the Glass-Steagall Act were later tempered. In 1999, the Act was repealed allowing banks that accept consumer deposits to once again make loans that may be risky. Retail depositors have limited protection from a potential bank collapse through deposit insurance. The merits and disadvantages of separating investment and commercial banking remain a matter of debate.

[185] Francis Reid was a secretary/treasurer of the Company, not a member.

Pasadena, where they were living at the turn of the century. [186] Prior to their donations, the university occupied only rented facilities.

The first challenge to confront the Company in the 1930s came in the form of a fire that started in a boathouse. The conflagration swept through four cottages, including those of Sam McLaughlin and William Woodruff. Many valuable antique furnishings were lost. [296] Later, the same year, a fire on Courtright Ridge burned a thousand acres. [297] There was a fire on Squire's Ridge as well.

There had been no heavy logging on the island for half a century. The Company resumed logging the year following the fires. Although staff wages were cut slightly when the Depression took hold the Company's motivation for the resumption of logging was not likely financial. Fire-damaged timber was removed, and the trees along the ridges were thinned to make it less likely future fires would spread. A temporary sawmill placed on Squire's Ridge was used to cut the logs into lumber, which was then hauled to the south beach. The Jeep trails that run across the ridges today are former logging roads. Some of the pine two-by-fours (which were rough and un-planed) found use for framing the cottages that were just starting to be built in Long Point Park. Logging continued until 1936.

The biggest challenge the Company faced during the decade was that there were few ducks to shoot, because the marsh dried out. (Photo 43) The same weather pattern that created the Dust Bowl led to lower levels in the Great Lakes. In 1934, the level in Lake Erie was the lowest in recorded history —about 1.2 metres below the high level. In his memoir, Junius Morgan recalled how he walked from The Cottages to where Deep Pond and Center Pond had been, kicking up dust along the way. [293] A further disappointment was that the Company had planted wild rice and celery in the marsh just three years earlier, only to have the effort fail due to the drought.

Another major factor that led to the decline of ducks was the widespread draining of wetlands to create agricultural land. Fledglings need access to some kind of pond to survive. A foundation named More Game Birds in America, Inc. began studying duck decline in 1930. It vigorously lobbied the government to address the issue. President Roosevelt was sympathetic. In 1933, he announced the creation of the President's Committee on Wildlife Restoration. The committee quickly produced a report, and a few months later, the United States funded an $8,500,000 wetlands restoration program managed by the United States Biological Survey. The following year, Congress passed the Migratory Bird Hunting Stamp Act. If anyone 16 years of age or older wanted to hunt migratory waterfowl, they had to purchase a stamp. Ninety percent of the revenue was allocated to conservation measures.

In 1935, the More Game Birds Foundation completed a scientific census which concluded there had been an 80% reduction in the population of ducks since the beginning of the century. [298] The United States Biological Survey concluded the figures were even worse. More Game Birds concluded that the duck population could only be substantially increased if wetland restoration not only in the United States but also in Canada. (Most of the continent's ducks hatch their young in Canada's prairie provinces.) However, U.S. law prohibited government conservation funds from

---

[186] Arthur Fleming later left his entire estate to Cal Tech.

being used outside the country. The More Game Birds Foundation concluded there was an urgent need to raise funds privately to get projects underway north of the border. It underwrote the formation and operation of two not-for-profit corporations, Ducks Unlimited and Ducks Unlimited (Canada.) Private donations raised in the United States could be used in either country, thereby addressing the critical circumstances on the Canadian prairies. Over the next few years Ducks Unlimited completed more than 100 wetland creation projects. Robert Winthrop, an American who joined Long Point Company in 1937, is believed to have been a major benefactor of Ducks Unlimited (Canada). He was the managing director of the Long Point Company for 34 years and he also served as a president of Ducks Unlimited.

Photo 43. The Marsh Center, located about one mile south of The Cottages. (Public Domain) [295]

Needless to say, duck hunting was dismal at the Long Point Company in 1934. The managing director at the time, Louis Thompson, was frustrated and left for home.[187] Junius Morgan, his brother, Henry, and Wilton Lloyd-Smith wondered how to make the best of an unpleasant situation.[188] They decided to declare "summer rules," which allowed them to invite their wives to Long Point. They did so by telephone, apparently with success. Morgan later wrote

---

[187] ibid
[188] Sam McLaughlin and Joseph Wheelwright were present as well.

this was the first time since the Company's founding that women guests had visited the cottages during the hunting season.[189]

Junius Morgan established the tradition of hosting members to the cottage he shared with Wilton Lloyd-Smith for before-dinner cocktails. The cottage became known as the "Sin Center" a name given to it by Horatio Hathaway Jr. When Mrs. Morgan later visited Long Point, she thought the bar in the cottage was shabby, so she sketched a design for a new one. Punter Charlie Reeves built and installed it.

The last remaining member from Boston, Horatio Hathaway Jr., dropped out the following year. His shares went to Marshall Field III, the heir to a Chicago department store fortune who happened to be Lloyd-Smith's next-door neighbor. Their Gold Coast estates on Long Island were beside each other. Although they were next-door neighbors, visiting would require some travel as Field's estate exceeded 1,000 acres. Today the acreage is the Caumsett State Historic Park Preserve.

Photo 44. From left to right, Henry Morgan, Louise, Morgan (spouse of Junius,) Wilton Lloyd-Smith, Catherine Morgan (spouse of Henry,) Junius Morgan, Marjorie Lloyd-Smith (knitting.) 1934. (Public Domain) [295]

During the week, discussions occurred about the state of the parched-out marsh. Company president Dr. Joseph Wheelwright proposed creating canals that would help reflood the area should the water rise in future years. His suggestion found favor, and Wilton Lloyd-Smith then retained an engineering firm named the New York Sewage Disposal Co. to design a network of channels. An engineer from the company by the name of Dobson expeditiously traveled to Long Point where he sketched out a plan. Sam McLaughlin offered to procure the needed dredging equipment.

---

[189] ibid

The following year, Lloyd-Smith became the managing director and the Company commenced dredging. The first channel completed was aptly named the Wheelwright Canal. It ran west then south from The Cottages. (Photos 45 & 46) Over the next few years, further dredging completed tens of miles of additional channels.

Photo 45. The Wheelwright Channal, the Company's first, was dug in 1935. It extends west then south from the Company's headquarters. (Public Domain) [295]

Photo 46. The Wheelwright Channel. c. 1935. (Public Domain) [295]

Another event that occurred during the hunting lapse of 1934 was Lloyd-Smith requesting that his flying boat, the *Rubber Duck* be brought to Long Point.[190] Steve Parkinson, his personal pilot, flew the aircraft from Long Island. Two passengers who went for sightseeing flights around Long Point were Hanson Ferris and his wife.

Lloyd-Smith enjoyed photography, and he used his Leica camera to compose quite a few pictures that year, some of which he compiled into a book which he gave to the other members during the following year's Christmas season.[191]

Photo 47. The "Rubber Duck" departing Cottage Creek. 1934. (Public Domain) [295]

---

[190] The *Rubber Duck* was a four-place Keystone-Loening Commuter.
[191] Company members typically registered their books with the U.S. Copyright Office. Lloyd-Smith did not register his.

Photo 48. Pilot Steve Parkinson prepares to take punter Lou Snooks for his first aircraft flight. 1934. (Public Domain) [295]

Photo 49. The eastern tip of Long Point, 1934 (Public Domain) [295]

Photo 50. The eastern tip of Long Point. 1934. (Public Domain) [295]

Photo 51. Long Point's ridges and Ryerson's Island. 1934. (Public Domain) [295]

Marshall Field and Wilton Lloyd-Smith were affected by the utility of aircraft, particularly flying boats which the press referred to as air yachts. [192] Lloyd-Smith was among the first to use a flying boat to commute from a Long Island estate to Wall Street. Both men joined the Long Island Aviation Country Club, where they socialized with like-minded wealthy individuals and the aviation leaders of the day. [193] A group formed at the club to visualize an improved, grander flying boat. Among them were Charles Deeds, co-founder of the Pratt & Whitney company and president of United Aircraft Exports Corporation; Robert McCormick, owner of the Chicago Tribune; Cornelius Vanderbilt Whitney, and Long Point Company members Henry Morgan, Roland Harriman, Marshall Field, and Wilton Lloyd-Smith. [194] [299] Other members of the group were Captain Boris Sergievsky of Sikorsky Aircraft, Powell Crosby, and Garfield Wood. Under the management of Lloyd-Smith, the group funded a syndicate that reached out to Grover Loening to design and build the new aircraft. Loening however, had already sold his aircraft company and invested some of the proceeds in the newly formed Grumman company. Although he sketched out a preliminary design, he asked the group to work with Leroy Grumman to build it.

Roy Grumman accepted the assignment. Production of three G-21 Goose flying boats, the largest aircraft Grumman had yet undertaken, and the first with twin engines, commenced at Bethpage, N.Y., in late 1936. The aircraft had a design range of 1,300 kilometres miles at a speed of 174 knots. The first test flight occurred in May 1937. Two months later, Lloyd-Smith and Marshall Field took delivery of it as co-owners. [195] The second aircraft went to Henry Morgan. The base cost of each aircraft was $60,000, and a crew of two professional pilots was necessary. At a time when North America was experiencing the throes of the Great Depression, this was a considerable amount of money to spend in such a manner.

Junius Morgan wrote that the amphibious aircraft made traveling to Long Point much easier. What had previously been a long journey from New York was reduced to three to four hours. [293] He acknowledged that weather was sometimes a challenge that caused delays and told of one such occasion when the Company's board was to hold a formal meeting at Long Point. They were waiting for managing director Wilton Lloyd-Smith to arrive. By means of a telephone call they learned the weather in New York was preventing his departure. It was raining, the ceilings were low and the visibility poor. When a break in the weather occurred, Lloyd-Smith's pilots called him to rush to the plane. The members at Long Point were informed he was on his way. A few hours later, Lloyd-Smith stepped onto the dock at The Cottages still in his dressing gown and pajamas.

---

[192] The Lloyd-Smith's Gold Coast estate named Kenjockety was a wedding present from Mrs. Lloyd-Smith's father, Arthur Fleming. While the estate was being constructed, Mrs. Smith and Henry Davison had the 60-foot yacht *Argo* built. Such yachts were crewed and their owners occasionally used them to commute to Manhattan. [368]

[193] Some of the leaders in aviation at the time who were members of the Long Island Aviation Country Club were Leroy Grumman, Walter Beech, Charles Deeds, Sherman Fairchild, Elmer Sperry, and Grover Loening.

[194] United Aircraft Exports Corporation was the predecessor to today's United Technologies Corp.

[195] The first aircraft carried registration number NC16910. The second NC16911, and the third NC16912. [301]

Two estates were cleared in 1935, allowing new members to join. The shares in Harry Payne Whitney's estate passed to his son-in-law, Barklie Henry. Edward Roland Harriman acquired the shares in Augustus Hemenway's estate. His father had controlled the Union Pacific railroad and served as its chairman and president. The younger Harriman eventually assumed the role as the chief executive of the railway, albeit somewhat reluctantly. He was more interested in his position as a vice-president of Brown Brothers & Harriman. It was Harriman who took delivery of the third flying boat to come off the Grumman production line.

Photo 52. Grumman G-21 owned by W. Lloyd-Smith and M. Field, at Manhattan Skyport
The large building in the right background is 120 Wall St. The skyscraper is the Cities Service building.
(Margarette Bourke-White, LIFE Magazine, 1937)

Photo 53. The Grumman G-21 co-owned by W. Lloyd-Smith and M. Field, at the Manhattan Skyport.
(Margarette Bourke-White, LIFE Magazine, 1937)

Photo 54. Grumman G-21 cabin. (Public Domain) (Margarette Bourke-White, LIFE Magazine, 1937)

Photo 55. Grumman G-21 owned by W. Lloyd-Smith and M. Field clearing Canadian customs at Port Dover.
A uniformed pilot is sitting on the aircraft nose. 1937.
(Clayton Scofield family collection)

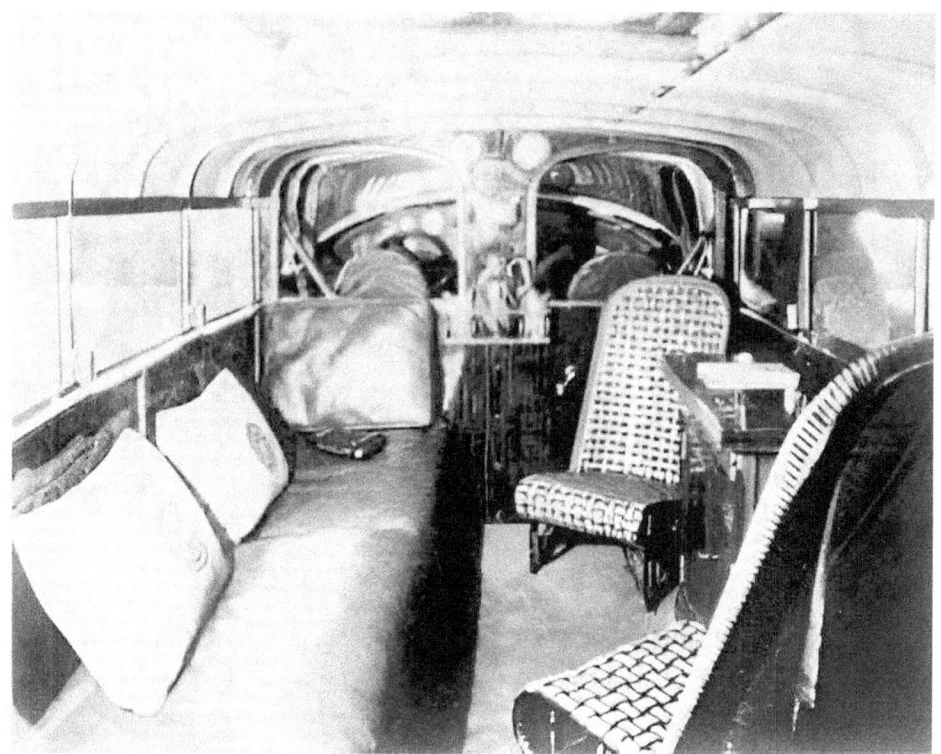

Photo 56. The interior of John Hay Whitney's Sikorsky flying boat. c. 1928. (Public Domain)

177

Discussion of the Long Point Company's members from the 1930s wouldn't be complete without mentioning Labrador Retrievers because certain members were instrumental in popularizing what was at the time an uncommon breed. Dogs were an on-again-off-again prospect at the Company throughout its history. Mostly off —because members generally felt that dogs caused ducks to avoid the marsh. Moreover, a dog isn't a practical skiff passenger. Occasionally, a special exception would allow a single member to bring his dog.

Members did not just hunt ducks at Long Point, however. They hunted elsewhere where assistance from dogs was more practical. Their preferred breed was the Labrador Retriever. Some of the members and their spouses bred Labs on their Gold Coast estates. They included Henry Morgan, Richard Howe, and Roland Harriman. Mrs. Marshall Field and Mrs. Harriman kenneled their Labs at Wilton Lloyd-Smith's estate. Mrs. Field was the founding president of the Labrador Retriever Club, and her next-door neighbor Wilton Lloyd-Smith was the first secretary/treasurer. (He was also on the board of The Seeing Eye, Inc., a non-profit organization still operating today that performs research and trains guide dogs for use by the blind.) The kennel at Lloyd-Smith's estate was as large as an average family home. (Photo 57) Comprehensive information about the structure and its associated facilities appears in a 1932 American Kennel Club article. [300]

Photo 57. The kennel on Wilton Lloyd-Smith's estate. [300]

The first field competitions of the breed occurred under the auspices of the Labrador Retriever Club in 1931. Thereafter, they were held annually. Because the dog's owners were such prominent individuals, the competitions were conspicuous Gold Coast social events. The New York Times covered them with full-page articles that included photographs of the owners wearing their finest sporting attire. The newspaper coverage brought considerable public attention to the breed. Today the Labrador Retriever is North America's most popular dog, probably because of its gentle disposition, rather than its swimming and retrieving ability.

The Long Point Company's keepers hunted regularly so that they could eat meat at their isolated shanties. When he was the Company steward, Hanson Ferris was known to give keepers a Labrador Retriever. Both for companionship and to retrieve the ducks they shot.

The 1940s and the Impact of World War II

The commencement of World War II abruptly ended public use of flying boats. The Royal Canadian Airforce (RCAF) was anxious to acquire the aircraft for search and rescue operations. Accordingly, Henry Morgan and Roland Harriman donated or sold their aircraft to the RCAF in 1940. [301] Wilton Lloyd-Smith, who had long suffered from brucellosis acquired during a safari to India, died the same year. The flying boat he and Marshall Field jointly owned was sold to an oil company. As part of the war effort, Grumman developed a military version of the aircraft and many were built.

Joseph Wheelwright stepped down as company president in 1940 and Junius Morgan was elected to replace him. Wheelwright had a stroke while at Long Point the following season and passed away in his cottage. Morgan later wrote, "…he died peacefully at the place he liked better than any other." [293]

Childs Frick became a member in 1940. His father, Henry Clay Frick, had been a coke manufacturer who supplied Andrew Carnegie's steel business in Pittsburgh. In 1881 he and Carnegie merged their businesses. In the ensuing years, Carnegie's health deteriorated. and he began spending his winters in New York and his summers in Scotland. His brother Tom managed much of the integrated business. Tom died in 1886, and leadership of the Carnegie Steel company fell to Frick. Compared to Carnegie, Frick was an even tougher, hard-nosed manager. He cut wages and increased working hours. His darkest side was apparent during the summer of 1892 when he hired hundreds of armed Pinkerton detectives to confront locked-out steelworkers. A gun battle left six steelworkers and a few Pinkerton detectives dead. A month later, Frick was shot in his office, the victim of an assassination attempt. He survived, and by 1918 Forbes magazine concluded he had become the second wealthiest individual in the United States, only John Rockefeller was wealthier.

Childs Frick led a very different life. He briefly assisted his father in the steel business after graduating from Princeton but found it not to his liking. He was inducted into the Signal Corps during World War I and stationed in California. While there, he took university science courses and became fascinated by paleontology. After completing military service, Frick shunned business altogether. He joined the staff of the American Museum of Natural History and later applied his Gilded Age inheritance as a huge benefactor and trustee of the institution. He was given the honorary title, Curator of late Tertiary and Quaternary Mammals. Over the course of his life, the expeditions he led or funded gathered more than 300,000 artifacts, an individual attainment that will never be replicated. Like other Long Point Company members of the era, Frick lived on an imposing Gold Coast estate named Clayton, that his father paid for. The former estate is now the home of the Nassau County Museum of Art.

Frick was one of the rare Company members who authored a book about Long Point. His book is unusual in three respects. He wrote under a pseudonym, namely *A Long Pointer.* Second, the book is entirely written in verse. Third, it is the only member's book dedicated to the

Company's punters. Comprised of three poems and a few illustrations, it is exceedingly rare, suggesting few if any punters received a copy.

Frick's name appears nowhere in the book. Perhaps that reflected a concern for personal security and he may have preferred his identity be unknown when he traveled to places such as Long Point. Frick did use his name when he registered his book with the copyright office in Washington.

Copyright renewal was required to retain long-term rights during the era when Frick registered his book. No renewal was ever submitted. Consequently, Frick's book has passed into Public Domain. Two of the three poems from his book, Long Point Glimpses and Oh Don't Forget Your Gear, are reproduced in Appendix B, together with a few illustrations.

Frick wouldn't have had the companionship of some of the Company's members and usual guests when he wrote his poems at Long Point in 1942. The United States had entered World War II. Reserve officer Junius Morgan was serving as the lieutenant commander on a destroyer and his is brother Henry was also on active navy duty. John Hay Whitney had joined the Army, and his frequent guest and soon-to-be Company member Barklie Henry was flanking convoys as the commander of the destroyer escort *Gantner*.

Unlike Britain, the United States did not have an intelligence agency at the commencement of the World War II. The British encouraged the United States to develop one. The outcome was the formation of the Office of Special Services (OSS), the predecessor of the Central Intelligence Agency. The British trained the first American agents at Special Training School No. 103, near Oshawa, Ontario. The facility was also known as Camp X. Long Point Company member Sam McLaughlin frequently hosted the camp's officers on Sundays at his nearby Parkwood estate.[196] He was later awarded the honorary rank of Colonel. As the OSS program matured, training commenced at two National Parks of the United States —the Chopawamsic Recreational Demonstration Area in Virginia and Catoctin Mountain Park at Thurmont, Maryland. (The latter is the site of Presidential retreat Camp David.)

All foreign intelligence operations depend highly on money, particularly the secret allocation, authorization, movement, and disbursement of funds. Because they were bankers, Junius and Henry Morgan were eventually billeted to the OSS.[197] The elder Junius held the more senior position. He headed the three-person committee responsible for the approval and outlay of all unvouchered funds. [302] A fact-checking effort for the preparation of this book revealed a large number of declassified documents in the CIA archives that attest to Junius' position. Two examples are presented in Appendix I. (Figures 64 & 65) Other declassified documents in the CIA archives demonstrate that Henry Morgan was responsible for managing the agency's document control system.

---

[196] Today, McLaughlin's Parkwood estate is a National Historic Site. The Site's curator provided the information on Camp X.

[197] Another reason they were billeted to the OSS was General William (Wild Bill) Donovan, the agency's director, was himself an Ivy League educated lawyer who preferred to place other wealthy Ivy League graduates in critical positions.

John Hay Whitney attended officer school and was commissioned as a captain in 1942. After further training at the Army Air Corps Intelligence School he was assigned to the Eighth Fighter Command headquarters and to the European Wing of Air Transport Command in London. [257] [303] There, he became friends with the Wing's chief of staff, Lt. Col. Roy Atwood and attorney William Jackson. After the war ended, Atwood would be Whitney's regular guest at Long Point and Jackson would oversee Whitney's vast wealth, considered by many at the time to be the world's largest fortune.

Whitney had long wanted to get into action on the continent, but his superiors deemed any such deployment an undue risk because of the extent of his air operations knowledge and refused his requests. Ranked as a colonel by 1944, he finally got his opportunity when he was assigned to North Africa that year. On August 21st he embarked on a mission into southern France.

The next day, a French resistance group Whitney was traveling with were engaged by Germans in a firefight. Whitney was captured. Although he was interrogated several times over the next week and a half, he managed to conceal his identity as an intelligence specialist. On September 4th, his captors ordered him into a box car destined for a POW camp in Germany. There were 44 others on board. Because most of the men were battle fatigued and weary, they had little interest in trying to escape. However, among them were a B-17 air crew who were fresh and had only seen combat from altitude. They were determined to return to duty. Of the 45 men on board, only 11 agreed to participate in an escape attempt, one of whom was Whitney.

That night, the airmen managed to open the box car door. Whitney, wrapped in a blanket and very frightened, jumped from the moving train, landed beside the roadway, and tumbled down an embankment. Bruised but not seriously injured, he collected himself and assembled with the others. They split into groups of three, and Whitney's trio forebodingly made their way into a dark forest. When morning came, they encountered a young boy. He summoned the French resistance who rescued Whitney and his two compatriots. Whitney provided a more detailed account of his entire adventure to his biographer. [252]

After the war, with the help of attorney William Jackson, Whitney set up a scheme whereby one third of his wealth was dedicated to philanthropy, another third to venture capital, and the remainder to his personal endeavors. He continued to visit Long Point where he was reputed to have been a patient hunter. In 1949, he had noted New York interior decorator Mimi Rand fashion new curtains for his cottage.[198]

Whitney was close to President Eisenhower, who appointed him Ambassador to the United Kingdom in 1957. Although he had been appointed by a Republican president, Whitney's politics gradually drifted toward the center. Because he was more liberal than the other Long Point Company members, he found himself less comfortable socializing with them. When he was at Long Point, he preferred to play cards before and after dinner alone with his regular guest, Roy Atwood, with whom he had served overseas.

The Long Point marsh can be a bleak place on a cold, damp, and blustery fall morning. Whitney began to find the early, cold mornings were becoming less to his liking. His final season

---

[198] Mimi Rand was a professional name. Her legal married name was Emilie Bushnell Lineaweaver II.

came when someone insulted him for spending his evenings alone in his cottage with Atwood. Whitney never returned to Long Point after that but he continued to pay his Company dues for the rest of his life. [15] When reminiscing to his biographer, he derided the social atmosphere at The Cottages, referring to it as "a stuffy place". [252]

The end of World War II brought new members. One was Malcolm Greenough, an investment banker who captained the Harvard football team and commanded the destroyer escort *Rudderow* during WWII. The others were Gold Coast neighbors Gen. Trubee Davison and Lt. Cmdr. Henry Coe. Davison, whose career assignment at the time was to set up the personnel system for the newly formed Central Intelligence Agency (CIA), had a physical disability. Although he could stand, he was unable to do so in a punt. Staff at the Company equipped his punt with a special chair and they would hoist him from the boardwalk into it. The chair could be jacked up, making it easier for Trubee to shoot.

Davison's courage, patriotism, public service, and the extraordinary circumstances that led to his paraplegia converge to form a truly remarkable story. John Pierpont Morgan had chosen Trubee's father, Henry Davison, to succeed him as the head of J. P. Morgan & Company, allowing Trubee to enjoy a privileged youth. While much had been given to the children in America's wealthiest families, much was expected of them. World War I was underway while Trubee was in his freshman year at Yale. He spent the following summer as an ambulance attendant in France transporting the injured from combat zones to hospitals in Paris.

By the time he was back at Yale, Trubee had developed a fascination for airplanes. He convinced his parents to procure a flying boat so he and his Yale contemporaries could form a militia and learn to fly. J.P. Morgan & Company provided $100,000 to get the militia started and Long Point Company member Harry Payne Whitney contributed $25,000. Someone who would be a future Long Point Company member, Louis Thompson, also contributed funds. Beyond his monetary contribution, Thompson served as the militia's administrative supervisor.

To make a long story brief, Trubee and his colleagues at Yale were successful at learning to fly, and to their credit they convinced the military to embrace them and their vision of the utility of flying boats for naval reconnaissance. The entire history of what became known as the First Yale Unit is detailed in the lengthy book *The Millionaires' Unit.* [304] [199] The day the young men took their military flight tests was a Long Island social event. Yachts moored in the sound so families and friends could observe the flight tests. Even though Trubee was the militia's leader, it wouldn't be his best day. He was nervous performing before the prominent crowd and fell victim to anxiety. He crashed on landing, breaking his back. Many of his militia contemporaries flew overseas during the war and some never made it home.

Trubee never let his disability impede him. He completed a law degree at Columbia. In 1925, he was elected chair of the National Crime Commission, which had been formed to address the rampant violence that occurred during prohibition. The following year, he was appointed

---

[199] An easier way to learn the story of The Millionaire's Unit is to view the two-hour documentary film with the same title.

Assistant Secretary of War for Aviation.[200] He would also be the longest-serving president of the American Museum of Natural History, where he engaged with several Long Point Company members who were trustees of the institution, including Junius Morgan, Roland Harriman, George Bowdoin, Childs Frick, and Wilton Lloyd-Smith. Davison relinquished his membership in the Long Point Company in 1965 and was succeeded by his two sons, Endicott and Daniel. As their father had been, they, too, were Skull and Bones Society inductees.

During World War II, there was considerable aircraft activity around Long Point and Turkey Point. In fact, Turkey Point marsh was a bombing range where live munitions were regularly dropped. The spotter's cabin on the north side of Lakeshore Road overlooking the marsh still stands. Today, it appears to be a cottage; few people know its original purpose.

One Saturday evening in 1943, William Mussel, a Long Point Company employee staying at The Cottages, heard a group of aircraft fly over, and shortly later, a crash. It was 8:30 PM. He went outside and saw two returning aircraft and another circling over the lake off the south beach. An Avro Anson bomber from the military airport at Hagersville had crashed into the lake.

Mussel tied a skiff to a powerboat and made his way three miles through the marsh and its channels to the south shore. Once there, he dragged the heavy cedar skiff 150 yards across the foredune and to the water's edge. Then, with a single paddle, he headed out into the darkness to the bomber, which was about one mile offshore. Another aircraft dropped flares and a raft, but the raft landed too far for the crew of four to try and reach it in the cold water. It took Mussel two hours to get his skiff to the bomber. Apparently, the aircraft sank about 15 minutes after he rescued the crew. Mussel spent the next two hours paddling them to the shore. For his fortitude, he was inducted to the Order of the British Empire.

Logging resumed on Long Point in 1947. The areas cut were the Anderson property and a small area south of Allen's Ridge. Like others before them, the contractor, in this instance the Pittman Company of Port Rowan, left behind limbs and debris. [168] Scientists believe the debris contributed to subsequent fires on Long Point. Bulldozers had to be used to create fire breaks to bring a weeks-long fire under control in 1962.

---

[200] The position would be equivalent to today's Secretary of the Air Force.

The Threat of Eminent Domain 1950 - 1980

Pressure came to bear on the Long Point Company following the election of Wally Nesbitt to the House of Commons in 1953. As soon as he was in office, Nesbitt encouraged the federal government to expropriate Long Point. How he developed passion for his proposal is a partial mystery. His father, Judge Wallace Nesbitt, had some familiarity with Long Point through his acquaintance with Samuel Woodruff. Before he was appointed a judge, the elder Nesbitt had been associated with Britten Osler's firm, Osler, Hoskins, and Creelman. He and Harry Collier represented Samuel Woodruff's estate, which became a messy affair after Ontario officials accused the estate of having hid assets from taxation. Wally probably became familiar with Long Point and who owned it from his father.

On April 29, 1954, he stood up in the House of Commons and pleaded to his fellow Parliamentarians to expropriate Long Point. His speech was replete factual errors and inaccuracies. He would repeat it yearly. Each time, it became a little more accurate. An abridged version of his first speech follows:

> On this opening item of the Department of Northern Affairs and National Resources there is a matter that I should like to call to the attention of the minister. It has to do with the subject of an island in Lake Erie, Ontario. This island is a very interesting place indeed from many points of view. It is approximately 14 miles long and varies in width from approximately 1 mile to 3 miles and averages approximately 14 miles in width. [*sic*] There are more than 17,000 acres of land on this island. It juts out from the Canadian shore of Lake Erie and stretches out toward the middle of Lake Erie almost to the international boundary line. The start of the island, which, owing to the filling in of the marshes, makes it in reality a sort of peninsula rather than an island, forms a long bay about 18 miles wide at the mouth and diminishes to only a few hundred yards in width at the narrow end. This particular island to which I refer would probably make a wonderful site for a national park for various reasons, which are as follows: First of all, this large island is located within 150 miles of probably the most thickly populated part of the Dominion of Canada. It is in southwestern Ontario and is part of the county of Norfolk. If this island were made a national park it would then be available as a playground and a place which could be visited not only by our own people there but by tourists from the United States as well, and we all know that tourist trade from the United States is very valuable indeed. In addition, this island is a veritable paradise for wildlife. I understand there are more snakes on the island per square foot than anywhere else in the world, but none of the snakes are poisonous.
> The island also has a very large stand of virgin timber, which is a rarity in that part of Canada. And, particularly, some of the

hardwoods grow to a great size, which is also unique. Unfortunately the present owners of the island are cutting down this timber and selling it.

When there is still all this wildlife on this island and it is still in the virgin state, there may be many who are wondering why people are not allowed to go on it.

It has been a well-known fact-and [sic] to everyone in that part of the country it is common knowledge- [sic] that the in-fact [sic]owners of the company have ever since that date been a number of extremely wealthy men from New York city and the surrounding areas. Occasionally there has been a Canadian member. At the present time I believe there are two and possibly three Canadian members of this club. The rest of them are all citizens of the United States. The late J. P. Morgan, of considerable financial fame, was one of the owners, or was one of the members and shareholders of this company. Many other men with prominent names in American business and financial history have been owners and members of this club. I do not wish to take up the time of the committee to go into this matter at any great length, but the information is easily available. As I understand it this club-and I say this in order to be fair-has kept up the objects and purposes that were set out in the original charter. They have been scrupulously careful about the taking of game. It is my understanding that the members of this club go to the club only during the duck-shooting season in the fall and that they take only a few ducks, something which is extremely admirable indeed. I understand that they seldom if ever attended the place during the bass-fishing season. I may say that there have been some extremely noted visitors to the club. His Majesty King Edward VIII, while Prince of Wales, was a guest at the club, and I understand he did some shooting there at the time of his visit. Of course that was quite a number of years ago. To get back to the original suggestion, I feel that this island should become a national park and the property of all the people of Canada, not only for the use of our citizens but as a wonderful attraction for tourists as well. It is quite true that the Long Point Company and its shooting and game club have done a very good job of preserving the wildlife there; and I think they should be commended for what they have done. While it is true that it may not have been all a matter of altruism, because by keeping everybody else off the island they actually protected the game and fish there for themselves, the fact remains that, no matter what was their reason for doing it, this is a wonderful preserve of wildlife and it is one of the few places of its kind anywhere in the settled or populated parts of Canada.

I am quite sure that the members of the Long Point Company do not need an island nearly fourteen miles long and a mile and a half wide purely for their own purposes. There should be a good road through the island so that the public can come in, as they do in other natural parks, and see nature as it is under unique circumstances. There is one other thing of interest about this island and that is what I may call the bay side, which is very swampy and full of wildlife such as snakes and so on, and which would be ideal for setting up any type of reserve. The southern or lakeside shore of the island has one of the most beautiful natural beaches in Canada with very fine, hard, white sand stretching for miles and would be suitable for holidayers. Now the far end of the island, that is the end closest to the mainland, which was never acquired by this company, is at the present time leased by the province of Ontario to cottagers on a 99-year lease basis with certain restrictions on the type of cottages that can be put up there. There are many hundreds of cottages, though in fact only a few have the advantage of a lakefront site. Most of them are in plots of sand toward the middle of the island. These cottagers come largely from places such as London, Woodstock, Tillsonburg, Brantford, Simcoe, Toronto, Hamilton and many other places, as well as from the United States. I know that a great many people from my own riding have summer cottages there and a great many people also have small cabins which they use on fishing and shooting expeditions.

I would like to wind up these remarks by emphasizing that such natural assets showing Canadian wildlife as it is in that part of Ontario, and which have remained unspoiled, should become the property of everyone in Canada and should not remain the property of a few very wealthy people from the United States. [305] 201

Photo 58. The Long Point Park Gift Shop and Post Office.
J.E. Evans, 1958. (Courtesy, University of Western Ontario Archives)

---

201 https://www.lipad.ca/full/1954/04/29/29/#1764046

Year after year, until he died in 1973, Nesbitt made the same plea. He also introduced resolutions and private member's bills. None got traction, but members of the Long Point Company became uneasy. Complicating the circumstances was the death of Junius Morgan, whose steady leadership and gracious deportment had sustained stability and goodwill among the members for decades. He had become ill at Long Point in 1960. To the extent it was feasible to rush him from The Cottages, Morgan was hurried to the hospital in Simcoe. Although Dr. Ross Parker performed emergency surgery, Morgan died that evening. The New York Times reported he had suffered an ulcer attack, a notably vague characterization of the actual cause of his death.

In his memoir, *Further Tales of Long Point*, Danny Davison wrote of his fondness for Morgan:

> Junius Morgan, who became president of the Long Point Company in 1940 was a class act. No one could be mean or selfish in his presence. He was contagious of goodwill and friendship. He really set the tone that makes this such a happy place. Junius loved Long Point... [15]

Davison remembered Junius's brother, Henry Morgan, the co-founder of Morgan-Stanley, with a little less approbation. He wrote that although Henry could be funny, he could also be "downright aggressive if the situation warranted it."

Sam McLaughlin succeeded Morgan as president and served for eight years. William C. Harris, a Canadian investment banker who held a seat on the Toronto Stock Exchange, became president in 1968. One year later, he was confronted with major embarrassment. Following up on information revealed by a Company punter, a joint law enforcement task force that included RCMP officers, swept into the marsh and confronted several members and guests. Company managing director Daniel Davison, and others were charged with possessing more ducks in their collection bags than permitted by regulation. Among those charged were punters. Officers confiscated the shotguns and skiffs.

Everyone charged had to appear for trial at Simcoe. Davison traveled all the way from the United Kingdom. Other members and guests came from New York City. Eight individuals, punters among them, pled guilty and were sentenced to a fine, or in lieu of payment, a jail term. The Company incurred bad publicity when newspapers reported the convictions.

Details of discussions held among the members over the next few years are presumably sensitive, and appropriately private. What is known, however, is that Harris eventually formed an opinion that the Company should phase itself out of existence. While he did not support Nesbitt's vision that the public gain access to Long Point, he was willing to see the island become a wildlife conservancy owned by the government. Harris eventually proposed that the members should transfer Long Point to the government in exchange for a lease that would terminate after 25 years. Not wanting to see the Company sunset, the members rejected Harris's proposal, and he stepped down and relinquished his membership. Regardless of the differences of opinion, there must have been considerable goodwill among the membership toward Harris as his son William, who was to a degree of like mind to his father, was elected the Company's next president.

Facing political pressure, fearing expropriation, and seeking to do the right thing while protecting their opportunity to hunt ducks, the Company's members sought a compromise. Over the next few years, they developed a plan to give one half of Long Point to the Crown. A complex series of transactions, including dissolution of the Company and the formation of a new corporate entity, would be necessary.

While noting that a full explanation "would require the writing of many volumes... and an advanced legal education to understand it," Daniel Davison provided a simplified account of what subsequently occurred.[202] Ownership of an 8,000-acre tract on the eastern part of the island was transferred to members individually in separate parcels. The Canadian members then donated their parcels directly to the Crown. The American's member's interests in the 8,000 acres were placed in a new U.S. corporation. Following a brief holding period, the Americans donated their shares in the new company to the Nature Conservancy, U.S.A. That organization, having effectively become the owner of the residual land on the eastern part of Long Point, then donated it to the Government of Canada. As a condition of their donation, the members had stipulated that the land be maintained as a wildlife sanctuary and Canada designated the 8,000 acres a National Wildlife Area.

When the negotiations for the donation were ongoing, the Canadian government flagged the Company's title to its part of the Anderson property as a potential problem. Ultimately, the government decided not to assume that tract, so the Company gifted its interest in the Anderson property to the Nature Conservancy Canada. One thing the Company did not yield was its rights over Long Point's oil and gas. While the Company surely has no interest in oil, one or two gas wells within the property boundary are likely still producing, and the revenue from the gas may be being used to defray property taxes on the part of the island that the Company retained.[203]

To complete such a complex series of transactions, required the assistance of legal counsel in Canada and the United States. One of the American attorneys who assisted was Stanley Weithorn. At one time he had overseen the section in the U.S. Internal Revenue Service that is responsible for evaluating regulatory compliance pertaining to gifts. After the transactions were completed, the Canadian and American members of the Long Point Company were able to take credit under the tax provisions of their respective countries for charitable donations.

A commemorative cairn was placed on Long Point in 1979 to memorialize the Long Point Company's donation. Over time, it became covered by blown sand. Although the relocation of the cairn was appropriate, the National Wildlife Service performed less than graciously. The torpid federal bureaucracy in Ottawa wasn't about to expend funds for the relocation. Local citizens stepped up to get it done. The Long Point Fish and Game Club and the Long Point Foundation for Conservation obtained permission from Ontario Parks to move the monument to the provincial park and gathered the funds to have a concrete pad poured to support the cairn. Port Rowan resident Keith Harvey put his heavy equipment to work to excavate the monument and carry it to its new location. (Photo 59)

---

[202] ibid
[203] The producing wells are likely those located in Helmer's Pond and Bouck's Pond.

Twenty-five years after the donation, long-time Company managing director Daniel Davison reflected on how well it had worked out:

> You can argue forever on the subject as to whether the Canadian government would have been a faithful custodian of the marsh but for the 25 plus years it has occupied the upland property it has struggled to preserve it, always hampered by a lack of funds and subject to public pressures. They have done the job, but a history, I believe, proves that the combination of public and private conservation has been a happy solution. [15]

Davison's words were prescient. The Canada Wildlife Service's portion of Long Point remains infested by phragmites, a tall, dense invasive grass. The weed had plagued the Long Point Company's marsh as well, but the Company brought most of it under control early. During the last two decades, non-governmental organizations including the Long Point Biosphere Reserve Foundation, the Long Point Ratepayer's Association, private donors, and especially the Nature Conservancy of Canada, sponsored the eradication of most of the weed at the far eastern end of Long Point. Ontario Parks and the Canada Wildlife Service have commenced control on their portion of the island. All tallied, millions of dollars have been spent on the overall effort.

Photo 59. The cairn commemorating the donation of lands on Long Point. 2020. (Author's photo)

The Second Long Point Park

By 1950, the notion that the intention of the Long Point Park Act had gone unrealized had surfaced. An investigator for the province's Department of Municipal Affairs, which had oversight responsibility for the Long Point Park Commission, wrote:

> Generally speaking the development which has taken place at Long Point has tended away from the conception that the park was to be an area for general use of the public ... towards the creation of a colony of summer cottage occupants, whose desires and interests clash with the valid purposes for which the park was set aside. [306]

This was also the era when the province recognized that it lagged far behind its American neighbor in providing readily accessible parkland to the public. In the United States during the Depression, funding from President Roosevelt's New Deal initiative, and the formation of the Civilian Conservation Corps, spurred the creation of many new parks. Ontario had just eight. In 1954, the legislature passed the Provincial Parks Act. Subsequently, a contingent of Department of Lands and Forests personnel was dispatched to travel throughout the United States for the purpose of examining its many parks and how they were formed and administered by all levels of government, municipal, state, and national. [268] Over the next six years, Ontario created 64 new parks, bringing its total to 72.

Francis Reid, the Simcoe lawyer who was the Long Point Company's secretary/treasurer (but not a member), anticipated at the beginning of the decade that the government was likely to seek more parkland on Long Point. Accordingly, he formulated a defensive strategy for the Company. The idea was to insert a buffer between the Company's land and the existing Long Point Park. The Company implemented the plan in 1952 when head keeper Hanson Ferris retired. As part of his retirement package, the Company gifted Ferris a large tract of land east of the Old Cut lighthouse. That way, if the government were to seek more parkland, negotiations would likely be limited to Ferris and the government. The Company would remain out of the public eye. It was a well-conceived approach.

Hanson Ferris died about a year after his retirement, and the tract the Company had given him passed to his four sons. They commenced leasing lots on the property. Access was through a locked gate at the east end of Beach Avenue. In the end, only four cottages were built there: one by Norman Bosworth of Toronto, an executive with the Canada Dry Co.[204] Two by Port Rowan businessman Leighton Cronk, and a fourth built by my father, Mike Selk, also of Toronto. He received his lease as compensation for professional services he had performed for the Ferris brothers. Today, the foredune where the cottages were located is just within the western boundary of the "new" Provincial Park.

The Provincial Parks Act transferred responsibility for Ontario's parks to the Department of Lands and Forests. It established a new entity, the Division of Parks. While the Division could

---

[204] Sam McLaughlin's brother formed the Canada Dry Company.

have retained the commission governance structure at Long Point, it recommended it be terminated. The Ontario cabinet accepted the recommendation and disbanded the Long Point Park Commission effective July 1, 1956. Administration for the public part of Long Point was transferred to a local forestry superintendent.

The Division of Parks then set out to rectify the situation that Long Point Park had become a largely private community by seeking to expand the park. It developed a plan to expropriate the tract that the Long Point Company had given to Norman Ferris four years earlier, About the same time, it offered leaseholders at Long Point the opportunity to purchase their lots. This same opportunity was not given to the four leaseholders who had built cottages on the Ferris tract. Expropriation of the Ferris tract was completed in 1961. The province compensated Leighton Cronk $3,500 for his two small cottages. Norman Bosworth received $5,800 for his, and my father received $5,000. For the land, Hanson's sons Arthur, Vernan, Norman, Paul, and Harry received $215,000 to divide among themselves. [307]

Construction of the "new" provincial park commenced immediately after the Ferris property was expropriated. Around the same time the province excavated a dozen ponds to create waterfowl hunting areas accessible to the general public.

The Bluffs Shooting and Fishing Club

Dr. James Salmon died in 1919. As mentioned in a previous chapter, the Long Point Company had granted him hunting rights for the area east of Spain's hotel to Bluff Point in 1871. The grant was associated with the transaction whereby Salmon sold the small tract he owned near Gravelly Bay to the Company.

Harry Collier, a St. Catharines attorney, had assisted the Long Point Company on several occasions. In appreciation of Collier, after Salmon's death the Company granted him a lease for a new entity, The Bluffs Shooting and Fishing Club. In a manner like what had been granted Salmon, the lease restricted the Bluffs Club to hunting in the lower marsh and permitted members to shoot one deer annually. The lease allowed the club to have just four shooters. They were given the use of Dr. Salmon's old cottage at Bluff Point. The yearly fee charged by the Company for the lease was initially $400 and the term was five years.

The first Bluffs Club members were Collier, Bruce Smith, an executive with the Royal Trust Company in Toronto, and Henry and Albert Taylor, both of St. Catharines. The Taylors were heirs to an Ontario brewery; Henry Taylor was a lawyer who practiced corporate law and Albert was an accountant by profession who also served as the Justice of the Peace for Lincoln County. Being *officers of the court* did not inspire Collier and the Taylors to be compliant with hunting regulations. They often exceeded the lawful daily duck limit by wide margins, as did Smith.

The Long Point Company extended the Bluffs Club lease beyond the initial five-year term. By 1933, the only remaining member still alive was Bruce Smith.[205] At the Company's urging, Collier's estate surrendered the Bluffs Club lease, and the Company granted a new one to Smith. The next club members were from Hamilton and Brantford. As the years passed, the Bluffs Club, which remained restricted to just four members, became very exclusive. Two members who passed away in recent decades were Sam Johnson of Racine, Wisconsin, heir to the Johnson's Wax Co. and the sole owner of its successor, the S. C. Johnson Co., and Ron Joyce, who developed the Tim Horton's coffee shop chain into a large enterprise.

After the Long Point Company donated the eastern part of Long Point, the lessor for the Bluff's Club became the Canada Wildlife Service. The Wildlife Service had little enthusiasm for renewing the Bluffs Club lease. To facilitate renewal, the members of the club liberally funded a not-for-profit corporation dedicated to conservation research with millions of dollars.

The Bluffs Club lease came up again for renewal in 2023. The Canada Wildlife Service chose not to renew it, and consequently the Bluffs Club is now inoperative.

Over the last century, stewards at the club included James Smith, Jack Gleadall, Thomas Cope, Charles Leighfield, and Bill McDonald. Smith had previously served as a member of the life-saving station at the tip of Long Point and Gleadall had been a Long Point Company punter.

---

[205] Harry Collier died in 1931.

Photo 60. The Bluff's Club. c. 1934. [308]

The Rice Bay Club and the Bayside Hotel

The Rice Bay Club has a clubhouse on a one-acre plot just west of The Cottages. Eighty years ago, it had a much more substantial presence. There was a lodge, a boathouse, and at least two outbuildings. The club's origins are related to late 19th century uncertainty about the boundary line of the Long Point Company's marsh. At some juncture, a scow broke free from its mooring on the bay and drifted into the marsh. Because the boundary was unresolved, the grounded scow continued to be used by individuals who were not members of the Long Point Company.

Research for this book did not uncover the identities of the individuals who formed the Rice Bay Club, but it is evident that the organization eventually attracted prominent and influential members. Most of them were from Woodstock or Toronto. (A list of individuals who had been members of the Rice Bay Club up to 1940 is presented in Appendix E.) By 1920, the boundary had been clarified, and it was apparent the Rice Bay Club was encroaching. Seeking an amicable settlement, the Long Point Company offered the club a draft lease.

In response, the Rice Bay Club adopted a strategy of procrastination. Year after year, for one reason or another, the club's officers canceled planned meetings with the Long Point Company. In frustration, the Company turned to outside counsel Harry Collier. Collier reported that the Rice Bay Club had come to include members who were politically well-connected. Moreover, so much time had passed that the possibility existed the club might obtain their one-acre plot by adverse possession.[206] As the club's members by this time seemed more interested in fishing than shooting ducks, Collier suggested the Company not commence an action to expel the club from its premises.

High water and a storm eventually undermined many of the Rice Bay Club's buildings, and they collapsed. A small cottage stands elevated over the one-acre plot today.

The Bayside Hotel was a turn of the century venture of Henry Teeple and Frank Pearsall, who was the postmaster in Port Rowan. Located west of the Rice Bay Club, it was a swanky summer place with a large screened-in veranda, guest rooms, dining hall, icehouse, electrical generator and three separate guest cottages. Visitors typically reached the hotel on the 63-foot steamboat *Zara*.[207] Americans, such as Rowland Hill who owned a whiskey distillery in Buffalo, were frequent guests.[208] After boundaries were clarified, the Long Point Company offered Pearsall a lease and he accepted it. He was permitted to host guests provided they refrained from trespassing.

The Bayside Hotel met the same fate as the Rice Bay Club. It was destroyed by high water and storms. While areas of dry ground may emerge on Long Point and endure for years, they are likely to once again be flooded.

---

[206] Adverse possession can occur after a party takes up occupancy on land it does not own. If the owner of the land does not take legal action to force the party from the land, the party may eventually claim it as their own. In such an instance, the party is referred to as the adverse possessor. In colloquial terms, they have claimed "squatter's rights."

[207] The *Zara* was built by Messrs. Mason & Robbins at Port Rowan and commissioned in 1903.

[208] Rowland Hill and Hanson Ferris were good friends. In his last will and testament Hill apportioned money from his estate to Hanson and his sons Arthur, Vernon, Norman, Paul, and Harry. [450] Whether Rowland Hill and Hanson Ferris's close friendship was related to the whiskey trade is uncertain.

Photo 61. The Rice Bay Club. c. 1940. (Private collection)

Photo 62. The Bayside Hotel with the steamboat Zara in the right foreground. Date unknown.
(Port Rowan/South Walsingham Heritage Association Archives)

Photo 63. A picnic at the Bayside Hotel. Date unknown.
(Port Rowan/South Walsingham Heritage Association Archives)

Photo 64. The steamboat Zara. Date unknown.
(Port Rowan/South Walsingham Heritage Association Archives)

197

Artists and Artisans

The first acclaimed artist to create scenes of Long Point seems to have been Lucius O'Brian. He was born in 1832 and graduated from Upper Canada College in 1847. O'Brian first worked as a draftsman in an architectural practice. An eclectic career followed, but by the 1870s O'Brian was working as an artist in Toronto and had found acclaim for his landscape paintings. O'Brian visited the Lake Erie region in 1873 and the following year. [309] His visits to Long Point inspired several sketches. Three were published as a montage in 1880. (Figure 50)

Figure 50. Lucius O'Brian's montage of Long Point sketches. (Public Domain) [310]

Charles Whymper was an accomplished British painter, illustrator, and wood engraver. While the subject matter Whymper tackled was wide-ranging, he was adept at depicting birds in their natural surroundings. He is credited as the principal illustrator for the book *Birds of the Wave and Woodland*. [311] Whymper never visited Long Point, but he did create a series of illustrations depicting scenes on the island by referring to photographs that had been taken during a visit by the Marquess of Lansdowne in 1887.[209] The illustrations were assembled by another accomplished wood engraver named John Greenaway and printed in the *London Illustrated News*.[210,211] (Figure 51) The circular image depicts the Marquis shooting from a skiff. Also present are images of The Cottages, rice beds, a pool with lilies, and a pond on which decoys have been set.

Louis Agassiz Fuertes was the next eminent artist/illustrator to visit Long Point. Considered to have been exceeded only by Audubon as an ornithologist-illustrator, Fuertes was a guest of Company member Henry Sage in October 1915. While on the island, he wrote a letter to his wife relating that he shot 65 ducks one day. The letter also included the following passage:

> The flat black-blue horizon of sparse trees, the ruddy beds of quill reeds, and the rustling rushes that the boat slides past, and the vibrant and brilliant air cut everywhere with the swift steady flight of ducks, ducks, ducks —some sifting straight overhead, silent except for the icy whisper of their wings, only heard for a second or two when they are nearest, others lining their straight course into the sunset—the darting teal, going as though they were hurled out of a gun—the frosty marsh smell everywhere and a cool wind in your neck, all gets to you in a wonderful way. Then, when it is almost dark, suddenly there is a roaring, rushing, splash, all over in less than a second, and dimly against the darkening sky a broad line of velvet, silent birds deploys, rises and falls into its formation and melts into the sky beyond. [312]

[209] Henry Petty-Fitzmaurice, the 5th Marquess of Lansdowne, served as Governor-general of Canada from 1883-1888. He was preceded by John Sutherland Campbell, the 9th Duke of Argyll, Marquess of Lorne, who served from 1878. He also shot at Long Point.
[210] A. J. (John) Greenaway was born in 1816. Whymper was born in 1853.
[211] The montage also appeared in a German publication.

Figure 51. Montage of Charles Whymper's woodcuts. (Public Domain) [313]

During or shortly after his visit, Fuertes painted a Long Point scene depicting canvasbacks in flight. The painting was hung in the Company dining room. It is still there today, although its condition has suffered. A color reproduction of the painting appears in a rare book that the Company's board of directors authorized in 1932 for the purpose of documenting the Company's history. Louis Steenrod Thompson, the managing director at the time, was assigned the task of preparing the book. He made a weak effort, merely assembling a set of historical documents and having them printed as a single volume. He wrote nothing himself except a one-page introduction. The book, which is titled *The Long Point Company*, was printed by Scribner in New York City sparing no expense. Among all books prepared by the Company or its members, the 1932 book is unique in that it is the only one that includes the members' names and their home addresses. The Library of Congress in Washington, DC, has two copies, catalogued as "socially significant." The Archives of Canada has one, and the American Museum of Natural History in New York City has another. Queens University in Kingston has a copy in its W.D. Jordan Rare Books Collection. Others are held in private collections. Copies of the book are rarely offered for sale, and when they are they fetch a price of a few thousand dollars. Even though it is a large, physically impressive volume, Louis Thompson's lackluster effort renders the book rather uninteresting.

Frank W. Benson was one of America's foremost impressionist painters. He took his initial formal training at Boston's Museum of Fine Arts, before going overseas to attend the Académie Julian in Paris. Upon his return to the United States, he taught at the Portland Museum of Art. He later went back to Boston to teach at the museum school in Boston where he had first studied. In the 1890s, the American government commissioned Benson to paint murals for the Library of Congress in Washington, D.C. He must have been given wide discretion, because his murals are portraits of his wife and daughters. I frequent the Library of Congress, and the murals never cease to impress me. Benson went on to make a good living painting portraits for wealthy New Englanders and their family members.

Benson first visited Long Point in 1916 as a guest of Augustus Hemenway. He returned roughly every other year until 1929, two years prior to Hemenway's death. He made entries to his diary during his journeys. These are among the few publicly available first-hand accounts of what it was like to travel to and hunt at the Long Point Company in the early 20th century. His entries for the years 1916, 1918, & 1920 are reproduced in Appendix D. When describing his first trip, Benson wrote that he departed Boston by train late in the afternoon together with Company members Augustus Hemenway and George Richards. They arrived at Waterford by 10:30 the next morning. From there, they traveled by car to Simcoe and then by train to Port Rowan. They ate lunch in a hotel in town and by mid-afternoon they were hunting in the Long Point marsh. Benson mentioned that in the evening they dined on duck, venison, and peach pie. The entry for his 8th day at Long Point stated he was running up against the seasonal shooting limit for members and guests of 500 ducks.

Photo 65. Frank W. Benson (foreground) at the Long Point Company. (Courtesy of Faith Andrews Bedford)

Benson's art depicts idyllic views of Long Point. But he had occasion to experience the raw force of nature that is sometimes to be had there. An entry in his diary describes one of Lake Erie's fierce fall storms. He wrote, "My bed shook all night in the howling gale, and we heard the hotel at Port Rowan was un-roofed…. the papers call this a West India hurricane, and it seems all of that." The weather event Benson was referring to has since come to be known as Lake Erie's Black Friday. It occurred after a hurricane passed over the U.S. Gulf Coast, then moved up into the Midwest as a tropical storm. There, it merged with another cyclonic system. The combined depression then moved east over the Great Lakes, hitting Lake Erie hard. Four ships were lost on the lake that day, and 49 crew perished.

Another entry in Benson's diary states a punter was curious about the etching process and Benson explained it to him.[212] This suggests Benson may have scribed some plates while at The

---

[212] To make an etching, the artist scratches a coating on a metal plate and later washes it in an acid bath so that the scratched areas become incised. Paper prints can be made from the plate because ink settles into the incised areas. When making a dry point, the artist uses an edging tool to incise the plate directly.

Cottages. However, his usual practice was to take photographs and draw sketches in the marsh. He would later use them as references in his studio while creating drypoints, etchings, watercolors, and oil paintings.

Signed original prints made by Benson are affordable. They can typically be purchased for about $1,000. Titles that depict scenes at Long Point include:

Over Sunk Marsh

Sunset at Long Point

Second Island Outlet

Blackbirds and Rushes

Souvenir of Long Point

In Island Pond

After Sunset

Redhead Grounds

The Punter

Marshes of Long Point

Figure 52. Benson's dry point Blackbirds and Rushes. 1920. (Public Domain) (Library of Congress)

Figure 53. Benson's drypoint Souvenir of Long Point. 1918. (Public Domain)

Figure 54 Benson's etching Marshes of Long Point. 1916. (Public Domain) (Library of Congress)

Figure 55. Benson's drypoint Over Sunk Marsh. 1920. (Public Domain)

Some of Benson's watercolors and oil paintings that were inspired by Long Point can be seen in museums and galleries, but many reside in private collections. At auction, the watercolors may sell for five-figure sums. However, one, *Redheads in Flight,* sold in 2021 for $270,000 US plus a buyer's premium.[213] Benson's Long Point oil paintings, when they become available, tend to sell for high six figures prices, with an occasional sale reaching beyond a million dollars. Readers interested in learning more about Benson's sporting art and seeing reproductions can refer to Faith Andrews Bedford's book, *The Sporting Art of Frank W. Benson.* [314]

Figure 56. Benson's watercolor Redheads in Flight. 1916. (Courtesy of Faith Andrews Bedford)

---

[213] A buyer's premium is an additional fee imposed by the auction house on the purchaser. It could be ten or as much as 20 percent of the bid price.

Figure 57. Benson's oil on canvass Marshes of Long Point. was purchased by Horatio Hathaway Jr. in 1925. (Courtesy of Faith Andrews Bedford)

Ogden Pleissner was another prominent American artist who was a guest at the Long Point Company. Schooled at the Art Students League in New York City, he taught there for decades. During his formative period, he attended a summer school for art in Nova Scotia. It was there that he advanced his landscape painting skills. One of his paintings was purchased by the Metropolitan Museum of Art in New York, while he was in his mid-twenties, making him the youngest artist to have a work on display there.

Stylistically in comparison to Benson, Pleissner was a realist. In 1942, the United States Government retained him to paint scenes of the World War II industrial effort. After being commissioned as an Army captain and serving in the Aleutians for a brief time, he was placed on an inactive duty to take on a role as an overseas war artist-correspondent for *Life* magazine. In this new capacity, Pleissner created more than 80 paintings. Many of them are on permanent display in the corridors of the Pentagon in Arlington, Virginia. His military background probably explains why it was General Trubee Davison who first brought him to Long Point in 1952, as Davison had served as Secretary of War for Air.

Because Pleissner's Long Point art is relatively recent (approximately 70 years old,) it is still protected by copyright and can't be reproduced herein. However, one of his watercolors depicting Howard Moulton punting Junius Morgan back to The Cottages can be seen by conducting an internet search. His realistic style contrasts with Benson's impressionism by the way he portrays The Cottages as background.

While at Long Point, Pleissner took notice of a stern plate nailed to a cabin wall. (Photo 66) The number of stars on the plate suggests it was crafted in the mid-19th century. Hanson Ferris told Pleissner he found the artifact on Long Point's south beach when he was a teenager. Pleissner traded a painting to Ferris for the plate, then repatriated it to the United States, where he had it restored. (There was yet no treaty between Canada and the United States in the 1950s addressing repatriation of antiquities.)[214] The plate is currently displayed in Vermont's Shelburne Museum.

Photo 66. Stern plate nailed to an exterior wall at the Long Point Company. c. 1960. (Public Domain) [162]

Other artists who have been Company guests include Roland Clark and Chet Reneson. Clark admired Frank Benson's art, and like Benson he created etchings, watercolors, and oil paintings. His Long Point etching *Inbound* (Figure 58) is more than reminiscent of Benson's *Souvenir of Long Point*. Clark also made decoys.

---

[214] A treaty addressing antiquities has since been implemented by Canada and the United States.

Figure 58. Roland Clark's drypoint, Inbound. 1925. (Public Domain)

Decoys are an essential component of a duck hunter's kit. Local artisans have crafted them for Long Point Company members since the time of the Company's founding. Antique specimens can be highly valued by collectors, depending on their age, condition, and craftsmanship. Enthusiasts have even had decoys examined using non-destructive methods such as X-ray and computed tomography (CT Scanning) to identify the techniques that were used to make them.

Two mid-19th century Port Rowan carvers whose decoys are highly lauded were Phineas Reeves and Isaiah Brown. Phineas was born in County Wiltshire, Britain in 1833, the same locale where Harry Woodward was born. He arrived in Canada in the mid-1850s and found work in a St. Williams furniture and carriage plant, becoming a skilled carpenter. Among his various assignments was painting the finishing details on carriages. Phineas later moved to Port Rowan, where he made furniture, built at least one house, and worked as a tinsmith.

Photo 67 Phineas Reeves. He was born in 1833 and died in 1892. Date unknown. (Public Domain)

Phineas carved the bodies of his decoys from cedar, and the heads from basswood. How he and others in the local area created a smooth surface prior to finishing is uncertain and would be a worthy topic for further research. Experts state that skilled carvers can achieve a smooth surface by using only hand tools such as draw knives, spokeshaves, files, and hand planes. If polishing was done, scouring rush or a mixture of pumice and oil might have been used.[215] At some juncture, likely during the 1870s, sandpaper would have overtaken those abrasives.[216] Mass

---

[215] Scouring Rush, or Horsetail, is a read-like plant that contains a high concentration of silicon dioxide. Native People used it to make an abrasive for scrubbing.

[216] Records indicate sandpaper —which would have been hand-made —was imported to the United States from Britain during the late 18th and early 19th centuries. It was probably imported to Canada as well. There were also individuals in the colonies who reported their trade occupation as being sandpaper makers. Hand-made sandpaper might have been too expensive to use for making a utility object such as a decoy.

industrial production of sandpaper began in the United States in 1858. By 1872, hundreds of thousands of reams were being produced annually in one Philadelphia factory.[217] Some of it likely made its way to Ontario. Cork sanding blocks are among the inventory of historical tools cabinet makers in Ontario used. [315]

A fraction of the decoys Phineas made were solid, but the majority he partially hollowed out to make them lighter and easier to handle. After hollowing the body, he planed the bottom and then sealed it with a board.

Photo 68 Phineas Reeves goose with original paint, branded J. A. Hewlett, attributing ownership
to James Hewlett of New York City
(Private collection)

---

[217] The sandpaper factory was owned by the Baeder-Adamson Co. Their primary business was manufacturing glue.

Photo 69 Long Point Pintail decoy with original paint. The graceful rearward sloping neck and other factors suggests the decoy was made by Phineas Reeves. Branded DT, indicating ownership by David Tisdale of Simcoe, ON. (Private collection)

Photo 70 Phineas Reeves Redhead hen, branded DT indicating ownership by David Tisdale of Simcoe, ON. (C. Moribella collection)

Reeves also made decoy bodies from cork, presumably when he was able to obtain the material. The heads were still made from basswood. The advantage the cork offered was a major reduction in weight; a disadvantage was fragility. Cork decoys were sometimes tarred or painted. Others were coated with lamp oil, which was then ignited and let to smolder, leaving a blackened surface. [316]

Another type of decoy Reeves made was the tin silhouette. These were flat tin plates cut so that the side-on profile resembled a duck, goose, swan, or shorebird. Reeves painted an image of the bird on the plate. Obviously, these decoys could not float. To stand one, the hunter used a sapling. They would push the sapling into the mud below the surface of the water, then split its top with a hatchet or other tool. The tin decoy was then wedged into the top of the sapling.

Photo 71 Phineas Reeves Tin Redhead silhouettes, marked E.H. indicating ownership
by Edward Harris, of London, ON.
(Private collection)

Isaiah Brown was thirty years younger than Phineas Reeves, so he started making decoys much later. Some of his decoys that were used at the Long Point Company are covered with a thin layer of canvas. When the sun shines on a smoothly finished wooden decoy, it may emit a glare. It was believed ducks sensed the glare, causing them to become suspicious. The mottled surface of canvas scatters light, so a decoy emits no glare. Whether Brown applied the canvas at the time the decoy was made or whether others added it later is uncertain.

Photo 72 Isaiah Brown Canvasback species, canvas covered and painted.
The hen in the foreground is branded GHR, indicating ownership by George Richards of Boston, MA.
It also has a second brand, R. Winthrop indicateding later ownership by Robert Winthrop.
The drake in the background is branded GHR
(Courtesy, Philp family collection)

Phineas Reeves had four sons. John, Charles, and Francis became skilled decoy makers and punters. The eldest, John, began making decoys in the 1880s. He left Port Rowan later that decade to manage the St. Clair Flats Shooting Co. He returned home a few years later only to die at the young age of 31.

Photo 73 Francis, John, & Charles Reeves.[218] Unknown dates, (Public Domain)

Charles and Francis, known locally as Charlie and Frank, are reputed to have punted for Toronto Big Creek Shooting Club Ltd. before taking up with the Long Point Company. They were crafting decoys no later than the early 1890s. Many are of the canvas-covered style. Their wives sometimes did the canvass cutting and application, fixing it to the body with as many as 200 tacks.

---

[218] John Reeves b. 1860 d. 1896, Frank Reeves b. 1870 d. 1938, Charles Reeves b. 1872 d. 1941

Decoys made by the first two generations of the Reeves family are highly sought after, especially those in good condition. Ten thousand dollars might be considered a notional price. The best among them command higher prices.

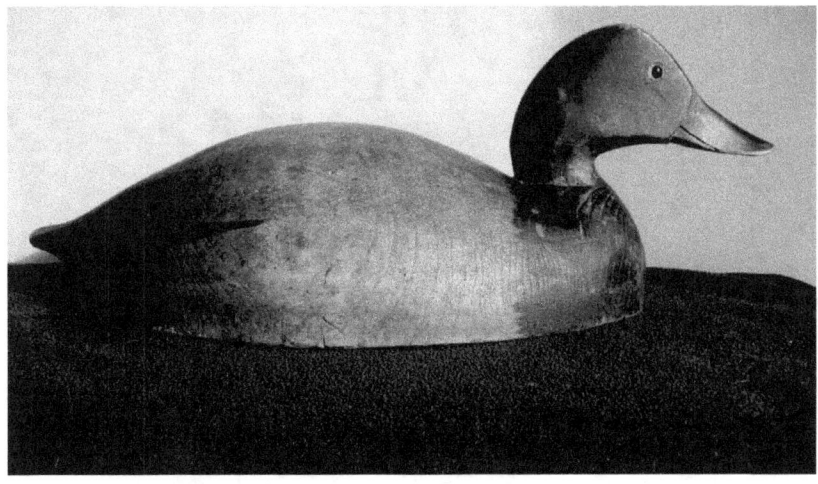

Photo 74 Jack Reeves Canvasback Drake, original paint,
branded LPC for Long Point Company & HSM. Attributed to Henry S. Morgan.
(Private collection)

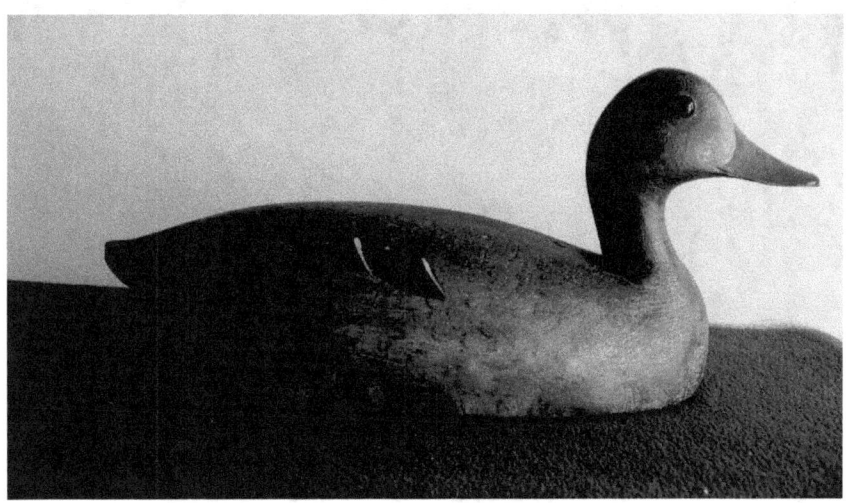

Photo 75 Charles Reeves Blue-wing Teal, original paint, branded W.L-S attributed to Wilton Lloyd-Smith.
(Private collection)

Photo 76 Frank Reeves Pintail. (C. Moribella collection)

Photo 77 John Reeves Canada Goose. (Used with permission, Guyette & Deeter, Inc.)

Charles's son Jack, who was born in 1904, continued the family tradition of carpentry, making decoys, and punting. He built about a dozen skiffs for Company members. The Mystic Seaport, (the largest maritime museum in the United States) has in its collection a Jack Reeves-built Long Point skiff.[219] The museum also has a half-scale model, that Jack built. Historically, Long Point skiffs were constructed from cedar strips affixed to hardwood ribs. Punters pushed and paddled them through the marsh using a very long oar. Sails were later added and raised when conditions were favorable. Gasoline-fueled outboard motors followed but were later succeeded by quieter 24-volt electric motors. The lead-acid batteries required for the electric outboards proved heavy and inconvenient to handle and charge. Today, four-stroke gasoline outboards are used. Cedar skiffs have given way to innovative designs constructed from fiberglass by Ron Bankes of Port Rowan. [317] Bankes also holds the current honor of being the Company's longest-serving punter.

Other 19th century local artisans who made decoys that are highly regarded were Walter Bailey of Forestville and William Harrison of St. Williams.[220] Decoys used at the Long Point Company were also sourced from Toronto maker John R. Wells and brothers George and James Warin. The Warins were principally boat builders who began making competition rowing boats around 1873. Their decoys are hollow, light, and were carefully crafted. If in outstanding condition, they may sell for tens of thousands of dollars at auction. Wells, who was born in 1861, was also a long-time boat builder. The finishing on many of his decoys has accurate presentations of the species' plumage.

While age is a factor in the collectability of the decoys made by all the individuals identified so far, the tradition of carving in the Long Point region is longstanding and continues to this day. Other local decoy makers include members of the Post, Ferris, Helmer, Kenline, and Oakes families. Factory-made decoys were produced at the McCall furniture factory in St. Williams.

Long Point Company decoys were traditionally branded with a member's initials, or sometimes with his initial and surname. The decoys customarily passed from a member to the successor who acquired his shares. The specimen shown in was originally owned by Wilton Lloyd-Smith. (Photo 79) After his death, it was rebranded for George Bowdoin and later again for his son-in-law, Russell Train.

The first shows of old wooden decoys were held on Long Island and in New York City during the 1920s, but their recognition as art came about slowly in the Long Point region. [318] Although decoys are anchored when in use, they can occasionally drift away. Over the years, many have been found by fishermen and boaters, some far east on Long Point's shores. Eventually, decoys used at the Long Point Company and the surrounding area slowly make their way to auction houses and private collections. Many had been lost during Lake Erie gales, including a great storm in 1975 and another in 1979, when one of the Company's decoy sheds washed away into the bay along with its historic contents. Others were donated by Company members to conservation groups to be sold at auction or gifted to Company staff and patrons. A few, no doubt, were removed without

[219] The skiff was donated by Henry Morgan.
[220] Late in the 19th century, Harrison began working as the assistant keeper for the lighthouse at the tip of the island.

permission. However, the great majority arrived to collections or at auction legitimately. Today, many of the important North American decoy collections contain specimens that originated at the Long Point Company. With the recognition of the historic and monetary value of these artifacts, beginning in the early 1970s, the Company and its managers moved to safeguard those remaining.

Photo 78 Warin Canvasback Drake, original paint. c. 1875.
Branded three times, first by the maker G&J Warin builders Toronto, then E.H. and A. Cochrane.
Attributed to Edward Harris and Alexander Cochrane (Private collection)

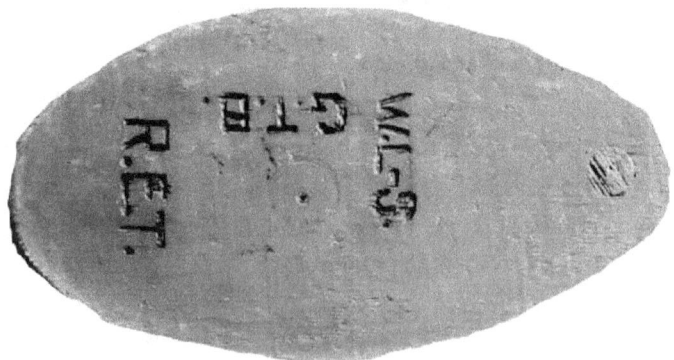

Photo 79 Decoy with Wilton Lloyd-Smith, George Bowdoin, and Russell Train's initials.
(Private collection)

Transportation

Early Long Point Company members traveling to Long Point from towns east such as Samuel Woodruff and Lauchlin McCallum, probably reached Port Rowan by steamboat. Others from the Hamilton area may have taken stages or buggies along the Plank Road to Port Dover and transferred to a boat.[221] David Tisdale reached Port Rowan from Simcoe by horse or horse and carriage then hired a sailor or oarsman to take him across Long Point Bay.

Egerton Ryerson, an intrepid individual, usually rowed himself from Port Ryerse to Long Point, even when the bay was icy cold. One day, his son Charles accidentally shot his own hand while on the island. Ryerson rowed him 16 kilometers to the mainland for treatment. On five occasions, including once when he was in his seventies, Ryerson traveled from Toronto to Long Point on his 20-foot (6-metre) sailing skiff *Seabird*.[222] Upon reaching Port Dalhousie, he traveled overland while the skiff was taken along the canal to Port Colborne. From there, Ryerson resumed the nautical portion of the journey.

One Englishman who was a guest at the Company in 1871 described his particular route.[223] He arrived in Paris via the Great Western Railway. From there, he took the daily stage to Simcoe, where he hired a horse and buggy to take him to Port Rowan. He quite enjoyed the latter part of his voyage writing:

> The beautiful drive in the early morning along the road which skirts the many indentations of the great Bay, the pure fresh nourishing air so peculiar to the North American continent, the spotless sky overhead, the pleasant voices of the early morning which every sportsman knows and loves so much to hear—birds, frogs the (nightingales of Canada), the hum of insects of every variety waking into life under the influence of the rising sun and, above all, the prospect before one of excellent sport, all combined to enslave the whole senses, producing a feeling of buoyancy and exuberance of spirits ... [319]

Before the Long Point Company was formed, many hunters paid Port Rowan's Captain Watts to reach Long Point on the yacht *Dan*. Watts unfortunately fell overboard on a cold voyage in 1862 and drowned. [320] His body wasn't discovered until the following Spring. William Bantam replaced him as the *Dan*'s captain, until he launched his own sloop, the 40-foot *Adra* in 1867.[224]

---

[221] Built by the VanNorman brothers, the Plank Road was completed in 1843. Planks were fixed perpendicularly to two parallel log stringers to form the roadbed.

[222] Although long, *Seabird* was only half a metre deep and less than a metre of beam. Ryerson equipped the boat with a sail and a canvass cover under which he could climb to protect himself from the elements when necessary.

[223] The Englishman identified himself only as H. J. P.

[224] *Adra* was built on the banks of the Port Royal Ship Canal, then taken to Port Rowan for final outfitting.

> Bantom's [sic] new yacht made its appearance at Port Rowan dock on Thursday, where it remained for a few days for some finishing touches. This little craft reflects great credit on its enterprising owner and principal builder, William C. Bantom, [sic] the hospitable proprietor of Ryerson's Island. Mr. Bantom [sic] has named his yacht Adra. She is intended for sporting, picnic and pleasure parties, having sufficient cabin room for a large number. The Adra will be perfectly safe in any storm on the Bay; she is thirty four feet keel, four feet in the hold, forty feet over all, ten feet bean, and is owned and commanded by the well known old mariner W. C. Bantom [sic]. [321]

During its first years, the Company also made use of the yacht *T. C. Kerr* captained by Port Rowan shipwright Nathan Woodward. (Thomas C. Kerr was the Company's first president) Likely a sloop, the *Kerr* ferried members, staff, provisions and game. It also carried Charles Brown, the Company's first steward through the Welland Canal to Hamilton to attend an annual meeting of the Company's board. The *Kerr* handily defeated the *Dan* in a race during Dominion Day celebrations at Port Rowan in 1870, only to suffer its fate the following year while carrying supplies from Port Ryerse to Long Point. Nathan Woodward, his wife, and their child clung to the overturned vessel and fortunately were rescued. [322] [323]

Another vessel that serviced visitors to the Long Point Company was John Spain's steamer *Norfolk*. The Company contracted with Spain one year (and perhaps another) to make a return trip from Port Rowan to Long Point every day during October and November. Beyond passengers and supplies, he was expected to carry the mail daily and any telegrams that had been received at the Stearn's Hotel in town. For his services, the Company paid Spain a $40 seasonal retainer plus one dollar each way for every passenger he carried.

After Spain sold the *Norfolk*, the Company made use of the sailboat *Hunter,* built at St. Catharines, and the *Teal*, a yacht owned by William Leary, the Company's head keeper. Both typically harbored in Port Rowan. On April 14, 1874, *Teal* capsized, tumbling the occupants into frigid water. News of the occurrence reached New York City by telegraph within hours, and *The New York Times* covered the story that day reporting that those who had been on board were rescued in a "perishing condition." The overturned sloop was later towed to St. Williams by the 173-ton schooner *Bay Trader*, a vessel which had been built on the bank of the Port Royal Ship Canal by John Glover and just launched the previous year.

Further arrangements began in the 1880s. For the convenience of members arriving by rail, the Company contracted with Captain Foster of Port Dover to have his steamboat *Annie Craig* ferry them. [324] Members paid a fee of $4 to Foster for every one-way passage. Members were to telegraph their expected time of arrival at the Hagersville railroad station so that carriages could be dispatched in advance, to bring them to Port Dover. Later in the decade, members departing from Port Dover traveled on either the steamer *W. L. Alderson* or the yacht *Ivey Alderson*. After the South Norfolk Railway established service to Port Rowan in 1888, the Company contracted with James Dease for the use of his steamboat.

About 1904, managing director George Richards ordered a new sloop for the Company. Norman Skene and Hollis Burgess, the foremost yacht architects in the United States, were contracted to design and build it.[225] [325] (Figure 59) Although it is uncertain when the yacht was completed, when it reached Long Point it was christened the *Gadwall* (after that species of duck.) The vessel was listed in the Lloyd's Register no later than 1912. [326]

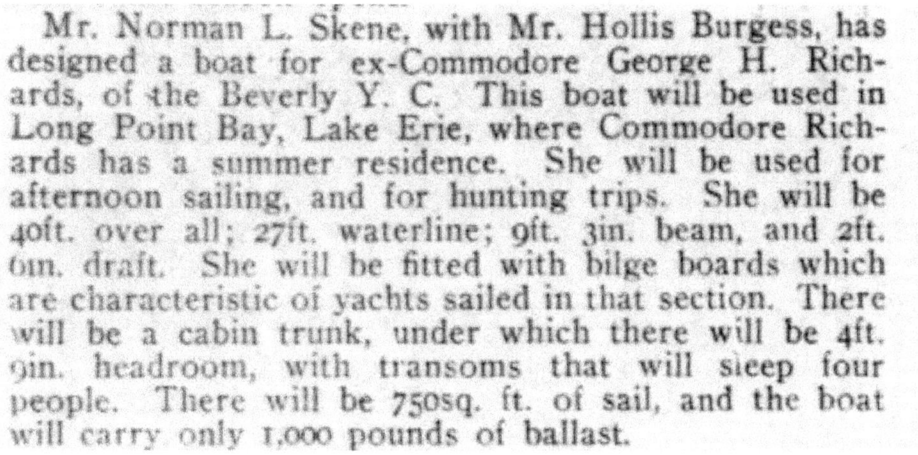

Mr. Norman L. Skene, with Mr. Hollis Burgess, has designed a boat for ex-Commodore George H. Richards, of the Beverly Y. C. This boat will be used in Long Point Bay, Lake Erie, where Commodore Richards has a summer residence. She will be used for afternoon sailing, and for hunting trips. She will be 40ft. over all; 27ft. waterline; 9ft. 3in. beam, and 2ft. 6in. draft. She will be fitted with bilge boards which are characteristic of yachts sailed in that section. There will be a cabin trunk, under which there will be 4ft. 9in. headroom, with transoms that will sleep four people. There will be 750sq. ft. of sail, and the boat will carry only 1,000 pounds of ballast.

Figure 59. Report about the yacht under construction for the Long Point Company. [325]

Long Point Company members from places such as Boston, Montreal, and New York would have traveled to Ontario in Pullman sleeping cars. Some, such as the Whitneys and Roland Harriman, may have traveled in their own private Pullman cars. Generally, they only went as far as Waterford, Ontario, although at least one private car appeared in Port Rowan during the 20th century.[226] [327] Townspeople attributed it to J. P. Morgan. However, he had died in 1913, and the car was observed after that date. It might have brought his son, J. P. (Jack) Morgan Jr., who occasionally visited Long Point, including in 1939, as a guest.

---

[225] Norman Skene, a graduate of the Massachusetts Institute of Technology, (MIT) authored *Elements of Yacht Design,* first published in 1901. He and Burgess designed the Americas Cup racers *Puritan, Mayflower,* & *Volunteer.*

[226] J. P. Morgan Sr. held a significant financial interest in the Pullman Car Company.

*Photo 80 The36-foot Sea Queen, the Company's first powered work boat. c. 1940
(Public Domain) (Port Rowan/South Walsingham Heritage Association Archives)*

*Photo 81 A Company launch ferrying men from Port Rowan to Long Point. c. 1960.
(Public Domain) (Port Rowan/South Walsingham Heritage Association Archives)*

Russel Train's Description of a Typical Day at the Company

Russel Train married Eileen Bowdoin, the daughter of Long Point Company member George Bowdoin and later inherited Bowdoin's Company shares. Following five years of military service during World War II, he studied law at Columbia. He then worked as a legislative aid on Capitol Hill specializing in tax law. In 1957, President Eisenhower appointed Train a judge of the U.S. Tax Court. After eight years on the court, he left to become president of the Conservation Foundation. Train later became the first chairperson of the White House Council on Environmental Quality and was the second individual to lead the Environmental Protection Agency (EPA). While at EPA, he spirited promulgation of the regulations that mandated cars be equipped with catalytic converters, an initiative that was strongly opposed by automakers because of the cost of the devices. Train was also in charge at EPA when the pesticides aldrin, dieldrin, chlordane, and heptachlor were banned. These regulatory initiatives led conservatives to put a target on Train's back in Washington. At the same time, he was concerned about his image with the progressive conservation community. He avoided Long Point altogether while heading the EPA, because he did not want to reveal that he was a sport hunter.

After leaving the EPA, Train accepted a position on the board of the National Resources Defense Counsel and was elected president of the World Wildlife Fund (USA). He returned to Long Point in 1977 and annually thereafter for 30 years. Train was very taken by the island. So much so he dedicated an entire chapter of his autobiography to describing his enjoyment there. [328] His prose offers readers a mind's eye tour of the dining room, the walls of which are oiled chestnut.[227] Above the fireplace hangs a portrait of Queen Victoria's son, Prince Arthur, who shot as a guest in 1869. Also hanging on the wall is a massive four-gauge shotgun. Train mentions King George V shot at Long Point in 1883 when he was still the Prince of Wales. Photos hang in the dining room to credit staff and punters, including three generations from the Reeves family, Phineas, Charles, and Jack.

Train relates that there is an "immutable" daily routine at the club. At 6:30, a punter arrives with a thermos of hot coffee and lights the cottage fireplace. At 8 AM the members and their guests gather for breakfast in the dining room. Train recalls breakfast to be an imposing meal of many courses. The senior member sits at the head of the table and signals for the staff to bring the next course by ringing a bell. Lots are drawn during the meal to determine the order by which shooting locations will be chosen. Members receive their precedence this way, but by tradition it will be their punter who chooses the location where the duo will hunt. All are expected to be in their skiffs, ready to go at 9 AM at which time the head keeper rings a bell signaling the day's hunt has begun. On board each skiff will be lunch. Because tradition imbues the day, the lunch will make the journey in a bucket —a picnic container of sorts —that has been Company property since the 1880s.

---

[227] The dining room is considered venerable. The Long Point Company asks visitors to be respectful and refrain from indoor photography on the premises. Nonetheless, many surreptitious photographs exist, particularly in personal collections of residents on the nearby mainland. Interior photographs of the dining room have been respectfully omitted from this book.

Photo 82 Headed out to the marsh in the morning. Date unknown. (Private collection)

The decoys are typically in the water by 9:45, and the hunters wait patiently for ducks to arrive. Everyone is expected to be back at The Cottages by 5 PM. After cleaning up, members and guests gather at one of the cottages for cocktails, a tradition begun by Junius Morgan in the early 1930s. Dinner begins at 7:30. It will again be a multicourse meal beginning with soup, followed by fresh fish, such as pickerel, perch, or sometimes planked whitefish. Everyone is then served a duck that has been roasted in a 19th century woodstove at a temperature exceeding 700⁰ F. Each is prepared to the individual member's or guest's preference. A rare bird cooks for just six minutes; a well-done one, twelve. There is also a nine-minute medium-done choice. Both red and white wine accompany the meal. After dessert, a night cap might be had at a gathering in a member's cottage. It's a long day.

One year, a few days prior to the commencement of the shooting season, Train was accompanied by his wife for three nights at The Cottages. They hiked across Courtright Ridge, strolled the beaches, and picnicked. David Walmsley, the head keeper at the time, stated that except for Sam McLaughlin's private nurse, Mrs. Train was probably the first female guest to stay at The Cottages since the fall of 1934.

Epilogue

As mentioned at the beginning of this book, Long Point was spared from the land grants of the early colonial era because a group of influential British military officers enjoyed shooting waterfowl. Disparate ownership was thereby precluded, and public access to the island sustained.

By the middle of the 19th Century fifty years later, there were no fewer than three hotels on the island, all operated by squatters. The development of railroad infrastructure not only facilitated visits by sport shooters from afar, it also enabled forwarding of game shot by local hunters to distant markets. The result was relentless slaughter. Although regulations were introduced to prohibit hunting during the breeding season, they were challenging to enforce and shooters frequently violated them.

The acquisition of the island by a syndicate of Canadian businessmen in 1866 did not bring an end to the slaughter, nor did it completely curtail hunting during the breeding season, at least initially. What changed was that most of the ducks shot at Long Point were no longer sold by individual hunters, but rather by a corporation. The shareholders of the corporation soon adopted an unyielding policy. They resolved that, "It is the aim of the members of the Company to make and maintain their property a private estate." Because these shareholders, and those that succeeded them, made use of only a small portion of the island for hunting, the remaining parts were mostly left alone as a natural wilderness, except for occasional limited logging. Consequently, much of the island's unique and vital ecosystem was preserved.[228]

With respect to vitality, one needs only to consider birds. Experts advise that North American birds are declining. There may be many reasons for the decline, but we can be confident that Long Point, with its location along two of the continent's migration corridors and its undisturbed marshes and woodlands, remains highly supportive of birds.

Many people have been rankled that a privileged few, mostly Americans, have owned a large slice of Canadian property that has recreational potential. The fact that these owners' wealth, in many instances, traces back to the Gilded Age —a time of adverse inequality —generally compounds the sentiment.

But what might have become of the island had its sociological evolution been different? Although Pelee Island had a mid-19th century limestone quarry, it evolved agriculturally and has remained that way. Pelee's geology and soil are very different from that of Long Point, where agriculture, except for perhaps orchards, would have failed.

Lake Erie's South Bass Island serves as an example of the crassest form of commercial development. It is a place crowded with honky-tonks and bars, two of which are astounding in their physical dimensions. (Photos 83 & 84) The island is serviced by fast ferries, and many visitors lament being onboard with the drunks who vomit over the gunwales on the return trip to the mainland.

---

[228] Although the island was protected against development and human intrusion, preservation was by no means all-encompassing. For example, there were no predators to prevent the deer the company imported to the island from flourishing. The deer thrived and the consequence was overgrazing that impaired flora. Eventually, conservation authorities culled much of the herd. Today, coyotes may be keeping the deer population controlled.

*Photo 83 The Beer Barrel Saloon on South Bass Island claims to have the world's longest bar.
2016 (Author's photo).*

Photo 84 The Boardwalk Bar. South Bass Island, 2016 (Author's photo)

Directly across from Long Point, Presque Isle shelters the harbor of Erie, Pennsylvania. (Photo 85) The island, which has a lighthouse, is very similar to Long Point although it is much shorter. The entirety of Presque Isle was set aside as a State Park in 1921, the same year the Ontario

226

legislature passed the act to create Long Point Park. Camping is not permitted in Presque Isle Park. Its biggest attraction is its sandy beach which has undergone fortification and renourishment due to erosion. An astonishing fact attests to how great public demand can be for beach recreation opportunities. A report prepared for the Pennsylvania Department of Conservation and Natural Resources notes that Presque Isle receives more than four million visitors annually.

Photo 85 Presque Isle State Park and Erie Harbor, 2019. (Author's photo)

Long Point stands alone as a unique southern Great Lakes island serving as a refuge for nature, largely protected from human encroachment. Although the public loves beaches, and those on Long Point are unrivaled, construction of a road along the island as envisioned by Wallace Nesbitt M.P., would not have been appropriate. Long Point is simply too changeable and fragile. Although the province of Ontario recognized the folly in Nesbitt's vision, provincial analysts did prepare white papers 60 years ago that proposed using tour boats to open distant regions of the island to campers. That too, would have been a bad idea. The far reaches of Long Point are best left to its spiders and snakes, mosquitos, deer flies, midges, ticks, stable flies, and especially birds and waterfowl.

The Long Point Company deserves some measure of commendation, particularly for the generous donation of the eastern half of Long Point, and for their stipulation that the island remains a wildlife preserve. For decades, the Company has unwaveringly accommodated scientific researchers, by granting them access to the island.

The Company has also tried to stay in tune with the times. Unlike days long past, the current regulatory limit for shooting ducks is six per day per person. Accordingly, the Company has devised a way to continue the spirit of competition that has always been a part of its culture. A member and punter try to shoot just one duck of a different species on any given day while being faithful to the regulatory limit. Not every member participates, but the initiative demonstrates adaptation.

As for the built-up community of Long Point and the provincial park, these places have given generations of cottagers, fishermen, hunters, vacationers, birders, beachgoers, and more recently full-time residents, much enjoyment. The community and park are pleasant, but during some summer weekends traffic and crowding are excessive. For many years, Norfolk County has promoted the island as a tourist destination. While tourism supports a few small businesses, it also brings the inevitable downside of increased wildlife roadkill —a condition that clashes with the island's designation as a UNESCO Biosphere.

The concluding topic I aim to address in this book is the need for Long Point residents to remain vigilant against the hazards posed by powerful Lake Erie storms. Although the probability of a life-endangering storm may be low, the following photographs demonstrate that it can occur. Over the course of my 70-year association with Long Point I can recall three such storms.

Photo 86, Ted Whitworth's Studebaker car buried in sand, March 1955. (Courtesy of Jeff Helsdon)

The following forewarnings can be anticipated. The first would be if the authorities advise leaving the island. The other two should be based on situational observation. If the storm surge on the south beach becomes severe enough to threaten washing across the island, it would be wise to leave. The third warning arises when the wind reaches sufficient strength to lower the water level by a metre or more in the boat channels at Long Point or the Port Rowan harbour. In such circumstances a seiche of significant consequence is possible. The severity of the seiche will be dependent not only on how far the water has fallen, but also on how the wind eventually subsides. Should the wind speed fade gradually without a directional change, the seiche will be less severe. Flooding may not even occur at Long Point. On the other hand, if the wind suddenly changes direction flooding is likely to occur.

The decision whether to evacuate should be based on cognizance of historic precedent, the warning principles discussed herein, and one's own risk tolerance. Recognize too that during darkness fewer cues will be available to assess the severity of a storm, whether a seiche may be pending, whether flooding has already occurred, and if it has, the depth of the floodwaters.

Photo 87, Long Point, March 1955. (Courtesy of Jeff Helsdon)

Photo 88, Long Point, March 1955. (Courtesy of Jeff Helsdon)

Appendices

Appendix A.   Long Point Company Members

Andrew A. Allan

Membership Years: 1875-1881

Birth: 1822

Birthplace: Saltcoats, Scotland

Death: 1901

Occupation: Businessman, banker

Positions: Co-founder and president, Merchants Bank of Canada
Chairman, Allan Line Steamship Co., Ltd.
Co-founder, Citizens Gas Company of Montreal
President, Montreal Rolling Mills
President, Cornwall Woolen Manufacturing Company
President, Dominion Oil Cloth Company.
President, Montreal Telegraph Company
Chairman, Montreal Harbor Commission
Director, Confederation Life Association
Director, Asbestos & Asbestic Co.
Governor, Montreal Protestant House of Industry and Refuge
President, Montreal Sailors Institute

Andrew Allan was the brother of **Sir Hugh Allan**. He was the first of the pair to be a member of the Long Point Company. After Hugh's death, Andrew took on the role of leading his brother's businesses.

The Allan brothers were founders and directors of the Merchant's Bank of Canada They were known to borrow from the bank, which was Canada's second largest, for their own purposes. Regulations have since been imposed to prohibit such self-dealing.

Photo 89 Andrew A. Allan, (Unknown Date) (Public Domain)

Sir Hugh Allan

Membership Years: 1881-1882   **Birth:** 1810

Birthplace: Saltcoats, Scotland

Death: 1882

Occupation: Businessman, financier, banker

Positions: President, Montreal Board of Trade
President, Merchants Bank of Canada
President, Montreal Ocean Steamship Co.
President, Provincial Loan Co.
President, Montreal Telegraph Co.
President, Canada and Newfoundland Sealing and Fishing Co.
President, Montreal & Western Land Co.
President, Vale Coal, Iron & Manufacturing Co.
President, Canadian Rubber Company of Montreal
President, Cornwall Woolen Manufacturing Co.
President, Thunder Bay Silver Mining Co.
President, Canada Cotton Manufacturing Co.
President, Montreal Warehousing Co.
President, Montreal Northern Colonization Railway
President, North-West Cattle Co.
President, Adams Tobacco Co.
Director, Montreal Railway Terminus Co.
Director, Canada Paper Company
Director, Canadian Railway Station Co.
Director, Canadian Railway Equipment Co.
Director, Ontario Car Co.
Director, St Lawrence International Bridge Co.
Director, Marine Mutual Assurance Co.
Director, Acadian Coal Co.
Director, Vermont and Canada Marble Co.
Director, St Lawrence Marine Insurance Company of Canada
Director, Citizens' Insurance & Investment Co.
Director, Canada Life Assurance Co.
Director, Director of the Western Union Telegraph Co.
Director, Confederation Life Association
President, Montreal Curling Club

Hugh Allan learned the importing and merchandising business as a young man working for Millar, Edmonstone, and Company in Montreal. After he became a partner in the firm, it was subsequently renamed Edmonstone, Allan, and Company. Assisted by capital loaned from his shipowner father, the firm began building both ocean-going ships and schooners for use on Canada's inland waters.

233

In the 1850's Allan formed a syndicate to create a new shipping company. He secured the contract for mail service between Britain and Canada and the new company grew to be a large enterprise, frequently by using anti-competitive practices.

The list of positions Allan held (which is partial,) speaks loudly of his reputation as the most aggressive capitalist in Canadian history. He wasn't just adept at business, he influenced and manipulated politicians, including Canada's first Prime Minister, Sir John A. McDonald.

Many of the industrial facilities Allan established were sweatshops that exploited children. Although he ultimately became Canada's wealthiest individual and lived in a 72-room mansion, he was not benevolent. Perhaps the only institution he offered financial support to, was the measurably religious Montreal Sailors' Institute.

Because Allan's ships carried troops and freight for the British military, Queen Victoria knighted him in 1871. Allan died in 1882, one year after he joined the Long Point Company.

Photo 90 Sir Hugh Allan, (Unknown date) (Public domain)

William. A. Allan

Membership Years 1890-1901   **Birth:** Uncertain

Birthplace: Uncertain

Death: Uncertain

Occupation: Mining engineer

Positions:
Joint owner, Mica Manufacturing Co.
Joint-owner, Pike Lake Mica Mining Co.
Joint-owner, Silver Star Mining Co.
Joint-owner, Portland Asbestos Mining Co.
Joint-owner, Ottawa Phosphate Mining Co.
Joint owner, Villeneuve Mining & Mica Co.
Founder & joint-owner, *Canadian Mining Review*
Co-founder, Railway Safety Appliance Co. of Canada
Co-founder, Brantford, Waterloo & Lake Erie Railway Co.
Co-founder, New Ontario Cobalt & Silver Mining Co.
Co-founder, Wellington Silver Mining Co.
Principal, Allan Gold Reefs Co.
President, Wellington Silver Mining Co.
Vice-president, General Mining Association of the Province of Quebec
Director, Austin Mining Co.
Director, Crowfoot Coal Co.
Director, Fleming Phosphate Mining Co.
Director, Red Point Gold-Mining Co.
Director, Larder Golf Reefs Co.
Director, Kootenay & Columbia Prospecting & Mining Co.
Director, Canadian Yukon Prospecting and Mining Co.
Director, North Star Mining and Development Co. of Toronto
Director, Ontario Peat Fuel Co.
Co-owner, Little Rapids Mining Co.
Member, Ontario Mining Institute
Member, American Institute of Mining Engineers
Member, Governing Council of the Art Association of Ottawa
Member, Executive Committee, Carleton Club
Member, Management Committee, Rideau Club
Member, General Committee, Ottawa Valley Tourist Assoc.
Member, Provisional Committee, Lady Stanley Inst. for Trained Nurses

William A. Allan and Sanford Fleming were long-time business partners engaged in the mining business and infrastructure development.[229] They managed their affairs from an imposing office building they built and owned in Ottawa. The structure, which they haughtily named Victoria Chambers, was strategically located directly across the street from Parliament. In addition to housing their own staff, Allan and Flemming, —operating under that business name —leased space to prominent attorneys and businessmen. The Bank of Ottawa placed its head office in the building. In later years, high-ranking civil servants had offices there.

Allan operated a pit mine near Gatineau, Quebec that was one of North America's earliest phosphate producers. He enjoyed the good fortune of selling it to investors in New York for a handsome sum before cheap phosphate from newly developed mines in Florida flooded the market and drove down prices for the commodity.

Allan was acquainted with Long Point Company president **John Manuel**. He gained membership in the Company by acquiring the shares of **Dr. J.T.D MacKenzie**.

---

[229] Sir Sanford Fleming served as chief engineer for the transcontinental railway project. He was a founder of the Royal Society of Canada and is recognized as the originator of the concept for *standard time*, which was ultimately adopted globally. Queen Victoria knighted him in 1897.

Francis B. Arnold

Membership Years: 1890-1901

Birth: 1845

Birthplace: Uncertain

Death: 1906

Occupation: Tea and coffee importer/wholesaler

Positions: Member, New York City Chamber of Commerce
Member, the Coffee Exchange
Trustee, Orient Mutual Insurance Co.
Member, Importers and Grocers Exchange

Francis Arnold was the son of Benjamin G. Arnold, the largest coffee importer and wholesaler in the United States. He acquired his shares from **William B. Hunter.** The elder Arnold, his son Francis, and Long Point Company member **Lyman R. Green** made a play to further dominate the coffee market. They entered firm contracts with growers, rather than just bidding on shipments arriving to New York harbor. After coffee prices temporarily collapsed in 1880, the Arnold firm got caught with too much leverage and a devalued inventory. Consequently, the firm suffered a spectacular bankruptcy. That ended **Francis Arnold**'s association with the Long Point Company and **Lyman Green**'s as well. Arnold died in Rome, Italy, in 1906 at the age of 62.

William M. Barnum

Membership Years: 1903-1926

Birth: 1865

Birthplace: Lime Rock, Connecticut

Death: 1926

Occupation: Attorney, investment banker

Positions: Member, Skull & Bones Society
Co-founder, Simpson Thatcher, & Barnum
President and Chairman, Pacific Coast Coal & Oil Co.
Director, First National Bank
Director, Henrico Coal Co.
Director, Bethlehem Steel Co.
Director, Montreal Locomotive Co.
Director, United States Guarantee Co.
Director, Manhattan Railway Co.
Partner, Harvey Fisk & Sons
Director, Pennsylvania Water & Power Co.
Director, Electrical Securities Corp.
Director, New York & Jersey Railroad Co.
Director, Railway Steel-Spring Co.
Director, Greely Square Realty Co.

William Barnum was the son of U.S. Senator William H. Barnum, who had been the Chairman of the Democratic National Committee. Willam M. graduated from Yale in 1877 where he was inducted into the Skull & Bones Society. He then studied law at Columbia. Barnum practiced corporate law for many years before joining Harvey Fisk & Sons as an investment banker. He is most remembered for assembling the financing that facilitated the construction of New York City's tunnels. Barnum served as president of the Long Point Company for four years and was in the position at the time of his death in New York City in 1926.

Photo 91 William M. Barnum, Date Unknown

Lt. Col. Arthur L. Bishop

Membership Years: 1927-1937   **Birth:** 1895

Birthplace: Brantford, Ontario

Death: 1967

Occupation: Military officer, civil engineer, businessman

Positions: Military Officer, World War I
President, Consumers Gas Co.
President, Sturgeon River Gold Mines
Vice-president, Coniaurum Mines
President, Coniagas Mines
Vice-president, Coniagas Reduction. Co.
President, Electric Steel & Engineering Ltd.
Director, Manufacturers Life Insurance Co.
Director, Imperial Bank of Canada
Chairman, Executive Committee of the Canadian Red Cross Society
Member of the Executive Board, Boy Scouts of Canada

Arthur Bishop was a nephew and ward of **Reuben Leonard**. He was born in Brantford, Ontario and schooled at Ridley College in St. Catherines. Like his uncle, Bishop graduated from the Royal Military College. He suffered a serious gunshot wound to an eye while serving in France during WWI. Bishop later joined his uncle in the mining business and succeeded him as the head of the Coniagas Mines. The positions listed above represent only a portion of his many business interests.

Photo 92 Arthur L. Bishop

239

Lt. Cmdr. George T. Bowdoin

Membership Years: 1937-1967   **Birth:** 1898

Birthplace: New York City

Death: 1967

Occupation: Military officer, banker

Positions: Pilot, Army Signal Corps, World War 1
Assistant Treasurer, Bankers Trust Co.
Partner, Winslow, Lanier & Co.
Mayor, Oyster Bay, New York
Reserve Officer, U.S. Navy
Trustee, Children's Aid Society of New York
Trustee, American Museum of Natural History
Chairman, New York Hospital
Board member, Nassau Hospital
Commodore, New York Yacht Club
Commodore, Seawanhaka Corinthian Yacht Club
Treasurer, New York Yacht Club
Member, Jupiter Island Club

George Bowdoin was a descendant of the second governor of Massachusetts. His great, great grandfather was Alexander Hamilton. His father and his grandfather were partners in J.P. Morgan & Co.

After his father died in 1914, George was raised by his aunt. Like many Long Point Company members, he attended the Groton School. He left in 1917 before graduating to enlist in the Army Air Corps and flew as a pilot during World War I.

After the war, Bowdoin worked for the Bankers Trust Co. He then joined one of Wall Street's oldest firms, Winslow, Lanier & Co. Upon turning 30 years old, he finally inherited the estate his father had left him. He then oversaw the shutdown and liquidation of Winslow, Lanier & Co., and retired to pursue a leisurely life of yachting and various philanthropic interests.

Bowdoin returned to military service during World War II, this time with the Navy. In the 1960s, he was a member of the syndicate that developed the Americas Cup winner *Constellation*. Bowdoin was philanthropic and remained closely associated with the New York Children's Aid Society for almost his entire adult life. About 1929, he donated his country estate to the Society. In 1952, he was a recipient of an honorary degree from Bowdoin College.

Bowdoin acquired shares in the Long Point Company from J.P. Morgan partner **Dwight Morrow**. The shares later passed to Bowdoin's son-in-law **Russell Train**.

Photo 93 Geo. T. Bowdoin, 1952

Frederick K. Broughton

Membership Years: 1877-1879

Birth: Uncertain date

Birthplace: Britain

Death: 1889

Occupation: Railroad manager

Positions: General Manager, Ulster railway
General Manager, Mid-Wales Railway
General Manager, Neath and Brecon Railway
General Manager, Great Western Railway
General Manager, Detroit, Grand Haven & Milwaukee Railway
General Manager, Chicago & Atlantic Railway

Fred Broughton, an uncompromising, hard-nosed cost cutter, was sent to Canada in 1875 to turnaround the British-owned Great Western Railway which had suffered financially during the recession that followed the Panic of 1873. It is very likely that **David Tisdale**, who was deeply involved in the railroad business, recruited Broughton to the Long Point Company.

Fatalities among railroad workers were very common at the time. In response, the Province of Ontario struck a committee to examine the circumstances. Broughton testified that a railway job was no more hazardous than any other occupation, even though the Great Western's workforce 0f just 800 was incurring about five fatalities each year and dozens of grave injuries.

After the Grand Trunk and Great Western were amalgamated in 1882, Broughton was retired. Two years later, he landed a position running the Detroit, Grand Haven & Milwaukee line, and by 1884 he had been hired as the general manager of Chicago & Atlantic Railway, for which he enjoyed a handsome salary of $8,000 per year.

No friend of the working man, whenever anything went wrong, Broughton blamed them. (That was a common management philosophy at the time.) After a series of major losses due to accidents on the Chicago & Atlantic line, he issued the following directive:

> With the object of protecting the public, by ensuring as far as possible the safe working of the line, every casualty, however slight, will be investigated by a committee composed of the heads of departments. All of the employees concerned in an accident will be suspended from duty until it can be carefully inquired into, by which means it is hoped that the cause may be discovered. I hope that all will cheerfully aid me. [329]

Broughton's philosophy was that even before a cause or causes had been established, it should be assumed the workforce had done something wrong. A year after issuing the directive, he encountered his own problem as an employee. At a meeting of the railway's board, a director claimed to have come upon Broughton drunk in his private railcar. The board then fired him. No longer able to find employment, Broughton launched a slander lawsuit against the director. A jury ruled against him after deliberating for just 10 minutes. [330] For reasons unknown, Broughton's membership in the Long Point Company lasted just two years. He died at Eastwood, Ontario, in 1889.

Maj. Adam Brown

Membership Years: 1867-1870   **Birth:** 1826

                                             Birthplace: Edinburgh, Scotland

                                             Death: 1926

Occupation: Wholesale importer, railroad developer, capitalist, politician

Positions: President, Hamilton Board of Trade
                  President, Hamilton Coffee Tavern Co.
                  Postmaster, City of Hamilton
                  President, Wellington, Grey & Bruce Railway
                  President, Northern and Pacific Junction Railway
                  President, Royal Canadian Humane Assoc.
                  Member of Parliament
                  Vice-consul to the Kingdom of Hawaii.
                  Member, St. Andrews Benevolent Society
                  President, Athenaeum Club of Montreal
                  Director, Great Northwestern Telegraph Co.

Adam Brown was a partner in the wholesale importing firm Brown, Gillespie & Co. When he joined the Long Point Company in 1867, he was organizing the Wellington, Grey & Bruce Railway, a public stock company. Brown was elected to Parliament as a Conservative for the riding of Hamilton in 1887. He lived to the age of 100.

Photo 94, Adam Brown, Unknown date, (Public Domain)

John Brown

Membership Years: 1866-1871   **Birth:**

                                        Birthplace: Scotland

                                        Death:

Occupation: Importer, wholesale grocer

Positions: Founding member, Hamilton Board of Trade
                   Director, Wellington, Grey & Bruce Railway

John Brown was a founding member of the Long Point Company and a partner in the Hamilton wholesale grocery and dry goods firm Kerr, Brown & MacKenzie. (His partners in the business were **Thomas Kerr** and **John Mackenzie**.) The business must have provided Brown with a handsome income, as he had a mansion built in Hamilton that had metre-thick stone walls. The residence was completed in 1861 and Brown named it Highfield. It was eventually sold to **James Turner**, who became a member of the Company in 1868 and later a member of the Senate.

Brown's brother, **Adam Brown**, who was a partner in the wholesale grocery firm Brown, Gillespie & Co., bought shares in the Long Point Company in 1867, one year after it had been founded.

Maj. Louis Cabot

Membership Years: 1877-1914

Birth: 1837

Birthplace: Brookline, MA

Death: 1914

Occupation: Military officer

Positions:
Member, Hasty Pudding Club
Member, Harvard Porcellian Club
Member, Cosmos Club, Washington, D.C.
Member, Union Club of Boston
Fellow, American Academy of Arts & Sciences
Member, Boston Society of Natural History
Member, National Association of Audubon Societies
Member, American Jersey Cattle Club
Member, Essex Country Club
Resident Member, Colonial Society of Massachusetts

Louis Cabot was the son of Samuel Cabot, a physician and ornithologist. He graduated from Harvard in 1858. He then went oversees to continue his studies. After returning to the United States, he commenced an architectural apprenticeship.

The Civil War led Cabot to join the Union Army in 1861. He was commissioned a 2nd lieutenant but soon suffered combat injuries and was hospitalized. There is persuasive evidence Cabot was afflicted by post-traumatic stress syndrome. He spent almost two years recovering in a private home before returning to duty in 1863. He was promoted to Captain and continued to experience battle. At the end of the war, Cabot was a major and a commanding officer in the 3rd battalion, 4th Regiment of the Massachusetts Cavalry.

Cabot married **Augustus Hemenway's** sister Amy in 1869. Her vast wealth enabled him to forego any type of hands-on business activity for the rest of his life. He lived as a country gentleman, sportsman, and a less than amateur scientist. (He was a Fellow of the Zoology & Physiology Division of the American Academy of Arts & Sciences.) In 1877, Cabot purchased the remaining shares of **Thomas Kerr**, a founder, and the first president of the Long Point Company. As the years went on, he purchased additional shares and assigned them to his Boston contemporaries. Sometimes, while at Long Point, Cabot would collect an interesting bird specimen and return it to Boston for examination at Harvard.

After their home was destroyed by fire, Cabot and his wife Amy built a 39-room mansion in Brookline which had 30-acres of ground designed by famed landscape architect Frederick Law Olmstead. Cabot also owned a 2,000-acre estate/farm in Dublin, New Hampshire that he used for shooting, and timberlands that extended 39 miles along the Gaspe´ Peninsula's Grand River, where he engaged in salmon fishing. He also had a quail-hunting preserve in the Carolina's.

By the dawn of the 20th century, Cabot's extensive ownership of land in the Gaspe´ Peninsula, and his claim to exclusive salmon fishing rights for tens of miles of the Grand River had drawn the ire of Quebec authorities. They began selling fishing licenses to residents, thereby challenging his claim. Cabot died at Aiken, South Carolina in 1914.

Photo 95 Louis Cabot, 1877 (Public Domain)

Arthur Tracy Cabot, M.D.

Membership Years: 1895-1912

Birth: Boston

Birthplace: 1852

Death: 1912

Occupation: Surgeon, public health advocate

Positions:
Instructor, Oral pathology & surgery, Harvard Medical School
Instructor, Genito-urinary surgery, Harvard Medical School
Visiting Surgeon, Massachusetts General Hospital
President, Massachusetts Medical Society
President, American School Hygiene Association
Trustee, Boston Museum of Fine Arts
Chairman, Board of Trustees, Massachusetts Hospitals for Consumptives
Member of the Board of Harvard College
Clinical Instructor in Surgery, Harvard Medical School
Fellow, American Academy of Arts & Sciences
Member, Corporation of Harvard College
Member, Boston Society of Natural History
Member, Dedham Polo Club
Member, Swan Island Club (Currituck)

Dr. Arthur Cabot was the maternal grandson of Patrick Tracy Jackson, who in 1832 introduced the power loom to the U.S. cotton industry. His father Samuel was a surgeon. Cabot graduated from Harvard in 1872 and from its medical school in 1876. After interning at Massachusetts General Hospital, he briefly studied abroad in Berlin, Vienna & London. He pioneered the operation for removing pus from the chest cavities of children when he worked at the Boston Children's Hospital. It was there that he also developed a wire split for stabilizing leg fractures. The design, which found worldwide use for decades, became known as the Cabot splint. He is also reputed to have been the first surgeon at the Massachusetts General to successfully perform abdominal surgery for resolving a strangulated umbilical hernia.

Beginning in 1904, Cabot began to focus on public health and the prevention of tuberculosis. By 1910, he had closed his surgery practice to dedicate himself entirely to the effort. Cabot understood that the tuberculosis bacterium survived on surfaces and could be spread by surface contact. Accordingly, he strenuously advocated for better hygiene and cleanliness in schools. Additionally, he advanced the policy that when a state made schooling compulsory, it became responsible for the care of children who became infected.

Cabot was brought into the Long Point Company by his uncle, **Louis Cabot**. He sold his shares the year before his death in 1912 and used the proceeds for philanthropy.

Figure 60. Portrait of Dr. Arthur Cabot. Date unknown. Etching by Frank W. Benson. (Public Domain)

Lt. Paul C. Cabot

Membership Years: 1954-1987   **Birth:** 1898

Birthplace: Brookline, MA

Death: 1994

Occupation: Financial professional

Positions: Founder, State Street Investment Corp.
Partner, State Street Research & Management Co.
Treasurer, Harvard College
Member, Dedham Country and Polo Club

Paul Cabot was the son of attorney Henry B. Cabot. He completed an undergraduate degree at Harvard before graduating from the Harvard Business School in 1923. The following year, he formed the State Street Investment Corporation and created the first mutual fund in the United States. He married Virginia Converse, whose sister Louise was married to **Junius Morgan**.

Cabot was appointed Treasurer of Harvard University in 1948. He would later be the recipient of honorary doctoral degrees from Harvard and Yale. Cabot was reputed to turn the air blue when he became frustrated hunting in the marsh at Long Point. He died in 1994.

Col. Eli Clinton Clark Jr.

Membership Years: 1867-1874

Birth: Uncertain

Birthplace: Uncertain

Death: 1913

Occupation: Lumberman

Positions: Principal, Clark, Sumner Co.

Eli Clark's father owned a sawmill in Albany, New York. His son continued the enterprise. As local resources became depleted, Clark began acquiring rights in Ontario and began forwarding timber from there to Albany. He commenced cutting on Long Point in the 1850's in association with **William Little**. Although Clark was an American, he held the timber license for the entirety of Long Point when the island was put to auction in 1866. By that time, he was residing in New York City. He managed his Canadian operations by traveling to and from a hotel in Toronto. Evidence suggests Clark also stripped timber from the Georgian Bay region. It is unlikely he ever hunted at Long Point. His only interest in the island was to timber it. He died at Galveston, Texas in 1913.

George A. Clark

Membership Years: 1871-1874   **Birth:** 1824

Birthplace: Paisley, Scotland

Death: 1873

Occupation: Industrialist, businessman

Positions: Principal, George A. Clark & Brothers
                 Principal, Clark Thread Co.

George Clark was the son of John Clark, one of the founders of the J & J Clark thread company of Paisley, Scotland. James Clark, his great uncle, is credited with having invented the bobbin.

While still a teenager in 1840, George was sent to Hamilton, Ontario to serve an apprenticeship with Kerr & Company. That very likely explains how he became acquainted **Thomas Kerr,** who would later be one of the founders of the Long Point Company and its first president. After completing his apprenticeship, Clark returned to Scotland.

In 1856, Clark emigrated to New York City. Together with two of his siblings, he incorporated George A. Clark & Brothers to import the family's Scottish thread. After the U.S. imposed import tariffs in the 1860s, George, his brothers, and Robert Kerr, established a very large manufacturing complex in Newark, New Jersey. Clark oversaw the construction and operation of the facility.

Clark died in 1873, less than two years after he joined the Long Point Company. He willed a substantial sum to fund the construction of a new city hall in his hometown of Paisley, Scotland. He also left a bequest to the University of Glasgow.

An interesting sidenote is the scale of the thread manufacturing facilities in Paisley and New Jersey. After the Clark facility in Paisley was amalgamed with that of J. P. Coats Ltd. in 1896, the combined enterprise had half a million spindles and consumed 400 tons of coal per day. The workforce exceeded 10,000 and included girls and boys as young as 14. Their hours were 6 AM to 6 PM, with two one-hour meal periods. Actual paid working time was about 55 hours per week. The demand for bobbins became so high it contributed to the denudation of Scotland's forests. Thousands of tons of lumber needed to be imported annually from North America to support continued bobbin production.

The American facility near Newark, New Jersey was also large. *Scientific American* reported the factory's 338-foot-tall smokestack was the highest in the United States.

Photo 96, George Clark, unknown date, (Public Domain)

Alexander Cochrane Jr.

Membership Years: 1902-1915   **Birth:** 1840

                                                Birthplace: Barrhead, Scotland

                                                Death: 1919

Occupation: Chemical industry executive, financier, investor

Positions: President, Cochrane Chemical Co.
President, Manufacturing Chemists Assoc.
Interim president, American Telegraph & Telephone Co. (AT&T)
Founding director, New England Telephone Company
Director, National Bell Telephone Co.
Director, American Bell Telephone Co.
Director, American Telephone & Telegraph Co.
Director, Eliot National Bank
Director, New England Trust Co.
President, New England Navigation Co.
President, New Haven & Hartford Railroad Co.
President, Boston & Maine Railroad Co.
Director, Boston & Lowell Railroad
Vice-president, New England Trust Co.
President, Board of Trustees, Peter Bent Brigham Hospital
Director, Maine Central Railroad
Vice-president, Union Club
Director, Massachusetts Electric Cos.
President, Maine Central Railroad Co.
President, Chicago, Burlington & Northern Railroad Co.
Member, Restigouche Salmon Club
Member, Jekyll Island Club
Member, Somerset Club
Member, Canaveral Club
Member, Myopia Hunt Club
Co-founder, Permanent Wildlife Protection Fund

In 1865, **Alexander Cochrane** and his brother inherited their father's pioneering chemical works at Malden, Massachusetts. It manufactured sulfuric, nitric, & hydrochloric acids, and later indigo dye. Under Alexander's leadership as president the firm grew larger via acquisitions and mergers. Without going into the details, through various mergers, Allied Chemical and Monsanto are in one way or the other descendants of the Cochrane firm. Honeywell Corporation is as well because it acquired Allied-Signal Corp.

Cochrane invested in early telephone companies, and railroads that owned the rights of ways over which telegraph and telephone lines were built. He was such a large shareholder in the amalgamated entity, AT&T, that he served briefly as president while the firm searched for a new chief executive. Cochrane died in 1919.

Photo 97 Alexander Cochrane Jr., Unknown date, (Public Domain)

Thomas Cochran III, L.L.D.

Membership Years: 1924-1936

Birth: 1871

Birthplace: St. Paul, Minnesota

Death: 1936

Occupation: Lawyer, investment banker

Positions: Member, Skull & Bones Society
Coach, Minnesota Golden Gophers
Founder, Ardsley Hall Co.
Vice-president, Astor Trust Co.
Director, Bankers Trust Company
President, Liberty National Bank of New York
Partner, J.P. Morgan & Co.
Partner, Drexel & Co.
Partner, Morgan-Grenfell
Director, Chase National Bank
Director Chase Securities Corp.
Director, Morris Plan Co. Of New York
Director, General Electric Co.
Associate Member, Jekyll Island Club
President, Board-of Directors, Doctor's Hospital

Thomas Cochran III was the son of a real estate lawyer. He attended the Phillips Academy, then Yale where he played football and edited the *Yale Record*. He was inducted into the Skull & Bones Society. After graduating from Yale, Cochran coached the University of Minnesota Golden Gophers football team. He then studied law at Columbia.

Cochran founded the Ardsley Hall Co., a real estate investment firm in New York City in 1904. He was soon appointed a vice-president of the Astor Trust Co., and not long later, president of the Liberty National Bank of New York. In 1917, he became a partner in J.P. Morgan & Co.

Cochran was a widower who had no descendants and had amassed a fortune. He gave almost all his money to the Phillips Academy in Andover, Massachusetts and he funded the Addison Gallery of American Art which was constructed on the school's campus.

Cochran introduced his fellow J. P. Morgan & Co. partner **Junius Morgan** and **Dr. Joseph Wheelwright** to Long Point. He died in 1936 at the age of 65.

THOMAS COCHRAN
1871–1936

Photo 98 Thomas Cochran, Unknown date

Lt. Cmdr. Henry E. Coe Jr.

Membership Years: 1946-1954   **Birth:** 1894

Birthplace:

Death: 1954

Occupation: Attorney, financial professional

Positions:
Member, New York Stock Exchange
Partner, Mallory, Adee Co
Trustee, Yale Library
Director, Niagara Fire Insurance Co.
Director, Improved New York Properties Corp.
Director, Dolphin Jute Mills
Director, Philharmonic Society of New York City
Trustee, Village of Oyster Bay Cove

Henry Coe Jr.'s grandfather was a founder of the Metropolitan Museum of Art and served as its first president. Henry prepared at the Groton School. He graduated from Yale in 1917 and then studied law there. Coe obtained a seat on the New York Stock Exchange in 1926 when he was working for Reynolds, Fish & Co. In 1944, he was a founding partner of Mallory, Adee & Co. Coe was an associate member of the Jekyll Island Club. He died in 1954.

Henry E. Coe III

Membership Years: 1969-1998   **Birth:** 1925

               Birthplace: New York City

               Death: 1997

Occupation: Banker

Positions: Vice-president, Chase Manhattan Bank
      Managing Director, Chase Manhattan Overseas Corp.
      National Secretary, Ducks Unlimited
      Chairman, Waterfowl Research Foundation

Henry (Tony) Coe prepared at the Groton School before attending Yale. He graduated in 1946 and died in 1997 at the age of 71.

Gen. Frederick Trubee Davison

Membership Years: 1945-1965   **Birth:** 1896

Birthplace: New York City

Death: 1974

Occupation: Naval aviator, government executive

Positions: Member, Skull & Bones Society
Militia leader
Assemblyman, Nassau County
Chairman, National Crime Commission
Assistant Secretary for War
President, American Museum of National History
Honorary Trustee, American Museum of National History
Member, New York State Assembly
Trustee, Yale University
President, Air Power League
President, National Air Council
Member, Boone & Crockett Club
Director, personnel, Central Intelligence Agency
Assistant to the Director, Central Intelligence Agency

J.P Morgan chose Trubee Davison's father, Henry Davison, to succeed him as the managing partner of J.P. Morgan & Co. Trubee was educated at the Groton School, which his grandfather, Endicott Peabody, had founded in 1884.

Trubee enrolled at Yale in 1914. After his freshman year, he spent the summer overseas working as an ambulance attendant and driver transporting the wounded to Paris for treatment. Back at Yale, Trubee developed an interest in airplanes —particularly flying boats. He foresaw them being used for coastal defense against ships and submarines. Remarkably, he convinced his parents to fund a militia so he and his contemporaries at Yale could learn to fly. J.P. Morgan & Co. put up $100,000 to get their program started. Long Point Company members **Harry Payne Whitney** and **Payne Whitney** each contributed $25,000. **Louis Steenrod Thompson** also assisted.

Davison and his contemporaries spent the following summer at his father's Long Island estate and began learning to fly nearby. A few of the young men soloed before they returned to Yale for the next school year. The militia continued training the following summer. At first, the military took no interest in them, or in the concept the young Davison was promoting. However, he eventually convinced the Navy to allow him to participate in a coastal exercise. From the air, in the aircraft his group had trained in, Trubee demonstrated he could locate the dummy subservice mines that had been laid for the exercise. Naval officers were impressed. The militia continued their training and eventually the Navy decided to induct the young airmen, provided they demonstrated their skill through individual flight tests.

The day of their tests was somewhat of a social event, as the wealthy families and their friends embarked on their yachts to watch the young men take off from and land on Long Island Sound. The day went well for everyone, except for Trubee, who was the militia's de facto leader. The stress of the event overcame him, and he stalled while attempting to land. His aircraft plummeted into the Sound and Trubee suffered a broken back. The injury rendered him paraplegic. All the others passed their tests, and all but four ended up going overseas to participate in the war. Three were killed. A detailed account of the militia is the topic of the book, *The Millionaires' Unit,* by Marc Wortman. However, viewing a 2-hour documentary by the same name that was released in 2015, is a far easier way to learn more about the story.

After a long hospitalization and rehabilitation, Davison was able to stand and get around on crutches. Although he remained disabled for the rest of his life, he forged a distinguished career. After graduating in law from Columbia, Davison commenced working as an attorney. President Coolidge appointed him Chair of the National Crime Commission in 1925. The following year, Davison was appointed the Assistant Secretary of War for Air, a position he held for many years. (He ceremoniously landed a Fokker aircraft in 1927.) In 1941, he served as the Acting Deputy Chief of Staff, Army Air Force Combat Command. Later in the war, he worked in the Office of Strategic Services, the predecessor of the Central Intelligence Agency (CIA). When the CIA was formed, Davison set up its personnel system and served as the Assistant to the first Director. He was a recipient of the Navy Cross and the Distinguished Service Medal. Davison appeared on the cover of *Time* magazine twice.

Davison was the longest-serving president of the American Museum of Natural History. He initially served from 1933 to 1941 then took a break while he was on active military duty. He resumed the position from 1947 to 1951.

Because of his disability, Davison's Long Point skiff was equipped with a special chair. Staff used a lift to get him from the dock into the punt. He died in 1974.

Photo 99 Trubee Davison, 1927, (Public Domain)

Daniel P. Davison

Membership Years: 1965-2010   **Birth:** 1925

Birthplace: New York City

Death: 2010

Occupation: Lawyer, banker

Positions: Secretary, J. P. Morgan & Co.
                Vice-president, J. P. Morgan & Co.
                President, United States Trust Co.
                Chairman, Christie's Americas
                Chairman, Burlington Northern Railroad

Like his father, **Trubee Davison, Daniel Davison** was educated at the Groton School. During World War II, he piloted a B-17 Flying Fortress for the Army Air Corps. After the war ended, Davison attended Yale, graduating in 1949. He was inducted into the Skull & Bones Society. After completing a law degree at Harvard he practiced publicly for a few years and then joined J.P Morgan & Co., where he soon became secretary of the firm and later a vice-president. He is most often remembered for greatly expanding the business of the United States Trust Co., where he served as the chief executive officer.

Davison served as the managing director of the Long Point Company for three decades. He wrote a memoir about the Company that he dedicated to head keeper, Buck Walmsley, and his son and successor, David, and their wives. Titled, *Further Tales of Long Point*, it is a delightful and informative memoir. Like all the books written by members, it was privately printed and is therefore very rare. Davison was once charged in the marsh at Long Point for possessing more than the permissible limit of ducks and was subsequently convicted. He died in 2010 at the age of 85.

Endicott P. Davison

Membership Years: 1965-1967   **Birth:** 1923

             Birthplace: New York City

             Death: 1996

Occupation: Attorney

Positions: Partner, Winthrop, Stimson, Putnam & Roberts
      Director, Institutional Development and Capital Support, Yale University
      Board Member, American Museum of Natural History
      Board member, Union Theological Seminary
      Trustee and President, National Recreation and Park Assoc.
      Trustee, Groton School
      Member, Skull & Bones Society

Endicott Davison was educated at the Groton School. Like his brother **Daniel Davison**, he served as a pilot in the Army Air Corps during World War II. Following the war, he attended Yale, where he was the captain of the football team.

Davison graduated in law from the University of Virginia in 1951. He worked as a securities lawyer and became a partner in the firm Winthrop, Stimson, Putnam & Roberts. A Skull & Bones Society member, he successfully represented the Society in a dispute with a Apache Tribal leader pertaining to the alleged display of Geronimo's skull in the Society's building at Yale.

Davison maintained his interest in flying and owned a Grumman flying boat. He was less interested in duck hunting. His membership in the Long Point Company lasted just two years. Davison died in 1996.

Watson Bradley Dickerman

Membership Years: 1891-1923

Birth: 1846

Birthplace: Mt. Carmel, CT

Death: 1923

Occupation: Stockbroker, investor, trustee

Positions: Founding partner, Dominick & Dickerman
President, New York Stock Exchange
Partner, Moore & Schley
President as Receiver, Norfolk & Southern Railroad
President, Zoological Society of New York
Director, New York Stock Exchange Building Co.
Assistant Treasurer, J.P. Morgan & Co.
Director, Long Island Loan & Trust Co.
Director, Long Island Railroad
Director, Morning Star Mining Co.
Director, Ward Consolidated Mining Co.
Co-founder, Westchester Mutual Trust Co.
Member, Union League Club
Member, New York City Yacht Club
Member, Century Association
Founding Associate, New York Zoological Society
Member, Board of Managers, New York Zoological Society
Member, New York Farmers organization
Founding sponsor, Permanent Wildlife Protection Fund
Member, Suburban Riding & Driving Club
Member, Jekyll Island Club
Member, Westchester Country Club

Watson Dickerman grew up on a farm and was educated at the Williston Academy in Massachusetts. At the age of 17, he went west and began working as a bank clerk in Springfield, Illinois. Two years later, he moved to New York City. In 1870, when he was still in his early twenties, Dickerman and William Dominick formed the stock brokerage firm Dominick and Dickerman which survives to this day. In 1890, the members of the New York Stock Exchange elected Dickerman president. He served two terms. In 1899, he became one of the three partners in the brokerage Moore & Schley.

Dickerman joined the Long Point Company in 1891 and quickly took an active role in managing its affairs. He was also a full member of the Jekyll Island Club. After his wife died in 1908, Dickerman retired to the large, elaborate farm he had established on Long Island in 1884 to breed trotting horses, dogs, and cattle. He was posthumously inducted to the Harness Racing Hall of Fame in 1976.

Dickerman was a generous patron of the American Museum of Natural History and a founding associate and president of the New York Zoological Society. He was philanthropic and an advocate for wildlife conservation. He died in 1923, leaving a five-million-dollar estate to his second wife and their single child.

WATSON B. DICKERMAN
DOMINICK & DICKERMAN. PRESIDENT 1890-91

Photo 100 Watson Dickerman, c. 1891, (Public Domain)

Sir George Alexander Drummond

Membership Years: 1870-1907

Birth: 1829

Birthplace: Edinburgh, Scotland

Death: 1910

Occupation: Chemist, businessman, Canadian Senator

Positions: Chemist, John Redpath Co.
Member, Montreal Board of Trade
Partner, John Redpath & Son
Vice-president, Montreal Board of Trade
President, Montreal Board of Trade
President, Canada Sugar Refining Co.
Director, Bank of Montreal
Member, Canadian Senate
Vice-president, Bank of Montreal
President, Bank of Montreal
Director, Royal Trust Co.
Director, Canada Jute Co.
Director, Canadian Pacific Railway
Director, Ogilvie Milling Co.
Director, Labrador Co.
Director, Intercolonial Coal Mining Co.
Director, Mexican Light & Power Co.
Director, Trinidad Electrical Company
Commander, Royal Victorian Order
President, Royal Edward Institute

Sir George Alexander Drummond studied chemistry at the University of Edinburgh. He emigrated to Canada to assist John Redpath, who was building a sugar refinery in Montreal. Drummond married Redpath's daughter, and he soon became a partner in Redpath sugar. He died in 1910.

Photo 101 Sir George Drummond, Unknown date, (Public Domain)

Frederik S. Eaton

Membership Years: 1979-2021   **Birth:** 1938

Birthplace: Toronto

Death: 2021

Occupation: Lawyer, businessman, capitalist, diplomat

Positions: Director, T. Eaton Co.
President, T. Eaton Co.
Chairman, White Raven Capital Corp.
High Commissioner for Canada to the United Kingdom
Chancellor, University of New Brunswick
Member, Restigouche Salmon Club
President, Art Gallery of Ontario
President, Toronto Club
Fellow, Royal Society for the Encouragement of Arts, Manufacturing & Commerce
Board Chairman, Canadian Museum of History,
Director, TD Bank,
Director, Baton Broadcasting Co.
Director, *The Toronto Telegram*,
Officer, Order of Canada

Frederik Eaton graduated in law from the University of New Brunswick and then entered his family's retail business. He served on the boards of many Canadian businesses beyond those named above, including Trizec, Norcen, Hollinger, Abitibi, and Canada Packers. Controversy surrounded his appointment as High Commissioner for Canada to the United Kingdom after the press reported Eaton was a member of a club (the Long Point Company) that did not admit women. [331]

Frank H. Ellis

Membership Years: 1901-1924

Birth: 1845

Birthplace: Philadelphia

Death: 1925

Occupation: Sportsman

Positions: Director, Empire Passenger Railway Co.
Director, Citizens' Passenger Railway Co.

Frank Ellis was the son of lumberman Amos Ellis, who developed and owned Philadelphia's first public transit system, the Citizens' Railway Company. Amos' son Charles Ellis went on to manage his father's various business interests, while his younger brother, Frank, lived a leisurely sportsman's life of fishing, shooting, and breeding horses.

Frank lived in Philadelphia's Stratford Hotel for many years. Late in life, (1921) he moved to Orlando, Florida where he was prominent in the equestrian community. He died there four years later. The portion of his estate that passed through probate amounted to 4.3 million dollars. Ellis is most remembered for his passion for harness racing.

Marshall Field III

Membership Years: 1935-1947   **Birth:** 1893

Birthplace: Chicago

Death: 1956

Occupation: Investment banker, publisher

Positions: Director, Guarantee Trust Co.
Founder & Publisher, *Chicago Sun*
Publisher, *Parade*
President, Child Welfare League of America
Owner, Simon & Shuster
Owner, Pocket Books
Trustee, Roosevelt University
Vice-president, Long Island Biological Association

Marshall Field III was the grandson of the founder of a Chicago department store. His father died at an early age due to a gun accident. After his brother died, Marshal Field III became the sole heir to his grandfather's huge fortune.

Field was educated in England and graduated from Cambridge. He served in France during World War I. During the Roaring Twenties, Field built a grand estate on Long Island's Gold Coast that he modeled after those he had known in Britain. The estate, which he named Caumsett, encompassed well over 1,000 acres. Next door (so to speak) was the estate of Marjorie Lloyd-Smith, that her father Canadian-born Arthur Fleming had built for her when she wed Wilton Lloyd-Smith. Today, Caumsett is a state park.

Field's wife was the founding president of the Labrador Retriever Club of America (1931) and **Wilton Lloyd-Smith** served as the organization's first secretary and treasurer.

Field purchased a Loening Commuter flying boat in 1929. He introduced Lloyd-Smith to flying boats and both men became members of the Long Island Aviation Country Club. Together in 1937, they took joint delivery of the first Grumman G-41 Goose.

Photo 102 Marshal Field III, Unknown Date, (Roosevelt University)

George J. Forster

Membership Years: 1868-1869   **Birth:**

                                               Birthplace:

                                               Death:

Occupation: Importer and wholesale merchant

Positions: Principal, G.J. Forster & Co.
                  Member, Hamilton Board of Trade
                  Director, Canada Life Assurance Co.

George J. Forster was a wholesale merchant in Hamilton who imported groceries, wine, and liquor. He left the Company following a dispute about which members would be permitted to bring guests to Long Point and when.

Childs Frick

Membership Years: 1940-1953   **Birth:** 1883

Birthplace: Pittsburgh

Death: 1965

Occupation: Vertebrate paleontologist

Positions: Member, Board of Managers, New York Botanical Garden
Trustee, New York Zoological Society
Chairman, Conservation Committee, New York Zoological Society
Trustee, American Museum of Natural History
Honorary Staff Member, American Museum of Natural History
Honorary Curator of Mammals, Carnegie Museum
Member, Boone & Crockett Club
Member, Jekyll Island Club
Director, Mellon National Bank and Trust Co.
President, Board of Trustees, the Frick Collection

Child Frick, the son of Henry Clay Frick, was born in Pittsburgh in 1883. His father was a partner of Andrew Carnegie and served as the chief executive of the Carnegie Steel Co. According to *Forbes* magazine, Henry Clay Frick was the second wealthiest individual in the United States as of 1918. He left an estate valued at $94 million three years later.

Childs attended Princeton, graduating in 1905. He traveled, seeing the world, and collected game for a few years before moving home to Pittsburgh to assist his father in business. During World War I, he served in the Signal Corps in California, where he had the unusual privilege of taking courses in paleontology while serving. After the war, he moved to Long Island and joined the staff of the American Museum of Natural History in New York City. He is credited as the author of *Horned Ruminants of North America*

Frick was a major benefactor of the Museum. He funded a great many paleontological expeditions and created the Childs Frick Corporation to inventory and store the fossil artifacts the expeditions uncovered. At the time of his death, the collection contained hundreds of thousands of specimens. These, Frick left to the Museum, together with a large building to store them. [332]

Frick was a reserved individual who kept a low profile and avoided drawing attention to himself. In 1942, he wrote under a pseudonym when he penned a brief book of verse about Long Point that he dedicated to the Company's punters.

Frick's former Long Island estate, Clayton, is now home to the Nassau County Museum of Art.

George H. Gillespie

Membership Years: 1866-1871   **Birth:** 1827

Birthplace: Biggar Park, Scotland

Death: 1900

Occupation: Importer and wholesale merchant, securities broker, insurance executive

Positions: Partner, Brown, Gillespie & Co.
Member, Hamilton Board of Trade
Member, Arbitration Committee, Hamilton Board of Trade
Director, Dundas Cotton Mills
Director, Canada Life Assurance Co.
Vice-president, Canada Life Assurance Co.
President, Hamilton Provident & Loan Soc.

George H. Gillespie came to Canada as a young man in 1844. He learned the wholesale trade in Montreal, before moving to Hamilton to work for Denholm & Co. Together with **Adam Brown**, he formed Brown, Gillespie & Co. to import tea, wine, groceries, and dry goods. After suffering financial difficulties in 1867, he embarked on a new career selling securities and insurance.

John Gillespie

Membership Years: 1867

Birth:

Birthplace: Biggar Park, Scotland

Death:

Occupation: Uncertain

Positions: Principal, Brown, Gillespie & Co.

John Gillespie likely resided in Edinburgh, Scotland. It is improbable that he attended the meeting held at the Royal Hotel in Hamilton on January 29, 1867, when the founders were allotted stock in the Company. Nonetheless, he was allocated twelve shares. It is possible he provided financing to **George H. Gillespie** to assist him in making bids when Long Point was put up for auction in 1866.

A year later, acting as trustee for **George H. Gillespie**'s affairs, he took possession of George's shares. He disposed of them, as well as his own shares over the next few years. It is unlikely he ever visited Long Point.

Col. Allan Gilmour

Membership Years: 1877-1885

Birth: 1816

Birthplace: Shotts, Scotland

Death: 1895

Occupation: Lumberman

Positions: Principal, Gilmour & Co.
President, Ottawa Curling Club
Founder, Art Association of Ontario

Allan Gilmour emigrated to Canada in 1832. He first worked for the William Ritchie Co. in Montreal but eventually established his own lumber business. A steam powered mill he had constructed at Trenton was for a time reputed to be one of the largest sawmills in the world. Gilmour also owned mills at Gatineau.

Gilmour was a veteran of the Fenian conflict. As his wealth increased, he became an avid art collector. He acquired his shares in the Long Point Company from **William Hunter**.

Gilmour never married. In the later years of his life, he resided with his companion **John Manuel** to whom he transferred his shares in the Long Point Company through a trust. When he died in 1895, the amount of his estate that passed through probate amounted to $1,452,824, most of which passed to **John Manuel**.

Photo 103 Allan Gilmour, Unknown date, (Public Domain)

Maj. Melville Ross Gooderham

Membership Years: 1922-1937　　　　**Birth:** 1877

Birthplace: Toronto

Death: 1951

Occupation: Lawyer, insurance executive

Positions:　President, Manufacturer's Life Insurance Company
Director, Canada Permanent Trust Co.
Director, Consumers Gas Co.
Chairman, Board of Governors, Ridley College

Melville Ross Gooderham prepared at Ridley College and later graduated from Osgoode Law School. He was called to the bar in 1900. Gooderham worked for the Manufacturer's Life Insurance Company prior to and after serving overseas during World War I. He succeeded his father as president of Manufacturers Life. Gooderham died in 1951.

C. Athol Gordon

Membership Years: 1980-1991   **Birth:**

                                         Birthplace:

                                         Death: 2006

Occupation: Civil engineer, stockbroker

Positions: Director, MacDougall, MacDougall & MacTier Inc.
                   Trustee, Mount Royal Cemetery
                   President, Douglas Hospital Foundation
                   President, Orleans Fishing Club

Athol Gordon prepared at Bishop's College School, Lennoxville, Quebec and the Institute Le Rosey in Switzerland. He graduated in engineering from McGill and the Massachusetts Institute of Technology. After working for his family's Pentagon Construction Co., which was absorbed into the firm that has since become SNC-Lavalin, he entered the securities sales business. In 2002, he was disciplined by the Bourse de Montreal for failing to act in a client's best interest and was fined $30,000. Gordon died in 2006.

Lyman R. Green

Membership Years: 1877-1881   **Birth:**

                                        Birthplace:

                                        Death:

Occupation: Tea importer

Positions: Partner, B. G. Arnold & Co.
Member, New York City Chamber of Commerce
Member, New York Importers and Grocers Exchange
Member, Board of Managers, Brooklyn St. John's Hospital

Lyman Green was a partner in New York's B. G. Arnold & Co. He handled the firm's tea business. Green acquired his shares in the Long Point Company from fellow tea importer **William Hunter**. While he took an active role managing the affairs of the Company, his tenure was brief because his shares were transferred to a bankruptcy trustee when the B.G. Arnold & Co. suffered an insolvency.

Cmdr. Malcolm W. Greenough

Membership Years: 1947-1948   **Birth:** 1904

Birthplace:

Death:1948

Occupation: Investment banker

Positions: Partner, Hutchins & Parkinson
Member, Perkins Institution and Massachusetts School for the Blind
Trustee, Essex Institute
Trustee, Massachusetts Public Reservations
Vice-commodore, Eastern Yacht Club
Member, Hasty Pudding Club[230]
Member, Harvard Memorial Society

Malcolm W. Greenough enrolled at Harvard in 1921, at the age of 16. In 1924 and 1925, he captained the football team, the youngest individual to ever hold the position. After graduating in 1925, he attended Harvard Business School.

Greenough became a naval reserve officer in 1937. During World War II, he commanded the destroyer escort *Rudderow*. He was inducted to the Order of the British Empire. Greenough's membership in the Long Point Company lasted only one year because he died shortly after joining at the age of 44.

Photo 104 Malcolm Greenough, 1924 (Public Domain)

---

[230] The Hasty Pudding Club is a Harvard student social club founded in 1795. Over the years, five members have served as President of the United States. Lore is that early members ate a pudding made from corn meal, milk & molasses, as a desert at meetings.

Clement A. Griscom Jr.

Membership Years: 1900-1924   **Birth:** 1868

Birthplace: Philadelphia

Death: 1912

Occupation: Businessman

Positions: General Manager, International Mercantile Marine Co.
President, National Transit Co., (a Standard Oil pipeline.)
Director, Pennsylvania Railroad
Director, United States Steel
Director, Long Island Railroad
Director, Bank of North America
Director, Insurance Company of North America
Director, Empire Trust Co.
Director, New York Real Estate Security Co.
President, Reilly Repair & Supply Co.
President, Society of Naval Architects and Marine Engineers
Director, Development Company of America
Director, Maritime Association of the Port of New York.
Senior Editor, Theosophical Quarterly
Member, New York Yacht Club

Clement A. Griscom Jr.'s father founded the International Navigation Company, a major ocean shipping and transit enterprise that expanded by acquiring the Inman and Red Star Lines. Later, through financial engineering from J.P. Morgan & Co., the firm consolidated the White Star Line, American Line, Leyland Line, Atlantic Transport Line, and Dominion Line to form the International Mercantile Marine Co. The younger Griscom graduated from the University of Pennsylvania and later took over management of the enterprise.

Together with J. P. Morgan and John Rockefeller, **Clement Griscom** served as a member of the American National Red Cross Relief Committee of New York. As an editor of Theosophical Quarterly, he sometimes wrote under the name Acton Griscom.

Griscom's son, Ludlow Griscom, was a friend of Louis Agazzis Fuertes. Like Fuertes Ludlow Griscom became a prominent ornithologist. He was member of the staff of American Museum of Natural History. Ludlow greatly advanced the principle that birds could be identified by being viewed in their natural environment, rather than being shot. Clement Griscom's shares in the Long Point Company remained with his estate for 12 years before being acquired by **Richard Howe**. Whether Ludlow ever visited Long Point could be a topic for further research.

John H. Hale

Membership Years: 1973-2002   **Birth:** 1924

                                                    Birthplace: London, England

                                                    Death: 2002

Occupation: Businessman

Positions: Vice-president, Finance, Alcan Aluminum Ltd.
Chairman, Pearson, Plc.
Director, The Economist Newspaper

John Hale served as president of the Long Point Company from 1983 until his death in 2002. He held the position even while he was living in London. Hale left a bequest to the Company. Some of the funds were used to purchase a sterling silver bowl. It is awarded to a member and punter if they shoot ten different species of ducks or more in a single day, while remaining below the combined regulatory limit for two men of 12 ducks.

Ferris F. Hamilton

Membership Years: 1969-1985   **Birth:** 1925

                                        Birthplace:

                                        Death: 1985

Occupation: Oil industry executive

Positions: Co-founder, Hamilton Brothers Oil Company

Ferris Hamilton studied engineering at Princeton. He left school to fly as a pilot during World War II and did not return to his studies afterward. Instead, he went to work as an oilfield roustabout. In 1949, Ferris and his brother bought a drilling rig and formed the Hamilton Brothers Oil Company. The firm was active in Texas and Alberta. Notably, even though their company was small, the Hamilton brothers were the first to produce North Sea oil.

Ferris was the first Westerner to be a member of the Long Point Company, probably because he married the stepdaughter of Company member **John Pratt Jr**. and inherited his shares.

Hamilton, who had heart disease, suffered a fatal heart attack in the Long Point marsh and died there in 1985 at the age of 59. His punter, Pete Overbaugh, was unable to recover the body into the skiff from which Ferris had fallen. Sadly, Overbaugh had to tow Hamilton's body back to The Cottages.

Lt. E. Roland Harriman

Membership Years: 1935-1946   **Birth:** 1895

Birthplace: New York City

Death: 1978

Occupation: Investment banker, railroad executive

Positions: Director, Union Pacific Railroad
Chairman, Union Pacific Railroad
Director Union Banking Corp.
President, American Red Cross
Founder and Chairman, U.S Trotting Assoc.
Treasurer, American Museum of Natural History
Chairman, Boys' Club of New York

    E. Roland Harriman attended the Groton School then studied economics and history at Yale. He was a member of the crew team and was inducted into the Scull & Bones Society. His father had controlled the Union Pacific Railroad, and Roland was a member of the railroad's board of directors from 1920 until the time of his death. He assumed the role of chairman of the railway in 1946, perhaps reluctantly. During World War II, he was the chairman of the American Red Cross.

    Like other Long Point Company members, Harriman was a member of the syndicate that sponsored production of the Grumman G-21 flying boat. He took delivery of the third aircraft to come off the production line. Harriman died in 1978.

Photo 105 E. Roland Harriman [295]

Edward W. Harris

Membership Years: 1877-1906   **Birth:** 1832

Birthplace: Long Point settlement

Death: 1925

Occupation: Lawyer, businessman

Positions: Director, Port Ryerse Harbor Co.
Co-founder, Ontario Loan & Debenture Co.
Co-founder, London Life Insurance Co.
Director, London and Port Stanley Railway
Vice-president, Canada Car Co.

Edward Harris was born in the Long Point settlement in 1832. In 1860, he married Sophia Ryerson, a daughter of Col. Joseph Ryerson. Harris was called to the bar in 1854 and went to London, Ontario where he practiced with his brothers **George B Harris** and John Harris. In 1870, together with Joseph Jeffery, he organized the Ontario Loan & Debenture Co. Four years later, the two men formed the London Life Insurance Co.

In 1869, Harris purchased the mill right at Port Ryerse for a mill that had previously burned. Together with John Potts, he redeveloped the facility. It burned on Sept 27, 1888. He also engaged in the commercial fishing business on Long Point Bay, although his venture was unsuccessful.

Harris was the author of *History and historiettes: United Empire Loyalists* (1897), *Is Game of Any Value to the Farmer* (1891), *The Quail* (1905), *Our Great Lakes Fisheries: a Vanishing Heritage (1905), Canada, the Making of a Nation* (1907), *A Review of Civic Ownership* (1908), and *Recollections of Long Point* (1918). He resided at Elden House in London, an estate his father had built. After he experienced serious financial challenges in the 1880's, he sold the house to his brother **George B. Harris**. Today, the house is a historical site open to the public. Harris served as president of the Long Point Company from 1886-1898. He died in 1925.

Lt. George B. Harris

Membership Years: 1877-1902

Birth: c. 1836

Birthplace: London, Ontario

Death: 1923

Occupation: Lawyer, insurance executive

Positions: Director, Northern Life Assurance Company of Canada
Director, London and Western Trust Co.
Director, London Life Insurance Co.

George B. Harris was educated at the Bayly Grammar School. He practiced law with his brothers, Edward, and John. Like them, he was instrumental in the organization of the Ontario Loan & Debenture Co. and the London Life Insurance Co. George also practiced real estate law. In the 1880's he acquired the family's ancestral home, Elden House in London. It is an historical site open to the public. He died 1923.

Photo 106 George B. Harris, Unknown date (Public Domain)

William C. Harris

Membership Years: 1955-1980

Birth: 1900

Birthplace: Toronto

Death: 1987

Occupation: Stockbroker, bond dealer, banker

Positions: President, W. C. Harris & Co.
Chairman, Harris & Partners
Member, Toronto Stock Exchange
Director, Imperial Life Assurance Co.
Vice-president, Bank of Nova Scotia
Director, Bank of Nova Scotia
Director, Canada Packers Inc.
Director, Canadian General Electric Co.
Director, Toronto General Trust Corp.
Director, Brazilian Light & Power Co.
Director, Canada Permanent Mortgage Co.
Director, Imperial Life Assurance Co.
Director, Ralston Purina Co.
Chairman, Osler & Hammond Ltd.
Member, Rolling Rock Hunt Club
Member, Caledon Mountain Trout Club
Member, Jupiter Island Club
Member, Board of Governors, York University
Trustee, Hospital for Sick Children

William Harris, was born in 1900. He was not related to Long Point Company members **Edward Harris** or **George Harris**. He graduated from Toronto's Riverdale Collegiate and then from the University of Toronto in 1925 with a degree in commerce. His firm Harris & Partners was merged with Dominion Securities in 1973.

Harris was elected president of the Company in 1968 and served for seven years. Later in his tenure, he proposed the Company donate Long Point in exchange for a fixed lease from the government. Because the proposal would have led to the eventual sunset of the Company, it was not accepted by a majority of the members and Harris relinquished his position as president. His son, William B. Harris, succeeded him as president and during his tenure the Company did donate about half of Long Point.

Photo 107 William C. Harris

William B. Harris

Membership Years: 1967-1982　　　**Birth:** 1930

　　　　　　　　　　　　　　　　　　Birthplace: Toronto

　　　　　　　　　　　　　　　　　　Death: 2022

Occupation: Banker

Positions:　Co-chairman, Dominion Securities
Chairman, Barclay's Bank of Canada
Chairman, Mercantile and General Reinsurance
Chairman, BPI Financial
Director, Empire Life
Director, Alcan Aluminum Co.
Board member, Key Publishing Co.
Board member, Toronto Symphony Orchestra
Board member, National Ballet of Canada
Board member, National Ballet School
Board member, Ballet Jorgen
Board member, Royal Ontario Museum.
Board member, Hospital for Sick Children
Member, Board of Governors, University of Toronto
Chairman, Board of Governors, University of Toronto
Chairman, World Wildlife Fund, Canada
Founding director, Nature Conservancy of Canada

William B. Harris was the son of member **William C. Harris**. He was educated at Upper Canada College, the University of Toronto, and Oxford. He served as president of the Long Point Company from 1975 to 1982 and was instrumental in the Company's decision to donate half of Long Point.

Horatio Hathaway

Membership Years: 1879-1897   **Birth:** 1831

Birthplace: New Bedford, MA

Death: 1898

Occupation: Textile industrialist

Positions: Member, Harvard Porcellian Club
President, Acushnet Mill Corp.
President, Hathaway Manufacturing Co.
Director, Wamsutta Mills
Director, Mechanics National Bank
Director, Potomska Mills
Treasurer, Potomska Mills
Trustee, New Bedford Institute for Savings
Co-founder & President, St. Luke's Hospital
President, New Bedford City Council

Horatio Hathaway 's father was a far east trader and tea importer. The younger Hathaway attended Phillips Academy, then Harvard, graduating in 1850. He then went to sea, sailing on merchant ships traveling to and from China.

After inheriting a considerable fortune, Hathaway entered the textile business and became a prominent industrialist. His Wamsutta Mill was the largest cotton weaving factory in the world and employed 2,000 workers. Remnants of Hathaway's business were eventually acquired by Warren Buffet's Berkshire Hathaway holding company.

Hathaway died in 1898. His Long Point Company shares passed to his son **Thomas S. Hathaway.**

Photo 108 Horatio Hathaway, unknown date. (Public Domain)

Capt. Thomas S. Hathaway

Membership Years: 1899-1924

Birth: 1866

Birthplace: New Bedford, MA

Death: 1924

Occupation: Capitalist

Positions: President, Acushnet Mill Corp.
President, Hathaway Manufacturing Co.
President, National Bank of Commerce of New Bedford
President, Trustee, New Bedford Institute for Savings
Director, Mechanics National Bank
Director, Wamsutta Mills
Director, Union Cotton Manufacturing Co.
Director, New Bedford and Onset Street Railway Co.
Director, Union Street Railway Co.
Director, First National Bank
Director, Pocassett Manufacturing Co.
Director, Border City Manufacturing Co.
Director, Morse Twist Drill & Machine Co.
Member, New Bedford Yacht Club
Member, New York City Yacht Club
Member, India Wharf Rats Club

Thomas Hathaway graduated from Harvard then entered his father's textile business. He never married and died in 1924 at the age of 57.

Photo 109 Thomas Hathaway, Unknown date, (Public Domain)

Lt. Horatio Hathaway Jr.

Membership Years: 1924-1934

Birth: 1870

Birthplace: New Bedford, MA

Death: 1934

Occupation: Sportsman

Positions: Director, Acushnet Mill Corp.
Director, Wamsutta Mills
President, Fairfield Ice. Co.
Member, Massachusetts House of Representatives
Member, India Wharf Rats Club

Horatio Hathaway Jr. was convicted for shooting shore birds in Massachusetts when he a young man. He graduated from Harvard in 1893. After inheriting a fortune from his father, Hathaway largely eschewed business to live a leisurely, sporting life. Some of his avocations were fox hunting, breeding hounds, raising Guernsey cattle, and yachting. He was a member of the Norfolk Hunt Club in Dedham, where he rode regularly.

During World War I, Hathaway recruited men to the Merchant Marine. He inherited his brother's shares in the Long Point Company in 1924. Hathaway died in 1934.

Photo 110 Horatio Hathaway Jr., 1911 (Public Domain)

Thomas J. Havemeyer

Membership Years: 1877-1881

Birth: 1845

Birthplace: New York City

Death: 1899

Occupation: Financier

Positions: Partner, American Sugar Refining Co.
Member, Currituck Shooting Clu*b*
Member, New York Club
Member, New York Yacht Club
Member, South Side Sportsmen's Club
Member, Cuttyhunk Club

Thomas Havemeyer's father essentially monopolized the sugar refining industry in the United States. After their father's death, his sons inherited the enterprise.

Thomas was educated at Heidelberg University in Germany. Flush with inherited wealth, he lived a high life at the family estate at Throggs Neck, N.Y., a summer residence in Maine, and at various New York City apartments. He traveled and entertained guests on his 38-metre-long steam yacht *Ideal*. **William Hunter** likely introduced Havemeyer to the Long Point Company.

Throughout his life, Havemeyer professed to be a bachelor. When he was 37 years of age, a women named Helen Havemeyer sued him, claiming they had been married on Sept. 26, 1875, and that they had lived together until 1882. After Havemeyer died at 53 in 1899, another woman, Anna Wright sued his estate claiming she and Havemeyer had been married since Sept. 8, 1884. Research into the outcomes of these litigations revealed nothing, suggesting both claims may have been settled confidentially.

Augustus Hemenway

Membership Years: 1883-1931

Birth: c. 1853

Birthplace: Boston

Death: 1931

Occupation: Ship, mine, and timberland owner, philanthropist

Positions: Member, Massachusetts House of Representatives
Director, Chicago, Burlington & Northern Railroad
Trustee, Boston Museum of Fine Arts
Secretary, Board of Directors, Sharon Sanitarium
Founding member, Metropolitan Park Commission
Founding member and Trustee, Massachusetts Public Reserves
Member, Board of Overseers, Harvard University
Treasurer, Boston Eye & Ear Infirmary
Trustee, Peter Bent Brigham Hospital
Rear Commodore, Eastern Yacht Club
Member, Boston Yacht Club
Vice-president, Massachusetts Fish & Game Protective Association

Augustus Hemenway graduated from Harvard in 1875. The following year, he and his sister Amy inherited a fortune, likely the largest in Massachusetts up to that time, and Hemenway gifted the university a new campus gymnasium. Their father had established trade between the U.S. and South America where he developed copper, silver, and saltpeter mines. He also owned a 2,500-acre sugar plantation in Cuba that was worked by 160 enslave people, and lumber mills in Maine. His fleet of at least eight ships serviced these various ventures.

Hemenway's spouse, Harriet spearheaded the effort to stop the trade of wild bird feathers. Together with her cousin, she founded the Massachusetts Audubon Society (the first such organization in the United States) and successfully lobbied the Massachusetts legislature to ban the wild bird feather trade.

Amy Hemenway married **Louis Cabot,** and it was Cabot who brought his relatively young brother-in-law Augustus into the Long Point Company. Hemenway was an avid sailor, who together with fellow Long Point Company member **Charles J. Paine** and others, owned the America's Cup defender *Puritan*. During the last decade of his life, he visited Long Point infrequently, instead delegating his club privileges to his friend the artist Frank Weston Benson. Hemenway died at the age of 77 in 1931.

Figure 61. Portrait of Augustus Hemenway. Etching by Frank Weston Benson. Unknown Date, (Public Domain)

Lt. Cmdr. Barklie M. Henry

Membership Years: 1935-1945   **Birth:** 1902

Birthplace: Rosemont, Pennsylvania

Death: 1966

Occupation: Military reserve officer, investment banker, intellectual, trustee

Positions: Director, U.S. Trust Co.
Director, AT&T
Director, Texas Co.
President, John Hay Whitney Foundation
Vice-chairman, Carnegie Institution
President, Community Service Society of New York
President, New York Association for Improving the Condition of the Poor
Honorary Governor, Payne Whitney Psychiatric Clinic
President, Board of New York Hospital
Trustee, Vincent Astor Foundation
Trustee, the Rockefeller Institute
Trustee, Community Services Society of New York
Director, Milbank Memorial Fund
Trustee, Cooper Union
Member, Harvard Board of Directors
Trustee, American Academy in Rome

Barklie (Buz) Henry was the son of prominent Philadelphia investment banker W. Barkley Henry. He prepared at St. George's School in Newport, Rhode Island and then attended Harvard where he served on the Board of the *Lampoon* and as its Ibis. He was also captain of the crew team. In his final year at Harvard, Henry published a novel titled *Deceit*, which found considerable acclaim. After graduating in 1924, he went on to further studies at Oxford.

On returning to the U.S., Henry worked as a writer for *Atlantic Monthly*, the *Boston American* and served as the editor of *The Youth's Companion* magazine. His first exposure to the financial realm was a position with the Guarantee Trust Co.

During World War II, Henry served as the commanding officer of the destroyer escorts *USS Gantner* and *USS Jesse Rutherford*. Highly respected for his intellect, he later became a member of the Princeton Consultants advisory board, an entity well known for its association with the Central Intelligence Agency's. President Eisenhower subsequently appointed him to the four-person Committee on International Information Activities.

Henry's association with the Long Point Company was a consequence of his marriage to Barbara Vanderbilt Whitney, a daughter of **Harry Payne Whitney.** Henry died of a heart attack in 1966 at the age of 64.

Photo 111 Barklie Henry [295]

James Augustus Hewlett

Membership Years: 1868-1891

Birth: 1835

Birthplace: Rock Hill, New York

Death: 1891

Occupation: Importer and wholesale merchant

Positions: Principal, Hewlett & Torrance
Member, Importers and Grocers Exchange.
Member, Maritime Association of the Port of New York
Member, Board of Arbitration, Maritime Assoc. of the Port of New York
Trustee, Sugar Exchange
Trustee, Atlantic Mutual Insurance Co.

Importer **James Hewlett**'s business was located at 67 Wall St., very close to that of **William B. Hunter**. He imported tea, coffee, spices, and other goods from distant sources. Hewlett's business partner in New York was Henry Torrance, whose father had been the first merchant in Montreal to directly import tea from China.

For decades, Long Point Company members only drank coffee supplied by Hewlett when they stayed at The Cottages. After he died in 1891, a portrait of Hewlett was hung in the Company dining room.

Photo 112 James A. Hewlett

Lt. Col. Henry L. Higginson

Membership Years: 1889-1906   **Birth:** 1834

Birthplace: New York City

Death: 1919

Occupation: Military officer, investment banker

Positions: Director, National Shawmut Bank of Boston
Director, New York and New England Railway Co.
Director, Mexican Telegraph Co.
Director, General Electric Co.
Treasurer, Archeology Institute of America
Trustee, Carnegie Institution of Washington.
Member, Harvard College Board
President, Harvard Club of Boston

Henry Higginson was raised in Boston and schooled at the Boston Latin School. He attended Harvard, but left in 1856, his freshman year, to study music in Vienna. He returned in late 1860. At the outset of the Civil War, Higginson entered the 2nd Massachusetts Infantry Regiment. He was shot and slashed on the battlefield at Aldie, Virginia in June 1863. After suffering a difficult journey back to Boston in a wagon, he was discharged.

After recovering Higginson joined his father's investment bank, Lee, Higginson & Co. He remained interested in music his entire life and he founded the Boston Symphony Orchestra. Higginson preferred and used the title Major, instead of his higher rank. Yale awarded him an honorary L.L.D degree in 1901. He died in 1919.

Photo 113 Henry L. Higginson

Richard Flint Howe

Membership Years: 1924-1943   **Birth:** 1863

Birthplace: Green Bay, Wisconsin

Death: 1943

Occupation: Lawyer, businessman

Positions: Secretary/Treasurer International Harvester Corp
Member, Aircraft Production Board

Richard Flint Howe graduated from Harvard Law School in 1884. He married Abby Deering, the daughter of William Deering who co-founded the International Harvester Co. Howe served as Harvester's first corporate secretary and treasurer. President Woodrow Wilson appointed him to the Aircraft Production Board during World War I.

Howe, resided at Jericho on Long Island, lived a high life. His avocations included breeding horses, raising Guernsey cattle, and sailing on his 57-metre yacht *Seaborn*. He died at the age of 79 in 1943 after falling from a horse at his winter "cottage" in Aiken, SC. The 17,000 square-foot cottage is now the home of the Aiken County Historical Museum.

Figure. 62 Richard F. Howe. Portrait by Zorn Anders. 1904 (Public Domain)

William Deering Howe

Membership Years: 1945-1948   **Birth:** 1900

Birthplace: Chicago, Illinois

Death: 1948

Occupation: Businessman

Positions: President, Transair, Inc.
Co-founder United Airports Exports, Inc.
Director, Lehigh Coal & Navigation Co.

William Howe graduated from Harvard in 1922. He inherited his Long Point Company shares from his father, **Richard Howe**. His maternal grandfather co-founded International Harvester. He died of a heart attack while swimming at Veradero Beach, Cuba. He was just 48 years old.

Lt. William B. Hunter

Membership Years: 1867-1885   **Birth:** c. 1825

Birthplace:

Death: 1888

Occupation: Tea importer and wholesaler

Positions: Principal, Wm. H. Hunter & Co.
                  Director, Knickerbocker Life Insurance Co.

William Hunter was listed as a member of the Norfolk 1st Battalion as of 1850. He moved to Hamilton where he learned the wholesale trade. By 1852, he was residing in New York City and working for himself as a commission merchant. His place of business was at the corner of Old Slip and Water Street, close to both Wall Street and the wharfs where ships docked.

Hunter became a member of the New York City Chamber of Commerce, the Tea Exchange, and later the Grocer's Exchange. He took on George Wykes Jr., John R. Steven, and Canadian Thomas B. Robb as partners. Their firm grew to be a major importer of English tea, much of it for the Canadian market. The recession that followed the Panic of 1873 impacted the firm and it went bankrupt in 1875. Hunter, who had diversified his investments, seems to have successfully coped with the circumstances.

Hunter's vision was for the Long Point Company to be an exclusive, stable club for upper class sportsman. Accordingly, he recruited wealthy individuals from New York City that he was acquainted with from his business dealings. For a very brief period, he held 40% of the Long Point Company's shares. Hunter was an aggressive shooter. He died at home in Brooklyn in 1888 at the age of 64.

Thomas C. Kerr

Membership Years: 1866-1871　　　　**Birth:**

Birthplace: Scotland

Death: 1878

Occupation:　Grocery wholesaler, financier

Positions:　　Partner, A. & T.C. Kerr & Co.
　　　　　　　Partner, Kerr, Brown, & MacKenzie
　　　　　　　Director, Canada Life Assurance Co.

Thomas Kerr was a founder of the Long Point Company and served as its first president. In 1836, he and his brother Archibald established the import firm A. & T.C. Kerr & Co. in Hamilton. To support their trading, they became involved in shipbuilding and ownership beginning in 1847. The first sailing vessel the Long Point Company made use of was the *T. C. Kerr*, captained by Nathan Woodward of Port Rowan.

　　Kerr later went into business with **John Brown** and **John MacKenzie**, and their firm became a very large wholesale importer of dry goods, groceries, wine, and liquor. Kerr co-founded the Canada Life Assurance Co., a stock company with Hugh Baker in 1847. He died overseas in London in 1878.

Robert A. Laidlaw

Membership Years: 1958-1976   **Birth:** 1886

Birthplace: Barrie, Ontario

Death: 1976

Occupation: Businessman

Positions: Chairman, National Trust Co.
Board member, DeHavilland Aircraft Co.
Director, Bell Canada
Director, Bank of Montreal
Board member, British American Oil Co.
Vice-president, Canada Life Assurance Co.
Director, de Havilland Aircraft of Canada, Ltd.
Director, Canada Life Assurance Co.
Director, Steel Company of Canada
Director, Moore Corp.
Director, British American Oil Co.
Director, Gulf Oil Canada, Ltd.
Director, Toronto Savings & Loan
Director, Maple Leaf Gardens,
Governor, Upper Canada College
Chairman, Board of Trustees, Hospital for Sick Children
Founding member, Quetico Foundation

Robert A. Laidlaw prepared at Upper Canada College before attending the University of Toronto. He then worked for his father, R. A. Laidlaw, in the family's lumber business. A noted philanthropist, Laidlaw died 1976.

Lt. Allen T. Lambert

Membership Years: 1976-1980   **Birth:** 1911

Birthplace: Regina, Saskatchewan

Death: 2002

Occupation: Banker

Positions: President, Toronto Dominion Bank
Board Chairman, Toronto Dominion Bank
President, International Monetary Conference
Director, Brascan Corp.

Allen T. Lambert joined the Bank of Toronto while still a teenager. During World War II, he served in the Navy on a corvette. After being released from duty, Lambert returned to the Bank of Toronto. He was named the manager of the bank's branch in Yellowknife in 1947.

When the Bank of Toronto and the Dominion Bank merged, Lambert was put in charge of the new entity, the Toronto Dominion Bank.

Lambert, who was an Officer of the Order of Canada, left a significant bequest to the Nature Conservancy.

Lt. Col. Reuben W. Leonard

Membership Years: 1922-1927   **Birth:** 1860

                                                  Birthplace: Brantford, Ontario

                                                  Death: 1930

Occupation: Military officer, engineer, capitalist

Positions: Engineer, Canadian Pacific Railway
                 Chief Engineer, Cumberland Railway and Coal Co.
                 Chief Engineer, St. Lawrence & Adirondack Railway
                 Chief Engineer, Cape Breton Railway
                 Founder, General Manager & President, Coniagas Mines Ltd.
                 Founder & President, Coniagas Reduction Company
                 President, Engineering Institute of Canada
                 Vice-president, Canadian Mining Institute
                 Vice-president, Canadian Society of Civil Engineers
                 Director, Bank of Montreal
                 Member, Governing Council, University of Toronto,
                 Governor, Wycliffe College
                 Chairman, National Transcontinental Railway Commission
                 President, Royal Military College Club
                 Member, Board of Governors, Ridley College
                 Member, Canadian Battlefields Memorials Commission
                 Governor, Kingston School of Mining
                 Founder, Leonard Foundation

Reuben Leonard attended Brantford Collegiate Institute, then enrolled at the Royal Military College at Kingston. He graduated as a civil engineer and began his working career with the Canadian Pacific Railway. Later, he became closely involved with the construction of the first hydroelectric plant at Niagara. During the Northwest Rebellion of the Métis under Louis Riel, he was assigned the position of Staff Officer for Transport.

In 1905, Leonard developed a silver and nickel mine at Cobalt, Ontario that he named CONIAGAS. The name was derived from the terms in the Periodic Table of Elements for metals that were prevalent in the ore, namely Co (Cobalt), Ni (Nickel), Ag (Silver), and As (Arsenic). He served overseas very briefly during WWI.

Leonard and his wife had no children, but they were guardians to Leonard's nephew **Arthur Bishop**. They were philanthropic. One of Leonard's gifts was the establishment in 1923 of an educational trust for scholarships. He stipulated that only Protestant, white, British subjects could be recipients of funds from the trust. That, and his contempt for labor unions, put him in conflict with other members of the Governing Council of the University of Toronto on which he served. The terms of Leonard's educational trust remained in effect until 1980, at which time the Ontario Court of Appeals ruled them invalid.

Leonard was also a large benefactor of Queens University, which led to him being the recipient of an honorary doctoral degree from that institution in 1930, the year of his death.

Photo 114 Reuben W. Leonard, Unknown date (Public Domain)

Maj. Gen. Harry F. G. Letson

Membership Years: 1949-1969   **Birth:** 1896

Birthplace: British Columbia

Death: 1992

Occupation: Military officer, mechanical engineer

Positions: Director, Powell River Co.
Director, Powell River Co.
President, Professional Engineers Association of British Columbia
President, Dominion of Canada Rifle Assoc.
Commander, Order of the British Empire

Harry Letson was seriously injured at Vimy Ridge during WWI. Following the war, he studied engineering. After graduating he went overseas and completed a PhD at London University in 1923. During World War II, he served as chairman of the Canadian joint staff in Washington, D.C.

Letson and **Trubee Davison**, both being generals, and both having physical disabilities, were good friends while at the Long Point Company. **Daniel Davison**, Trubee's son, wrote that Letson, whose one leg was shorter than the other, would support himself on the handles of Trubee's wheelchair while pushing him along the wooden walkways at The Cottages. Daniel jokingly added that although his father and Letson imbibed, neither ever fell into the water.

Another account asserts that Letson's influence in Ottawa led to the Company obtaining aerial photos of Long Point that were useful for preparing new maps of the marsh, which had evolved over time.

Letson was honored with the title, Commander, Order of the British Empire in 1944. He died in Ottawa in 1992, at the age of 95.

Photo 115 Maj. Gen. Harry Letson, Unknown date, (University of Victoria Archives)

William Little

Membership Years: 1866-1867   **Birth:** 1836

Birthplace: Caledonia, Ontario

Death:

Occupation: Lumberman

Positions: Principal, James Little & Son
Vice-president, Canadian Forestry Association

William Little's father, James Little, was one of the earliest lumberman in Canada West, and among the first to export lumber to the United States. By the early 1860s, he had formed the view that America's demand for lumber was insatiable, and if export tariffs were not imposed, Canada's forests would quickly be depleted, while American forests would be conserved. Although he was ridiculed for many years, James Little eventually became quite influential and an advocate for sustainable forestry.

William joined his father in the lumber business and their enterprise was active cutting along the lands flanking Big Creek and on Long Point in the 1850s in association with American sawmill owner Eli Clark. The area on Long Point where their business staged timber for rafting, Sawlog Creek, was close to the marshes west of Ryerson's Island. That likely explains how William became acquainted with the other Long Point Company founders. Together with them, Little successfully bid for parcels on Long Point at the auction in Toronto that was held in 1866. However, after the founders incorporated the Long Point Company, Little revealed he was indebted to Eli Clark and his shares in the Company were transferred to Clark.

William and his father relocated to Montreal about 1872. After his father died, William carried on his father's advocacy for sustainable forestry. Eventually, those principles found favor in the industry, and he was elected vice-president of the Canadian Forestry Association. William resided in Westmount, where he lived to an old age.

Capt. Wilton Lloyd-Smith

Membership Years: 1931-1940   **Birth:** 1894

Birthplace: Elmira, New York

Death: 1940

Occupation: Attorney, investor

Positions: Trustee, American Museum of Natural History
President, Mammoth-St. Anthony, Ltd.
President, St. Anthony Mining and Development Co.
Founding Secretary/Treasurer, Labrador Retriever Club
Board member, Seeing Eye, Inc.
Board member, Long Island Biological Assoc.
Member, Council on Foreign Relations
Associate member, Jekyll Island Club.
Chairman, Block Community Assoc.
Member, Advisory Council, Seeing Eye, Inc.

Wilton Lloyd-Smith was the son of Judge Walter Lloyd-Smith. He graduated from Princeton in 1916 and then served overseas in an artillery unit during WWI. Following the war, he studied law at Harvard. After being admitted to the bar in 1921, he joined the Wall Street firm Cotton & Franklin.

Lloyd-Smith was not an heir to great wealth. However, he married Marjorie Fleming, the daughter of Canadian-born and educated lawyer Arthur Henry Fleming. Fleming had emigrated to Detroit, where he married Clara Fowler, the daughter of very wealthy Eldridge M. Fowler, who owned vast timber holdings and iron reserves on the Mesabi Range and held a large interest in the McCormick agricultural works at Chicago.

Fleming later moved his family and Marjorie's mother to California where he found fortune in the lumber and mining industries. He and his daughter Marjorie's wealth (sourced from her father Eldridge Fowler) bankrolled the initial development of the California Institute of Technology (Cal Tech.) Fleming would eventually place almost all his wealth in trust for Cal Tech. Regardless, his daughter Marjorie remained independently wealthy and was the major source behind Wilton Lloyd-Smith's wealth. He was recruited into the Long Point Company by Junius Morgan in 1932, and he served as the Company's managing director from 1935 until his death in 1940.

Lloyd-Smith was a big game hunter, an activity justifiably offensive to many today. It wasn't perceived that way 100 years ago, and Lloyd-Smith's safaris were as much about the discovering the natural world and bringing specimens back to the American Museum of Natural History as they were about the excitement of pursuit. He was always accompanied by one of his teenage daughters when on safari and they would return to New York with samples of flora, not just wildlife.

One of Arthur Fleming's assets was a mine in Arizona that produced gold, molybdenum, and vanadium. Lloyd-Smith served as president of the mine. He also held shares in the firm that published Time magazine, and he was a large initial investor in Newsweek.

Lloyd-Smith was one of the first to commute to Wall Street from an estate on Long Island's Gold Coast in an amphibious airplane, and he may have been the first Long Point Company member to have his aircraft brought to Long Point. Aerial photographs he took of the island in 1934 might be the only such photos taken of the island that decade.

Lloyd-Smith contracted brucellosis while on safari in India. The disease caused him to suffer a heart attack in 1935, and he retired the following year. It was at that time he headed a syndicate with the aim of developing a more modern and capable amphibian aircraft. Leroy Grumman took on the project and in 1937 Lloyd-Smith and his neighbor **Marshall Field III** took delivery of the first Grumman G-21 Goose. Lloyd-Smith used the aircraft to reach Long Point as well as a summer home on Michigan's Upper Peninsula. He died in 1940 at the age of 45.

Photo 116 Wilton Lloyd-Smith deplaning from the Grumman Goose at the New York City Skyport
(Margarette Bourke-White, LIFE Magazine, 1937

John T. Lord

Membership Years: 1869-1901   **Birth:** 1834

Birthplace:

Death: 1903

Occupation: Merchant

Positions: Principal, Lord & Taylor
                      Member, New York City Yacht Club

John Lord's father, Samuel Lord, co-founded the merchant firm Lord & Taylor. After his father retired and returned to England in 1864, John took over management of the business.

Lord was an aggressive shooter who retained membership in the Long Point Company for 32 years. For a time, he harbored a small, crewed, personal steamboat in Port Rowan.

Lord maintained residences in London, England, in New York City, where he was active in real estate investing, in New Brunswick, New Jersey, and at Cannes on the French Riviera. He fell into ill health in 1901 and went overseas. He died 14 months later in Cannes. His shares passed to New York City financier **William Barnum**.

Charles E. Lord

Membership Years: 1969-1993   **Birth:** 1928

Birthplace:

Death: 1993

Occupation: Banker, public servant

Positions: President, West Hartford Police and Fire Commission
Member, West Hartford Council
Chief Executive Officer, Hartford National Corp.
First Deputy Comptroller of the Currency
Acting Comptroller of the Currency
Chief Administrative Officer, Central Intelligence Agency
Vice-chairman, Import-Export Bank
Senior advisor, Dillon, Read & Co.
Chief Executive Officer, Prudential Bank & Trust Co.
Director, Institutional Development, Yale University
Vice chairman, Madison Financial Group
National Trustee, Ducks Unlimited
Member, Council on Foreign Relations
Trustee, Vertical Flight Foundation
President, Project Orbis

Charles Lord 's father's name was John T. Lord. However, his father was not the same individual by that name who was a member of the Long Point Company. Charles' father had made a fortune in the textile industry and Charles was raised on a Long Island Gold Coast estate. He prepared at the Hotchkiss School and then attended Yale, graduating in 1949. He was inducted into the Skull & Bones Society.

Lord first worked in public service as a bank examiner, but soon after joined the Hartford National Bank and Trust Co. in a junior position. He rose steadily and became the bank's chief executive officer in 1972.

For a brief period, Lord served as the chief administrative officer of the Central Intelligence Agency. He was awarded an honorary master's degree by Yale. Lord was the president of Project Orbis, the organization that developed the first flying ophthalmic hospital. He died at the age of 64, in 1993.

Richard. A. Lucas

Membership Years: 1876-1888   **Birth:** 1844

Birthplace: Richmond, England

Death:

Occupation: Importer and wholesale grocer

Positions: Salesman, G. J. Forster & Co.
Principal, Lucas, Park & Co.
Member, Board of Arbitration, Hamilton Board of Trade

Richard Lucas came to Canada in 1857and settled in Hamilton. He worked for G. J. Forster & Co., wholesale grocers, and later acquired ownership of the firm and renamed it Lucas, Park & Co. Lucas served as the Long Point Company's third president.

Maj. John I. MacKenzie

Membership Years: 1884-1890

Birth: 1835

Birthplace: Ross-shire, Scotland

Death: 1927

Occupation: Importer and wholesale grocer

Positions: Partner, Kerr, Brown & MacKenzie
President, Hamilton Board of Trade
License Inspector, City of Hamilton
Vice-president, Dominion Telegraph Co.
Chairman, Hamilton Water Works Committee
Director, Wellington, Grey, & Bruce Railway

John MacKenzie worked as an apprentice in a retail store in Scotland while he was a young teenager. He emigrated to Canada at the age of 20 and commenced working for a grocery importing firm in Hamilton, likely that of **Thomas Kerr** and his brother. In 1846, he set out on his own by opening a general store in the town of Ingersol. The store was a successful venture and MacKenzie sold it after eight years and used the proceeds to enter partnership with **Thomas Kerr** and **John Brown**. He moved to London to manage their new wholesale outlet there. While in London, MacKenzie served in local government and co-founded a militia with James Moffat. In 1866, he returned to Hamilton where he served as a reserve officer with the rank of major. He was also an alderman in the city government.

MacKenzie served as the Long Point Company's secretary/treasurer from 1870 to 1886. He died at his daughter's residence in Chicago in 1901.

Surg. Maj. John T. D. MacKenzie

Membership Years: 1884-1890
Birth: 1822

Birthplace: Ross-shire, Scotland

Death: 1901

Occupation: Surgeon, military officer, educator

Positions:
Acting Civil Surgeon
Acting Professor of Anatomy & Physiology, Grant Medical College
Assistant Surgeon, Sir Jamsetjee Hospital
Professor of Anatomy & Physiology, Grant Medical College
Professor of Surgery, Grant Medical College
Professor of Anatomy & Physiology, Grant Medical College
Curator of Museum, Grant Medical College
Acting Professor, Comparative Anatomy, Grant Medical College
Professor, Dental Surgery, Grant Medical College

Dr. John MacKenzie joined the British Army in 1858 as a surgeon and was immediately attached to the 92nd Highlanders in India. After being engaged in field operations, and following the establishment of British rule, he was named acting civil surgeon for the district of Nimár. In 1861, he was assigned to the Grant Medical College in Bombay, where he taught and performed surgery at the resident hospital associated with the college.

After spending 18 years in India, MacKenzie retired and settled in Kingston, Ontario. In 1883, he advocated for a ban on the export of Canadian game to the United States.

John Manuel

Membership Years: 1885-1914   **Birth:** 1830

Birthplace: Muirhead, Scotland

Death: 1914

Occupation: Lumberman, capitalist

Positions: Cashier, Gilmour & Co.
Vice-president, Ottawa Electric Co.
Vice-president, Ottawa Gas Co.
Director, Ottawa Light, Heat & Power Co.
Director, Carlton Protestant Hospital
Vice-president, the Canadian Club
President, Metropolitan Rifle Assoc.
President, Ottawa Curling Club

John Manuel, a nephew of **Allan Gilmour,** emigrated to Canada at the age of 24. He worked for Gilmour's lumber business. Neither he or Gilmour married, and eventually the two men resided together as companions, with Manuel tending to Gilmour's financial affairs.

Manuel inherited a very large portion of Gilmour's assets including his shares in the LPC. He accumulated an interest in the Canadian Bank of Commerce, becoming one of its largest shareholders. Manuel served as president of the Long Point Company from 1898 until the time of his death in 1914.

Photo 117 John Manuel, Unknown date, (Public Domain)

Capt. Lachlan McCallum

Membership Years: 1866-1869   **Birth:** 1823

Birthplace: Argyleshire, Scotland

Death: 1903

Occupation: Shipyard owner, tugboat fleet owner, farmer

Positions: Commanding Officer, Dunnville Naval Brigade
Principal, Canada Towing & Wrecking Co.
Principal, International Wrecking & Transportation Co.
Member, Legislative Assembly of Ontario
Member of Parliament
Member, Canadian Senate

Lachlan McCallum began his career as a shipwright while still a teenager in Scotland. He arrived in Canada with his mother and two siblings in 1842. He later settled in Stromness, near Dunnville, and established a boat building business at Port Maitland. He retained ownership of many of the boats he built. His fleet carried freight and towed rafts of timber.

McCallum formed and equipped a local militia known as the Dunnville Naval Brigade. When the Fenian invasion occurred, he immediately put one of his tugs, the *T.J. Robb,* into military service. He and the forces he commanded during the conflict experienced considerable combat.

McCallum was elected to the Ontario Legislative Assembly as a Conservative in 1871, and to Parliament in 1874. He was appointed to the Senate in 1887. When the transcontinental railway was being planned, he advocated for an all-Canadian route. McCallum was also a farmer reputed to have more than 1,000 acres under cultivation.

Photo 118 Lachlan McCallum, 1899, (Public Domain)

Capt. James E. McConnell

Membership Years: 1971-1991   **Birth:** 1912

Birthplace: London, Ontario

Death: 1998

Occupation: Advertising executive

Positions: President, McConnell, Eastman & Co.
President, Canadian Assoc. of Advertising Agencies
Board member, Union Acceptance Corp.
Board member, Canerina Petroleum Corp.
Board member, Bureau of Municipal Research
Board member, Great Northern Gas Utilities Ltd.
Board member, Great Northern Capital Corp. Ltd.
Board member, Hospital for Sick Children
Chairman, Board of Governors, Ridley College.

James McConnell attended Ridley College. After graduating from the University of Western Ontario in 1936 with a business degree, he joined his father's advertising agency, McConnell, Eastman & Co.

During World War II, McConnell served in the Canadian Army. In 1962 he, was elected President of the Canadian Association of Advertising Agencies. He died in 1998.

Alexander McInnes

Membership Years: 1868-1874

Birth:

Birthplace:

Death:

Occupation: Wholesale merchant, clothing and shoe industrialist

Positions: Principal, Sanford, McInnes & Co.

Alexander McInnes, of Hamilton, was the brother of dry goods wholesaler Donald McInnes. With financing from his brother, Alexander formed a joint venture with William Sanford to produce clothing. Their firm, Sanford, McInnes & Co., established a factory in Hamilton in 1861. A male workforce patterned and cut fabric. Women picked it up and sewed it into clothing at home on a piece work basis The company encouraged skilled German seamstresses to move from New York City to Hamilton. The enterprise was highly successful for its owners. One reason it did so well was the American Civil war constrained clothing imports to Canada. By 1871, the year Sandford bought McInnes out, the company was one of Canada's leading clothing manufacturers. With an inside workforce of 455, it was the fourth largest employer in Ontario. Sanford and McInnes also operated a shoe and boot factory in Hamilton.

Neil McKinnon

Membership Years: 1962-1975

Birth: 1911

Birthplace: Cobalt, Ontario

Death: 1975

Occupation: Banker

Positions: Chairman, Canadian Imperial Bank of Commerce
Director, Canada Life Assurance Co.
Director, Royal Insurance Co., Ltd.
Director, Brazilian Light & Power Co.
Director, National Trust Co. Ltd.
Director, Allied Chemical Canada Ltd.
Director, Trans Canada Pipelines Ltd.
Director, Ford Motor Co. of Canada Ltd.
Director, Campbell Soup Co.
Director, Honeywell, Inc.
Director, Holt, Renfrew & Co. Ltd.
Director, Crown Zellerbach, International Inc.
Member, Board of Governors, Ridley College
Member, Board of Governors, University of Toronto

Neil McKinnon began working for the Canadian Bank of Commerce in Cobalt, Ontario in 1925 at the age of 14. In 1956, he was named president of the bank. Following its merger with the Imperial Bank of Canada he became the chief executive officer of the combined entity, the Canadian Imperial Bank of Commerce. McKinnen was a member of the Long Point Company at the time of his death in 1975.

Robert Samuel McLaughlin

Membership Years: 1932-1968   **Birth:** 1871

Birthplace: Enniskillen, Ontario

Death: 1972

Occupation: Industrialist

Positions: Partner, McLaughlin Carriage Co.
Director, McLaughlin Carriage Co.
Secretary/Treasurer, McLaughlin Carriage Co.
President, McLaughlin Motor Car Co.
Director, General Motors Corp.
Director/Treasurer, Chevrolet Motor Co. of Canada Ltd.
Vice-president, General Motors Corp. (USA)
President, General Motors of Canada Ltd.
Director, Toronto Dominion Bank
Director, Canadian Pacific Railway Co.
Director, Consolidated Mining & Smelting Co. of Canada
Councilor, Town of Oshawa
President, Oshawa General Hospital
Director, International Nickel Co. of Canada
Director, Canadian General Electric Co.
Director, McIntyre-Porcupine Mines Ltd.
Director, Moore Corp.
Director, Ontario Jockey Club

Sam McLaughlin joined his father's carriage making business at Enniskillen near Oshawa in 1887. The firm grew to become a mass producer of carriages. In 1907, Sam formed the McLaughlin Motor Car Co. He entered a stock exchange arrangement with Michigan carriage and Buick manufacturer Bill Durant and began building automobiles in Canada using imported Buick drive trains.

Durant experienced financial difficulties after he formed General Motors and in 1910 temporarily lost control of the new company. With financial backing from Sam, Durant and Swiss national Louis Chevrolet formed a new Company under Louis' name. With help from investment bankers Lee, Higginson & Co., Durant recovered control of General Motors in 1916 and McLaughlin, a significant shareholder, was named a director and vice-president. He remained an executive and director of the parent corporation for the rest of his life, while serving as president of General Motors Canada.

One year after he joined the Long Point Company, McLaughlin's cottage caught fire and burned. He furnished his rebuilt cottage with steel art deco furniture. McLaughlin served as the president of the Company from 1960 until 1968.

During World War II, McLaughlin opened his Parkwood home and estate as a mess for military officers who were training individuals to be covert agents at Camp X in Oshawa. He was subsequently given the honorary title Colonel. He was later inducted into the Order of Canada as a Companion. Today, McLaughlin's Parkwood home and estate is a National Historic Site open to the public. The library in the home has approximately 5,000 books which are largely uncatalogued. Sam carefully retained his Long Point Company memorabilia, and staff at Parkwood provided material that was helpful for the preparation of this book.

Sam McLaughlin was highly philanthropic. His donations to public causes amounted to hundreds of millions of dollars. During his old age, a rules exception was made for him, and his private nurse, Margaret Nelson, would accompany him to Long Point. He ceased to be a Company member at the age of 96 and died in 1972.

Photo 119 Sam McLaughlin and his private nurse Margaret Nelson on Long Point Bay. Date unknown.
(Port Rowan/South Walsingham Heritage Association Archives)

Capt. Junius S. Morgan

Membership Years: 1929-1960   **Birth:** 1892

Birthplace: New York City

Death: 1960

Occupation: Capitalist, investment banker

Positions: Director, Morgan Guarantee Trust Company
Director, Liberty National Bank
Partner, J. P. Morgan & Co.
Board member, General Motors Corp.
Director, United States Steel Corp.
Trustee, American Museum of Natural History
Trustee, J. Pierpont Morgan Library
President, J. Pierpont Morgan Library
Commodore, New York Yacht Club
Associate member, Jekyll Island Club

Junius Morgan was a grandson of J.P. Morgan and the older brother of **Henry Morgan**. He attended the Groton school. A year after graduating from Harvard in 1914, he married Louise Converse, the great granddaughter of Frederic "the Ice King" Tudor. (See member **William Tudor**) He then served in the U.S. Navy during World War I.

In 1920, Morgan was admitted as a partner in J. P. Morgan & Co. He is reputed to have been a kind gentleman who did not have the predilection to be an investment banker. Morgan was elected president of the Long Point Company in 1940 and is known to have fostered camaraderie among the members for 20 years.

As a reserve naval officer, Morgan was called back to duty during World War II, first as a lieutenant commander on a destroyer, and later as a captain in the Office of Special Services, the predecessor of the Central Intelligence Agency. In his latter capacity, he headed the three-person committee that approved and disbursed all funds for clandestine operations.

To a degree, Morgan made the Long Point Company somewhat of a social club for his Long Island Gold Coast neighbors. He was a terrific writer, and in 1953, he penned a short memoir titled, *Further Recollections of Long Point.*

Morgan died at the Simcoe hospital on Oct. 19, 1960, at the age of 68 after falling ill at Long Point. At the time of his death, he had been president of the Company for 20 years.

Photo 120 Charles Reeves punting Junius Morgan (Public Domain) [295]

Cmdr. Henry S. Morgan

Membership Years: 1929-1960 **Birth:** 1900

Birthplace: London, England

Death: 1982

Occupation: Capitalist, financial executive

Positions: Co-founder, Morgan-Stanley
Director, Morgan Guarantee Trust Company
Director, Liberty National Bank
Member, Board of Overseers, Harvard University
President, U.S. International Sailing Assoc.
President, J. Pierpont Morgan Library
Director, General Electric Co.
Director, Aetna Insurance Co.
Board member, Pullman Palace Car Co.
Commodore, NYC Yacht Club
Associate member, Jekyll Island Club.
Trustee, Groton School.
Trustee, Museum of Modern Art
Vice-president, Metropolitan Museum of Art
Trustee, New York City Community Services Society
Vice-chair, Carnegie Institution of Washington

Henry Morgan was a grandson of J.P. Morgan and the younger brother of **Junius Morgan**. He attended the Groton School and graduated from Harvard in 1923.

Henry was admitted to partnership in the J.P. Morgan & Co. in 1929. However, after regulatory changes forced the separation of commercial banking and investment banking, he and two other firm partners, Harold Stanley, and William Ewing, took their capital and formed the investment firm Morgan-Stanley. He was a Director of the Aetna Insurance Co., which his great-grandfather founded in 1850.

Henry was a member of the syndicate that sponsored the development of the Grumman G-21 flying boat and in 1937 took delivery of the second unit to come off the production line. With the break-out of World War II, the aircraft was donated or sold to the Canadian military. During the War, Morgan served first in a procurement role, but later transferred to the Office of Special Services, the predecessor of the Central Intelligence Agency, where he managed the Office's document control system. Morgan died in 1982.

Photo 121 Henry Morgan (Public Domain) [295]

Dwight Whitney Morrow

Membership Years: 1925-1931   **Birth:** 1873

Birthplace: Huntington, WV

Death: 1931

Occupation: Attorney, investment banker, diplomat, American Senator

Positions: Attorney, Simpson Thacher & Bartlett
Director, Pacific Coast Co.
Director, Railway Steel-Spring Co.
Director, American Locomotive Co.
Director, Erie Railroad Co.
Director, Anniston Electric & Gas Co.
Palisades Trust & Guarantee Co.
Director & Trustee, Provident Loan Soc. of New York
Co-founder, British & Continental Investment Co.
Member, New Jersey State Board of Charities & Corrections
Partner, J.P. Morgan & Co.
Partner, Drexel & Co.
Partner, Morgan Grenfell & Co.
Partner, Morgan, Harjes & Co.
Director, War Savings Committee
President, Tuberculosis Bureau of the Civic Assoc. of Englewood
Adviser, Allied Maritime Transport Council
Chairman, Committee of Arrangements, NY State Chamber of Commerce
Member, Executive Committee, Roosevelt Memorial Assoc.
Member, Board of Regents, Smithsonian Institution
Member, Administrative Board, Institute of International Education
Member, Executive Committee, American Assoc. Intl. Conciliation
Chairman, Aircraft Board of Inquiry
Ambassador to Mexico
Member, United States Senate

Dwight Morrow became a friend of Calvin Coolidge when they attended Amherst College. Morrow went on to study law at Columbia. He became a partner in J.P Morgan & Co. in 1914.

Morrow was extraordinarily influential in American business and international relations, particularly during the Coolidge administration. He authored *The Society of Free States*, published by the League of Nations. Coolidge nominated Morrow to be the U.S. Ambassador to Mexico. When Charles Lindbergh flew to Mexico on his 1927 Goodwill Tour, he met Morrow's daughter Anne for the first time. They were married in 1929.

After serving as the U.S. Ambassador to Mexico, Morrow returned to the United States to fill a vacant U.S. Senate seat. He died a year later in 1930 at the age of 58.

Photo 122 Dwight Morrow. Unknown date. (Public Domain)

Sir William Mulock

Membership Years: 1899-1907

Birth: 1844

Birthplace: Bond Head, Ontario

Death: 1944

Occupation: Lawyer, politician

Positions: Chief Justice, Exchequer Division, Ontario High Court of Justice
Acting Lieutenant Governor, Province of Ontario
Chief Justice, Supreme Court of Ontario
Member of Parliament
Minister of Labour
Postmaster General
President, Victoria Rolling Stock Co.
President, Farmers' Loan and Savings Co.
Vice-chancellor, University of Toronto
Chancellor, University of Toronto
President, Canadian Peace and Arbitration Society

William Mulock attended the Newmarket Grammar School. Later, as a student at the University of Toronto, he excelled at linguistics. He was called to the bar in 1868.

Although Mulock practiced corporate law and had many business interests, he was supportive of the labour movement. He was highly instrumental in the formation of the cabinet level Department of Labour in 1900 and served as its first minister.

After he was elected vice-chancellor of the University of Toronto, Mulock led the effort to bring together Toronto's disparate denominational colleges into a single federation. He also promoted the establishment of the university's professional schools of engineering, medicine, and law. He died at the age of 101 in 1944.

Photo 123 Sir William Mulock, Unknown Date, (Public Domain)

David Morton

Membership Years: 1991-2017

Birth: 1929

Birthplace: Devonport, England

Death: 2017

Occupation: Businessman

Positions: Managing Director, Alcan Booth Industries Ltd.
Vice-president, Planning, Alcan Aluminum Ltd.
President & Chief Executive Officer, Alcan Aluminum Co. of Canada Ltd.
Director, Bank of Nova Scotia,
Director, McCain Foods Ltd.
Director, Methanex Corporation Inc.
Director, Canadian Overseas Packaging Industries, Ltd.
Director, The Laird Group PLC
Chairman, International Primary Aluminum Institute
Member, Board of Governors, McGill University

David Morton attended Devonport High School and Cambridge University. He joined the Alcan corporation after graduating in 1954. Morton remained with the company for his entire career and was named president and chief executive officer in 1981. He died in Montreal in 2017.

Lt. Orsun D. Munn Jr.

Membership Years: 1986-2000   **Birth:** 1924

Birthplace: New York

Death: 2011

Occupation: Lawyer, investment banker, stockbroker

Positions: Director, Canada Oil Lands, Ltd.
Chief Executive Officer, Wood, Walker & Co.
Principal, Orson Munn & Co.
Partner, Munn, Bernhard & Associates
Assistant Treasurer, Ducks Unlimited
Member, Board of Trustees, Southampton Village

Orson Munn was the son a New York patent lawyer whose family published *Scientific American* magazine. The younger Orson served in the U.S. Navy for three years during World War II and was assigned to a PT boat as an ensign. After the war, he attended Princeton. He then completed a law degree at Fordham.

Munn served as the assistant treasurer of Ducks Unlimited. When he passed away at the age of 86 in 2011, his descendants faced the challenge of handling a collection of 10,000 toy soldiers, many of which had been painted by Munn himself. The collection was appraised at $400,000.

Lt. John Lang Nichol

Membership Years: 1969-2020

Birth: 1924

Birthplace: Vancouver

Death: 2020

Occupation: Businessman, Canadian Senator

Positions: Director, Adanac Mining & Exploration Ltd.
Director, Alcan Aluminum Ltd.
Director, Alcan Aluminum Co. of Canada Ltd.
Director, Canadian Pacific Enterprises Ltd.
Director, Crown Zellerbach Canada ltd.
Director, Alcan Group of Companies
Director, Placer Dome Inc.
President, Liberal Party of Canada
Chairman, Board of Directors, Pearson College

John Nichol was born in Vancouver in 1924. During World War II he served in the Royal Canadian Navy in the North Atlantic. Morton graduated with a degree in commerce from the University of British Columbia. He later became the president of the Liberal Federation of Canada and then the Liberal Party of Canada. He was a close associate of Prime Minister Pierre Trudeau, who appointed him to the Senate in 1966. Morton was honored with the title, Companion of the Order of Canada. He died in 2020.

Brig. Gen. Oliver Hazard Payne

Membership Years: 1898-1911

Birth: 1839

Birthplace: Cleveland

Death: 1917

Occupation: Military officer, oil industry pioneer, capitalist

Positions: Partner, Clark, Payne & Co.
Vice-president, Standard Oil Co.
Treasurer, Standard Oil Trust
Director, Standard Oil Co.
Trustee, Manhattan Trust Co.
Director, American Tobacco Co.
Director, Continental Tobacco Co.
Director, Havana Tobacco Co.
Director, Consolidated Tobacco Co.
Director, International Cigar Machinery Co.
Director, Chase National Bank
Director, Virginia & Southeaster Railway Co.
Director, Coal Creek Mining & Manufacturing Co.
Director, Tintic Copper Co.
Director, Croesus Gold Mining & Milling Co.
Director, Chihuahua & Pacific Railroad Co.
Trustee, Chihuahua Mining Co.
Director, Manufacturing Investment Co.
Director, New York Loan & Improvement Co.
Director, New York & Northern Railway Co.
Director, Pacific Mail Steamship Co.
Director, National Union Bank
Director, International Traction Co.
Director, Helena Mining Co.
Director, Tennessee Coal, Iron & Railroad Co.
Director, Virginia & Southeastern Railway Co.
Director, Interlake Pulp & Paper Co.
Trustee, Central Trust Co.
Member, Suburban Riding & Driving Club
Member, New York City Yacht Club
Member, Oketee Club
Co-founder, Great Northern Paper Co.
Co-founder, Jockey Club

Oliver Payne was born in Cleveland in 1839, the son of lawyer and railroad executive Harry B. Payne. He was sent to the Phillips Academy in Andover, Massachusetts and after graduating he enrolled at Yale. Following the commencement of the Civil War, Payne left the university and joined the Union Army. By 1863, he had participated in numerous battles and was ranked a colonel. He was seriously wounded by a gunshot at Chickamauga, Georgia. After a long recovery, he returned to duty and participated in further encounters. He retired after serving for three years. Payne was later brevetted a brigadier general, although he never referred to himself as such, preferring instead to be addressed as Colonel.

Payne returned home to Cleveland and borrowed money from his father to enter the iron business, then oil refining —an industry that had begun less than a decade earlier. John Rockefeller, who had attended school with Payne in Cleveland, approached him and proposed a merger. Payne agreed and swapped his shares in Clark, Payne & Co. for shares in Rockefeller's oil company. The transaction made Payne the third largest shareholder in Standard Oil and a vice-president. Later, in 1882 when the various Standard Oil entities were rolled up into a trust, Payne took the role of the trust's treasurer.

Payne used the dividends he received from the Standard Oil Trust to invest in other businesses. The many corporate directorships he held reflect the breadth of his investments. He sometimes wielded influence. His father was a member of the U.S. House of Representatives, and in 1884, Oliver assisted him in securing nomination as a candidate for a Senate seat. He was accused of disbursing funds from the Standard Oil Trust to bribe party officials so that they favored his father's nomination. Regardless, the elder Payne won the seat and served in the U.S. Senate for one term.

Payne could be influential in other ways. His preferred stockbroker was the Moore & Schley firm (where **Watson Dickerman** was one of the three partners.) The Panic of 1907 resulted in Moore & Schley experiencing a liquidity crisis while holding a large number of shares in Tennessee Coal, Iron, & Railroad Co., an enterprise Payne held many shares in. As soon he became aware the brokerage might have to sell the shares to address its liquidity crisis, Payne took immediate action to protect the value of his own shares. He proposed U.S. Steel buy the stock in Moore & Schley's account. Payne reached out to Henry Clay Frick, U.S. Steel's chief executive, and J. Pierpoint Morgan. Because Tennessee Coal, Iron, & Railroad Co. happened to be U.S. Steel's leading competitor, antitrust issues were at stake. Frick rushed to Washington to convince President Theodore Roosevelt to support what would effectively amount to a merger of the two companies.

With Roosevelt's support, a transaction whereby U.S. Steel exchanged bonds for the stock of Tennessee Coal, Iron, & Railroad Co. was promptly completed. For the first time in U.S. history, two companies that were components in the Dow Jones Index were combined into a single entity. Roosevelt was accused of being controlled by capitalists and enabling monopolization. Congressional pressure followed and the United States later sued to block the transaction. However, the merger was never overturned.

After the Civil War, a few Long Point Company members acquired southern plantations from struggling owners; Payne was one of them. (There has never been a Southerner in the Long Point Company.) In 1899, he bought the Greenwood plantation and its Greek Revival mansion at Thomasville, Georgia. He also had a 303-foot yacht built at the Bath Iron Works. Placed in service in 1899, the yacht which Payne named *Aphrodite,* was the largest private yacht in the U.S. registry. Payne circumnavigated the globe on a world cruise and later used the yacht to travel to Europe seasonally and to a fourth home he had in Bermuda. After World War I broke out, it was too risky for Payne to use the yacht, so he leased it gratis to the U.S. Navy.

Two of Payne's nephews, **Payne Whitney** and **Harry Payne Whitney** joined the Long Point Company while he was still living. His great nephew, **John Hay Whitney**, would become a member later. When his will was probated, **Oliver Payne**'s estate was recorded to be just 32 million dollars. About three million of it passed to his nephew **Payne Whitney**. There was no Standard Oil stock in the estate. It is highly likely that Payne transferred most of those shares and much of his other wealth to his nephew, **Payne Whitney** via a trust before he died in New York City in 1917. Estimates vary, but the amount given in trust was likely on the order of 60 million dollars. His palazzo at Esopus, and eight million dollars, Payne left to another nephew, Harry Payne Bingham.

Photo 124 Oliver Hazard Payne, Unknown date, (Public Domain)

Maj. Gen. Charles J. Paine

Membership Years: 1881-1885

Birth: 1833

Birthplace: Boston

Death: 1916

Occupation: Military officer, capitalist

Positions: President, Houghton Copper Co.
President, Mayflower Copper Co.
President, Winona Copper Co.
Vice-president, Champion Copper Co.
Director, Chicago, Burlington, Quincy Railroad Co.
Director, Atchison, Topeka & Santa Fe Railroad Co.
Director, Mexican Central Railway Co.
Treasurer, Pacific Copper Co.
Director St. Mary's Canal Mineral Land Co.
Director, Colorado Power Co.
Director, Boston Elevated Railway Co.
Director, Pureoxia Co.
Director, Rolfe Coal Mining Co.
Member, New York Yacht Club
Member, Union Club
Board member, Massachusetts Institute of Technology

Charles Paine was born in Boston in 1833, the great-grandson of Robert Paine, who had been a signer of the Declaration of Independence. Charles attended the Boston Latin school and graduated from Harvard 1853. He rowed on the crew team in 1852 in a competition against Yale. The event is considered to have been the first inter-collegiate contest in the United States and has since been a long tradition. Paine then studied law and was admitted to the bar in 1856.

With the breakout of the Civil War, Paine entered the Union Army and was commissioned a captain. He served for the duration of the conflict and led Black troops in the attack on New Market, Virginia in 1864.

Following the war, Paine married Julia Bryant, the daughter of wealthy New England merchant John Bryant. He worked for the investment bank Lee, Higginson & Co. and invested his wife's money in railways and copper mines, accruing a fortune.

Paine is probably most remembered for his Americas Cup racing. He was a triple defender who led the syndicate that built the *Puritan*. He owned the *Mayflower* and the *Volunteer*. Paine captained all three boats, and Long Point Company member **George Richards** was his steadfast crew member.

In 1897, President McKinley appointed Paine to the three-person commission on bimetallism which was struck to advance the concept of having a monetary standard based not just on gold, but silver as well. Paine died in 1916.

Photo 125 Charles Paine, Unknown date, (Public Domain)

Lt. Cmdr. John T. Pratt Jr.

Membership Years: 1942-1969

Birth: 1903

Birthplace: Greenwich, CT

Death: 1969

Occupation: Investment banker, capitalist

Positions: Partner, Charles Pratt & Co.
Vice-president, United Chromium Inc.
Vice-president, Chromium Corp. of America
Director, Transcom Electronics Inc.
Director, Birmingham Realty Co.
Trustee, U.S. Trust Co.
Member, Board of Trustees, Pratt Institute
Director, Motion Picture Capital Corp.
Trustee, Pratt Institute
Trustee, Museum of the American Indian (Heye Foundation)
Director, Glen Cove Community Hospital

John Pratt Jr. was a grandson of major Standard Oil shareholder Charles Pratt, and a nephew of Herbert L. Pratt, a Standard Oil president. He attended the Groton School and graduated from Harvard in 1925. In 1930, he purchased a New York Stock Exchange seat.

Pratt commanded the destroyer escort *Douglas L. Howard* during WWII. He died at Glen Cove on Long Island in 1969 at the age of 65.

John Rankin

Membership Years: 1870-1871

Birth: 1845

Birthplace: Greenbank, NB

Death: 1928

Occupation: Shipowner

Positions:
Chairman, Rankin, Gilmour & Co. Ltd.
Member, Mersey Docks & Harbour Board
Director, Bank of Liverpool
Director, Royal Insurance Co.
Chairman, Royal Insurance Co.
Chairman, Bank of Liverpool
Director, British & Foreign Marine Insurance Co.
Director, Pacific Steam Navigation Co.
Vice-president, Canada Guarantee Co.
Director, Consolidated Bank of Canada
Member, Liverpool Shipwreck and Humane Society
Chairman, Liverpool Shipwreck and Humane Society
Chairman, Soldiers & Sailors Club
Governor, Sedbergh School
Council member, Liverpool University

John Rankin was born in Greenbank, New Brunswick. He attended the Liverpool Institute High School for Boys in England and then Madras College at the University of St. Andrews.

In 1861, Rankin joined his family's ship owning and merchant marine business. He was a member of the Long Point Company for only one year and likely never visited Long Point.

George H. Richards

Membership Years: 1883-1922   **Birth:** 1838

Birthplace: Gardiner, Maine

Death: 1922

Occupation: Attorney

Positions: Director, Massachusetts Title Insurance Co.
Trustee, Massachusetts Scholl for the Blind
President, North American Fish & Game Protective Assoc.
Member, Boston Society of Natural History
Commodore, Beverley Yacht Club

George Richards was the son of a Boston dry goods merchant. His grandmother, Emma Jane Gardiner, was Frederic "the Ice King" Tudor's sister. Richards was sent overseas for schooling in Rugby, England. He graduated from Trinity College, Cambridge, then returned to the United States to study law at Harvard.

Richards served as the managing director of the Long Point Company and was president from 1914 to 1922, the year he died. He was elected President of the North American Fish & Game Protective Association, a cooperative conservation effort between the U.S. and Canada on Feb. 15, 1911. Richards was a regular crew member in Americas Cup races for his friend and business associate **Charles Paine.** He was also a close friend of **Louis Cabot** and shared Cabot's interest in the natural world.

Henry W. Routh

Membership Years: 1867-1868   **Birth:**

Birthplace:

Death:

Occupation: Wholesale grocer

Positions: Partner, Brown, Gillespie & Co.
Member, Hamilton Board of Trade

Henry Routh apparently managed sales for the wholesale grocery firm Brown, Gillespie & Co. Earlier he had worked with **Adam Brown** at the Hamilton wholesale firm W.P. McLaren & Co.

Routh held his Long Point Company shares for approximately one year. The reason for his short tenure was very likely the financial collapse of Brown, Gillespie & Co. in 1868. Routh's shares passed to **James Hewlett** of New York.

Dean Sage

Membership Years: 1897-1902

Birth: 1841

Birthplace: Ithica, NY

Death: 1902

Occupation: Lumberman, capitalist

Positions:
Director, Norfolk Southern Railroad
Director, Kinderhook & Hudson Railroad
Director, Kings County Water Supply Co.
Vice-president, Civil Service Reform Association of Albany
Trustee, Atlantic Trust Co.
Member, Boone & Crockett Club
Member, Grolier Club
Member, New York Association for the Protection of Game
Member, Executive Committee, Road Horse Assoc. of New York

Dean Sage was the eldest son of Henry W. Sage, an Ithica, NY lumberman who harvested timber from Ontario's Lake Simcoe area where he had built a steam-powered sawmill. Although Dean attended law school in Albany, it is not likely he was ever called to the bar. His father loaned him and his brother money so they could each purchase a one quarter share in his lumber business. Dean worked as a sawmill manager. After their timberlands in Ontario that fed the sawmill at Bell Ewert were fully harvested, the Sage's moved on to Michigan and Wisconsin. Eventually, they moved to New York and invested their capital in other enterprises.

Dean was well-acquainted with **Watson Dickerman** and **Oliver Payne**, as like them he had railroad investments. He bred trotting horses, an avocation he shared with **Frank Ellis**. Sage founded the Camp Harmony Angling Club in New Brunswick and was the author of the extravagantly printed standard, *The Ristigouche and its Salmon Fishing*. He was also the author of several magazine articles and book chapters. A bibliophile, he assembled a noteworthy collection.

Members of the Safe family were major benefactors of Cornell University. **Dean Sage** died while on a salmon fishing trip to the Ristigouche River with other Long Point Company members on June 23, 1902. He was 61.

Photo 126 Dean Sage, Unknown Date, (Public Domain)

Henry M. Sage

Membership Years: 1902-1933

Birth: 1868

Birthplace: Albany, NY

Death: 1933

Occupation: Lumberman, businessman, capitalist

Positions: President, Colonie Electric Co.
Director, Flint Granite Co.
Director, Albany Insurance Co.
Director, New York State National Bank
Vice-president, New York State National Bank
Trustee, Albany Savings Bank
President, Cincinnati Gas & Electric Co.
President, New York State Forestry Assoc.
Principal, Sage Land & Improvement Co.
Trustee, Cornell University
Member, Deer Island Club

Henry M. Sage was the son of **Dean Sage**. He graduated from Yale in 1890 and then operated his family's lumber business. He became a member of the New York State Senate and chairman of its finance committee. One of Sage's avocations was breeding Guernsey cattle. He died in 1933. His descendants bequeathed his Georgian mansion Fernbrook at Menands, NY to the Rensselaer Polytechnic Institute.

Henry W. Sage

Membership Years: 1913-1929   **Birth:**

Birthplace:

Death:

Occupation: Lumberman, businessman, capitalist

Positions: Vice-president, Sage Land & Improvement Co.
Treasurer & Assistant Secretary, Cincinnati Gas & Electric Co.
Trustee, American Museum of Natural History
President, New York Society for the Prevention of Cruelty to Children
President, National Steeplechase & Hunt Club

Henry W. Sage was the son of William H. Sage, who was **Dean Sage**'s brother. He graduated from Yale in 1895, before working in the family lumber business. He served as president of the Long Point Company beginning in 1926. After three years in the position, he resigned because of a dispute. Jack Morgan, J.P. Morgan's son, bought Sage's shares and gave them to his son, **Junius Morgan**.

J. Michael G. Scott

Membership Years: 1980-2009

Birth: 1927

Birthplace:

Death: 2009

Occupation: Investment banker

Positions: Vice-chairman, Wood, Gundy Inc.
Vice-chairman, Scotia McLeod
Board member, Bombardier Inc.
Board member, Weyerhaeuser Canada Ltd.
Chairman, Sunnybrook Health Sciences Centre
Honorary Director, Atlantic Salmon Federation
Director, Toronto Mendelssohn Choir,

Michael Scott was educated at the University of Toronto Schools, graduating in 1945. He then attended the University of Toronto where he completed a degree in commerce.

Harold Stanley

Membership Years: 1937-1940　　　　　　　**Birth:** 1885

Birthplace: Great Barrington

Death: 1963

Occupation:　Investment banker, financial executive

Positions:　　Co-founder, Morgan-Stanley
　　　　　　　Assistant treasurer, J. G. White & Co.
　　　　　　　Vice-president, Guarantee Trust Co.
　　　　　　　President, Guarantee Co.
　　　　　　　Partner, J.P. Morgan & Co.
　　　　　　　President, Morgan, Stanley Inc.
　　　　　　　Partner, Morgan-Stanley

Harold Stanley graduated from Yale in 1908. He was captain of the hockey team and was inducted into the Skull & Bones Society. After graduating, Stanley joined the National Commercial Bank in Albany, NY. He later moved to New York to work for the bond house, J.G. White & Co. After working for the J.P. Morgan affiliated Guarantee Trust Co., he was admitted to partnership in J.P Morgan & Co., where he specialized in utilities financing.

After the Banking Act of 1933 forced the separation of commercial and investment banking, Stanley, **Henry Morgan**, and William Ewing co-founded the investment firm Morgan-Stanley. When the firm was later reorganized into a partnership, Stanley served as the senior partner.

Photo 127 Harold Stanley appearing before the National Monopoly Committee
1939 (Library of Congress)

Gen. Horace Chase Stebbins

Membership Years: 1910-1931   **Birth:** 1873

Birthplace: Boston

Death: 1947

Occupation: Commission textile merchant, capitalist

Positions: Partner, Ridley Watts & Co.
Principal, Watts, Stebbins & Co.
Director, National Park Bank of New York
Director, Lincoln Trust Co.
Member, Union Club
Member, Santee Club
Member, Seawanhaka Corinthian Yacht Club

Horace Stebbins was born in Boston. Later, his father was sent to Tombstone, Arizona to assist in the management of a silver mine there. While in Tombstone, the elder Stebbins met pastor Endicott Peabody. When Peabody decided to leave Tombstone in 1884 to form the Groton School in Massachusetts, Stebbins father placed his son Horace under Peabody's guardianship. Thus, **Horace Stebbins** attended the Groton School, graduating in 1892.

Stebbins began his career with the wholesale cotton cloth firm Grinnell, Willis & Co. He later entered into a partnership with Ridley Watts. As a commission agent for New England's textile mills, including the Wamsutta Mills, Stebbins eventually became very wealthy. He would have had business relationships with **Horatio Hathaway Jr.** and **Thomas Hathaway** and likely learned of Long Point from them.

Stebbins served as a lieutenant colonel in France during World War I. He retired from business in 1920 to become the head of the Military Training Camps Association. Stebbins was a recipient of the Distinguished Service Medal. His title, General would have been honorary. Stebbins died in New York City in 1947 at the age of 73.

357

William Payne Thompson

Membership Years: 1916-1922

Birth: 1872

Birthplace: Petersburg, VA

Death: 1922

Occupation: Sportsman

Positions: None beyond club memberships

William Thompson's father was Col. William Payne Thompson, an associate of John D. Rockefeller who served as secretary, vice-president, and treasurer of the Standard Oil Trust.

William attended Lawrenceville School in New Jersey, then Harvard. Sickness prevented him from graduating. Thompson was generally inactive in business and having inherited great wealth, he lived as a Gatsbyesque socialite. He was reputed to be an outstanding fly caster and marksman. After he died in 1922 at the age of 50, his shares in the Long Point Company passed to his older brother **Louis Thompson.**

Col. Louis Steenrod Thompson

Membership Years: 1923-1936

Birth: 1865

Birthplace: Wheeling, WV

Death: 1936

Occupation: Sportsman

Positions: Member, Boone & Crockett Club

Louis Thompson, also known as Lewis Thompson, was another son of Col. William Payne Thompson, who had been a secretary, vice-president, and treasurer of the Standard Oil Trust.

Although Thompson graduated as a civil engineer from MIT in 1888, he had limited business and professional interests. He drew on inherited fortune to live a sporting life.

In 1896, Thompson married Geraldine Morgan. They resided on the 800-acre Brookdale Farm estate in Lincroft, New Jersey, a property Thompson had inherited from his father. In 1904, **Harry Payne Whitney** leased a portion of the farm for horse breeding.

Thompson was a major funder of the First Yale Unit, the flying militia formed and led by **Trubee Davison**. Although he was twice the age of the militia's pilots, he contributed his time and energy by working closely with them on a daily basis and he was the unit's administrator.

Thompson acquired his shares in the Long Point Company following the death of his brother, **William Thompson**. He served as managing director from 1930 to 1935. In 1932, he compiled a book documenting the Company's history titled, *The Long Point Company*.

Thompson died at his multi-thousand-acre Sunny Hill plantation in Thomasville, Georgia in 1936 at the age of 71. His wife bequeathed most of Brookdale Farm to Monmouth County for use as park land. The former farm is listed on the U.S. National Register of Historic Places.

Lt. Col. David Tisdale

Membership Years: 1866-1891   **Birth:** 1835

Birthplace: Norfolk,

Death: 1911

Occupation: Attorney, railroad developer, lumberman, capitalist, politician

Positions: Captain, Fenwick Rifle Co.
Master, Court of Chauncery, Simcoe
Lieutenant-Colonel, 9th Norfolk Rifles battalion
Council Member, Norfolk County
Reeve, Town of Simcoe
President, Port Dover & Lake Huron Railway
Member of Parliament
Minister, Militia & Defense
President, Crown Life Assurance Co.
President, St. Clair & Erie Ship Canal Co.
Honorary President, Veteran's Assoc. for Norfolk County
President, J. E. Potts Salt & Lumber Co.

David Tisdale was born on the mainland across from Long Point in 1835. He attended the Simcoe Grammar School, then began studying law at the age of 18 in the offices of G. R. Van Norman. He went on to study further in Toronto and was called to the bar in 1858. He returned to Simcoe where he practiced with partners for most of his working life.

Tisdale was adept at finance. One of his common areas of practice was structuring loans and capital for businesses. He was also a colonial agent for the Standard Life Assurance Co. of Scotland. While in Simcoe, Tisdale joined the Fenwick Rifle Company. He was elected Captain in 1862. At the same time he served as the Master of the Masonic Lodge in Waterford. Tisdale was a defender during the Fenian conflict in 1866. The following year he was appointed Lieutenant Colonel of the Norfolk Battalion and had 250 men under his charge.

While his legal practice largely involved business matters, Tisdale might also represent members of his community when they needed help. A fascinating instance involved two children of a runaway slave. Their mother had escaped with them to Canada from Virginia. Once in Canada the slave married a Scotsman. They lived in Simcoe where she had another child —John. D. Lewis. While a teenager, Lewis made his way to New York City and found work first as a porter, then as a wholesale dry goods salesman. He was ambitious, and having come to understand the merchant trade, he set out in business on his own and was very successful. By the outset of the Civil War, his wholesale business in New York City which dealt in high quality goods, was well known.

A decade later, Lewis fell from his carriage and suffered a fatal injury. His estate was large and his will peculiar. Lewis lawyer undertook a search for heirs that lasted for years. Aware that

Lewis had once told him he had come from Canada, the lawyer placed an advertisement in a Toronto newspaper. So it was that David Tisdale came to appear in a court room in New York City in 1876 representing Lewis' Canadian family. During the proceedings, Tisdale demonstrated that Lewis had once traveled from New York to Simcoe for the purpose of having a tombstone placed over his mother's grave. He entered a photograph into evidence that showed Lewis in Simcoe, together with convincing deposition testimony. The outcome was a partial distribution of the Lewis fortune to his Canadian relatives.

Tisdale was an organizer of and an investor in railways. He served as the president of the Port Dover & Lake Huron Railway, the company that owned the harbor in Port Dover, as well as its successor by merger, the Grand Trunk, Georgian Bay, & Lake Erie Railroad. Overall, he had a rather stellar career both in business and politics. He was a candidate in the federal election in 1874. While he was defeated that year, Tisdale was elected as a Conservative in 1887. After parliament recessed that year, he celebrated his victory by traveling to California to visit his old friend Daniel Freeman.[231] Tisdale and was returned to office by the electorate until his retirement in 1908. He seems to have had just one major stumble. That was his investment in the J.E. Potts Salt and Lumber Co. That company's history is an interesting story.

John Potts was born in Vittoria in 1838. Together with William Dawson, he established a retail store in Port Rowan when he was just 19 years old. In 1865, he sold his interest in the store and moved to Simcoe to enter the lumber business. Six years later, his steam-powered sawmill in Charlotteville Township was the largest employer in Norfolk County. Potts also partnered with **Edward Harris** in the gristmill at Port Ryerse. In 1876, seeking greater fortune, Potts moved to Au Sable, Michigan, where he gained a reputation for being an uncommonly aggressive businessman. In just a few years, he was among the largest timber operators in the state.

Potts had a vision to build a private railway to move logs to a sawmill he would build. In 1884, he and David Tisdale, who was of course an expert in railway development, formed the J.E. Potts Salt and Lumber Company. Using financing from Canadian banks, the firm laid roughly 50 miles of narrow-gauge track in northern Michigan, purchased rolling stock, and founded a town with a company store and housing, called Potts.

In just a few years, the J.E. Potts Salt and Lumber Co. had grown to be a massive operation with a workforce of 1,400. Sixty-eight teams skidded timber to the railway. Twenty-two locomotives and 400 cars carried logs to Potts and to the company's Au Sable mill, which could process the equivalent of millions of board feet per season. One credible source states that during the 1887-8 season the facility Au Sable mill had an output of 100 million board feet. [333] To ship the massive volume, the enterprise owned two lake barges, the *Silana* and the *Cickands,* and it chartered others. The company had another mill at Green Bay, Wisconsin.

Potts set about expanding the railroad in the hope he would be able to convert it to a common carrier. However, he fell ill in 1890, becoming confined to his mansion in Detroit.

---

[231] Like David Tisdale, Daniel Freeman practiced law in Simcoe during the 1860s. Before he studied law, he taught school. Because his spouse suffered from asthma, Freeman moved his family to California in 1873. He developed a highly successful 25,000-acre ranch and founded the City of Inglewood. The home Freeman and his family shared on the ranch is listed in the U.S. National Register of Historic Places.

Meanwhile, David Tisdale, who owned most of the enterprise, was busy in Ottawa in his new capacity as a Member of Parliament. With Potts sidelined, the business, which was highly leveraged, experienced a cash flow crisis. Payroll for a workforce of 1,400 was missed. Tisdale responded by taking over as president. Although he seems to have handled the crisis with considerable aplomb, the company ended up in receivership. Four Canadian banks rushed to place claims on the firm's inventory, fixtures, and rolling stock. Other creditors were left with nothing. Years later, a court in Michigan held Tisdale personally liable for unpaid municipal taxes.

Tisdale ended his Long Point Company membership one year after the bankruptcy. He served as a Member of Parliament continuously until 1908. He died in 1911 at the age of 75.

Photo 128. The J.E. Potts Salt & Lumber Co. sawmill at Au Sable (Public domain)

Photo 129 The J.E. Potts Salt & Lumber Co. private railway (Public domain)

Photo 130 The Hon. Lt. Col. David Tisdale, Unknown date, (Public Domain)

Maj. Russell E. Train

Membership Years: 1967-2011

Birth: 1920

Birthplace: Jamestown, RI

Death: 2012

Occupation: Lawyer, judge, public servant, conservationist

Positions: Judge, U.S. Tax Court
Administrator, Environmental Protection Agency
Founder, African Wildlife Leadership Foundation
President, Conservation Foundation
President, World Wildlife Fund, USA
Chairman, World Wildlife Fund, USA
Treasurer, U.S. Polo Assoc.

Russell Train was schooled at St. Albans in Washington, D.C. He studied economics at Princeton, graduating in 1941. He then entered the Army but remained in the United States throughout World War II. Following five years of service, he studied law at Columbia. Train's first work assignment as a lawyer was for the Internal Revenue Service. He later became a staffer on Capitol Hill, assisting the Ways and Means Committee. President Eisenhower appointed him a judge of the U.S. Tax Court in 1957.

Train was an advocate for wildlife conservation. He founded the African Wildlife Leadership Foundation. After leaving the Tax Court, he served in the Nixon administration as the head of the Council on Environmental Quality, a new office which Nixon had created. Train's next assignment was as Administrator of the Environmental Protection Agency. During his tenure, the agency issued regulations to ban certain toxic pesticides and to require that cars be equipped with catalytic converters. After finishing his appointment as head of the EPA, Train took on the presidency of the American arm of the World Wildlife Fund. He was a recipient of the Presidential Medal of Freedom. Train included a chapter about the Long Point Company in his autobiography. He died in 2012 at the age of 92.

William Tudor

Membership Years: 1870-1876

Birth: 1848

Birthplace: Boston

Death: 1923

Occupation: Capitalist, mine developer, artist

Positions: President, Live Oak Phosphate Co.
Treasurer, Shawmut Consolidated Copper Company.

There is slight uncertainty about who Long Point Company member **William Tudor** was. Company records state he was from Boston. In all likelihood, he was the son of Frederic "the Ice King" Tudor, who commercialized the worldwide trade in natural ice and imported tea to New York. A book published in 1896, *Deacon Tudor's Diary,* edited by **William Tudor** and his brother, includes family genealogy. Review of genealogy suggests there was no other **William Tudor** among the extended Tudor family in Boston in 1870 whose age would make him eligible to be a member of the Long Point Company.

Because Frederic Tudor died in 1864, his sons would have become involved in the family business at an early age and would have been active in the tea trade. It follows that either **William Hunter** or **Thomas Kerr** recruited Tudor to the Long Point Company.

Tudor graduated from Harvard in 1871. Being of great wealth, he later spent much time in Europe studying art. Eventually, he became active in the mining business, developing copper mines in the West, and one of the first phosphate mines in Florida. Tudor died in Venice, Italy in 1923.

James Turner

Membership Years: 1868-1874

Birth: 1826

Birthplace: Glasgow

Death: 1889

Occupation: Importer and wholesale merchant

Positions:
Partner, Ferguson & Turner
Partner, Turner, MacKenzie and Co
Partner, Turner, Rose & Co.
Principal, James Turner & Co.
President, Hamilton Board of Trade
President, Hamilton & Lake Erie Railway
Director, Wellington, Grey & Bruce Railway
Director, Northern & Pacific Junction Railway
Vice-president, Bank of Hamilton
Member, Canadian Senate

James Turner came to Canada at the age of 22 and joined his brother as a partner in the Hamilton wholesale firm Ferguson and Turner. He was a co-founder of the Hamilton Board of Trade. After his brother died in 1864, Turner continued in the wholesale business with other partners. He was an agent for the New York tobacco supplier, A.H. Mickle & Sons. He also specialized in importing wine and liquor.

Turner was a supporter of Canada's first Prime Minister, Sir John A. MacDonald, and MacDonald appointed him to the Senate in 1884. He died in office 1889.

Figure 63. Portrait of James Turner. Unknown date. (Public Domain)

Carroll L. Wainwright Jr.

Membership Years: 1967-2011

Birth: 1925

Birthplace: New York City

Death: 2016

Occupation: Lawyer

Positions: Partner, Milbank, Tweed, Hadley & McCloy
Director, U.S. Trust Corp.
Director, Edward John Noble Foundation, Inc.
President, Waterfowl Research Foundation
Chairman, Trinity Church Grants Board
Trustee, New York City Boy's Club
President, New York City Boy's Club
Secretary, Rockefeller Fund for Music
Member, Distribution Committee, New York Community Trust
Trustee, American Museum of Natural History

Carroll Wainwright was a great grandson of railroad magnate Jay Gould. He graduated from Yale in 1949 and in law from Harvard. One of his avocations was decoy collecting. He died in 2016 at the age of 90.

Lt. Col. John Walker

Membership Years: 1876-1884

Birth: 1832

Birthplace: Scotland

Death: 1889

Occupation: Oil industry pioneer, businessman

Positions: Director, Imperial Oil Ltd.
Vice-president, Canada Pacific Railway Co.
Vice-president, Huron and Bruce Railway Co.
Director, Ontario Savings & Loan Co.
Director, Equitable Loan Co.
Director, Canada Chemical Co.
Director, Sovereign Fire Insurance Co.
Director, London City Gas Co.
President, Mechanics Institute
President, School of Art & Design

John Walker was born at Inverary, Scotland in 1832. He emigrated to Canada in 1864 and became a very early producer of Ontario oil. Walker first resided at Bothwell, but moved to London, where he established one of Ontario's first oil refineries. Later, he participated in the amalgamation of the refineries that had proliferated in London, and in the creation of the Imperial Oil Company. He served on Imperial's first board of directors.

Walker, who was a veteran of the Fenian conflict, sold his Long Point Company shares to **Dr. J.T.D. MacKenzie** in 1883. He died in 1889.

William H. Wheelock

Membership Years: 1930-1938   **Birth:** 1876

Birthplace: New York City

Death: 1942

Occupation: Real estate executive

Positions: Vice-president, Douglas Robinson & Co.
President, Brown, Wheelock; Harris, Vought & Co.
Partner, Brown, Wheelock, Harris & Co.
President, Brown Wheelock Co. Inc.
Treasurer, Five Points House of Industry
Director, New York Investors, Inc.
Director, Home Life Insurance Co.
Director, The Prudence Co., Ltd.
Director, Globe Indemnity Co.
Director, Liverpool & London & Globe Insurance Co. Ltd.
President, The Prudence Co. Ltd.
Member, New York City Chamber of Commerce
Trustee, Title Guarantee & Trust Co.
Trustee, Children's Aid Society
Member, Board of Managers, Presbyterian Hospital
Member, New York Athletic Club

William Wheelock prepared at the Cutler School in New York City before attending Harvard. He graduated in 1898. Intending to follow his father as a doctor, he entered medical school. Finding it too rigorous, he withdrew. By happenstance, he entered the real estate profession and eventually assembled the land for many major projects. Examples include the New York Hospital, the Presbyterian Hospital, Penn Station, Central Post Office, the 1931 Waldorf Astoria Hotel, Brooks Brothers, and department stores such as Gimbel Brothers. During World War I, he managed land acquisitions for the Army. A grand jury indicted him for fraud in 1934. However, he was acquitted of any wrongdoing.

Wheelock was a member of North Carolina's Narrows Island Club and a co-founder of the Freestone Point Gun Club in Virginia. He died in 1942 at the age of 66.

Surg. Mjr. Joseph S. Wheelwright

Membership Years: 1927-1941

Birth: 1875

Birthplace: Bangor, ME

Death: 1941

Occupation: Surgeon, military officer

Positions: Associate in Physiology, Columbia University
Co-founder, Southampton Hospital
Co-founder, Doctors Hospital
Trustee, Association for Improving the Condition of the Poor
Trustee, Community Services Society of New York
President, Medical Board, Southampton Hospital
Fellow, New York Academy of Medicine
Fellow, American College of Surgeons
Member, New York Zoological Society
Member, International Cat Society
President, Chesapeake Club of New York

Dr. Joseph S. Wheelwright was the son of a Bangor, Maine manufacturer. His grandfather had been a dry goods merchant who co-founded the Bangor Savings Bank. Wheelwright attended Yale where he captained the crew team and was inducted into the Skull & Bones Society. He went on to study medicine at Cornell Medical College, graduating in 1900. Wheelwright interned at New York's Presbyterian Hospital becoming a surgeon. He was duly engaged overseas during World War I. Following the war, he spent additional time as a military surgeon in Paris helping the injured recover.

Wheelwright served as president of the Long Point Company from 1930 to 1940. He was also president of the Chesapeake Club of New York, attesting to his interest in dogs as retrievers. His membership in the International Cat Society reflected his concern that cats should be licensed because of their tendency to kill birds when allowed to roam.

Wheelwright died at Long Point in 1941 at the age of 65 after suffering a stroke. In his Long Point memoir, **Junius Morgan** wrote that Wheelwright had died "at the place he liked better than any other."

Henry J. Wheelwright

Membership Years: 1943-1957

Birth: 1892

Birthplace: Bangor, ME

Death: 1956

Occupation: Capitalist

Positions: President, Columbia Investment Co.
Trustee, Bangor Savings Bank
Director, European and North American Railway
Director, Eastern Corp.
President, Common Council of the City of Bangor

Henry Wheelwright was the brother of **Dr. Joseph S. Wheelwright**. Following his brother's death, he inherited shares in the Long Point Company. One of his avocations was breeding trotting horses. He died in 1956.

William K. Whiteford

Membership Years: 1959-1968

Birth: 1900

Birthplace: Los Angeles, CA

Death: 1968

Occupation: Engineer, oil industry executive

Positions:
Vice-president, Barnsdall Oil Co. Ltd.
President, Toronto Pipeline Co. Ltd.
Vice-president, British American Oil Company
President, British American Oil Company
Director, Bank of Nova Scotia
Director, Bank of Nova Scotia Trust Co. of New York
Vice-president, Gulf Oil Corp.
President & CEO, Gulf Oil Corp.
Chairman, Gulf Oil Corp.
Director, General Motors Corp.
Director, Proctor & Gamble Co.
Director, Jones & Laughlin Steel Corp.
Director, Steel Company of Canada
Director, Canada Life Assurance Co.
Director, Mellon National Bank & Trust Co.
Director, Holiday Inns of America Inc.
Trustee, University of Pittsburgh

William Whiteford graduated in engineering from Stanford University in 1923. He began his career as a roustabout in the California oil fields. When he joined the Long Point Company in 1959, he was the president of the British American Oil Company. His membership may have reflected a renewed interest on the part of Company to drill for oil on Long Point, because a year later British American sunk two wells just east of the Provincial Park. One showed gas, and the other both oil and gas. Neither was put into production. Whiteford's next position was chief executive officer of the Gulf Oil Corporation.

Whiteford died after being in an automobile accident in Ligonier, PA in 1968. He was 67 years old, and he had been the recipient of three honorary L.L.D. degrees. However, his reputation was diminished six years later after an outgrowth of the Watergate investigation into the Nixon administration determined that more than a dozen large corporations had been making illegal contributions to legislators in Washington. The Gulf Oil Corporation was among them.

The Mellon family, whose ancestors had founded Gulf Oil and who were very large were shareholders, were unaware of the activity and insisted a thorough investigation be conducted. The investigation, which was noted for its transparency, found that Whiteford had for a decade overseen a scheme that siphoned money from the Gulf Oil Corporation, laundered it, and then funneled it to politicians. A Gulf Oil Corporation lawyer who was closely involved in the scheme spent a year in prison.

Capt. Robert D. Winthrop

Membership Years: 1906-1912

Birth: 1861

Birthplace: Boston, MA

Death: 1912

Occupation: Investment banker

Positions: Partner, Robert Winthrop & Co.
Director, Nassau Light & Power Co.
Director, Nassau County Trust Co.
Director, Deer Range Construction Co.
Member, Harvard Hasty Pudding Club
Member, Turf & Field Club
Member, Union Club
Member, New York Athletic Club
Member, Knickerbocker Club of New York
Member, Somerset Club
Member, Boone & Crockett Club

Robert D. Winthrop graduated from Harvard in 1883. Throughout his career, he was associated with his father's investment firm, Robert Winthrop & Co. Like some other Long Point Company members, two of his avocations were raising Guernsey cattle and horses. Winthrop, who never married, died in 1912 at the age of 51.

Capt. Frederic Winthrop

Membership Years: 1912-1913   **Birth:** 1868

Birthplace: Boston, MA

Death: 1932

Occupation: Investment banker, farmer

Positions: Partner, Robert Winthrop & Co.
Member, Massachusetts Historical Society
Member, New York Historical Society
Member, American Antiquarian Society
Member, New England Historical-Genealogical Society
Member, Colonial Society of Massachusetts
Member, Military Historical Society
Member, Bostonian Society
Member, Society of Colonial Wars
Member, Somerset Club
Member, Knickerbocker Club of New York
Member, Myopia Hunt Club

Frederic Winthrop graduated from Harvard in 1891, then joined his father's investment firm. He retired after just 10 years and established a farm that he called Groton House in Ipswich where he raised Guernsey cattle and bred horses. During World War I, he served overseas with the Red Cross.

Frederic inherited the Long Point Company shares of his brother **Robert D. Winthrop**. He must have had no interest in being a member of the Company, as he disposed of the shares a year later.

Robert Winthrop

Membership Years: 1937-1999

Birth: 1904

Birthplace: Boston, MA

Death: 1999

Occupation: Investment banker

Positions: Principal, Robert Winthrop & Co.
Partner, Wood, Struthers, & Winthrop Inc.
Board member, Winthrop University Hospital
President, Ducks Unlimited
Trustee, Wildlife Conservation Fund

Robert Winthrop was among the tenth generation of his family to attend Harvard. He graduated in 1926. His ancestor, John Winthrop, became the first colonial governor in Massachusetts in 1631.

To inform President Lyndon Johnson, who was a duck hunter, about the importance of wetlands conservation, Winthrop had people deluge the White House with postcards on which one word was written —Ducks. The campaign was supposed to be accompanied by a single explanatory letter to Johnson. However, after the letter was given to a Congressman to forward to Johnson, a staff error resulted in it being inadvertently delivered to the Interior Department. Meanwhile, White House staff were perplexed by the thousands of incoming postcards. An article about the mysterious postcards appeared in the news media. When Winthrop's letter finally surfaced publicly, he enjoyed a significant public relations accomplishment.

Winthrop, who was highly philanthropic, died in 1999 at the age of 95. He had been a member of the Long Point Company for 61 years and the managing director for 34 years.

Frederic B. Winthrop Jr.

Membership Years: 1938-1979   **Birth:** 1906

Birthplace: Boston, MA

Death: 1979

Occupation: Public servant

Positions: Founder, Winthrop Foundation for the Deaf
Member, Massachusetts Eye & Ear Infirmary
Member, Massachusetts Fisheries and Wildlife Board
Commissioner, Massachusetts Dept. of Food & Agriculture
Member, Massachusetts Society for the Promotion of Agriculture
Trustee, Trustees of Reservations
Trustee, North American Wildlife Foundation
Trustee, Essex Agricultural and Technical Institute
Chairman, Ipswich Conservation Commission
Director, Ipswich River Watershed Association

Graduating in 1928, **Frederic Winthrop** belonged to the tenth generation of his family to attend Harvard. His main interest became the family farm, Groton House, although he also served as Commissioner of the Massachusetts Dept. of Food & Agriculture. Winthrop died in 1979 at the age of 72.

Harry Payne Whitney

Membership Years: 1914-1930   **Birth:** 1872

Birthplace: New York City

Death: 1930

Occupation: Capitalist, sportsman

Positions:
President, Whitney Realty Co.
Director, Guarantee Trust Co.
President, New York Electric Vehicle Transportation Co.
Director, New York Transportation Co.
Director, Illinois Electric Vehicle Transportation Co.
Director, Metropolitan Street Railway Co.
Director, National Bank of Commerce in New York
Director, Morton Trust Co.
Director, Gaston, Williams & Wigmore Steamship Co. Ltd.
Director, Metropolitan Opera & Real Estate Co.
Director, Washington Life Insurance Co.
Director, Wharton Steel Co.
Director, Nassau Power & Light Co.
Director, Granby Consolidated Mining, Smelting & Power Co.
Director, North American Trust Co.
Principal, Metals Exploration Co.
Trustee, State Trust Co.
Trustee, Fifth Avenue Trust Co.
Director, Plaza Bank
Director, The Cuba Co.
Managing Director, Guggenheim Exploration Co.
Principal, Benson Mines Co.
Director, Vanadium Steel Co.
Director, Vanadium Corp. of America
Director, Electric Storage Battery Co.
Director, Wright Co.
Director, Wright-Martin Aircraft Corp.
Director, Cuba Cane Sugar Corp.
Director, Sinclair Oil Co.
Director, Metropolitan Opera Co.
Vice-president, Yaqui Land & Water Co.
Vice-president, Association for the Improvement of the Breed of Horses
Vice-president, Automobile Club of America
Member, New York Zoological Soc.
Trustee, Association for the Protection of the Adirondacks
Member, Restigouche Salmon Club

Member, Union Club
Member, Metropolitan Club
Member, Board of Stewards, Jockey Club
Member, Aero Club of America

Harry Payne Whitney was the son of railroad investor and Secretary of the Navy, William Collins Whitney. Some of his father's significant shareholdings were in Cape Breton's Dominion Coal Co. and Dominion Iron and Steel Co. His mother, Flora, was **Oliver Hazard Payne**'s sister and his brother was **Payne Whitney**.

After attending the Groton School, Whitney went on to Yale. He was inducted into the Skull and Bones Society and graduated in 1894. Whitney then studied law at Columbia. He married Gertrude Vanderbilt, the daughter of Cornelius Vanderbilt, in 1896.

Harry Payne Whitney might be best described as dynamic. He was a yacht racer, 10-handicap international polo champion, arctic explorer, socialite, and an enthusiast of new technologies such as automobiles and aircraft. Together with William Thompson, he purchased the Wright Brothers aircraft business; he owned one of the earliest flying boats; and he was a benefactor of **Trubee Davison** 's flying militia. His most favored avocations were equestrian. He leased the stable facilities at **Louis Thompson**'s Brookdale Farm and employed close to 100 people there to breed, train, and care for his horses.

One of Whitney's significant business achievements was the risky creation of Hudson's Bay Mining and Smelting. After he died in 1930, at the age of 58, his public value of his estate was valued at 69 million dollars.

Photo 131 Harry Payne Whitney (Public Domain) (Library of Congress)

William Payne Whitney

Membership Years: 1911-1927

Birth: 1876

Birthplace: New York City

Death: 1927

Occupation: Capitalist, sportsman

Positions: Director, United States Trust Co. of New York
Director, Great Northern Paper Co.
Trustee, United States Trust Co.
Trustee, Metropolitan Museum of Art
Trustee, New York Public Library
Vice-president, Society of New York Hospital
Governor, New York Hospital
Member, Jockey Club

Payne Whitney, as he was known, was the younger brother of **Harry Payne Whitney** and a nephew of **Oliver Hazard Payne**. Like his brother, he was educated at the Groton School, then at Yale. He captained the crew team and was inducted into the Skull and Bones Society. After graduating in 1898, he continued his studies by completing a law degree at Harvard. Payne married Helen Hay, whose father had been the U.S. Secretary of State, and Ambassador to the United Kingdom. Payne shared his brother's passion for equestrian sports.

Oliver Hazard Payne transferred a huge fortune to **Payne Whitney**, likely through a trust. A reasonable estimate of the size of the trust is 60 million dollars. The details of which investments from the trust Payne continued to hold are uncertain, but he is known to have had interests in the Great Northern Paper Co., First National Bank of New York, and the Northern Finance Company. His inherited wealth led to him being the third highest paying taxpayer in the United States in 1924. That year, only the taxes of Henry Ford and John Rockefeller exceeded Whitney's. He never really held a job, although he did maintain an office on Wall Street and he was involved in the Whitney Realty Co. together with his more dynamic brother.

Payne Whitney also inherited his uncle's Greenwood plantation at Thomasville, Georgia, and he employed hundreds of people to maintain the property. The plantation passed to his son, **John Hay Whitney**. After President Kennedy was assassinated in 1963, Jacqueline Kennedy secluded herself at the mansion on the plantation. Whitney's wife later donated the property, and it is currently managed by the Nature Conservancy.

The high life of the roaring twenties got the better of **Payne Whitney** and he suffered a heart attack in 1927 after playing tennis and died at the age of 51. His portion of his estate that passed through probate was appraised at 179 million dollars, a third of which he donated to philanthropic causes. His Long Point Company shares passed to his son, **John Hay Whitney**. Joan Whitney, Payne's daughter, was the first woman to purchase a major league baseball franchise —the New York Mets. ▯

Col. John Hay Whitney

Membership Years: 1928-1982

Birth: 1904

Birthplace: Ellsworth, ME

Death: 1982

Occupation: Capitalist

Positions: Director, United States Trust Co. of New York
Chairman, Freeport Texas Co.
Director, Pan American Airways Corp.
Chairman, Selznick International Pictures Inc.
Principal, John H. Whitney & Co.
Publisher, *New York Herald Tribune*
Chairman, *International Herald-Tribune*
Chairman, Whitney Communications Inc.
Founder, Corinthian Broadcasting Co.
Co-founder, *Newsweek*
Member, Commission on Foreign Economic Policy
U.S. Ambassador to the United Kingdom
Chairman, John H. Whitney Foundation
Vice-president, Society of the New York Hospital
Secretary, Helen Hay Whitney Foundation
Trustee, Museum of Modern Art
President, Museum of Modern Art
Vice president, National Gallery of Art
Member, Board of Governors, Payne Whitney Psychiatric Clinic
Chairman, American Thoroughbred Breeders Association
President, Thoroughbred Racing Association
Governor, Turf and Field Club
Director, Association for the Improvement of the Breed of Horses
Member, Board of Stewards, Jockey Club

     John Whitney was the son of **Payne Whitney.** He was schooled at Groton, then Yale, graduating in 1926. He went overseas to study at Oxford; but because his father died the following year, he returned to the United States. Although he inherited approximately 100 million dollars, making him one of the ten wealthiest individuals in the world, he entered the working world in a junior position for the investment bank Lee, Higginson, and Co. While that position may have been low-level, Whitney sometimes commuted to Wall Street from Long Island on his 72-foot yacht.

     Whitney later formed John H. Whitney & Co., one of the earliest private equity venture capital firms. Among his many investments was a 15% position in the start-up Technicolor. Thereafter, Whitney began financing the first color motion pictures. As the backer and chairman of Selznick International Pictures, he insisted a reluctant David Selznick to produce the movie Gone with the Wind. He also financed live theater productions.

Like many highly privileged heirs, Whitney was patriotic. He joined the Army during World War II. Although he spent almost all his time safely in London as an intelligence briefer, he traveled into the war zone on one occasion. A day later, he was engaged in a fire fight with German forces and was captured. After 18 days as a prisoner and several interrogations, Whitney found himself in a boxcar enroute to a German prison camp. At night an air crew who were among the prisoners managed to open the boxcar door. The crew, Whitney, and a few others jumped from the moving train. They were subsequently rescued by the French Resistance.

After the war, Whitney progressively invested in media. He co-founded *Newsweek* with Paul & Andrew Mellon, **Wilton Lloyd-Smith**, and others. He published the *New York Herald-Tribune.* Following the death of **Marshal Field III,** who had founded *Parade*, the nationally distributed insert to Sunday newspapers, Whitney bought it. He also acquired dozens of radio and television stations. An altogether different investment was his Minute Maid orange juice venture.

Dwight Eisenhower and Whitney were good friends. During his second term as President, Eisenhower nominated Whitney to be the U.S. Ambassador to the United Kingdom and Whitney served in the position for the duration of Eisenhower's time in office. Continuing his family's equestrian tradition, he was a was a championship polo player and a steward of the Jockey Club. He and his wife maintained a large stable on their Greentree estate at Manhasset on Long Island's Gold Coast.

Following World War II, Whitney dedicated one third of his income and wealth to philanthropy. He died in 1982 at the age of 77.

Richard Woodruff

Membership Years: 1876-1887

Birth: 1822

Birthplace: St. David's, ON

Death: 1887

Occupation: General merchant

Positions: Director, Security Permanent Building & Savings Soc. of St. Catharines

Richard Woodruff was a younger brother of Long Point Company co-founder **Samuel Deveaux Woodruff** and a general merchant in St. David's, Ontario. He died in 1887.

Photo 132 Richard Woodruff, Unknown date. (Public Domain)

Joseph Woodruff

Membership Years: 1877-1886

Birth: 1820

Birthplace: St. David's, ON

Death: 1886

Occupation: General merchant, businessman, banker

Positions: Co-founder, Zimmerman Bank
President, Niagara Falls Suspension Bridge Co.
Co-founder, Erie & Ontario Insurance Co.
Director, Woodstock & Lake Erie Railway & Harbour Co.

Joseph Woodruff was the younger brother of **Samuel Woodruff**. He owned a merchant business at Drummondville in Welland County in 1851 while simultaneously serving as Clerk of the Peace for Lincoln and Welland Counties, and the town of Cayuga. He later served as Sheriff of Lincoln County. He died in 1886.

Photo 133 Joseph Woodruff, Unknown date, (Brock University, Public Domain)

Samuel Deveaux Woodruff

Membership Years: 1866-1883　　　　　　　**Birth:** 1819

Birthplace: St. David's, ON

Death: 1904

Occupation:　Civil engineer, industrialist

Positions:　　Superintendent, Welland Canal
President, Lincoln Paper Mill Co. Ltd.
Chief Engineer, Port Dalhousie and Thorold Railway
Member, St. Catharines Water Commission

Samuel Woodruff was schooled at Upper Canada's second high school, the Grantham Academy in St. Catharines. Afterward, he trained in Lewiston, New York to be a civil engineer. Woodruff worked first on the Erie Canal at Lockport but returned to St. Catharines in 1841 to take a position as assistant engineer for the Welland Canal. No later than 1851, he was the canal's superintendent, a position he held for almost four decades.

Woodruff was the second individual to serve as president of the Long Point Company. He stepped down in 1881, likely to focus on forming the Turkey Point Co. He was a co-founder and president of the Lincoln Paper Mill Company. He seems to have had railway investments as well.

Woodruff was a full member of Georgia's Jekyll Island Club, and his son **Welland Woodruff** inherited his membership and was approved by the club's board. They were the only Canadians to have ever been members.

Woodruff died in 1904. The settlement of his estate became protracted. There were no income taxes in those days, but there were succession duties. Woodruff had created a trust in the state of New York for his children. While he was still living, his four sons were the beneficiaries of the trust's income distributions. When the sons received their annual distribution cheques, they endorsed them to their father. He, in turn, kicked back a small portion of the funds to them. Because Woodruff had derived income from the trust while he was still living, the Ontario Attorney General argued the trust was an invalid scheme undertaken by Woodruff to avoid succession duties.

Photo 134 Samuel Woodruff, Unknown date, (Public Domain)

Welland Deveaux Woodruff

Membership Years: 1912-1920

Birth: 1861

Birthplace: Lincoln, ON

Death: 1920

Occupation: Capitalist

Positions: President, Lincoln Paper Mill Co. Ltd.
Director, Coniagas Mines Ltd.
Vice-president, Coniagas Reduction Co. Ltd.
Director, Nicola, Kamloops, & Similkmeen Railway
President, St. Catharines Golf Club
Member, Jekyll Island Club

Welland Woodruff was the son of **Samuel Woodruff**. He prepared at Upper Canada College and attended the University of Toronto. He did further study at Eastman Business College in Poughkeepsie, NY, before taking on the role of overseeing the family's pulp and paper business. He died in 1920 at the age of 59.

Alfred S. Woodruff

Membership Years: 1919-1926

Birth: 1855

Birthplace: Lincoln, ON

Death: 1926

Occupation: Paper company executive

Positions: Superintendent, Lincoln Paper Mill Co. Ltd.
Vice-president, Lincoln Paper Mill Co. Ltd.

Alfred Woodruff was another son of **Samuel Woodruff**. He oversaw manufacturing operations in the family's pulp and paper mill. He died in 1926 at the age of 70.

Appendix B.   Long Point Glimpses

In 1942, Childs Frick published a book of verses for the members of the Long Point Company. Because copyright registration for the book was never renewed, the book is now in the Public Domain. Two of Frick's three poems are reproduced herein.

Note that when Frick mentioned the Sea Queen, he was referring to the launch that members traveled on to reach Long Point from Port Rowan. When he referred to the Sin Center, he was describing the cottage Junius Morgan and Wilton Lloyd-Smith co-owned. Morgan initiated the custom of having members over to his cottage for cocktails before dinner. Prohibition was active in the United States (but not in Canada) at the time, and Horatio Hathaway Jr. began referring to Morgan's cottage as the Sin Center. When Frick mentioned the Eternal Light, he was referring to an improvised electric lamp that Morgan and Lloyd-Smith built at Long Point one Sunday. They assembled it from items they found in their boathouse, including an archaic conical urinal and an old decoy. Lloyd-Smith had a fashionable shade made in New York and the lamp remained a fixture in the Sin Center for decades. (Frick provides a drawing of the lamp in his book.) Finally, when Frick mentioned the Battleground, he was referring to a large pond east of The Cottages. Before the Company adopted the policy of drawing lots each morning to determine who would hunt where in the marsh, William Hunter and Edward Harris simultaneously located there, shooting wildly over each other. That night, following a heated debate, the members developed new rules to prevent any such incident from recurring. The pond has since been known as the Battleground.

English scholars might not think much of Frick's poetic ability. As someone familiar with Long Point, I appreciate his verse. Long Point Glimpses, in particular, evokes memories of my own experiences in the marshes of Long Point.

LONG POINT GLIMPSES

OH DON'T FORGET YOUR GEAR

And

OLD FOWLER

By a Long Pointer

Privately Printed. Long Island, 1942

Long Point Glimpses

C. F., Long Point, October 6, 1942.

Port Rowan on the Bay
Whence flocks of ducks arise,
As Queen churns 'cross the way
To Long Point's Paradise—

Famed marsh and breeding ground
Of Long Point cottages,
Where whistling wings resound
O'er best of villages—

As spirits of the North
By flyways of the sky
From lands that brought them forth
October southward fly!

But not in forty-two
If that first week you drew
When wonderous was the view
But ducks themselves so few—

And only in your sleep,
In sweetest slumber deep
Could you then see them leap,
Those chicken with web feet!

The sun strikes through the willows
The wispr'ing breezes say
Come on you gunning fellows
There'll be sweet sport today—

For southwest wind's ablowing
And birds from roughened lake
Are to the marsh aflocking,
Winged bands in breezes' wake!

Punts rumble down the ways
With gear all neatly stored
While punters wait on quays
To hear the "all aboard"—

For Hanson's held the drawing
And you've got number four—
With southwest winds ablowing
How could man ask for more!

Ah well one yearns each day
To punt the winding way
Midst reeds of green and gray
That in the breezes sway—

O'er waters bluest blue
Touched by the sky's bright hue—
And ever thrill anew
For much is up to you!

Then as one paddles 'long
Through that dear marsh fecund
By clear canal and pond
Along old ways so fond—

Apushing thru the quill—
There comes that jolly thrill
A squawk that breaks the still,
Wings winging o'er the hill!

A thousand wings in flight,
Reeds nodding in the light,
The everchanging sight
In front, to left and right!

The twisted Indian root,
Or nightshade's scarlett fruit
Midst purple flowered thistle
Of hummochs all a bristle!

Arum and pick'rel weeds
And fat spiked sausages
Of waving tall cat-tails
Whose silver down 'er sails!

A Sparrow Hawk, Broadwing
By flock of bright Red Wing,
Great Blue on labored way,
Or Flicker gat at play.

A dark green dragon fly,
A tattered butterfly,
Two loons that wing us by,
An eagle soaring high—

A Bittern's shout from the grass,
Merganzer scooting past,
Pike's dash that water's roll
A mink's or muskrat's hole.

The Greebs that dive or hover
The Coots, trailing for cover—
The asters, golden rods
And milkweeds pointed pods.

Apunting through the quill,
The tasselated quill—
Bright red and yellow stalked
With green and silver topped!

The pads of pond lily,
The pods of celery,
The rushes and the rice—
For ducks and men, and mice!

The wild rice trampled down,
The droppings scattered round,
The muddy marled stream bed
Whence startled fowl have fled!

Unfathomed history
Of hosts that used to be—
Whence did they first emerge?
The secret of their urge?

The hosts that used to ride
Where instinct still doth guide,
The flocks that yet arrive
Of kinds that still survive—

The bands of sleek Pintail
Or Sprig that upward sail,
Red-head and Canvass-back,
Mallard, Green-head and Black—

The Blue and Green-winged Teal
So swift they seem unreal,
The Widgeon and Spoonbill
And small and large Bluebill,

The Ring-necked flying free
Or Buzzing Bumblebee,
The Golden-eye and Ruddy,
Old squaw and Rainbow buddy!

How well that morn begun—
Just sitting in the sun
Aholding of a gun
And letting old time run—

While munching of a bun
And waiting for the fun—
Assured that they will come
Before the hour's done!

395

But when you've lost your swing
And pellets fail to ping—
There is no use in grousing
Just concentrate on leading—

Oh best of gunning men
And tell that Jenny Wren
And grunting old Marsh Hen—
They both needs know you ken!

Oh when they come in nigh
So dark against the sky
And show their flashing eye
'Tis then you must let fly!

But when they come along
And you are all ayawn—
How everything goes wrong
And bingo they are gone!

But when they slant o'er quill,
When they about you mill
And you do swing until
You lead 'em by a bill—

Ah if you ever will!
'Tis then you'll feel a thrill,
'Tis then you'll see 'em spill—
Ah if you only will!

That day of hail and snow
With ole Jack Frost ablow
When flocks wing to and fro
And you old top do glow!

Or Blue-bird day serene
When languor reigns supreme
And you just drowse and dream
When sport's so very lean—

But when sport so doth lag
And empty is your bag
And you are skunked afair—
How you would stay in the air

And for one instant hold
Yon sinking crimson globe
That seeks earth's shadowed rim—
For you, might still then win!

But faithful eve hath come
That ends each day of fun
And punts for home must run
As soon as "tie-ups" done—

And now for that trip back
Straight up the sunset's track—
The muffled soft tap, tap
Of long strong pole of Jack!

And as the sun sinks low
And marshes' shadows grow
Mid silence here below
Now comes the afterglow—

When waters turn to gold
And lone trees stand so bold—
As crimson clouds unfold
In beauty manifold

And when the stars atwink—
How you of home do think,
Of that long waiting drink
And paddles deeper sink!

Ah happy hour you enter
Refulgent, warm "Sin Center,"
Where President doth reign
O'er that "Eternal Flame"—

For which men home forsake
In Eastern Erie Lake,
By Marsh and sandy ridge
And wings that years doth bridge—

From eighteenth centurie
And Ryerson fam'ly
To this exquisite night
Where by "Eternal Light"—

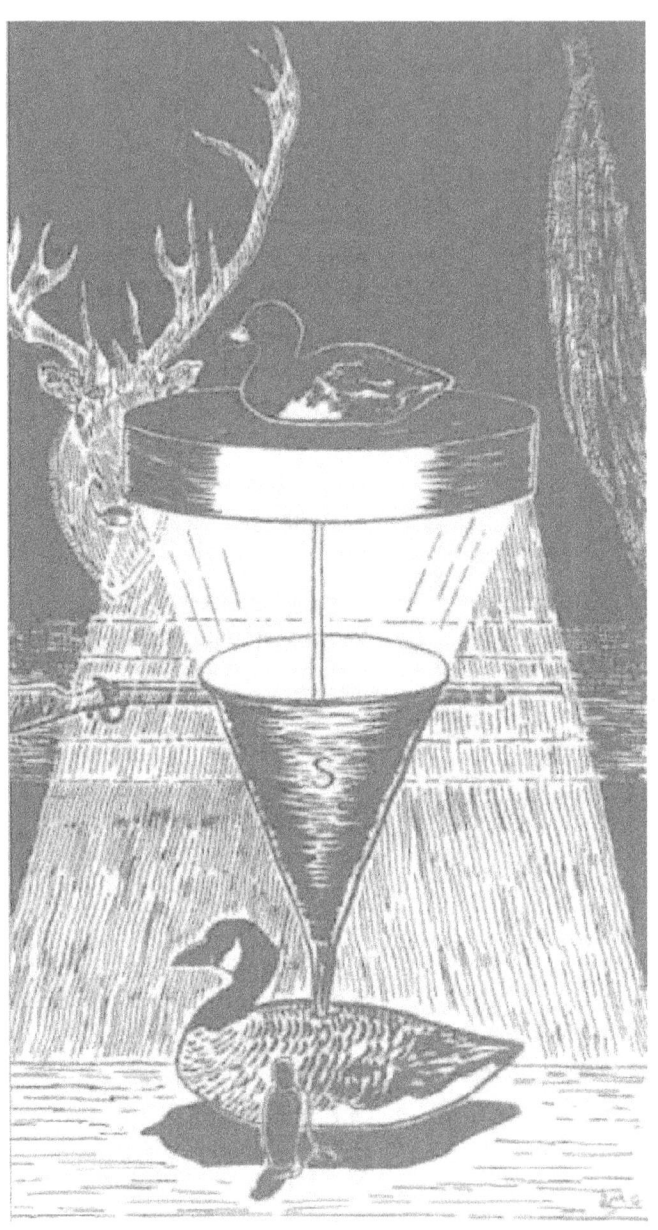

They gather as of old
To warm from out the cold
And steel the famished soul
For its appointed goal—

That wanton stroll below
By boardwalk's yellow glow
To Madame's planked whitefish
With dripping ducks delish—

An eve of camaraderie
In that fair marsh's lee
Where life runs merrily
As on the boundless sea!

Till breezes melody
Recalls to memorie
Of morrow bright to be
And leads you finally—

Into the chill night air—
With glimpse of Bear out there
A couched in starry sea—
To cot L., M., F. -B.—

And dreams of ridge remote
Of ash, white birch and oak,
"Trappers", "Umbrella Bunch,"
Or punter's lucky hunch!

Or dreams of "Battleground"
O'er which Red-head abound,
Or hole in marsh new found
With whistling wings all around!

To hear them in one's sleep,
In soundest slumber sweet
And watch them as they leap,
Those chicken of the deep—

Those flocks from out of the blue
Asearching for the sun
That holds their course so true—
The pace at which they come!

Those spirits of the North
The race they have to run,
Those birds from out of the North
Which still are left to come!

Oh Don't Forget Your Gear

The sun once more has risen o'er
The far flung marsh that round us rings
And now once more the whistling roar
That sings of Long Point's myriad wings!

Arise oh sons, pull on your gums,
Arub your eyes and grab your guns,
Your coffee strong, eggs, ham and buns!
The seconds tick and time 'er runs,

So if you must before the trip
Why hurry up but do be quick!
Bluebills and teal are trailing by—
The black duck sets his wings on high!

And punters strong with paddles tall
In lolling skiffs by wharves stand near—
As all await the welcome call
When loud the gong tangs out "the clear"—

And you yourselves will quick install
In punts as punters push from pier—
But in the hurry of it all
Oh don't alas forget your gear—

That case well filled with sixes chilled,
Decoys you'll need and calling read,
Those glasses strong and slicker warm,
That water jug and fleece lined rug,
Those thermos hot and sandwich box,

Your rubber mitts and smoking kits,
The fly dope two and counter true,
That wing tail and useful pail,
Pocket heater and light meter
And with the last a camera fast—

To snap in black or kodochrome
The feathered hosts that go and come,
To show the fair folk back at home
Just where and how the whole was done!

Arise oh sons, the seconds fly—
In Morpheus' arms you'll ill afford
No matter how for sleep you cry,
To miss the welcome "all aboard"!

O'er marches gray the shadows play,
Southwest the wind and clear the sky
And winging time urges away—
The perfect Long Point day is nigh!

Photo 135 The Eternal Light, Unknown date, (Private collection)

Appendix C. Oil and Gas History

French explorers who traveled through upstate New York and Canada in the early 17th century had never known or heard of flammable gases.[232] They were amazed to observe seeping natural gas ignite when native people put a torch to it.

The first commercial use of gas occurred for lighting in Britain during the late 18th century. However, that gas was not natural, it was synthetically manufactured town gas made by heating coal to a high temperature inside an industrial vessel. The first known commercial use of natural gas occurred just 60 kilometers from the tip of Long Point, at Fredonia, New York, where gas had been observed to seep from the rock along the banks of the nearby Canadaway Creek.[233] William Hart made the initial attempt to capture the gas in 1825 when he had a 27-foot well dug through the slate-like rock. Picks and shovels were used to create the well. Hart then built a pipeline, likely from bamboo, to convey the gas to a gristmill, two stores, and two shops, where it was used for lighting thereby replacing expensive tallow candles and whale oil.[234] [334]

Four years later, the U.S. Government built a lighthouse on the nearby shore of Lake Erie at Barcelona, New York. The light would be the first anywhere in the world to be fueled by natural gas, which was delivered through hollowed-out pine logs. The intent had been to commission the flame during Fourth of July celebrations in 1830, but a technical problem delayed the ignition until the next day. The use of natural gas remained a novelty for many years, although the use of synthetic gas made from coal had already taken hold in North America's towns and cities.

In 1857, Hart put down two additional wells about a mile from the initial one. Instead of using picks and shovels these new wells were sunk using a drilling technique that had been developed for drawing salt brine from underground.[235] After the gas flow from one of the wells was found to be disappointing, Hart surmised that to be flow the gas must necessarily seep through fissures in the rock. Drawing from his experience as a gunsmith, he had his drillers pack gunpowder into the well and tamp it down to the bottom. When the charge was ignited, the explosion fractured the underlying rock layer. The outcome was a copious flow of gas. Hart followed this production success by erecting a gas holder made of brick in downtown Fredonia. Using the holder as a reservoir, he was able to reliably distribute gas to users around the town.

---

[232] Although 17th century European explorers were unfamiliar with natural gas, ostensibly it fueled "eternal flames" in Greek temples such as the Temple of Apollo at Delphi.

[233] The general area was known as Canadaway, a *lingua franca* adaptation of Ganadawao, the name indigenous people used for the area.

[234] During precolonial times, there were areas of bamboo (canebrakes) as far north as Lake Erie. European settlers cleared much of the bamboo to render fertile bottomlands suitable for crops. [399] Bamboo groves are not uncommon where I reside in Northern Virginia.

[235] Salt was a vital commodity with many uses, just one being food preservation. Initially, it was imported to North America from Britain. By the middle of the 18th century, settlers learned from native people to extract it from brine. [397] To drill a brine well, a chisel was attached to a rope and strung over a Y-shaped tree branch. The rope was pulled to raise the chisel and then released, allowing the chisel to drop. Through repetition, a deep hole could be chipped in the rock, provided the chips were removed as drilling was underway.

Photo 136 Barcelona lighthouse. (Author's photo)

The following year, the first oil well in North America was drilled. Many non-academic American sources claim it occurred at Titusville, Pennsylvania, but the actual location was in Ontario, near the town now known as Oil Springs. [335] [336] Similar to the seepage of natural gas at Fredonia, the oil had been noticed oozing at a creek edge. Just three years later, there were at least 400 wells at Oil Springs. [337] Most of the oil was forwarded to London, Ontario, the location of Ontario's first refineries.[236]

The oil business made its Port Rowan debut in 1865. A news report stated that at a meeting held in town local investors subscribed to $1,200 worth of stock in a fledgling company. [338] The Port Rowan Petroleum Company commenced drilling the following year, likely along Dedrick's Creek. The activity amused many of the villagers because the drilling identified no worthy prospects and the principal shareholders in the company were from Buffalo. They were probably equally amused when town Reeve Richard Richardson (a.k.a. Richie Riches) set about drilling under his foundry for a source of fuel, also unsuccessfully. [339]

The first Canadian attempt to capture and market natural gas occurred at Port Colborne in 1885. A nominal well, fed a hotel and a few other establishments for lighting. As a commercial

---

[236] After the development of railways, refining activity moved away from London, and closer to the oil fields.

venture, it was a failure. The next efforts occurred in southwestern Ontario. Napoleon Coste was a French engineer who had worked on the Suez Canal and a failed effort to construct a Panama Canal. He then moved with his family to Amherstburg, Ontario. One of his sons, Eugene, was sent to Paris to study engineering. Upon his return to Ontario, he and his brother persuaded their father to form the Ontario Natural Gas Co. The following year, the company drilled a well east of Kingsville near Ruthven. It produced a massive 283,000 cubic metres daily. [340] The flow was so profuse Eugene Coste concluded the local market would never be able to consume it and a large a portion of the gas would need to be exported to the United States. A pipeline was constructed, and gas was soon flowing from Canada to Detroit and Toledo. Coste then formed the Provincial Natural Gas and Fuel Company of Ontario Ltd. and set sights on the Buffalo market. He drilled a well seven miles east of Port Colborne. These too, were successful, and after a pipeline was built gas flowed to Fort Erie and Buffalo. All these early Ontario wells depleted quickly and by 1903, gas exports to the United States were banned.

After the Coste brothers made another huge find near Tilbury, they teamed up with Niagara Falls engineering contractor Harry Symmes to form the Volcanic Oil & Gas Company. Volcanic built a pipeline to transport gas from Tilbury to Chatham in 1906, where Symmes planned it would be used to generate electricity and fuel industry. Over the next few years, Ontario became a hotbed for gas drilling activity.

Large towns already had gas service, but the gas was synthesized from coal, each town having its own manufacturing plant.[237] Because coal had to be imported to Ontario, and the manufacturing process was capital-intensive, the gas was costly. Moreover, it was malodorous and very toxic. The cause of the toxicity was the high concentration of carbon monoxide in the gas. Anyone unfortunate enough to feel deposed to suicide could "go home and stick their head in the oven," as the saying went; thereby expeditiously meeting their end. As soon as natural gas could be delivered to a town, it could be fed into the existing distribution infrastructure, instantly rendering the town's dirty coal-based synthetic gas plant obsolete.[238]

As the early 20th century progressed, gas drilling activity spread east from southwestern Ontario and west from the Niagara region, converging around Norfolk County.[239] By 1912, there was a drilling frenzy underway in Port Rowan and along the range from Port Royal to St. Williams. The drilling later moved offshore to Long Point's Inner and Outer Bays and eventually, far out into Lake Erie.

Junius Morgan wrote in his 1953 memoir that Long Point's oil & gas potential received considerable discussion among members, but no exploration or development was pursued. [293] However, the attitude of the Company's members later changed, perhaps because property taxes were becoming a burden. On July 14, 1958, the Company formed the Pintail Oil & Gas Development Corporation. The following year, William Whiteford, president of the British

---

[237] Gas manufactured from coal is commonly referred to as town gas.

[238] Natural gas service to London did not commence until 1935. In 1941, Toronto shad no natural gas service. Gas was still being made there from coal. Hamilton and some places west of there did have natural gas service [337]

[239] Many of these legacy wells were carelessly abandoned, have hazards, and present a serious challenge for property owners and local governments.

American Oil Co. was admitted as a member. In 1960, British American drilled two wells on the south shore of Long Point, about one mile east of the Provincial Park. One showed gas, and the other both oil and gas. Both wells were capped and never put into production.

The Ontario government's well database indicates Talisman Energy drilled a well in the southeastern part of Bouck's Pond in 1976. Place Energy drilled two in Helmer's Pond in the late 1980s. The database suggests these wells were put into production. However, this should be considered uncertain, because the facts are proprietary to Pintail Oil & Gas Development Corporation. The Ontario corporate registry lists Pintail as an active corporation with its office in Simcoe.

There are at least 14 gas wells in Long Point's Inner Bay, all of them abandoned. In their day, the wellhead pressures could be high.[240] In the Outer Bay, there are many wells, some still producing. On Long Point, or in its ponds, there are about a dozen wells. Those drilled by the Dominion Natural Gas Co. during the 1920s were never put into production.

Oil production directly through the lakebed is not permitted. Should a driller encounter oil, either the permit for the well must be surrendered, or a method to prevent production from the oil-bearing strata must be implemented.

Unlike Canada, the United States has never allowed oil or gas drilling on its side of the Great Lakes. Both countries allow drilling wells on land that extend horizontally below the lakes.

Photo 137 Drilling on Long Point Bay, 1967. [341]

---

[240] The Bluewater Oil & Gas company's 2-Port Rowan well, drilled in 1958 about one mile north of Big Rice Bay, had a shut-in pressure of 625 pounds per square inch and an initial flow of 11,600 cubic metres per day.

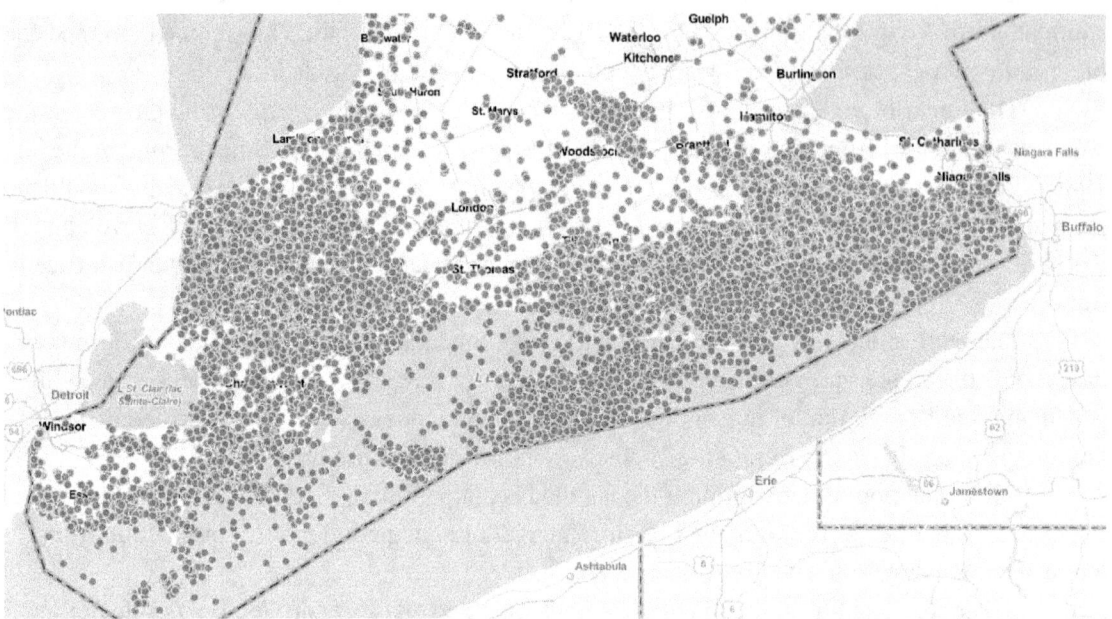

Figure 64. Petroleum & gas wells in Ontario, [342] *(Open Ontario Government License)*

Appendix D.   Frank Weston Benson's Diary Entries

1916

Oct. 8-9

Left Boston at 4:45 P.M. with G.H. Richards and A. Hemenway. Very warm day. Woke up at Buffalo and breakfasted on whitefish as we passed Niagara Falls. Rainy morning. Arrived at Waterford at 10:30. We took two motors and bumped over nine miles of road to Simcoe, where we took another train on a jerkwater railroad for Port Rowan, arriving there at one o'clock. We had a banquet at the local hotel and then took the club launch with all our luggage and ammunition and sailed for Long Point, where we landed at sharp three o'clock, seeing some ducks on the way over. The Point looks like a Florida mangrove key —just a few trees that appear to be growing out of the lake.

I was installed in Arthur Cabot's house, and my punter Snooks got the boat and decoys ready and took me out for a couple of hours. A.H. went with his man Spencer. Hundreds and hundreds of black ducks and green-winged teal, some baldpates and pin-tails and a few bluebills. Saw blue and green herons, marsh and sharp-shinned hawks, winter yellow-legs and beetle-head plover. Marsh wrens nest in the reeds. Saw ten muskrats. We set decoys hurriedly as it was late, and the ducks came often but not quite near enough. I shot down twenty-one and retrieved fifteen: twelve black, 1 pintail, 1 baldplate, 1 green-winged teal. The others fell in tall reeds at some distance. Paddled home in the dark with teal buzzing round our heads and many black ducks flying round. Saw a lot of mud hens. Had a wonderful dinner of venison and black duck with currant jelly, peach pie and cream and coffee. The prettiest afternoon's shooting I ever had.

Oct. 10

George Snooks called me at seven and brought in my bath and afterwards got the boat ready. Walked out by the cottages with A.H., and three snipe flew almost in our faces. From the observatory we saw a flock of red-heads come into the marsh. A fair day with light westerly wind. Not much of a day for ducks, one would say —but what one would say doesn't count here. After a very fine breakfast we all started out, I to what is called Head South about three miles away and between the ridges, A.H. to Corner Stake Pond. Saw lots of black ducks on the way. We found a blind made by Dr. Phillips for photographing purposes. It was out in the open where the rice was beaten down, and as soon as we pushed the boat in, the ducks began to come. I made the usual unnecessary misses and some rather good shots. The birds were mostly black ducks, and shooting from 10:30 to 3:30, I killed 52 of these that I was able to get. Three or four lay in the mud where we could not push the boat, and we had to leave them. Lots of yellow-legs and beetle-heads flying about the marsh and a few small flocks of red-heads. I shot also 1 shoveler, 1 gadwall, 3 teal (g.w.), 3 mallards, 18 baldpates and 17 pintails.

A.H. got 73 ducks, of which 40 were black ducks and the rest baldpates, pintails and 3 red-heads. Saw several big bunches of mud hens. Several snipe flying round the creek near the club. My legs are tied up in knots from crouching all day. This is the best shooting day I have ever had.

Oct. 11

Beautiful morning with a light westerly wind. Not good for duck shooting —in other places. After breakfast I took some photographs and then started out with Snooks for the middle of the marsh, having drawn No. 3. A.H. went to the ridges for a walk, taking his rifle. He brought back a small deer, the only one he saw. I set out decoys at about 9:45 on the edge of the wild rice, and the ducks came slowly and rather shy, but they kept coming at intervals till 4 o'clock when I picked up 57 black ducks, 5 pintails, 3 baldpates and a wood duck. Saw lots of snipe lighting in the rice but within 50 feet of the blind; also beetle-heads and yellow-legs. Teal were buzzing about my head all day and we saw quite a lot of red-heads going into Island Pond. All my ducks were long shots, not one falling in the decoys all day, so I wasted many cartridges.

Oct. 12

Warm summer day. Wind light from the S.W. I had first choice and tried Head of Creek Pond but nothing doing. All the ducks went out and nothing stirred all morning. Shot 3 or 4 and then moved to North Branch but no better. Made some sketches and photographs.
Got a few shots in the afternoon and killed 2 red-heads, 2 teal, 9 black ducks, 6 pintails. Saw lots of red-heads over Island Pond. A.H. went to Long Creek and had a fine day with the red-heads and black ducks.

Oct. 13

Woke this morning to find it raining hard and the wind a gale from S.W. The punters advised against going out so we stayed at home against our will. Went out behind the house and started some snipe and shot several. Later A.H. and I crossed the creek and after much shooting gathered in 18 fat snipe, which we are going to eat on Sunday. After lunch it began to clear with the wind N.W. and at 3 o'clock A.H. and I went out for a short shoot. He went to South Marsh and shot 40 ducks in an hour. I went to Teal Bend quite close by and after missing all the first birds that came to me I ended by shooting everything that came and got some long shots and good doubles. Shot one winter yellowlegs. The water in the marsh is higher than at any time since we came. A.H. brought me a beautiful pintail drake.

Oct. 14

Calm morning wind N.W. dropping to a calm S.W. later. Opening of the red-head grounds today, and A.H. drew first and I second. We went together to Island Pond where we drove out a great flock of red-heads. I set out to the eastward and then shifted twice as the birds would not come my way. A.H. began shooting at once. We moved nearer him and got a dozen birds when he generously came down and made me take his blind with the result that I had the greatest day's shooting ever. Gus had 23 birds when we changed blinds and he ended up with 51 including 3 canvasbacks. I missed as usual many shots I should have made but hit enough to count up 72 at sunset. Lost only 2 or 3 cripples. A splendid day's shooting, and I doubt if it could be had anywhere else. Saw few birds except red-heads and teal and millions of mud hens. They seem to attract the red-heads.

Oct. 15

Sunday, and no shooting. Fair and warm. Wind strong from the south-west veering to westward. We lay abed till 8 o'clock, glad of the rest after a strenuous week and breakfasted at 9 o'clock, after which we re-arranged the pictures and stuffed birds on the walls and mantel, making the dining-room more orderly. I took some photographs and loafed till lunch time and then had a short nap, later visiting in A.H.'s cabin. Clouding up at sunset.

Began reading "The Romance of the Martin Conner" and find it entertaining. Tried to photograph a kingfisher on the post outside my window but his eyes were too sharp.

Oct. 16

Light northerly wind and cloudy, shifting to southward and clearing at 11 A.M. Drew No. 1 again this morning and chose Head South. Saw more black ducks on the way over than on any day yet. Several eagles about the first ridge. Set out first opposite the ditch through the ridge and got one duck. Packed up and tried further north and shot 9 but the breeze shifted and blew on shore so we picked up again and went clear to the south end of the pond. Before Snooks could cut enough rushes for the blind I had shot 9 ducks, sitting in the boat. They had been feeding there and were eager to get back. To make it more favorable still a strong breeze struck in from the south and the air was full of ducks. They came streaming along, black ducks, pintails and widgeon, so thick that I soon let the two latter kinds pass by and devoted myself to the big black ducks. I shot better than usual and got 70 with 155 shells. When we tried to eat lunch they kept coming just the same and I almost loaded my gun with a sandwich. Lost only two cripples--a most successful day. A.H. was just west of me and I could hear his gun going at frequent intervals. He came home with sixty ducks and reported having dropped his gun overboard.

Saw many snipe on the way, also yellow-legs and plover. Saw two flocks of hooded mergansers and a lot of grass birds.

Oct. 17

Howling northwester and high sea in the creek. I drew No. 1 again to my shame and chose the Red-head Ground. Dolan with No. 2 took second choice of the same ground and set out in sight of me. I was at the foot of the creek. Shot a few, but most of the birds decoyed to a flock of coots between the two positions. We had to run our bow on a muskrat house to keep from drifting. Moved east and drove out the coot and set out against another rat house and began to pick up a few birds. Dolan moved east toward the outlet and I heard him shooting a good deal. Most of the birds that came to us visited him first and were very wild. None came down to the decoys, except two pair and I got the others by high-passing shots. Shot fairly well for me and picked up 55 red-heads, 1 black duck, 1 bluebill and 1 pintail. Lost a canvasback that I knocked down.

A.H. went to the ridge for deer and hunted carefully but saw none. The muskrats worked on their houses and didn't seem to mind the guns at all. I saw four working near us at once.

Oct. 18

Northeast wind fresh and cold with a partly cloudy sky growing threatening at sunset. I drew No. 3 and my punter chose the Umbrella Bunch hoping for some red-heads, but there were none there. I had few chances but took them all and got 28 birds with 65 shells. The ducks drifted the whole length of the pond, and we had to go a mile to leeward to pick them up. As my allowance is now small I let the pintails and baldpates go by except when they offered a double shot. I gathered 21 black ducks, 2 pintails, 2 baldpates, 1 mallard, 1 red-head, 1 bluebill. Much shooting to windward of me in the Second Island Pond where lots of red-heads have been feeding. Saw great quantities of black ducks at Head South and all over the marsh on the way home. Left at 3 P.M. as no birds were coming my way.

Oct. 19

Hard rain and N.W. wind shifting to S.E. and S.W. Everybody stayed in and kept dry. In the afternoon it let up a little, and Hathaway and Stone, who came up yesterday, went out at 3 and got a few ducks. A.H. and I went up the northern bay then with four men and saw them haul a draw net to the shore. They got 100 pounds of big pickerel, perch, cat fish and dog fish with several turtles. While waiting, several yellow-legs came along and we called them in and shot 7, which we take with us tomorrow for luncheon. I also shot a black duck at the Rice Bay inlet.

Oct. 20

Light southerly wind in the morning when we all set out together, seven boats. My position was back of the outlet near Second Island where I set out near a bed of rushes and hauled the boat in. The sky grew dark and we heard heavy thunder and soon were in the midst of such a squall I couldn't see my decoys. The birds had been acting very wild, and I had only occasional shots though I saw a good many. Occasional red-heads gave me shots and I killed perhaps a dozen, and four canvasbacks out of a flock of six. I also shot two ring-necked ducks and a dozen black ducks with one pintail. When the squall came from the west southwest the birds all went adrift and many of them so far to leeward that it was impossible to retrieve them. The spray blew off the water in sheets, and we had all we could do to get in our decoys. It took us two hours to get home, about two miles, working our hardest, and we took in a lot of water. Snooks says it is the hardest wind he ever saw in the marsh. I managed to pick up one canvasback, 8 black ducks, 4 red-heads, 1 pintail, and 2 ring-necked ducks.

Oct. 21

Last night I packed my bag and expected to go home today but was relieved to find the others did not want to go in the storm. My bed shook all night in the howling gale and we heard the hotel at Port Rowan was un-roofed. Hathaway did not turn up with his punter last night and we were somewhat worried but knew that there was a keeper's hut on the Island to leeward of him, and we found in fact that he passed the night there, the keeper and his wife cooking his meals and keeping him comfortable. We sent a boat and two men with a bottle of whiskey to find him this morning and they brought him back. The papers call this a West India hurricane and it seems all of that. In the height of the gale yesterday the air was full of ducks and they streamed past my blind and over my decoys often within fifty feet but I did not shoot as I could not have picked them up. After lunch today A.H., Mr. Richards and I called on Mr. Barnum at his house and while there we heard Carroll and Hathaway banging away at snipe across the creek. Dolan went up to Teal Bend, to windward, and I heard a lot of shots from his direction. Wind has hauled a little to the westward and has moderated a good deal at six o'clock. Telegraphed home that we were coming home tomorrow.

1918

Oct. 19

A day long to be remembered! Fine, cool with S.E. breeze and I drew No. 3. Snooks had the good judgment to choose the Battleground and when I got there I drove out 300 Redheads and Canvasbacks. We set our decoys and went ashore to get quills for the blind or "hide" as Snooks calls it. When we got back to the decoys which were at the edge of a rice bed on the windward side, there was a flock of Redheads sitting among the decoys. We paddled down quietly and when they flew I killed three. I got six on my next two shots and all day they came to me and disregarded everyone else. Apparently there were no ducks at all in the marsh except Redheads and they were only where I was and while the others had the poorest day I ever heard of here (only 25 in all for 5 guns) I had my best day and got 63 Redheads, 18 Canvasbacks and 1 Bluebill.

Oct. 21

Mild, summerlike day, wind light N.W. falling calm in P.M. Chose Long Creek. Few ducks flying and those decoyed poorly. Shot about ten in the forenoon. Wind shifted to South in P.M. and we changed blinds. Ducks few and far between. Managed to pick up 19 including 1 Redhead, 13 Black ducks, 3 Widgeon, 2 Pintails. An eagle tried to steal one of my ducks.

Oct. 23

Light N.E. wind. Partly cloudy. No. 2 choice. South end of Redhead Ground. Set out at our old blind built by Mr. Luce. Redheads and Canvasbacks began coming wide and I made some cripples at first. At lunch time I picked up 17. In the afternoon they came faster but very hard shooting, all over the right shoulder which is hard for me. At sunset I found I had 54. 45 Redheads, 7 Canvasbacks, 1 Black duck, 1 Bluebill. Breezing up tonight. Annual Meeting of the Long Point Co. and a large attendance at dinner.

Oct. 25

Saw Buffle Heads and Hooded Mergansers and at one o'clock when it threatened rain, thousands of ducks rose south of us and came overhead high up. My shoulder became so painful with the heavy load I am shooting that I had to pick up at 3 o'clock and come home. I could hardly raise my gun to my shoulder.
I believe that I saw this morning more ducks than I ever saw before at one time--I should say 25,000 at a guess.

1920

Oct. 10

Left Boston 7 P.M. with Aug. Hemenway, Lawrence H., Gee. H. Richards for Long Point.

Oct. 11

Arrived on time in a rattling thunderstorm. Two others shooting here, Knight and Johnston. Did not go out the first P.M.

Oct. 12

Fine A.M. Fresh N.E. wind dying away to calm at 9. Second choice fell to me and I took the Short Cut. Drove out many ducks and got set out about 10 o'clock. Calm and hot and ducks naturally did not decoy very well. At lunch time I picked up 19, all pintails but one. After lunch they came faster and at 4:30 I had 53, a remarkably good shoot for a calm day.

Oct. 13

Another summer-like day. Light-southerly breeze all day. Drew No. 1 and went to Second Island Pond. No ducks seen on the way down and after trying our stand for an hour with no results, we picked up and set out in the marshes further west. At noon I had about five ducks, all black. The day was hot and quiet and the ducks would only look us over without decoying but caused me to waste a lot of powder on long chances. A few birds kept coming at intervals all day and at 4:30 I picked up 35. One pintail, 1 teal, 4 mallards, 6 baldpates, 23 black ducks, very few redheads and canvasbacks to be seen in the marsh.

A.H. went today to the Bluffs to hunt deer and to spend the night. Hathaway arrived today. Saw a flock of snipe this morning before breakfast. Later, 3 yellowlegs and a duckhawk. Many muskrats swimming in the creek as I came home at sunset.

Oct. 14

Temperature 64" at 9 A.M. Light S.W. wind clear. Hardly a duck to be seen in the marsh as we went through in the boats though I saw great numbers going out at 7:30. I drew No. 2 and went to Irish Channel. Not a bird to be seen so we kept on west to Harry's Pond and found nothing; went ashore and loafed on the lake beach till noon. Then put out decoys in Harry's and ate lunch. In the afternoon a few high birds came along and now and then one or a pair would come to me. At three there was quite a little stir for a few minutes and I shot down ten birds in a quarter of an hour. I stayed till 4:30 and then as it fell quite calm I picked up and found I had 24 birds which was much better than I had expected in the morning. Almost no redheads yet, not enough to make a day's shooting. A number of snipe flying round at sunset and huge flocks of blackbirds that look in the distance like puffs of smoke. A.H. went to the Bluffs yesterday for deer and came home tonight with a doe. Lawrence went to the ridges today on the same errand but got none.

Oct. 15

Another hot, quiet day. Wind S.W. light. Drew No. 2 and went to Head South, where I had my first shoot four years ago. Found hundreds of ducks and windrows of feathers there but when we drove the birds out, they stayed out and all was quiet and hot till after lunch. Then it remained hot but I had some shooting, all at high passing birds for they refused to come down to the decoys. It resulted in my missing many birds but I also got a lot of satisfactory long shots. As we were far from home, we left at 4:45 and picked up 37 ducks. Found Barnum here when we got back. Johnston of Toronto left this morning, disgusted with the weather. In spite of the warmth which is unseasonable we have had good shooting.

Oct. 16

Sharp squall west with rain at breakfast time, clearing in an hour and wind falling to a moderate breeze. I drew No. 7 and went to Head South again. Ducks rising all over the marsh and lots of snipe flying about. Built a blind at head of the pond and everything was quiet for an hour or so, then many ducks passed over high up, occasionally one or two would drop to us, but most shots were very high so my average was low. At noon I had killed 19 birds besides several lost in the reed beds. About three o'clock they began to come better, flying lower, and though I missed a lot of shots, I killed enough to make my score 58 birds in the boat at 4:30. We had to go a long way to retrieve them as the wind was down the pond. Saw a large gray owl on the way home and started many ducks in the black rushes. Mr. Barnum shot a duckhawk that was chasing a Yellow-legs.

Oct. 17

Sunday. Again a warm day; wind E swinging round to S. and S.W. at noon, growing cloudy and threatening rain. After breakfast I took a walk up the shore of Rice Bay with A.H. to look for snipe. As soon as we left the house a crowd of birds got up from the grass and flew all about us--as many as 75 is our hunch. We kept on starting them all the way up to the Inlet, singly and in pairs. We must have put up 200 in going 500 yards. No fishing allowed on Sunday by order of the president.

Oct. 18

Foggy and quiet morning. Light easterly breeze. Poor prospects as the ducks go out very early these still days. Drew No. 4 and went to eastern end of the Irish Channel. There was a good flock of big ducks there but the fog was so thick you couldn't see much. An occasional bird shot out of the fog, seeing the decoys, and gave me a shot and I took advantage of all of them, missing but one before lunch. I picked up 12, then had lunch and watched the clearing of the fog which was very beautiful over the marsh. I never saw so few ducks in a day here. The marsh seemed absolutely deserted except for a pair of eagles and some hawks. One eagle came and looked over my dead ducks but none of them seemed to suit him so he went off. Then four airplanes appeared over Lake Erie and we watched them till they turned South.

Up to sunset I got a few more shots and collected 22 in all, coming home in the dusk with plenty of ducks fluttering up out of the rushes.

Oct. 19

Still foggy morning. Light Easterly. Fished in the creek with no results then went out after snipe. Found them very wild but managed to down 14 of which I found but nine. A.H. and Lawrence to the Ridges after deer. Nobody else went out this morning but all loafed about and lunched at the Club House.

Went out in the marsh at 1:30 and set out in Pearson's Pond. Got two shots at pintails and two at Redheads and killed 3 birds. Home at sunset. Nothing moving till dark. A. Thompson came tonight.

Oct. 20

S.W. wind fresh, diminishing to quiet breeze. Clear. 5th choice, Harry's. Went out full of hope but saw no ducks. Set out and waited and waited and waited. Up to sunset I had six shots and picked up 1 whitewing coot, 1 mallard, 1 bluebill and 1 baldpate. Absolutely nothing moving in my part of the marsh except hawks and cranes. Nobody did anything except Hathaway who got 16. Others 2, 3, and 4.

Unheard of weather for this time of year. Have worn my thinnest clothes and have yet been uncomfortable from heat. All ducks now go out at daylight and do not begin to return till dusk. No redheads as yet. Lawrence Hemenway got a doe at the Ridges yesterday and A.H. saw three others.

Oct. 21

Still another warm sunny day. Wind fresh S.W., nevertheless, all ducks left at sunrise. I drew 4 and went to the Doctor's blind but saw no signs and came back through the lower cut, having entered the Pond by way of the Lake and Second Island Inlet. Set out about 11 at East end of Irish Channel and from then to four o'clock never fired a shot nor did I see a dozen birds. At sunset I had eleven birds and came home by moonlight with lots of ducks all about.

Oct. 22

Hot again, wind S.W. moderate. Only Sage and Hathaway went out at 9. The rest of us loafed about and watched the snipe, of which hundreds were flying about. At noon down the shore to see a net hauled, hoping for a big lot of carp, but only a few fish were taken with some big 5 lb. pickerel and a bass or two. I went out at 3:15 and stayed till sunset and killed 3 black ducks and 4 pintails. Very few birds came into the marsh. Immense flocks of blackbirds. I saw a Duck Hawk.

Oct. 23

Woke to find a cool morning at last with an easterly breeze. Drew No. 5 and went to Pearson's Pond. Drove out about 5000 ducks, Black and Pintails. Set out in the corn at east end and began to pick up a few birds but shot rather badly at first. Ducks came at intervals all day. At lunch time I had about 20. Better flight in the afternoon and I also shot better. Stayed till sunset and picked up 58. Several in the bogs and marshes I could not reach.

Oct. 24

Sunday. Out here in the middle of a great lake the thermometer in the shade stands at 68 as we go to breakfast. No wind, sultry atmosphere, a perfect July day. Fortunately it wasn't a shooting day for it is the worst for that purpose we have had. Took a nap and visited round at the other houses. One of the punters expressed great interest in the etching process which I explained to him. Tomorrow is our last day for shooting.

Oct. 25

Dull cloudy, mild N. light falling calm at noon. Rain in P.M. I saw such a sight today as I never expect to see again. When we started out ducks rose in thousands and thousands all over the marsh and the whole sky was covered. With a breeze we should have had the greatest day ever. As it was we all did well and Thompson at Head South killed 130 in 51/2 hours. No one else had any such shooting. I shot 42 of which I could not retrieve 3 as they were in mud. Being calm they came from all directions and flew very high and made hard shooting. Dawson got 43, Sage 35. Thousands of Redheads and Canvasbacks were coming in from the North in lines and V's high up against the sky all the morning- and when we put the ducks up, the noise was like thunder. Saw a balloon passing to the south at 8 o'clock. Going home tomorrow in spite of pressing invitations to stay. Best time ever.

Appendix E.   Rice Bay Club Members

E.C. Fowell	Chicago	G. S. Gibbon	Toronto
C. C. Matheson	Embro	Dr. H. Beemer	Toronto
C. A. Thompson	Hamilton	J. P. Rogers	Toronto
R. Reynolds	Hamilton	A. C. Cameron	Toronto
C. M. Balwin	London	N. H. Gooderham	Toronto
T. A. Karn	London	F. H. Gooch	Toronto
J. S. Hobbs	London	Geo. H. Leslie	Toronto
E. A. Miller	London	Dr. Allan Canfield	Toronto
Stewart Jones	London	H. B. Smith	Toronto
L. H. Jones.	London	I. A. McCurdy	Toronto
C. A. Farmer	Montreal	J. T. Eastwood	Toronto
F. C. Whitney	New York	G. G. Plaxton	Toronto
L. Wicham	New York	Victor Ross	Toronto
C. B. Edwards	Norwich	J. Dockray	Toronto
W. Hamaker	Port Dover	C. L. Bailey	Toronto
Ewart McKay	Simcoe	W. Karn	Woodstock
Thomas Dunn	St. Louis	D. Miller	Woodstock
John Lind	St. Marys	J. D. Patterson	Woodstock
Walter Lind	St. Marys	A. S. Patterson	Woodstock
G. G. McPherson	Stratford	C. A. Pyne	Woodstock
Justice J. A. Makins	Stratford	Dr. A. B. Welford	Woodstock
D. M. Ferguson	Stratford	A. M. Scott	Woodstock
H. W. Strudley	Stratford	A. Pattullo, M.P.P.	Woodstock
James Pullen	Sweaburg	Geo. R. Pattulo	Woodstock
J. F. McKay	Toronto	R. N. Ball, K.C.	Woodstock
Wm. Stone	Toronto	Jas. Canfield	Woodstock
J. J. Palmer	Toronto	Hon. Jas. Sutherland	Woodstock
Wm. Hyslop	Toronto	Frank Hyde	Woodstock
M. I. Adams.	Toronto	J. H. Mcleod	Woodstock
T. W. Jull.	Toronto	A. W. Stone	Woodstock
T. Wibby	Toronto	J. M. Cole	Woodstock
G. G. S. Lindsay	Toronto	Colonel Ball	Woodstock
Wm. Pearson	Toronto	H. A. Little	Woodstock
H. A. Fleming	Toronto	T. L. Hay	Woodstock
T. A. Weldon	Toronto	John Butler	Woodstock
B. Blair	Woodstock	James C. Sutherland	Woodstock
Dr. W. T. Parke	Woodstock	E. F. H. Dutton	Woodstock
Dr. C. M. MacKay	Woodstock	Dr. W. Stevens	Woodstock
R. V. Sawtell	Woodstock	W. M. Boultbee	York Mills
Dr. C. R. Patience	Woodstock		

Appendix F. Books Written by Long Point Company Members

Recollections of Long Point
Edward Harris
Warwick Brothers & Rutter, Ltd., Toronto, 1918

The Long Point Company
Compiled by Louis Steenrod Thomson
Privately printed, Scribner, New York, 1932

The Long Point Company
A collection of photographs and captions by Wilton Lloyd-Smith
Privately printed, New York, 1935

Long Point Glimpses, Don't Forget Your Gear, and Old Fowler
A Long Pointer (a nom de plumes of Childs Frick)
Privately printed, James H. Knight Printing, Glen Head, NY. 1942

Further Recollections of Long Point
Junius S. Morgan Jr.
Privately printed, The Yale University Press, 1953

Further Tales of Long Point
Daniel Davison
Privately printed, Digital Printery, Glen Cove, New York, 2003

The Long Point Company, 150 Years
Robert Winthrop II
Privately printed, Design & Production by Frank Range, 2015

Appendix G.   Other Books and Papers About Long Point

A Synopsis of the History with Act of Incorporation, of the Long Point Company, of Hamilton, Ontario
The Long Point Company
Privately printed by R. Raw, book and job printer, Hamilton, 1872

Lore and Legends of Long Point
Harry B. Barrett
Burns & MacEachern, Don Mills, Ontario 1977

Long Point Photography
Tim Hagen
Self-published, Port Dover, 2001

Down by the Bay: a History of Long Point and Port Rowan, 1799-1999
Edited by Sharon Hazen, et al.
Boston Mills Press, 2001

A Faunal Investigation of Long Point and Vicinity
Snyder, L. and Logier, E.B.S.
Transactions of the Royal Canadian Institute, 1931, Vol. 18

Flora of Long Point, Regional Municipality of Haldimand-Norfolk, Ontario.
Reznicek, A.A. and P.M. Catling
The Michigan Botanist, 1989, 28: 99 – 175

Breeding birds of Long Point, Lake Erie: A study in community succession
McCracken, J.D., M.S.W. Bradstreet, and G.L. Holroyd
Canadian Wildlife Service Report Series Number 44

Overbrowsing of vegetation by white-tailed deer on the Long Point National Wildlife Area
McCullough, G.B. and J. Robinson.
Canadian Wildlife Service, Ontario Region, 1988

Thirty years of vegetation change at Long Point, Ontario
Bradstreet, M.S.W. and J.K. Pickering
Canadian Wildlife Service, Ontario Region, 2022

Less is more: vegetation community changes coincide with white-tailed deer (Odocoileus virginianus) suppression over 30 years at Long Point, Ontario
Pickering, J.K.
M.Sc. thesis, 2022, University of Guelph

Appendix H.   Understanding Great Lakes Level Fluctuations

Water levels in the Great Lakes fluctuate. When the level in Lake Erie is high, erosion can be expected. Worse, the lake may wash across Long Point. It has done so at different locations on many occasions. When the level has been unusually low, such as occurred in the early 1960s, larger boats have been unable to leave dockage to enter Long Point's Inner Bay.

Extremes in water levels, whether they are high or low, bring forth conspiracy theories. For the most part, the theories involve allegations that government agencies are controlling the lake levels. Such theories are invariably false, except as they apply to Lake Ontario.

Three types of level fluctuations occur in the Great Lakes. Short-term, seasonal, and long-term. Wind and storms cause short-term variation. Seasonable changes follow a predictable annual pattern. Near the end of winter, the melting of accumulated snow increases the level in the lakes. Spring rains lead to a further increase. About June, levels stabilize before beginning a slow decline. That rate of decline increases rapidly during the fall. The reason is during the fall, the average air temperature over the lakes is lower than the water temperature. Without getting into the nuances of the applicable thermodynamics, suffice it to say the increased temperature difference in the fall promotes increased evaporation. It is a fact that almost all the annual evaporation from the Great Lakes occurs during the autumn.

The source of all the water in the Great Lakes is in one way or another precipitation. Long-term changes in weather patterns impact the amount of precipitation that falls in the Great Lakes Basin. It follows that long-term fluctuations of levels in Great Lakes track long-term precipitation trends. These fluctuations are unpredictable because long-term changes in weather patterns are generally unpredictable.

Infrastructure developments have impacted on the dynamics of the Great Lakes. However, these alternations have been slight, and they occurred long ago. For example, the Chicago River used to flow into Lake Michigan, which is where the city draws its drinking water from. Because the water in the river was polluted, so became the water in the lake. Authorities decided 123 years ago to reverse the river's direction. It has since flowed from Lake Michigan toward the Mississippi River. Other examples of infrastructure changes were the development of small hydroelectric facilities north of Lake Superior in the 20th century. A minor volume of water that previously flowed to James Bay has since entered Lake Superior.

As for Niagara Falls, a control dam was built on the Niagara River 70 years ago. At night, the gates in the dam open, allowing some water to bypass the Falls and flow into the reservoirs that feed the hydroelectric plants. The control dam extends only halfway across the river. Therefore, water always flows naturally to the Falls.[241] The overall impact of the control dam on total water flow from Lake Erie to Lake Ontario is essentially nil. The dam merely directs the route that the some of the water takes —to the Falls or the power plants.

---

[241] The flow to the American falls was cut off on one occasion. Construction of a temporary river dam was necessary. The project allowed repairs to be made to the precipice of the American falls.

There are a couple of locations where authorities can exercise flow control. Generally, most of the water that flows out of Lake Superior passes through hydroelectric stations. However, a very limited control point is present at the entrance to the St. Mary's River. The amount of water that bypasses the generating stations and flows directly to the St. Mary's River can be increased or decreased, but just slightly.

More robust control exists on the St. Lawrence River where the flow can be increased or decreased through a control dam. Adjustments will impact Lake Ontario causing its level to rise or fall. The problem is that when water levels in Lake Ontario are high, increasing the flow through the dam in the river can cause flooding in communities downstream.

It is important to recognize that adjusting the level in Lake Ontario does not impact the other Great Lakes. The reason is Niagara Falls effectively decouples Lake Ontario and Lake Erie. When the level goes up or down in Lake Ontario, it doesn't affect how much water flows over the Falls. As for the power plants, what water does not go through them goes over the Falls and vice versa. That some of the flow is diverted to the power plants is immaterial because the water from the power plants is returned to the downstream Niagara River.

Appendix I.   Examples of Junius Morgan's OSS Correspondence

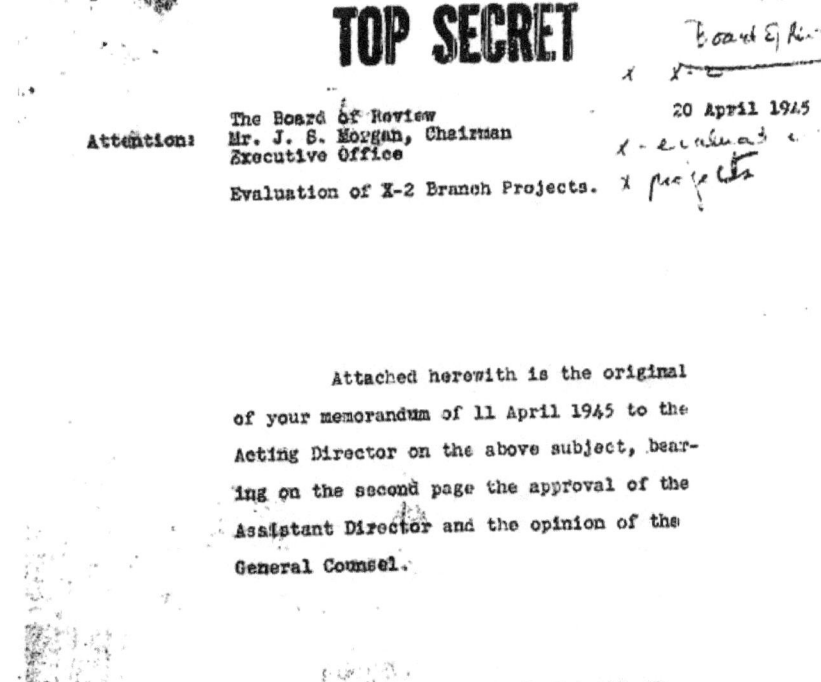

Figure 65. OSS memorandum to Junius Morgan. 1945, (Central Intelligence Agency Archives)

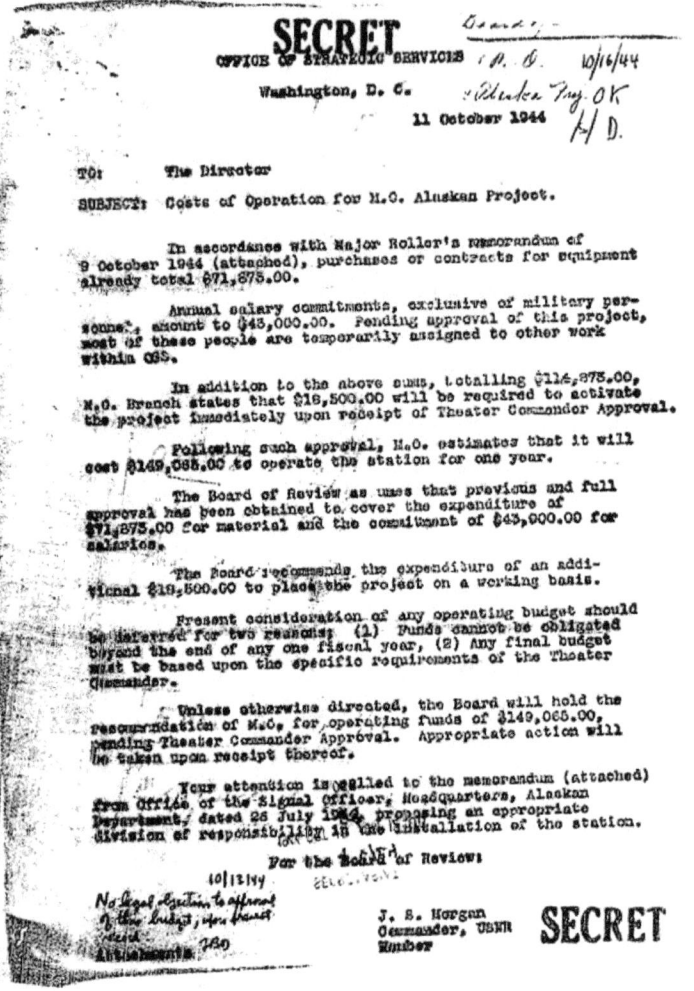

Figure 66. OSS memorandum by Junius Morgan. 1944. (Central Intelligence Agency Archives)

Appendix J.   Historical Nautical Maps and Map Excerpts

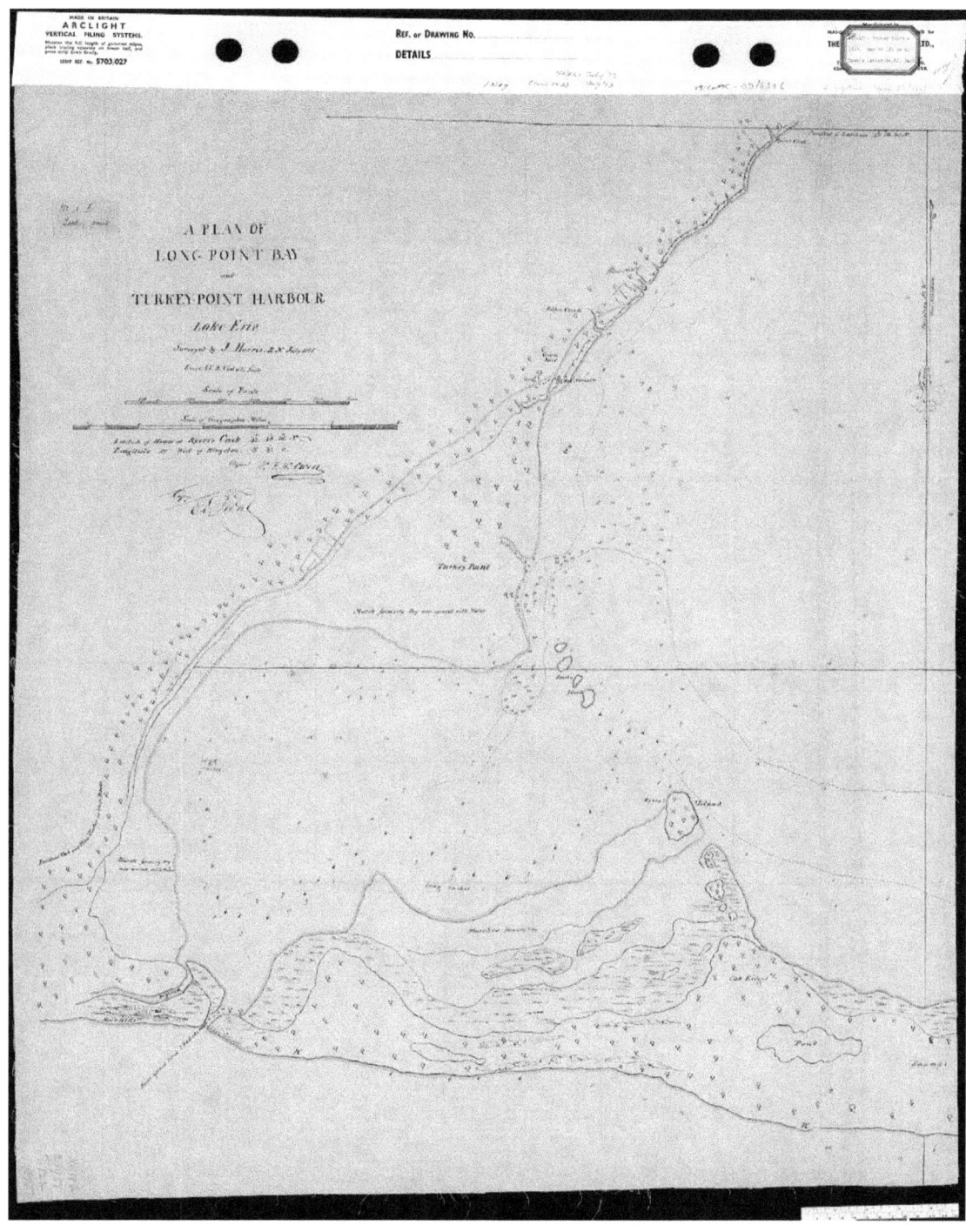

Figure 67. Royal Navy Chart for Long Point Bay. 1815.
Big Creek empties into Long Point Bay. A very narrow channel crosses the Long Point isthmus.

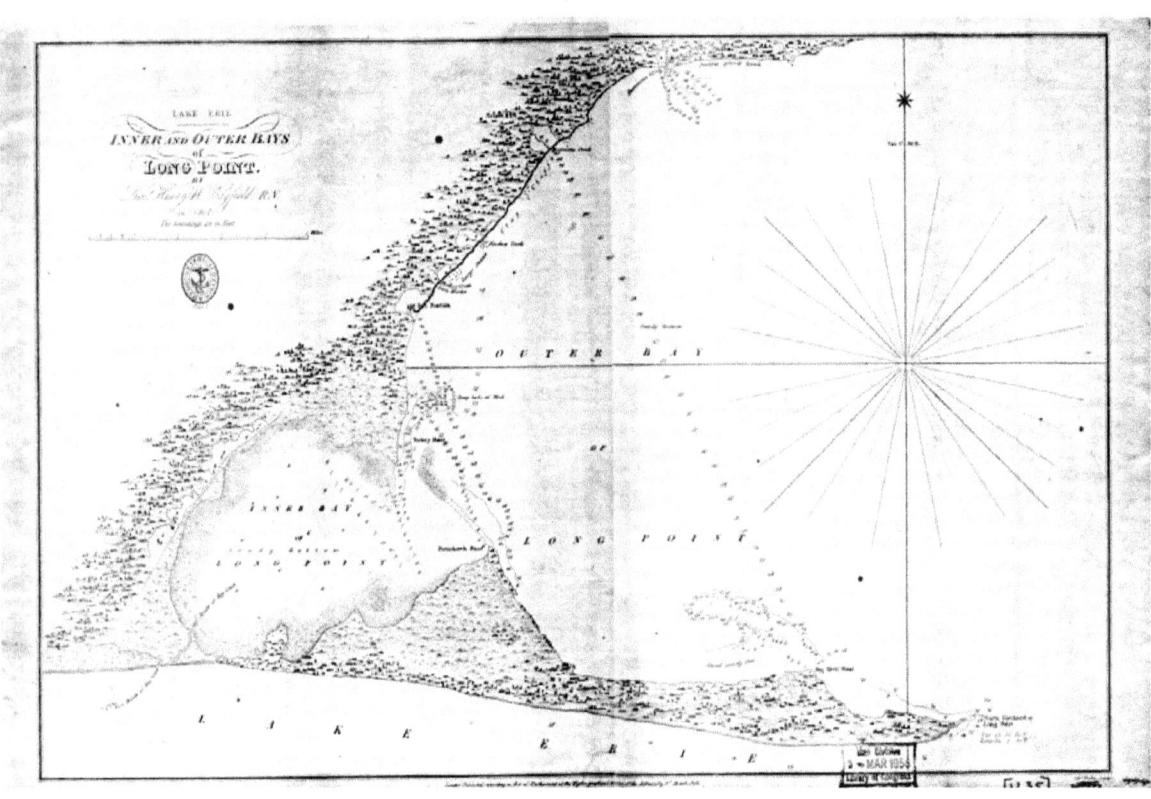

Figure 68 . Royal Navy chart for Long Point Bay. 1818. (Library of Congress, Washington, D.C.)
Big Creek is depicted emptying into Lake Erie. Long Point is depicted as a peninsula.

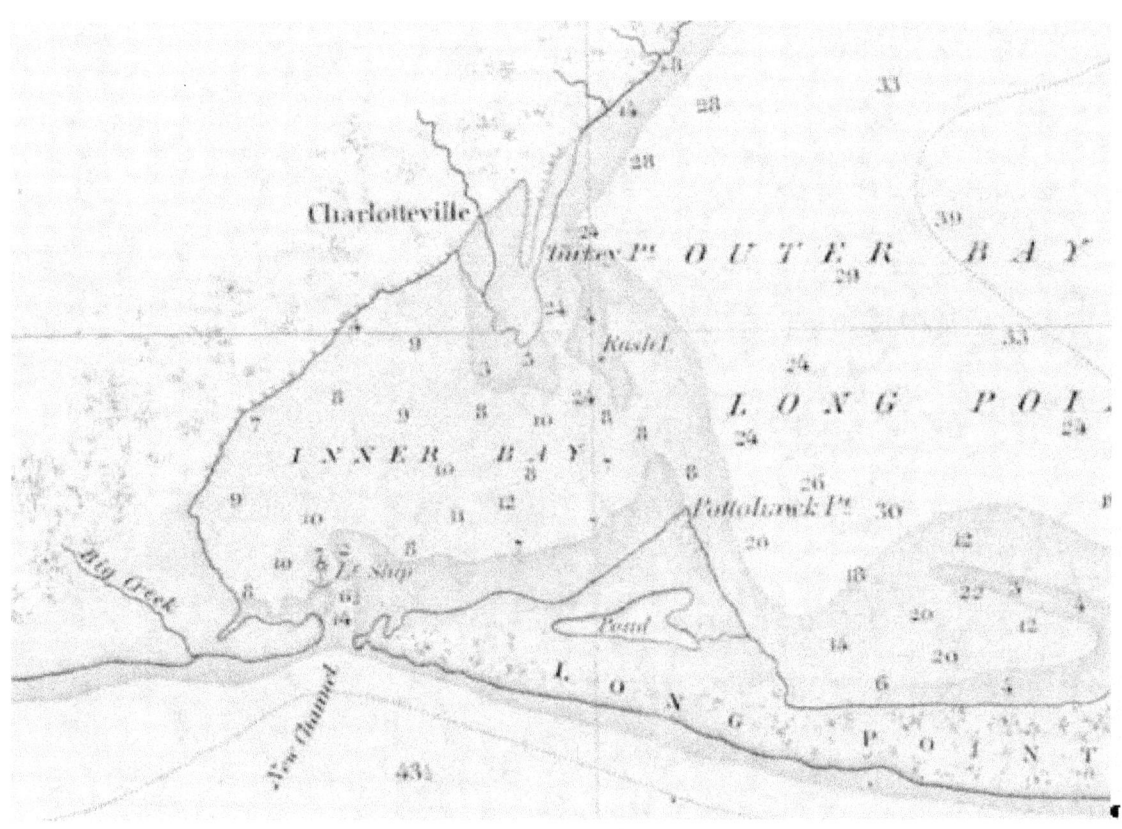

Figure 69. This excerpt from a U.S. War Department chart depicts both the 1833 channel and the lightship. 1849

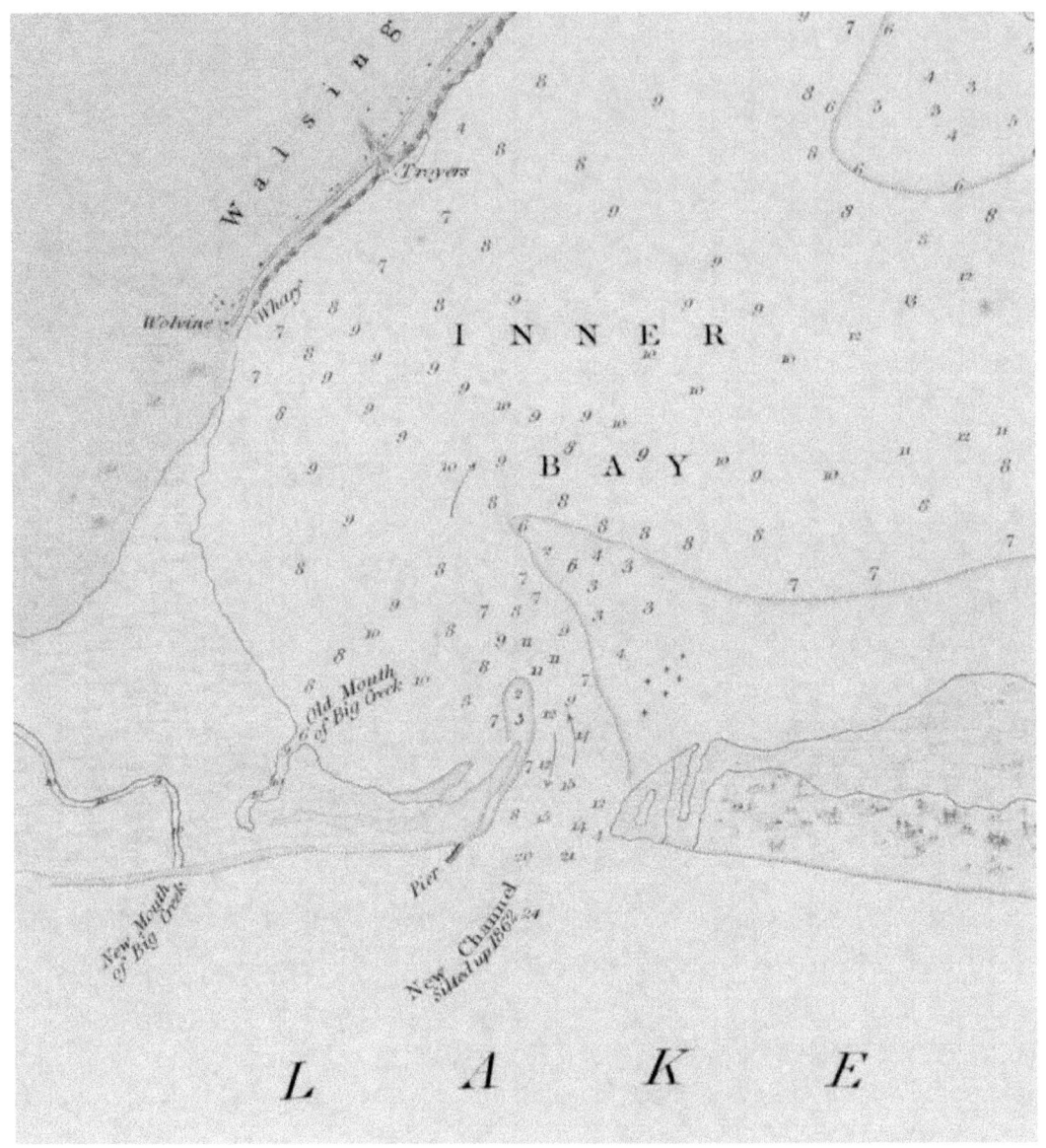

Figure 70. Excerpt from 1839 Royal Navy nautical chart with notes up to 1863.
The channel that formed in 1833 is shown as silted up in an 1862 note.
Port Rowan is labeled Wolvine and Troyer's landing is called out.

Acknowledgments

Researching and writing a lengthy historical treatment is a big undertaking. Had it not been for the COVID epidemic, I never would have written this book. Stuck at home for many days, I wanted to have a project to keep myself busy.

One of the most rewarding outcomes of the project was the many friendships it fostered, each of which led to invaluable assistance and encouragement. Bruce Malcolm was the first. He thought the story of the Long Point Company was worth telling. Marlene and Paul Smith also encouraged me, and Marlene reviewed the first manuscript. She and her daughter Heather promoted the first edition once it was available in print, and Heather shared information useful for the second edition. Douglas Glover generously reviewed my initial manuscript, coached me, and reviewed the first edition on his Substack blog and on Facebook. Kimberly Tisdale Lupal shared information about Long Point Company member David Tisdale. Karen Deans and Sharon Crockett promoted the book to the Long Point and Port Rowan communities.

Michael Bradstreet shares my interest in Long Point. His knowledge runs deeper than mine. Michael is a biologist who has published many scientific papers about the island and the birds who visit it. Jenny Lawrence is a descendant of a Long Point Company member from the era of *The Great Gatsby.* Graciously approachable, she shared details about her ancestor, sought out the Company's 1932 book, and copied it for me. David Mason shared historic photographs from his collection. Samantha George, the Curator for the Parkwood National Historic Site, searched for and found Col. Sam Mclaughlin's copy of Wilton Lloyd-Smith's 1934 book of Long Point photos among the 5,000 uncatalogued books at the site. Karen Barr read many chapters of the initial manuscript, annotated them, and gave me necessary coaching on writing. Sue Kociuk and Mike (Big Ike) Wilkins proofread the first edition.

Staff at the Norfolk County Archives and the Port Rowan/South Walsingham Heritage Association pulled materials for me. Staff in the rare book collections at Brock University and the University of Toronto did the same.

The Internet Archive and the Hathi Trust are invaluable repositories of historical information that can be accessed via the Internet. The research for this book would not have been feasible without access to these collections.

Most importantly, my spouse Grace has supported me throughout all my endeavors, and I can't thank her too much.

References

[1]   L. Snyder, "A Faunal Investigation of Long Point and Vicinity," *Transactions of the Royal Canadian Institute,* vol. 18, 1931.

[2]   B. Huis, et al, "Long Point National Wildlife Area: management plan (proposed)," Canadian Wildlife Service of Environment and Climate Change Canada, Gatineau, P. Q. Canada, 2020.

[3]   J. Macoun, Catalogue of Canadian Birds, Ottawa: Geological Survey of Canada, 1900.

[4]   W. E. Davis, Ed., Contributions to the History of North American Ornithology, vol. 4, Cambridge, Massachusetts: Nuttall Ornithological Club, 2019.

[5]   O. H. Marshall, The Historical Writings of the Late Orsamus H. Marshall, Albany: Joel Munsell's & Sons, 1887.

[6]   J. Coyne, "Galinee's Narative and Map Translated by J. Coyne," Ontario Historical Society, Toronto, 1903.

[7]   L. Hennepin, *A New Dicovery of a Vast Country in America,* vol. 1, A.C. McClurg & Co., 1697, p. 108.

[8]   L. Phelps, Journal of a Voyage Undertaken by the Order of the French King through North America, Vol 2, 1871, Translated by L. Phelps, Chicago: The Caxton Club, 1923.

[9]   D. W. Smyth, A short topographical description of His Majesty's province of Upper Canada in North America, W. Faden, 1799.

[10]   G. Laidler, "Long Point, Lake Erie, Some Physical and Historical Aspects," in *Ontario Historical Society*, 1944.

[11]   G. Sinclair, "Snakes Alive!," *MacLean's,* pp. 19-20,24, 26-27, 15 August 1945.

[12]   J. G. Spain, *Letter to the Editor,* Ontario, 1876.

[13]   J. McCracken, M. S. W. Bradstreet and G. L. Holroyd, "Breeding Birds of Long Point, Lake Erie," Canada Wildlife Service, Ottawa, 1981.

[14]   Government of Canada, "Wildlife Area Regulations," 2020. [Online]. Available: https://laws-lois.justice.gc.ca/eng/regulations/C.R.C.%2C_c._1609/FullText.html. [Accessed 4 November 2021].

[15]   D. Davison, Further Tales of Long Point, Glen Cove, NY: Privately printed by DigitalPrintery, 2003.

[16]   C. Lewis, "Late Quaternary History of Lake Levels in the Huron and Erie Basins," in *Proc. 12th Conf. Great Lakes Research, International Association for Great Lakes Research*, 1969.

[17]   R. W. Kelley, *Michigan Conservation,* vol. 24, no. 4, 1960.

[18]   P. Sly, "Lake Erie and its Basin," *J. Fish. Res. Board Canada,* 1976.

[19]   P. Barnett, "Quaternary Geology of the Tillsonburg Area," Ontario Geological Society, 1982.

[20]   N. Burns, Erie the Lake that Survived, Totowa, New Jersey: Rowman Allanheld, 1985.

[21]   Williams, S., Meisburger, E., "Geological Character and Mineral Resources of South
        Central Lake Erie," Army Corps of Engineers, Fort Belvoir, Virginia, 1982.

[22]   J. P. Coakley, "Evolution of Lake Erie Based on the Postglacial Sedimentary Record
        Below the Long Point, Point Pelee, and Pointe aux Pins Forelands, PhD thesis,"
        University of Waterloo, PhD dissertation, Waterloo, Ontario, 1985.

[23]   *Norfolk Reformer,* 14 January 1864.

[24]   *Norfolk Reformer,* 24 March 1864.

[25]   W. J. McInnes, *Deposition of Richard Johnson of Forestville,* Simcoe, Ontario: Norfolk
        Historical Society, 1901.

[26]   *Upper Canada Herald,* December 1833.

[27]   NOAA, "What is a seiche?," 22 February 2023. [Online]. Available:
        https://oceanservice.noaa.gov/facts/seiche.html#:~:text=In%201844%2C%20a%2022%
        2Dfoot,flooding%20near%20Buffalo%2C%20New%20York..

[28]   *Pittsburgh Morning Post,* p. 2, 25 Oct 1844.

[29]   S. E. Pugsley, *The Old Cut at Long Point,* 1906.

[30]   J. Morse, The American Gazetteer, Boston: Samuel Etheridge, 1804.

[31]   J. D. Stout, A Gazetteer of the Province of Upper Canada, Prior & Dunning, 1813.

[32]   M. J. Wright, "Excavation at the Glen Meyer Reid Site, Long Point, Lake Erie," Ontario
        Archaeological Society, London, 1978.

[33]   W. A. e. a. Fox, "The Shaman of Long Point," *Ontario Archaeology,* vol. 57, pp. 23-44,
        1994.

[34]   W. Canniff, History of the Serttlement of Upper Canada, Toronto: Dudley & Burns,
        1869.

[35]   G. Laidler, "John Troyer of Long Point Bay, Lake Erie," *Ontario History,* vol. 39, 1947.

[36]   W. B. Waterbury, "Sketch of Peter Teeple, Loyalist & Pioneer," in *Read before the
        Elgin Historical Society,* St. Thomas, 1899.

[37]   F. Eames, "Pioneer Schools of Upper Canada," *Papers and Records, Ontario Historical
        Society,* vol. 18, 1920.

[38]   F. J. Audet, Canadian Historical Dates & Events, Ottawa: George Beauregard, 1917.

[39]   Guillet, The Pioneer Farmer and Backwoodsman, Toronto: University of Toronto Press,
        1963.

[40]   C. Coons and H. Barrett, Alligators of the North: The story of the West & Peachey
        steam warping tugs, Toronto: The Dundurn Group, 2010.

[41]   J. B. Hurlbert, "Collection of the Products of the Waters and Forests of Upper Canada,"
        Longmoore & Co., Montreal, 1862.

[42]   *The Gazette,* 26 May 1798.

[43]   E. A. Owen, Pioneer Sketches of the Long Point Settlement, Toronto : William Briggs,
        1898.

[44]   J. M. Thoms, *PhD Thesis Dissertation,* Bristish Columbia: University of British
        Columbia, 2004.

[45] A. Fraser, "Eighteenth Report of the Department of Public Records and Archives of Ontario," Herbert H. Ball, 1929.

[46] *Minutes of the Executive Council,* 1808.

[47] B. Blakeley, The Civilian Soldier: a complete history of the Norfolk militia 1796-2007, Waterford: Norfolk Mercantile, 2007.

[48] C. Thomas, Ryerson of Upper Canada, Toronto: The Ryerson Press, 1969.

[49] *American Patriot,* p. 1, 11 June 1814.

[50] M. Conrad, A Concise History of Canada, 2nd Edition, Cambridge University Press, 2022.

[51] H. Bayfield, vol. 2, Quebec: Literary and Historical Society of Quebec, 1831.

[52] "Federal Heritage Designations," 1927. [Online]. Available: https://www.pc.gc.ca/apps/dfhd/page_nhs_eng.aspx?id=441. [Accessed 26 January 2021].

[53] J. H. Bartlett, "The Manufacture of Iron in Canada," in *Transactions of the American Institute of Mining Engineers*, Halifax, 1885.

[54] H. Bathurst, "Minutes of the Intended Arrangements between Earl Bathurst, His Majesty's Secretary of State, and the Proposed Canada Company," York, Upper Canada, 1825.

[55] *The Liberal,* 15 September 1836.

[56] M. Williams, Americans and Their Forests, Cambridge, UK: Cambridge University Press, 1989.

[57] H. B. Barrett, The 19th Century Journals & Paintings of William Pope, Toronto: M. F. Feheley Publishers Ltd., 1976.

[58] *Advertisement, The Long Point Advocate,* 16 September 1843.

[59] *Advertisement, The Western Liberal,* 23 Auguste 1850.

[60] R. Fowler, Hither and Thither; or Sketches of Travels on Both Sides of the Atlantic, London, England: Frederick R. Daldy, 1854.

[61] J. A. Temple, Annals of Two Extinct Families of the Eighteenth Century (Von Luders and Light), London, U.K.: F. V. White & Co., 1910.

[62] J. Farquharson, "Herons and Cobblestones, A History of Five Oaks and the Bethel Area of Brantford Township, County of Brant," Grand River Heritage Mines Society, Paris, Ontario, 2003.

[63] *American Lumberman,* p. 69, 6 Dcember 1919.

[64] *Norfolk Reformer,* 2 June 1864.

[65] "Gerald C. Metzler Great Lakes Vessel Database, Wisconsin Maritime Museum," 1 March 2023. [Online]. Available: http://www.greatlakesvessels.org/en-us/intro.aspx.

[66] "Lake Vessel Register," Association of Canadian Lake Underwriters, Toronto, 1866.

[67] "Canada at the Universal Exhibition of 1855," The Legislative Assembley of Canada, 1856.

[68] *Jackson v. Evans et al,* 1870.

[69] *Norfolk Reformer,* 25 December 1862.

[70]   S. Wingrove, "Letter of Sharlet Wingrove Nov. 1, 1868," *Waterloo Chronicle,* 19 November 1868.

[71]   *Norfolk Reformer,* 3 September 1868.

[72]   *Buffalo Express,* 22 Juner 1869.

[73]   *Map of the County of Norfolk, Canada West,* George C. Tremaine, 1856.

[74]   J. Earl, A Sketch of Norfolk County, Canada West, Simcoe, 1857.

[75]   C. J. Humber, C. J. Humber, Ed., Mississauga, Ontario: Humber, C. J., 1991.

[76]   C. W. Jefferys, The Picture Gallery of Canadian History, Ryerson Press, 1945.

[77]   *Medical & Surgical Reporter,* vol. 7, no. 6, p. 143, 9 November 1861.

[78]   *New York Times,* p. 5, 2 November 1861.

[79]   *Norfolk Reformer,* 23 January 1862.

[80]   *Evening Courier & Republic,* 5 October 1868.

[81]   *Norfolk Reformer,* 6 October 1864.

[82]   *Norfolk Reformer,* 21 May 1868.

[83]   *Norfolk Reformer,* 3 July 1862.

[84]   *Norfolk Reformer,* 18 December 1862.

[85]   "Journal of the House of Assembly of Upper Canada," 1834.

[86]   *The Nautical Magazine & Naval Chronicle,* pp. 234-235, 1844.

[87]   *Wellington Mercury,* 18 February 1854.

[88]   "General Report of the Commissioners of Public Works," Legislative Assembly, Toronto, 1858.

[89]   *Appendices to the Report of the Minister of Public Works for the Fiscal Year Ending June 30 1870,* 1871.

[90]   *Norfolk Reformer,* 8 September 1864.

[91]   *Erie News,* 19 April 1860.

[92]   Toronto: H.R. Page & Co., 1877.

[93]   *Toronto Telegram,* 5 April 1936.

[94]   *Toledo Blade,* 2 December 1867.

[95]   *Buffalo Morning Express,* 4 May 1868.

[96]   *Norfolk Reformer,* 7 May 1868.

[97]   *Norfolk Reformer,* 14 January 1864.

[98]   "The Timber Trade of Big Creek," *Norfolk Reformer,* 8 August 1861.

[99]   *Norfolk Reformer,* 19 May 1864.

[100]   *Norfolk Reformer,* 14 May 1863.

[101]   G. W. Hotchkiss, History of the Lumber and Forest Industry of the Northwest, Chicago: George W. Hotchkiss & Co., 1898.

[102]   *The Canadian Lumberman,* vol. 18, no. 2, February 1897.

[103]   *Buffalo Express,* 15 December 1870.

[104]   *Evening Courier & Rebulic,* p. 2, 23 July 1869.

[105] *Norfolk Reformer,* 7 July 1864.

[106] *Norfolk Reformer,* 25 August 1864.

[107] *Norfolk Reformer,* 7 August 1862.

[108] Hydrographic Office of the Admiralty, 1839 (Amended 1861).

[109] *Buffalo Express,* 22 June 1869.

[110] "Official Record of the Union & Confederate Navies in the War of Rebellion," Secretary of the Navy, Washington, DC, 1921.

[111] "Wikimedia Commons, File:USS Honeysuckle.jpg," [Online]. Available: https://commons.wikimedia.org/wiki/File:USS_Honeysuckle.jpg.

[112] *Norfolk Reformer,* 29 April 1869.

[113] *The Municpal World,* vol. 3, no. 5, p. 77, May 1893.

[114] *Ingersol Chronicle and Candian Dairyman,* p. 7, 5 August 1895.

[115] *Spirit of the Times,* 30 October 1841.

[116] H. Christmas, vol. 1, London: Richard Bentley, 1849.

[117] "Advertisement," *The Buffalo Commercial,* 21 April 1852.

[118] Indianapolis, Indiana: Umberhine & Gustin, 1861.

[119] *W. Haskins, Agricultural Surveyer, Letter to George H. Gillespie,* Hamilton, Ontario: Pivately Printed by R. Raw, 1872.

[120] *Genesee Farmer,* 1856.

[121] *Spirit of the Times,* 14 January 1854.

[122] H. B. Barrett, Lore & Lengends of Long Point, Don Mills, Ontario: Burns & MacEachern, 1977.

[123] R. W. Winks, Blacks in Canada: a history, First ed., New Haven: Yale University Press, 1971.

[124] *Norfolk Reformer,* 4 December 1862.

[125] *Norfolk Reformer,* 3 December 1868.

[126] *Norfolk Reformer,* 1 September 1864.

[127] *Norfolk Reformer,* 3 October 1861.

[128] A Synopsis of the History with Acts of Incorporation of the Long Point Company, Hamitlon: R. Raw, 1872, 1868.

[129] J. Spain, Normandlae Postal Office, 1863.

[130] The Long Point Company, Privately printed, 1966.

[131] E. Harris, Recollections of Long Point, Toronto: Warwick Brothers and Rutter, 1918.

[132] J. Deep, "The Daring 19th Century Reformers Who Sought to End Prostitution by Offering Financial & Emotional Support to Urban Sex Workers.," *Smithsonian,* 27 March 2025.

[133] "Found Drowned," *Norfolk Reformer,* 13 November 1862.

[134] *Norfolk Reformer,* 13 November 1862.

[135] *Ingersol Chronicle,* 21 November 1862.

[136] W. Witcher, "Long Point, Lake Erie, & the Protection of Game," *The Ottawa Times,* p. 2, 15 October 1870.

[137] E. J. Gorn, "Good-Bye Boys, I Die a True American': Homicide, Nativism, and Working-Class Culture in Antebellum New York City," *The Journal of American History,* pp. 388-410, 1987.

[138] "Heenan Obituary," *Huron Signal,* p. 1, 12 November 1873.

[139] L. Alan, The Great Prize Fight, New York: Coward, McCann & Geoghegan, 1977.

[140] *Springfield Weekly Republican,* 23 October 1858.

[141] D. Gildea, "The Heenan-Morrissey Fight of 1858 and Frank Queen's Attack on the Respectable Press," *Colby Quarterly, Vol 32, Issue 1,* 1996.

[142] *Frank Leslie's Illustrated Newspaper,* 30 October 1858.

[143] D. Gildea, "Science vs. Size," *American Journalism,* 1993.

[144] D. Gildea, ""Cross Counter": The Heenan-Morrissey Fight of 1858 and Frank Queen's Attack on the "Respectable Press"," *Colby Quarterly,* pp. 11-22, 1996.

[145] E. J. Gorn, The Manly Art: Bare-Knuckle Prize Fighting in America, Ithaca, New York: Cornell University Press, 2010.

[146] B. Mee, Bare Fists, the History of Bare-Knuckle Prize-Fighting, Woodstock, NY: The Overlook Press, 2001.

[147] "The Mace-Coburn Fizzle," *The New York Herald,* p. 8, 13 May 1871.

[148] *Norfolk Reformer,* 18 May 1871.

[149] "The Great Fight," *The Sun, New York,* p. 2, 12 May 1871.

[150] "The Mace-Coburn Fiasco," *Terre Haute Weekly Express,* p. 4, 17 May 1871.

[151] Brooklyn Eagle, "The Fight, Full Particulars of the Recent Mill," *Brooklyn Eagle,* p. 4, 9 May 1879.

[152] New York Times, "Beaten in Twelve Rounds," *The New York Times,* 8 May 1879.

[153] "The Death of a Prizefighter," *The Sun,* 11 March 1882.

[154] The Evening Star, "Canada Prevents the Donovan-Rooke Prize Fight," *The Evening Star,* p. 3, 12 May 1880.

[155] The Sun, "Preventing a Prize Fight, A Sheriff Meets Rooke & Donovan with a File of Soldiers," *The Sun,* p. 1, 12 May 1880.

[156] *The Daily Mail,* p. 1, 14 May 1880.

[157] *Brooklyn Daily Eagle,* 16 November 1881.

[158] *Norfolk Reformer,* 17 November 1881.

[159] *New York Times,* 17 November 1881.

[160] W. Herbert, Frank Forester's Field Sports of the United States and the British Provinces of North America, New York: Stringer & Townsend, 1849.

[161] *Norfolk Reformer,* 5 December 1861.

[162] D. A. Buscombe, Untitled, Port Dover: Privately published, 1975.

[163] *Evening Courier & Republic,* 5 November 1866.

[164] *Norfolk Reformer,* 12 April 1866.

[165] *Evening Courier & Republic,* 14 July 1865.

[166] J. A. MacDonald, Troubled Times in Canada A History of the Fenian Raids of 1866 and 1870., Toronto: W. S. Johnston & Co., 1910.

[167] *Los Angeles Herald,* 2 December 1887.

[168] S. E. Heffernan, "Long Point, Ontario: Land Use, Landscape Change, and Planning. Masters Thesis," University of Waterloo, Waterloo, Ontario, 1978.

[169] *Norfolk Reformer,* p. 2, 24 May 1866.

[170] *Norfolk Reformer,* 5 December 1867.

[171] S. Woodruff, *Private Instructions,* Long Point Company, 1882.

[172] *Norfolk Reformer,* 3 December 1868.

[173] Department of Marine & Fisheries, 1877.

[174] *Norfolk Reformer,* 13 August 1868.

[175] *Norfolk Reformer,* 4 June 1868.

[176] *Evening Courier & Republic,* p. 2, 1 October 1869.

[177] *Norfolk Reformer,* 7 October 1869.

[178] "Annual Archaeological Report and Canadian Institute Session," Canadian Institute, Toronto, 1892.

[179] "Annual Report of the Dept. of Agriculture," Legislatative Assembly of Ontario, Toronto, 1912.

[180] "Catalog of Specimens of the Ontario Archaeological Museum," Department of Education, Toronto, 1897.

[181] "ROM Collections," 2023. [Online]. Available: https://collections.rom.on.ca/objects/41628/axe?ctx=0a28f3de-4979-406b-b163-ed07cb91cc25&idx=16. [Accessed 27 April 2023].

[182] C. MacDonald, Port Dover: A Place in the Sun, Port Dover: Port Dover Board of Trade, 1998.

[183] *Montreal Herald Daily Commercial Gazette,* 26 October 1852.

[184] A. Wakeman, History and Reminiscences of Lower Wall Street and Vicinity, New York: The Spice Mill Publishing Co., 1914.

[185] "New York Market Report - Tea," *The London & China Telegraph,* 20 December 1870.

[186] "New York Market Report - Tea," *The London and China Telegraph,* 20 December 1870.

[187] "Marine Intelligence," *New York Times,* 2 October 1865.

[188] B. Crandall, "The Reeves of Long Point Company," *Decoy Magazine,* July 1992.

[189] *New Dominion,* 26 November 1869.

[190] G. Gillespie, 1868.

[191] J. Walter, Saratoga Springs, New York: Saratoga Springs Preservation Society, 2017.

[192] The Long Point Company, 100th Anniversary Yearbook, Privately published, 1966.

[193] *Buffalo Morning Express and Illustrated Express,* 26 November 1893.

[194] E. Ryerson, *Letter to His Daughter Sophie,* Toronto, Ontario: The Ryserson Press, 1866.

[195] G. Ryerson, Looking Backwards, Toronto: Ryerson Press, 1924.

[196] *Letter from W. Allan to George Gillespie, 1869,* Hamilton: The Long Point Company, 1872.

[197] W. A. Gordon, Lake Erie's Isle of Romance, Long Point Island, Port Dover: W. A. Gordon, Photgrapher, 1934.

[198] *Long Point Company v. Fick,* 1889.

[199] *Norfolk Reformer,* 3 October 1889.

[200] *Regina v. Spain,* 1889.

[201] *Regina v. Becker,* 1891.

[202] *The Saturday Globe,* 29 November 1890.

[203] *London Saturday Advertiser,* 4 November 1893.

[204] *Norfolk Reformer,* 16 January 1868.

[205] "Norfolk Reformer," p. 2, 3 December 1868.

[206] E. Ryerson, *Letter to His Daughter Sophie,* Toronto, Ontario: The Ryerson Press, 1869.

[207] W. Haskins, A Synopsis of the History with Act of Incorporation of the Long Point Company, Hamilton: R. Raw, Book & Job Printer 1872, 1869.

[208] *Norfolk Reformer,* 24 October 1873.

[209] Government of Canada, "Report of the Debates of the House of Commons," Ottawa, 1885.

[210] *Norfolk Reformer,* 10 March 1870.

[211] "Township of Walsingham vs. Long Point Company," *Local Courts and Municipal Gazette, Vol. VII,* April 1871.

[212] Province of Ontario, *Journal of Education, Vol 29, No. 10,* 1876 October 1876.

[213] *Municipal World,* vol. 16, no. 8, September 1906.

[214] A. McCullough, The Commercial Fishery of the Canadian Great Lakes, Ottawa: Canadian Parks Service, Environment Canada , 1989.

[215] *Norfolk Reformer,* 4 November 1869.

[216] "Norfolk Reformer," p. 2, 1 December 1870.

[217] *Forest & Stream,* vol. 4, no. 1, 11 February 1875.

[218] *Norfolk Reformer,* p. 2, 16 July 1868.

[219] E. Ryerson, *Letter to His Daughter Sophie,* Toronto, Onatrio: The Ryerson Press, 1869.

[220] "Norfolk Reformer," p. 2, 11 April 1872.

[221] *Forest and Stream,* 18 May 1880.

[222] "A Synopsis of the History with Acts of Incorporation of the Long Point Company," Hamilton, R. Raw, 1872.

[223] *The Canadian Gentleman's Journal & Sporting Times,* p. 5, 13 October 1876.

[224] *Outing & the Wheelman,* February 1885.

[225] *Forest & Stream,* vol. 7, no. 10, 10 October 1876.

[226] E. Ryerson, Toronto, 1869.

[227] M. Blair, The Paisley Thread Industry, Paisley, UK: Alexander Gardner, 1907.

[228] *Attorney General v. Tudor Ice Co.,* 1870.

[229] J. MacKenzie, *A Report and Financial Statement with Balance Sheet, Etc. of the Long Point Company,* Hamilton, Ontario, 1878.

[230] Long Point Company, *Minutes of the Long Point Company,* Hamilton: Times Steam Printing House, 1874.

[231] "Commercial Failures," *The New York Herald,* p. 5, 14 October 1875.

[232] T. W. Cobban, "The Role of Municipalities in Stimulating Economic Growth: Evidence from the Petroleum Manufacturing Industry, 1860-1960," University of Western Ontario, London, Ontario, 2008.

[233] *Chicago Tribune,* p. 3, 8 December 1880.

[234] *The Grocer,* vol. 10, 9 December 1880.

[235] *New York Times,* 8 December 1880.

[236] L. V. Briggs, History and Genealogy of the Cabot Family, Boston: C.E. Goodspeed & Co., 1927.

[237] *The Sun,* 10 July 1904.

[238] Commissioners Fish and Game, "4th Annual Report," Government of Ontario, 1895, 1895.

[239] *Norfolk Reformer,* 11 March 1915.

[240] *Norfolk Reformer,* 18 October 1883.

[241] *Toronto World,* p. 3, 13 December 1890.

[242] "Evidence Before the Royal Fish & Game Commission," *The Toronto World,* p. 1, 20 December 1890.

[243] "The Ottawa Convention," *Forest & Stream,* p. 188, 5 April 1883.

[244] *New York Times,* 15 October 1883.

[245] *Gleanings in Bee Culture,* vol. 24, no. 16, 15 August 1896.

[246] *London Advertiser,* 30 July 1989.

[247] *Gleanings in Bee Culture,* pp. 1257-1259, 15 October 1908.

[248] R. Chernow, Titan: the Life of John D. Rockefeller Sr., 2nd Ed., New York: Vintage Books, Div. Random House, 2004.

[249] K. Wimmel, Theodore Roosevelt and the Great White Fleet: American Seapower Comes of Age, Dulles, VA: Brassey's, 1998.

[250] H. H. Klein, "Standard Oil or the People," By the author, Tribune Bldg., New York City, 1914.

[251] G. Hughes, "Beaux Arts in the Forest? Stanfor White's Fishing Lodges in New Brunswick," *Journal of the Society for the Study of Architecture in Canada,* vol. 1, 2001.

[252] E. J. Kahn, "Jock: the Life and Times of John Hay Whitney," Doubleday & Co., New York, 1981.

[253] *Time Magazine,* 30 July 1934.

[254] A. Goodstein, Biography of a Businessman: Henry W. Sage, 1814-1897, Ithaca: Cornell Univerity Press, 1962.

[255] *Northern Advance,* 22 April 1897.

[256] *Turf, Field & Farm,* p. 630, 4 June 1902.

[257] E. J. Kahn, Jock: The Life and Times of John Hay Whitney, Garden City, N.Y.: Doubleday, 1981.

[258] *Time Magazine,* 30 July 1934.

[259] V. e. a. Hedman, Flin Flon, Flin Flon, Manitoba: Flin Flon Historical Society, 1974.

[260] *Woodstock Sentinel Review,* 10 October 1890.

[261] "Murdered by Poachers," *The Buffalo Enquirer,* p. 6, 2 November 1893.

[262] "Detective Allan's Death, Inquiry Regarding the Long Point Tragedy Resumed," *The London Advertiser,* p. 1, 7 October 1893.

[263] *The London Advertiser,* 1 November 1893.

[264] *The London Advertiser,* 31 October 1893.

[265] *Toronto World,* 17 November 1893.

[266] G. Richards, *Letter to David Tisdale,* Massachusetts, 1909.

[267] Burt, "Third Annual Report of the Games & Fisheries Department," Ontario Sessional Papers, No. 12-15, Ontario Legislative Assembly, Toronto, 1910.

[268] G. Killan, Ministry of Natural Resources Book No. 4763, the Queen's Printer, 1993.

[269] "Annual Report of the Fruit Growers' Assoc. of Ontario," 1879.

[270] E. C. Harris, Toronto: Edward Harris, 1891.

[271] Statutes of the Province of Ontario, Toronto: Clarkson W. James, Printer to the King's Most Excellent Majesty, 1921.

[272] *London Advertiser,* 18 August 1921.

[273] *Noble and Wolf v. Alley,* 1950.

[274] *Buffalo Express,* 1878.

[275] *Listowel Standard,* October 1879.

[276] S. e. a. Hazen, Down by the Bay, Erin, Ontario: Boston Mills Press, 2000.

[277] *Canada Lumberman and Woodworker,* 15 February 1919.

[278] *The Canadian Manufacturer,* 16 June 1905.

[279] "Report of the Bureau of Mines," Legislaature of Ontario, 1905.

[280] *Electrical World,* 16 February 1907.

[281] *Oil & Gas Journal,* 26 September 1912.

[282] *Oil & Gas Journal,* 18 July 1912.

[283] *Oil & Gas Journal,* 1 January 1913.

[284] *Oil & Gas Journal,* May 1939.

[285] *The Advance,* 19 June 1913.

[286] *Oil & Gas Journal,* vol. 12, no. 2, p. 6, 19 June 1913.

[287] *Oil & Gas Journal,* 16 April 1914.

[288] *American Gas Engineering Journal,* 22 May 1920.

[289] "FBI.gov," 15 April 2023. [Online]. Available: https://www.fbi.gov/history/famous-cases/wall-street-bombing-1920. [Accessed 15 April 2023].

[290] C. M. Fuess, Calvin Coolidge The Man From Vermont, Boston: Little, Brown & Co., 1940.

[291] *New York Times,* pp. 1, 26, 23 June 1969.

[292] *National Geographic,* vol. LIII, no. 1, pp. 8,9,11, January 1928.

[293] J. S. Morgan, Further Recollections of Long Point, New York: Privately printed, 1953.

[294] J. H. Whitney, *Letter from John Hay Whitney to Francis Reid,* Thomasville, Georgia, 1930.

[295] W. Lloyd-Smith, The Long Point Company, New York: Privately printed, 1935.

[296] *Windsor Star,* 6 May 1933.

[297] *Border Cities Star,* 11 September 1933.

[298] S. K. Farrington, The Ducks Came Back, New York: Coward-McCann & Co., 1945.

[299] R. Thruelsen, The Grumman Story, New York: Praeger Publishers, Inc., 1976.

[300] *The American Kennel Gazette,* pp. 9-13, 1 August 1932.

[301] J. Goodall, 10 February 2020. [Online]. Available: https://goodall.com.au/grumman-amphibians/grummangoose.pdf.

[302] S. P. Lovell, Of Spies and Stratagems, Prentice-Hall, 1963.

[303] V. Currier, Good-bye, Lord, I'm Going to New York, Xlibris, 2015.

[304] M. Wortman, The Millionaires' Unit, PublicAffairs, 2007.

[305] W. Nesbitt, "April 29, 1954," 24 January 2023. [Online]. Available: https://www.lipad.ca/full/1954/04/29/29/#1764046.

[306] *LR-30477, Vol. 5a,* Toronto, Ontario: Legislative Assembly of Ontario, 1950.

[307] Legislative Assembly of Ontario, 1961, 1962.

[308] W. A. Gordon, Lake Erie's Isle of Romance, Long Point Island, Port Dover, 1934.

[309] F. Halpenny, Dictionary of Canadian Biography, vol. 12, Toronto: University of Toronto Press, 1966.

[310] G. M. Grant, Ed., Picturesque Canada: the country as it was and is, Toronto: James Clarke, 1880.

[311] P. W. C. Robinson, Birds of the Wave and Woodland, London: Isbister & Co., 1894.

[312] M. F. Boynton, Louis Agassiz Fuertes, His Life Briefly Told and His Correspondence, New York: Oxford University Press, 1956.

[313] *London Illustrated News,* 5 January 1889.

[314] F. A. Bedford, The Sporting Art of Frank W. Benson, Jaffrey, NH: David R. Godine, 2000.

[315] L. A. Koltun, "The Cabinet Makers Art in Ontario c. 1850-1900," Government of Canada, Ottawa, 1979.

[316] G. R. Starr, Decoys of the Atlantic Flyway, New York: Winchester Press, 1974.

[317] 18 January 2023. [Online]. Available: https://www.bankesboats.com/.

[318] J. Barber, Wild Fowl Decoys, New York: Dover Publications, Inc., 1954.

[319] "Wildfowl Shooting on Lake Erie," *The Field Quarterly Magazine & Review,* Vol. 2 1871.

[320] *Norfolk Reformer,* 19 October 1862.

[321] *Norfolk Reformer,* 31 October 1867.

[322] *Norfolk Reformer,* 7 July 1870.

[323] *Norfolk Reformer,* 28 September 1871.

[324] J. MacKenzie, *Memorandum to members,* Hamilton, 1882.

[325] *Forest & Stream,* 23 January 1904.

[326] New York: Lloyd's Register of Shipping, 1912.

[327] M. Reeves, Interviewee, [Interview]. 29 June 2021.

[328] R. Train, A Memoir, Washington, D.C.: Privately published, 2000.

[329] *Railroad Gazette,* 25 July 1884.

[330] *Indiannapolis Journal,* 16 December 1887.

[331] *Toronto Star,* p. A13, 4 October 1991.

[332] J. Wallace, A Gathering of Wonders, Behind the Scenes of the American Museum of Natural History.,, New York: St. Martin's Press, 2000.

[333] J. Fitzmaurice, The Shanty Boy, or Life in a Lumber Camp, Cheyboygan: Democrat Steam Press, 1889.

[334] *Fredonia Censor,* 31 August 1825.

[335] V. Lauriston, "Ontario Natural Gas Industry," *American Gas Journal,* May 1939.

[336] F. Habashi, "The First Oil Well in the World," *Bulletin for the History of Chemistry,* vol. 25, no. 1, 2000.

[337] I. M. Drummond, Progress without planning : the economic history of Ontario from Confederation to the Second World War, Toronto: Government of Ontario, 1987.

[338] *Norfolk Reformer,* 17 August 1865.

[339] *Norfolk Reformer,* 7 September 1865.

[340] E. Coste, "The Journal of the Canadian Mining Institute," in *Papers and Proceedings of the Meetings of the Institute*, Montreal, 1900.

[341] *Hamilton Spectator,* 19 August 2019.

[342] "Ontario GeoHub," 7 February 2023. [Online]. Available: https://geohub.lio.gov.on.ca/datasets/lio::petroleum-well/explore.

[343] Holcombe et al, "Lake-Floor Geomorphology of Lake Erie, Research Publication RP-3," United States National Oceanic and Atmospheric Administration.

[344] Vronski, "Combat, Memory and Remembrance in Confederation Era Canada: The Hidden History of the Battle of Ridgeway, June 2, 1866," PhD Thesis, Department of History, University of Toronto, Toronto, 2011.

[345] L. M. E. Foreman, "Who was buried at the Varden Site," *Ontario Archaeology, No. 85-88/London Chapter, Occasional Pub. No. 9,* pp. 157-186, 2010.

[346] F. Weitzenhoffer, The Havemeyers: Impressionism Comes to America, New York: Harry N. Abrams Inc., 1986.

[347] L. S. Thompson, The Long Point Company, New York, NY: Privately printed by the Scribner Co., 1932.

[348] Chicago Tribune, "Prize Fight Between James Eliiott of Cleveland and William M. Davis of Detroit," *The Chicago Tribune,* p. 1, 11 May 1867.

[349] A. E. M. Paff, Etchings and Drypoints by Frank W. Benson, Boston & New York: Houghton MIfflin Co., 1919.

[350] Central Intelligence Agency, "The Career System in the CIA," Washington, DC, 1955, Declassified Jan. 7, 2002.

[351] "The Trigger," *The Canadian Gentlemen's Journal & Sporting Times,* 15 October 1876.

[352] E. K. Dodds, *The Canadian Sportsman Annual,* p. 136, 1885.

[353] *The Ottawa Times,* 2 December 1870.

[354] J. McCuaig, *Report of the Superintendant of Fisheries of Upper Canada,* Quebec: Legislative Assembley, Government of Canada, 1859.

[355] *Norfolk Reformer,* p. 2, 24 January 1867.

[356] *Norfolk Reformer,* p. 2, 17 May 1866.

[357] *Norfolk Reformer,* p. 2, 31 October 1867.

[358] Smith, W. H., Smith's Canadian Gazetteer, Henry Rowsell, 1849.

[359] Smith, W. H., Canada, Past, Present & Future, Vol. 1, Toronto: Thomas MacLear, 1851.

[360] *Hamilton Times,* p. 1, 11 August 1865.

[361] Boughner, "Notes on the Flora of Long Point Island," *The Ottawa Naturalist, Vol. 12, No. 5,* p. 105, August 1898.

[362] J. B. Brown, Views of Canada and the Colonists, Edinburg, Scotland: A & C Black, 1851.

[363] E. Ryerson, *Letter to His Daughter Sophie,* Toronto: The Ryerson Press, 1870.

[364] E. Ryerson, *Letter to His Daughter Sophie,* Toronto: The Ryerson Press, 1865.

[365] *Norfolk Reformer,* 6 December 1867.

[366] *Norfolk Reformer,* 23 September 1869.

[367] *Norfolk Reformer,* 23 September 1869.

[368] "Argo, Cooperative Commuting Becoming More Popular," *Motor Boating,* September 1926.

[369] M. Bourke-White, Artist, *1937.* [Art]. Life Magazine.

[370] MacKay, The Canada Directory, Montreal: John Lovell, 1851.

[371] "Long Point Cut Lighthouse," 5 November 2021. [Online]. Available: https://www.lighthousefriends.com/light.asp?ID=1078.

[372] L. A. M. Corkan, "The Beaver and Lake Erie Canal," in *Historical Society of Western Pennsylvania,* 1934.

[373] "Journal of the Legislative Assembly," Government of Canada, Toronto, 1856.

[374] W. B. Wilson, "The Sawmilling and Lumber Industry of Norfolk County," *Forestory,* vol. 8, no. 2, pp. 11-16, 2017.

[375] J. M. Thorington, American Entries in the Travellers' Book of the Grands Mulets, 1861-75, New York: The American Alpine Club, 1952.

[376] *Norfolk Reformer,* 4 December 1862.

[377] *Toronto World,* p. 1, 20 December 1890.

[378] W. E. Davis, Dean of the Birdwatchers, Washington: Smithsonian Institution Press, 1994.

[379] P. Ryan, "A River Running Out of Eden," *Sports Illustrated,* 25 May 1970.

[380] "Business & Finance: Flin Flon," *Time,* 29 July 1935.

[381] *Railroad Gazzette,* 28 August 1882.

[382] "Why a Well-known Railroad Man was Refused Damages in a Slander Suit," *Indiannapolis Journal,* 16 December 1887.

[383] *Canadian Lumberman,* February 1891.

[384] "Was a Bad Failure," *Eagle River Review,* 15 January 1891.

[385] "An Embarrased Firm," *Indianopolis Journal,* p. 3, 26 November 1890.

[386] *Forest & Stream,* 18 May 1880.

[387] Royal Navy, 1928.

[388] *Upper Canada Herald,* 1 December 1835.

[389] *Spirit of the Age and Journal of Humanity,* 13 March 1934.

[390] M. Reeves, *Personal Communication,* 2021.

[391] *Oil & Gas Journal,* 9 May 1912.

[392] G. Lash, "Early History of the Natural Gas Industry, Fredonia, New York," in *AAPG History of Geology Forum*, 2014.

[393] H. Saunders, "Letter," *Toronto World,* p. 1, 3 December 1901.

[394] "Advertisement," *Toronto World,* 10 October 1902.

[395] *Norfolk Reformer,* 21 November 1878.

[396] "Report of the Bureau of Mines," Legislative Assembley of Ontario, 1912.

[397] D. S. Kostick, "The Material Flow of Salt," Bureau of Mines, 1992.

[398] *Toronto World,* 21 July 1902.

[399] U. S. Dept. of Agriculture, "Why bamboo," [Online]. Available: https://www.nrcs.usda.gov/Internet/FSE_PLANTMATERIALS/publications/lapmcpg7408.pdf. [Accessed 23 January 2021].

[400] D. Sage, The Restigouche and its Salmon Fishing, Edinborough: Privately printed, 1888.

[401] *Norfolk Reformer,* 8 August 1861.

[402] The London Advertiser, London, Ontario, 1896.

[403] *Hamilton Times,* 22 April 1864.

[404] *Norfolk Reformer,* 12 September 1867.

[405] *Kingston Chronicle & Gazette,* p. 3, 1 February 1834.

[406] *Norfolk Reformer,* p. 2, 14 May 1863.

[407] *Norfolk Reformer,* 3 December 1863.

[408] L. H. Tasker, "The United Empire Loyalist Settlement at Long Point, Lake Erie," *Papers and Records,* vol. II, 1900.

[409] "Enclopedia of Cleveland History," [Online]. Available: https://case.edu/ech/articles/w/walk-water#:~:text=WALK%2DIN%2DTHE%2DWATER%2C%20the%20first%20steamboat%20on,the%20winds%20were%20strong%20enough.. [Accessed 30 April 2022].

[410] W. Lewis, "Transition from Sail to Steam on the Great Lakes in the Nineteenth Century," *The Northern Mariner,* vol. 25, October 2015.

[411] Quebec: Hunter, Rose & Co., 1863.

[412] E. C. Guillet, The Pioneer Farmer and Backwoodsman, vol. 1, University of Toronto Press, 1963.

[413] *New Dominion,* 19 March 1869.

[414] Fifty Years of Reforestation in Ontario, 1960.

[415] B. M. Pearce, "A Built to Order Forest," *MacLean's,* 1 April 1929.

[416] *Wages in the United States and Europe 1870 - 1898,* Washington, District of Columbia: Department of Labor, 1898.

[417] M. R. C. J. S. e. a. Nelder, "American dog ticks along their expanding range edge in Ontario, Canada.," *Scientific Reports,* vol. 12, June 2022.

[418] E. C. Guillet, Pioneer Travel in Upper Canada, University of Toronto Press (Reprint 1963), 1933.

[419] H. B. Barrett, "History of Human-Use Impacts on Long Point Bay," *Journal of Great Lakes Research,* vol. 7, no. 2, pp. 81-88, 1981.

[420] *Canada Lumberman & Woodworker,* p. 46, 15 December 1919.

[421] "Lloyd's Register," 1912.

[422] "A Report and Fiancial Statement of the Long Point Company," The Long Point Company, Hamilton, 1878.

[423] *Norfolk Reformer,* 29 September 1870.

[424] P. Mickwitz, *Gleanings in Bee Culture,* vol. 36, 15 October 1908.

[425] *Norfolk Reformer,* 1 September 1864.

[426] *Norfolk Reformer,* 8 September 1864.

[427] *St. Catharines Constitutional,* p. 1, 11 June 1868.

[428] "Report of the Board of Works," Legislative Assembly, Montreal, 1845.

[429] Hutchison's Hamilton City Directory, Hamilton: John Eastwood & Co., 1863.

[430] G. Laidler, *Long Point, Lake Erie: Some Physical and Historical Aspetcs,* vol. 36, The Ontario Historical Society, 1944.

[431] *Scientific American,* 20 October 1888.

[432] 22 February 2023. [Online]. Available: https://www.artnet.com/artists/ogden-minton-pleissner/junius-s-morgan-and-howard-moulton-approaching-v5rKoGgXqcU98OfnPjHV4A2.

[433]   Oxford and Norfolk Gazetteer and General and Business Directory, Woodstock: Sutherland & Co., 1867.

[434]   Buffalo, New York: C.F.S. Thomas, 1866.

[435]   *Ingersol Chronicle,* 24 August 1876.

[436]   *Hamilton Times,* 29 April 1864.

[437]   *The Bombay Gazette,* p. 2, 23 March 1867.

[438]   *The Bombay Gazette,* p. 2, 7 May 1866.

[439]   *The Canadian Gentleman's Journal & Sporting Times,* 1878.

[440]   "Advertisement, Hazell & Sons," *The Hamilton Times,* p. 1, 27 September 1900.

[441]   J. R. Wells, "Game Laws and Duck Shooting," *The Toronto World,* p. 3, 4 April 1900.

[442]   G. T. Bloomfield, "Canadian Industry in 1871," University of Guelph, Guelph, 1991.

[443]   Adam, G.M. *Prominent Men of Canada,* Toronto, 1892

[444]   Surveyor General's Dept.

[445]   *Brantford Daily News*

[446]   Toronto: O. L. Fuller, 1865.

[447]   H. Black, Doctor and teacher, hospital chief: Dr. Samuel Proger and the New England Medical Center, Chester, CT: Globe Pequot Press, 1982.

[448]   H. Hall, America's Successful Men of Affairs, The City of New York, vol. 1, New York: The New York Tribune, 1895.

[449]   J. Lennox, North of America, New Haven: Yale University Press, 2022.

[450]   *Record on Appeal, in the Matter of Proving the Last Will and Testament of Roland Hill,* 1934.

[451]   *Norfolk Reformer,* 13 August 1863.

[452]   *The Globe,* 14 March 1929.

[453]   *Millbrook Reporter,* 5 September 1895.

[454]   *Ottawa Times,* 8 May 1876.

[455]   *Ottawa Times,* 8 May 1876.

[456]   Commissioners, Fish & Game, "Annual Report 1892," Government of Ontario, Toronto, 1893.

[457]   E. Ryerson, *Various Letters to His Daughter Sophie,* Toronto, Ontario: The Ryerson Press, 1866-1874.

[458]   E. Ryerson, *Letter to His Daughter Sophie,* Toronto, Ontario: The Ryerson Press, 1865.

[459]   E. Ryerson, "*Letter to his Daughter Sophie,*" in *My Dearest Sophie,* Toronto, The Ryerson Press.

[460]   E. Ryerson, *Letter to his Daughter Sophie,* Toronto, Ontario: The Ryerson Press, 1869.

[461]   E. Ryerson, *Letter to his daughter Sophie,* Toronto, Ontario: The Ryerson Press, 1859.

[462]   *Erie News,* 19 April 1860.

[463]   *Port Royal Ship Canal,* Toronto: H.R. Page & Co., 1877.

[464]   W. Dickerman, *Letter to George Richards,* New York, NY, 1986.

[465] J. E. Bannister, *Western Ontario History Nuggets,* no. No. 5, pp. 1-8, 1944.

[466] W. Howells, Buffalo, New York: Commercial Publishing Company, 1880.

[467] *Norfolk Reformer,* 13 April 1865.

[468] "Letter to the Editor, Norfolk Reformer," *Norfolk Reformer,* 26 March 1863.

[469] R. Gillis, "Little, James," [Online]. Available: http://www.biographi.ca/en/bio/little_james_11E.html#:~:text=James%20Little%20immigrated%20to%20British,a%20contractor%20on%20the%20project.. [Accessed 10 February 2024].

[470] *Natural Gas Journal,* p. 333, July 1912.

[471] "Annual Report, Department of Marine & Fisheries," Government of Canada, Ottawa, 1909.

[472] C. Blanco, *Field & Stream,* 15 October 1905.

[473] MacDonald, John A., Troublous Times in Canada, a History of the Fenian Raids, 1910

[474] "For Commuters Only," *Flying Magazine,* September 1940.

Index

www.ingramcontent.com/pod-product-compliance
Lightning Source LLC
Chambersburg PA
CBHW080944120626
46546CB00010B/2828